Battle Hymn of China

STROZIER LIBRARY
FLORIDA STATE UNIVERSITY
TALLAHASSEE, FLORIDA 32306

MAY 10 1977

Battle Hymn of
CHINA

AGNES SMEDLEY

New York ALFRED A KNOPF
1943

THIS BOOK HAS BEEN PRODUCED IN FULL COMPLIANCE WITH ALL GOVERNMENT REGULATIONS FOR THE CONSERVATION OF PAPER, METAL, AND OTHER ESSENTIAL MATERIALS.

COPYRIGHT 1943 *by Agnes Smedley. All rights reserved. No part of this book may be reproduced in any form without permission in writing from the publisher, except by a reviewer who may quote brief passages or reproduce not more than three illustrations in a review to be printed in a magazine or newspaper. Manufactured in the United States of America. Published simultaneously in Canada by The Ryerson Press.*

PUBLISHED AUGUST 23, 1943
FIRST AND SECOND PRINTINGS BEFORE PUBLICATION

*To the soldiers of China,
poor, glorious pioneers in the world struggle
against Fascism*

Table of Contents

BOOK I Glimpses of the Past

THE PATTERN	3
ASIATIC MOTIF	8
EUROPEAN QUEST	11
FAR HORIZONS	22

BOOK II China, Past and Present [1928–1931]

INTO THE MIDDLE AGES	31
PATRICIANS AND PROLETARIANS	49
FIELDS OF LIFE AND DEATH	57
TERROR IN SHANGHAI	69
LU HSÜN	77
SOUTHERN EPISODES	86
SHANGHAI GUERRILLA WARFARE	92

BOOK III Imperialism and the Revolution [1931–1936]

MARCH OF DEATH	101
THE RIGHTS OF MAN	110
MOTOR CAR NO. 1469	115
SOVIET INTERLUDE	124

BOOK IV The United Front and War [1936–1937]

SIAN INCIDENT	133
MEN AND IDEAS	151
THE LION-HEARTED	164
NEWS BLOCKADE-RUNNERS	175
WAR	181

BOOK V The Last Days of Hankow [1938]

CROSS-CURRENTS IN HANKOW	205

RED CROSS PIONEERS 212
THE END OF HANKOW 231
THE STRUGGLE CONTINUES 236

Book VI   In Guerrilla Land [1938–1939]

NEW LAND 247
THE "NEW FOURTH" 259
DOCTORS NEED "TEACHING MATERIAL." 266
THE WOMEN TAKE A HAND 270
THE STORY OF A FARM 277
MEN IN TRANSITION: THE FIFTIETH ARMY 282
THE HOOFS OF THE JAPANESE 292
CROSSING THE YANGTZE 298

Book VII   Through Central China
[Late Autumn 1939]

COMMANDER CHANG YUN-EE AND THE FOURTH DETACHMENT 317
THE GUERRILLA WOUNDED 329
KWANGSI BASE 335
ANHWEI: THE PAST VS. THE FUTURE 345
ANHWEI INTRIGUE 356
DISCORD 364
SONG OF DESOLATION 372
MAN OF GOD 383
MY FRIEND THE NUN 389

Book VIII   Winter Offensive [1939–1940]

SWORDS FOR THE JAPANESE 401
THE CO-OPERATIVES 407
"TELL YOUR COUNTRYMEN —" 410
WINTER SOLDIERS IN HUPEH 426
THE COMMANDER WHO SANG 433

GENERAL WITH A CONSCIENCE 442
MUTINY 452

BOOK IX   With the Guerrillas Again [1940]

WITH THE GUERRILLAS AGAIN 459
MY CHINESE SON 463
STORM GUERRILLAS AND SALT-MINERS 475
TRAITORS AND PATRIOTS 481
FAREWELL! 488

BOOK X   Chungking and After [1940–1941]

CHUNGKING 497
THE MEDICAL CORPS FIGHTS ON 506
HONG KONG 511

Illustrations

	PAGE
It was a bloody era	36
Where child serfs slept	36
Dead bodies from Shanghai streets	46
Workers mowed down in December 1927	46
Demonstrations against Japan in Sian	146
(Left) A war orphan. (Right) Chu Teh	146
My friends of Hankow days	198
(Left) Lieutenant General Joseph Stilwell. (Right) Lieutenant Colonel Evans F. Carlson	198
Chinese currency and Japanese propaganda	262
Typical Japanese propaganda	262
The whole population gathered and I talked to the people	312
A column of peasant guerrillas	312
Lieutenant General Chung Yi and his aides	418
General Cheng Su-yuan and his Chief-of-staff	418
Civilians aiding in transporting the wounded	430
(Left) A "walking-wounded." (Right) Soldiers inside the barracks of the 173rd Division (Kwangsi Army)	430

BOOK I

Glimpses of the Past

The Pattern

THERE are tales, long whispered in my family, which, if true, explain the two strains that mingled when my father and mother married. One strain — my mother's — was of a hardworking, gentle, and devout folk. The other consisted of rebels, wanderers, tellers of tall tales, singers of songs.

My father eloped with my mother before she was of age. Her father, John, found them in the home of my father's sister, Mary. Aunt Mary was a widow with many children, but a woman of unusual capacity and determination. Her eyes fell approvingly on Grandfather John, a frail, gentle man resembling pictures of Jesus Christ. John's wife was still alive and, to judge by a faded tintype, very beautiful. But she died shortly after, following a long illness, and my grandfather married Aunt Mary. In the small, drab villages and isolated farmhouses of northern Missouri little rumors often grew to gargantuan proportions. The gossips specialized most of all in the gruesome and more than one farm woman was thereafter seen wagging her head and heard talking of the strange things that were supposed to have happened in my grandfather's house — of evil widows . . . and poor ailing wives . . . and poison. . . .

Finally Grandfather wasted away and died of tuberculosis. Mary cared for him with infinite tenderness, uttering never a harsh word at his endless exactions, warning her many children, and his, to behave as she did. There lingers in my memory a vision of this tall, strong woman, sitting or kneeling by his bedside, engaged in low conversation or silent waiting.

So John had died, said the gossips, shaking their heads knowingly. What else could you expect, when, as everyone

knew, he had spent his declining years walking the floor complaining that his first wife's spirit haunted him? As he lay dying, rumor ran, he wanted to cleanse his soul of the sin of poisoning his first wife, but Mary had smothered his confession by placing her hand across his mouth! Anything could be expected of that big woman, who came from God only knew where and could do anything from curing diseases with herbs to managing a big farm and rearing more than a dozen children!

If Aunt Mary had lived in an earlier period, her abilities might have caused her to be burned as a witch. Instead, she was well over ninety before she laid down her corncob pipe for the last time. People said she sped around the country in a Ford until her dying day, her white hair flying, her pipe in her mouth. She was so tall that when she died a special coffin had to be built for her. I have not yet heard just how many men were needed to carry the coffin, but by the time I get around to investigating the story, I'm sure the number will be fabulous. I've heard it said by the gentle branch of our family that Mary is most certainly not taking any back seat in the Hereafter.

All my mother's people died young — which, considering their goodness, was only natural. On the other hand, all my father's people, save one uncle who turned Christian missionary, lived to a ripe old age. The two family strains, meeting in me, made my spirit a battlefield across which a civil war raged endlessly.

When I was very young, my father dragged us from northern Missouri to southern Colorado, where Rockefeller's Colorado Fuel & Iron Company owned everything but the air. My father went to this region to make his fortune, but fell victim to a system the fruits of which were poverty, disease and ignorance for the miners.

We lived a primitive life in the camps, but I now understand that our intellectual poverty was far worse than our physical condition. When I try to recollect the impact of so-called cultural influences, I can recall only Scotch and English folk-songs, cowboy songs, and such ballads as those in praise of Jesse James — all of them sung by my father. I do not remember hearing my mother sing; she was too unhappy.

Until I was fifteen years old I knew little of the world beyond that Rockefeller domain of southern Colorado and northern New Mexico. My father did unskilled labor and drank to forget his hopes, and my mother worked intermittently as a washwoman and a keeper of boarders. We Smedley children — there were five of us — somehow managed to get to the poor local primary schools. But I never finished grade school and never attended a high school. Most high-school graduates of today inspire no regret in me, but I have always believed that had I had some basic knowledge of science, mathematics, literature, and language, I would have been better equipped to meet life. I have long felt that the poverty and ignorance of my youth were the tribute which I, like millions of others, paid to "private interests."

The schools my brothers and sisters and I attended were perhaps no more boring than most. However, my thinking was not to be disciplined, and not all the king's horses and all the king's men could teach me grammar or arithmetic. Even in later years my efforts to learn languages ended in dismal failure, although in the case of German I managed to absorb what I needed or whatever sounded beautiful or powerful. If I disliked a person, my mind closed and I could learn nothing from him. So I took from schools and from life what I found interesting, not what people thought good for me. But my mother and a red-haired woman schoolteacher in Tercio, a mining camp, must have regarded me with hope, for they kept urging me to get an education. Education seemed to consist in reading many books, but just which I did not know. For years I groped, reading anything between covers, often understanding hardly a sentence, but believing mystically that the key to knowledge lay buried in words. My reading covered everything from trashy romance to a ghastly book on school law and one called *Behaviorist Psychology*.

The nearest I ever came to the classics was a large volume

of something called "poetry." Because it was printed on very thin paper, it quite naturally hung from a string in a privy. A man by the name of Shakespeare seemed to have written it but I could make neither head nor tail of it. In later years I often read of men who received their first noble impulses from contacts with great minds; I was in my early twenties before I learned who Shakespeare was, and in my forties before I read his plays. In the mining camps he had made no impression whatsoever and I returned the volume of thin paper to its nail on the privy wall.

I disliked so many things in life and received so many humiliations from rich little girls that my teachers used to keep me after school and lecture me on the bourgeois virtues. It was in vain. I fought boys with jimson weeds and rocks, and nothing could make a little lady of me. When I was nine my mother put me out to work washing dishes and caring for squawling babies. I was later promoted to stripping tobacco leaves in a cigar store, but I dawdled so much over my work that I was fired. One employer told me that I was a bad worker because I read too many books. "Here's your wages for the week, and you needn't come back," he said. He gave me two dollars and a half. For years after that I did all kinds of unskilled labor.

Religion is sometimes considered a cultural influence. What I have known of it has made me content that I was not carefully trained in its principles. The virtue of submission to injustice, of rendering unto Cæsar that which Cæsar did not produce himself, made no impression on me. Beyond that, the belief in immortality has always seemed cowardly to me. When very young I learned that all things die, and all that we wish of good must be won on this earth or not at all.

When I was sixteen, my mother lay down and died from hard labor, undernourishment, and a disease which she had no money to cure. My father fell on his knees and wept dramatically, then rifled her old tin trunk. With the forty-five dollars he found hidden between the quilt patches he went to the saloon and got drunk with the boys. My elder sister had just died in childbed, leaving a baby boy, and I was thus the eldest child, with responsibility for this baby, as well as for my younger sister and two brothers.

Had I been more like my mother and less like my father, I would have accepted this burden as inevitable. But I resented my mother's suffering and refused to follow in her footsteps. I knew nothing of the world save the tales related by cowboys, miners, and teamsters. I knew that Columbus had sailed the seas and discovered a new continent and that my forefathers had fought in the American Revolution. The clatter of the hoofs of the horse of Jesse James as he robbed the rich to give to the poor echoed in my ears. It seemed that men could go anywhere, do anything, discover new worlds, but that women could only trail behind or sit at home having babies. Such a fate I rejected. After making a few rudimentary arrangements for the care of my sister and baby nephew and leaving my small brothers to my father, I began a life of semi-vagabondage that was to last for years.

That first period of life, which had ended with my mother's death, seemed to have little significance. I had been born and I had existed. I had no goal nor did I know enough to have one.

At the beginning of the second stage the primary need was, as always, to earn a living. An aunt helped me learn stenography, but I could seldom hold a job for more than a few days or a week. I might have learned to spell and punctuate correctly had I not seen girls about me who did it very well. Uncomplainingly they spent their lives taking down the thoughts of bosses, then turning away to type them out.

This resentment prevented me from becoming a good stenographer, and for years I wandered from one job to another — stenographer, waitress, tobacco stripper, book agent, or just plain starveling. My mother's voice urging me to "go on an' git an edjicashun" sent me to libraries, but I did not know what to read. Now and then I found a school where I could work as a waitress and attend lectures and one year I managed to spend as a special student in the Normal School at Tempe, Arizona.

While in this school, two events occurred which affected my life. The first was my introduction to natural science, in particular to biology. The second was a friendship with a Swedish-American woman, a university graduate from New York City who had come west to be near her brother, a civil engineer working in the Arizona desert. Shortly afterwards I married this brother but he soon divorced me. I didn't blame him at all; and once the humiliating bonds of marriage were removed, we became good friends. This friendship has continued throughout my life, and long after he had married a second time and had several lovely children, his wife and I also became close friends. I have always detested the belief that sex is the chief bond between man and woman. Friendship is far more human. I personally have never been able to reconcile myself to the sex relationship, for it seemed to me only a trap which limited women in every way. For women marriage is at best an economic investment; at its worst, a relic of human slavery. I have, however, heard of no society which has solved this problem; decades later I did not fail to tell men in the Soviet Union that I had listened to many men make speeches from the Tomb of Lenin in the Red Square, but only one woman — and that one on International Women's Day.

Asiatic Motif

IN my early twenties I left the Southwest for New York City. Here I spent nearly four years, working during the day and attending lectures at night at New York University. Among the friends I made was an old exiled professor from India, Lala Laipat Rai, who began tutoring me in Indian history, preparatory to sending me to India as a teacher. Some of his younger countrymen convinced me that India could not advance until it was freed from British rule — as America had been freed — by revolution. All my experiences predisposed me to believe this, and I became a kind of communication center for these men. I kept their correspondence, their codes, and foreign addresses. It was as a result of this work that I was arrested in 1918, held in solitary confinement in the Tombs in New York City, and charged with a violation of our Neutrality Law. Although I had never met a German and believed that I was only helping a subjugated people, I found myself accused of aiding in German espionage.

Years later I learned that Indian exiles in Europe had indeed formed a government-in-exile and taken a loan from the German Government to finance their work. They had shipped arms and ammunition from America to India, but had no more use for the Germans than the Germans had for them.

Soon after the Armistice I was released from jail and the charges against me were dismissed. I had spent the months of imprisonment studying and writing. Friends had sent me books, paper, and pencils, and for the first time in my life I had been able to study without being burdened with the necessity of earning my own living. My first short stories, *Cell Mates*, were written during that time.

Coming out of prison, I learned that, months before, my younger brother had passed through New York City en route to France as a soldier. He had tried to see me repeatedly but the prosecuting attorney had turned him away, telling him that I was a traitor. This, combined with news that my other brother had been killed while working as a day laborer, sickened me. The employer in whose service my older brother had been killed paid my father fifty dollars for his life. My younger brother, unable to earn a living, had offered himself to death before he was seventeen. Both had lived like animals without protection or education.

The problems of my own life had developed neurotic tendencies within me, and the fate of my brothers, combined with my imprisonment, deepened them. I came out of prison morose and miserable. I was in my early twenties, at an age when serious-minded middle-class men and women were completing their schooling and embarking on careers. They had homes, protection, and guidance. It was not that

I begrudged them these good things; it was merely that I thought the advantages they had should be made universally available.

I was a woman, and women were expected to marry and, if possible, "marry money." If you were not interested in marriage or money, you were doomed. As I saw it, I could hope to continue only as I was — slaving by day and striving desperately at night for some kind of meager education. And what after that? A shabby hall bedroom for the rest of my days?

I rejected such a life, yet I could envision no other. A World War had just ended and there was a sort of peace. The German Republic had come to life, but was held in pawn by the victors. The Russian Revolution had taken place, but the Russian people were still fighting on more than a dozen fronts against invading armies of World War victors, including one from my own country. The Russian people were learning the most brutal lesson in human history — that only by their own armed might could they have a civilization of their own choosing.

A Communist Party was being formed in New York, but I did not join it. I knew many of its leaders and had read books or articles written by some of them. For years I listened to Communists with sympathy and in later years in China I gave them my active support, but I could never place my mind and life unquestioningly at the disposal of their leaders. I never believed that I myself was especially wise, but I could not become a mere instrument in the hands of men who believed that they held the one and only key to truth.

Because of this I was often attacked from two sides: believers in capitalism called me a Communist, a Red, or an Anarchist; Communists called me an individualist, an idealist, or a bourgeois democrat. . . . One American woman Communist long delighted in dubbing me a "Smedleyite."

One day as the year 1919 drew to a close, I took my place in a line at the office of a shipping company on the New York waterfront and made application for a job as a stewardess on an old Polish-American freighter bound for Europe. It carried deck and third-class passengers, and another girl and I were hired to care for them. I had no definite destination, no clear aims, no connections with any organization save a weak link with Indian exiles who lived in Europe and published a small newspaper from Berlin. I merely entertained the hope that I could find them, live a short time in Europe, visit the Soviet Union, and, if possible, find work on some ship sailing for India. Whatever might result from this venture, I would at least see something of the earth on which I had been born. But live the life of a cabbage I would not.

European Quest

IN Danzig Harbor I deserted the freighter and journeyed to Berlin to look for the small office maintained by Indian exiles. The first person I met there was the Indian revolutionary leader Virendranath Chattopadhyaya. In New York I had often heard of him as one who had helped form an Indian government-in-exile and build up a world-wide network of Indian revolutionary activity. In fact, it was because of him and his colleagues that I had been imprisoned.

I found the personality and past life of Virendranath Chattopadhyaya compelling. In a very short time I had entered into a union with him; it was not a legal marriage, but I bore his name and was known as his wife. It was to last for nearly eight years, but became so complex that it tended only to aggravate my sick state of mind.

Whether or not I loved him I do not really know. Many years after I had left Viren I remember writing to an American friend that "to my astonishment and resentment Viren remains the center of my emotional life, and if he were in danger I suppose I would walk barefoot around the world to help him. Yet I would not live with him for a day." That was long ago, and time again proved the great healer. That he loved me there is no doubt. Neither I nor others understood why, for he had little interest in women.

Thirteen years before he met me, Viren had married an Irish Catholic girl. Because he was a pagan who rejected all her efforts to convert him, she bought a special dispensation from the Pope to marry him. After the ceremony she informed him that a condition of the marriage was that any issue was to be Catholic. They quarreled and parted, she becoming a nun in some hidden English convent and he trying for years to have the marriage annulled. He failed and we were never legally married. As a result my American citizenship was twice challenged in later years by the British Secret Service, which claimed, with no good intentions, that I was a British subject. To a shocked American consular official in China I once explained the situation thus:

"My husband was married to a Catholic nun and for this reason could not marry me. You may call me a concubine if you will, but not a British subject."

The official threw up his hands in despair.

Virendranath was the epitome of the secret Indian revolutionary movement, and perhaps its most brilliant protagonist abroad. He was nearly twenty years my senior, with a mind as sharp and ruthless as a saber. He was thin and dark, with a mass of black hair turning gray at the temples, and a face that had something fierce about it. He might easily have been taken for a southern European, a Turk, or a Persian. To me he seemed something like thunder, lightning, and rain; and wherever he had sojourned in Europe or England, he had been just about that to the British. His hatred for the islanders who had subjugated his country knew no bounds.

The foundation of his emotional life had been laid in the feudal Mohammedan state of Hyderabad. To this he had added a quarter of a century of intellectual training in England, Europe, and the Near East. His was a famous Brahmin family abounding in poets, singers, educators, and scientists. One of his sisters was the poetess and national leader Sarojini Naidu, and his younger brother was married to Kamala Devi, who later became a great leader. By race the family was Hindu, by culture a mixture of Hinduism, Mohammedanism, and the best of English liberalism. Viren's father had been one of the first Brahmins to defy caste laws by going to England and later to Germany to study science. An outcast, he was forced to emigrate to the Moslem state of Hyderabad, where he became a pioneer in modern university education.

Viren had been educated by his father, by Moslem scholars and English tutors. He grew up speaking Hindustani, English, a smattering of German, and the court language of the Moslem world, Persian. Throughout his childhood he had heard his mother — a poetess and an advocate of the emancipation of women — referred to with contempt by Moslems, and this had generated in him emotions which he had never been able to reconcile. This was only one of the many conflicts that went on within him and made his mind and emotional life remind me of one of those Hindu temples in south India — repository of all the cultural movements of the ages.

In Heidelberg and Jena Viren had pursued the study of comparative philology. He spoke English like a ruling-class Englishman and had learned French, German, Swedish, and some Italian and Spanish. He had lived in Sweden for a few years and had not only mastered the language but gone on to study Icelandic. When he and I went with an Indian delegation to the Soviet Union in 1921, shortly after my arrival in Germany, he soon assimilated Russian and in his leisure time sought out men from Lithuania or Iceland, or haunted the encampments of gypsies, in order to compare their languages with ancient Sanskrit.

Like Nehru and many other men of the upper classes of India, Viren had absorbed British traditions of liberty. These he had come to apply to his own country — a practice that enraged most Englishmen. He and his colleagues, some of them caste-ridden, orthodox Brahmins, were among the early nationalist terrorists of India — as they were also among India's early educators, scientists, artists, labor organizers, and, later, Communists. They hunted British rulers of India and Egypt with pistol, bomb, and knife. Some had been shot, some hanged, others imprisoned for life. In whatever sections of the world Indians gathered they were to be found.

Each summer, when groups of Indian students left England to spend their vacations on the Continent, one goal of pilgrimage was always Virendranath's home. Of this they never dared speak, and some even preferred not to recall their conversations with him, for he made violent attacks on Hindu caste prejudices and Moslem superstitions. He would eat pork in the presence of Moslems and beef in front of Hindus. To Hindus he spoke of Hinduism as a "cow-dung religion," and he made the adherents of both religions writhe under the sting of his tongue. He taunted them by asserting that even in poetry they learned not from India, but from England, and that they believed England was the paradise to which their souls would go after death. His contempt for Indians aspiring to official posts under the British Government was boundless. He warned his students that only clerks watched time-clocks or lived an orderly, respectable life. When told that one must live, he would answer in the words of Voltaire: "I don't see the necessity."

He practiced what he preached. He never possessed more than one suit of clothing, which I was constantly darning, patching, and pressing. Nor did he care what he ate. When he had money, he gave it to anyone in need, so that we were forever in debt. Money was merely a means of working for the independence of his country. His attitude toward it had been formed by the great joint families of India and in particular by that caste of Brahmin teachers and scholars who gave their knowledge freely. Years later I found the same attitude among those intellectuals of China who also came from families in which the clan cared for the individual.

Virendranath turned more and more to the study of Marxism as a means of gaining independence for India; and he eventually became a Communist Party member. I always wondered just what new design was added to the Hindu temple of his mind by this act. I could never imagine him being regimented by any political party or following "lines" of thought and action. His mind took the whole world as its province and drew nourishment from every age.

When Viren and I began life together, two eras and two cultures met. I was an American working woman, the product of a distorted commercial civilization, he a high-caste Indian with a cultivated, labyrinthine Brahmin mind and a British classical education. Though he hated everything British, he had an even deeper contempt for an American capitalism which judged all things by their money value. His mind was modern, but his emotional roots were in Hinduism and Islam.

Like a storm, he existed according to his nature, absorbing, influencing everything he touched. Our way of life was of his choosing, not mine; our home a small edition of that of a great joint family of India. Any Indian who became ill was brought to our home and nursed by me, and on one occasion I had two of them at once. Moslems and Hindus of every caste streamed through it as through a railway station or a hotel. Students came directly from their boats, carting all their bedding and cooking utensils. Some wore weird clothing. One student bought himself a woman's straw hat with a bunch of grapes hanging down the side; it looked somewhat like a turban, and only with difficulty could we induce him to cease wearing it.

We were desperately poor, and because Viren had no possessions, I sold everything I owned in order to get money. Just as the year 1923 began, protests from the British caused the German Government to order Viren to leave the country. We met the problem by moving repeatedly and changing our name. But our debts and difficulties seemed to increase by geometric progression.

Whenever things seemed about to improve, new problems would turn up. Sometimes Moslems with their wives still half in *purdah* came to live with us. At other times we visited some who were very much out of *purdah*, including, for example, the Moslem leader Mohammed Ali Jinnah and his wife. Cold, sleek, cruel-faced, Jinnah was a great landlord who had married a Parsi woman, daughter of a millionaire Bombay factory-owner. Certainly Mrs. Jinnah could never be accused of living in *purdah*. She was a beautiful but superficial society woman, whom Jinnah displayed as he would a jeweled shirt-stud. She often wore nothing above the waist except a brassiere carelessly covered by the sheerest of lace *saris*.

Viren had hopes of inducing the two of them to establish a scholarship fund for poor Indian students in Europe, and when they once wired him to visit them in a German spa where they were recuperating from night life on the Continent, he went in high anticipation. But they were not interested in scholarship funds. Bored, they had thought of Viren merely as a diversion. He was a brilliant conversationalist and Mrs. Jinnah was perplexed by a great problem: she could not find the rouge and lipstick she desired and wanted Viren to look for them in the shops of Berlin.

Such incidents engendered a cold disgust within me. I was, moreover, harassed by domestic difficulties. Hindu and Moslem religious festivals were sometimes celebrated in our home, with dozens of men sitting in a circle on the floor. In the manner of India, no man could be turned away hungry. The cooking and preparation for dinners were therefore endless and the very walls of our home seemed to be permeated with the odor of curry.

Viren thrived on company, but I began to wilt and sink under the complexity and poverty of our life. Everyone understood and loved Viren; few understood me. To them I was a queer creature who grew ever more strange — as indeed I did.

I was with Virendranath and witnessed the power of his personality when his youngest sister, Suhasini, came from Oxford to see him for the first time. She had been born after he left India, and her mother had sung her to sleep with lullabies about her exiled brother. The British Government had forced her father to leave Hyderabad and live in Calcutta under perpetual house-arrest and her childhood had been overshadowed by tragedy. British police were forever raiding their home, tearing up pillows, and disemboweling Suhasini's dolls to see if her father had hidden messages or codes from his exiled son. The old man had died a prisoner.

Suhasini was a musician and singer, a woman of striking beauty and noble bearing. When she stood before her brother for the first time, neither spoke, and I saw Suhasini trembling. Viren's face was tense with inner struggle; it was the first time in a quarter of a century that one of his family had come to share his life, and Suhasini must have reminded him of the tragedy of his father, his country, and his own long years of exile. In later years Suhasini returned to India as a Communist and labor organizer, earning her living as a singer. Her Communism had sprung from Viren's influence. But it was years before she would bow her handsome aristocratic head and meet on a plane of equality with men of lesser station. Thus it was that member after member of Viren's family, people of the highest caste and culture, broke the Brahmin bonds of privilege and placed their trained minds at the service of their country or of the dispossessed.

Perhaps my respect and admiration for such men and women robbed me of objectivity. As I saw Viren, his whitehot passion for liberty seemed never to wane; it communicated itself to every one of his countrymen who knew him. It was, in fact, the majesty of his life and intellect that bound me to him even in our most unhappy moments and long after our marriage had become a formality.

The circumstances of my youth, combined with the endless difficulties of my life with Virendranath in Germany, drove me almost to the verge of insanity. Twice I left him and sought rest and recovery in the Bavarian Alps, where I planned to continue my interrupted journey to India. Friends in London tried to secure a visa for me to enter India, but they failed because of my imprisonment in America in connection with the Indian exiles, my articles in the Indian press, and my association with Virendranath. My desire to live ebbed and I lay ill for nearly three years. For whole days I remained in a coma, unable to move or speak, longing only for oblivion. Nor could the best nerve specialists of Germany cure me. More than death I feared insanity, and the terror of this possibility haunted my very dreams. Once I attempted suicide, but succeeded only in injuring myself.

When all else failed, I was introduced to a woman nerve specialist, a former associate of Freud. An alienist in the Berlin courts, she was also connected with the University of Berlin. My psychoanalysis began, and continued torturously for two years. During this infinite suffering one image haunted my sleeping and my waking: I held a small Chinese vase in my outstretched palm and contemplated its beauty. A crack kept growing down the side, the vase broke, and the fragment rolled out of my outstretched palm. It seemed a symbol of my life. As I grew better, the image returned less often, yet seemed to hover, a menace, in the offing.

As my health returned, I began teaching English to university students and took up again the study of Indian history. I became a teacher in the English Seminar of the University of Berlin and, upon occasion, lectured before the seminar on Indian history. When plans were made for an English theater in Berlin, I coached actors and actresses, and in this way came into contact with the theatrical world. One of the friends I made here was Tilla Durieux, who was so often cast in psychological studies. She was one of the strangest of German actresses, but quite learned, having one of the best libraries of anyone in her profession. In a way she became my teacher in literature, architecture, music, and the theater. We spent one summer together in Austria, where we attended the Mozart Festspiel in Salzburg, then wandered through Austria and southern Germany, visiting historic cities and old cathedrals.

As a kind of counterthrust against growing Communism, the Hitler movement was rising in Germany, but to most of us it seemed just another fad that would soon die. Since I had to earn my living and struggle for health, I was too burdened to study it closely. Once when Virendranath had come to Bavaria to induce me to return to him and we were on our way back to Berlin we paused in Munich to attend Wagner's *Ring*. By chance one evening we followed a small crowd and found ourselves in a hall where Hitler was speaking. This event made so little impression on me that I recall nothing but Hitler's frothy shouting.

As my health improved I decided to shoulder another burden: attendance at the university and study leading to the Ph.D. degree. I did not have the academic qualifications, but by a law under the German Republic men and women could produce research work which, if accepted, would entitle them to work for their degrees. I produced two works on Indian history which were published by two leading German historical magazines; one was the *Zeitschrift für Geopolitik*, official organ for the Institut für Geopolitik, of which Professor Karl Haushofer was head. He had been a General in the World War, a military observer in Japan from the time of the Russo-Japanese War onward. Then he had founded the institute. Since he had published my thesis, I made a special trip to his home in the Bavarian Alps and secured his sponsorship for my entrance to the university.

It has since become clear that Haushofer was one of the men who made Adolf Hitler. His institute was even then the concealed General Staff of German Imperialism. It was he and this General Staff that furnished Hitler with such demagogic ideas as *Blut und Boden*, and, though his wife was part Jewish, Haushofer was perhaps one of those who helped write *Mein Kampf*.

Why Haushofer sponsored me, a woman, even though he and his class preached the inferiority of women, I do not know. Perhaps it was because of my Asiatic connections. I had prefaced my published thesis with the assertion that the nation that ruled India was the master of Europe. Haushofer apparently wanted to keep in touch with Asiatics, but when he once invited Virendranath and me to his place, there was nothing warm or friendly in his manner. He was wooden — a silent, suspicious man.

I was admitted to Berlin University to study for my Ph.D.,

but after a short time I realized that it was hopeless. I lacked a foundation in science and mathematics and I failed to keep pace with the thirty or forty older men in my seminar. Most of these men were already teachers in the Gymnasiums, who had returned to the university to take their final degree. I had to earn my living while studying and could find no time to master the language.

After a brief struggle I gave up my long-cherished plan.

The classes which I conducted in the English Seminar of the University resembled those automatic devices that pick up approaching sounds at a great distance. In them, liberals, Socialists, Communists, and Nazis defended their ideas with passion. Almost every class had at least one or more corps students, with dueling scars across their cheeks, who openly attacked the Republic, workers, Communists, Socialists, liberals, and Jews. One corps student once proclaimed to the class that degeneracy under the Republic was demonstrated even by the fact that Germans were forced to study under a foreign woman who wore her hair short and smoked cigarettes.

At this time I joined a group of Republican, Socialist, and Communist physicians trying to establish the first state birth-control clinic in Berlin. Margaret Sanger financed our first research branch and soon afterwards the Government took over the clinics and established branches in many cities. They continued until the Nazis came to power, after which women were ordered back to the bedroom. A German woman Communist doctor and I once got into a debate with her husband, a Communist physician in the Public Health Service, because he argued that if men could be conscripted to fight, women could be conscripted to breed. His attitude was no different from that of my Nazi students who sent a grievance committee to the head of the English Seminar of the University because my class had debated the question of birth-control.

The bitter fruits of defeat in war were eaten hourly by the German people and nourished only hatred for their conquerors. Month by month I saw people die of slow hunger and watched funeral processions enter and leave the little church on my street. One day in December 1923 I found a man, a shoemaker from the French-occupied Ruhr district, dying of hunger in the street near our house. He carried a dirty, ragged baby in his arms. A group of women gathered, each undertaking to do something for him, while I cared for the baby until the city welfare bureau could take it.

In the corner grocery I often observed gaunt workers pay out their week's wages, billions of paper marks, for a couple of loaves of bread, some potatoes, and margarine. Meat and fruit were beyond their reach. There was no sugar, only saccharine, and even this they could not afford. Families sought foreign boarders in order to get foreign currency, and decent foreigners were filled with shame. During this period I met American bankers and industrialists, among them a representative of General Motors, who regarded German poverty and helplessness as a gold mine for foreign investments: they could command very high rates of interest. What political guarantees they demanded against revolution I never knew, but they most certainly were demanded. The Nazis later came to power on such guarantees and with their help.

The Nazi movement was growing, loudly voicing revolutionary social ideas stolen from the Socialists and Communists, and utilizing the despair of the people and the Versailles Treaty with a masterly hand. With their coffers filled from mysterious sources, they were challenging Socialists and Communists and making a tremendous bid for power. But because they were still relatively weak, they revived a murder fraternity of the Middle Ages, the *Fememord*. Members of this group moved about at night, murdering trade-union leaders, Socialists and Communists, Jews, and professors who had enough integrity to defend the Republic. From the foreign bankers I heard no protests at such outrages; they talked only of "Communist violence."

Despite all their fierce talk, the Germans were still an orderly and disciplined people. Too disciplined, in fact. It was a Russian Communist who said that the German workers would revolt only if the Reichstag passed a law giving them permission. When the mounted police once charged a workers' demonstration in the Lustgarten in Berlin, the people who fled along the walks did not even step on the grass.

As an illustration of the servility of German womanhood, I recall the case of a woman from whom Viren and I rented rooms. She made a living for herself, her husband, and their son, but her husband beat her regularly, and once injured her so seriously that she nearly died. Viren and I took the case to police headquarters, but were informed that the police could not interfere in family affairs unless the wife was killed; in that case they could arrest the husband for murder.

It was the political confusion and inertia of the German people that left ajar the gates of the state and allowed the Nazis to move in. This attitude spread most rapidly during that era of heart-destroying insecurity; it grew out of hunger, despair, and political abuse until millions were willing to put their minds to sleep and follow anyone who promised them food, shelter, and peace. Of course, along with food, shelter, and temporary peace the Nazis assumed the right to feed the minds of the people. When the German people accepted this, they surrendered the one thing that separates man from beast — the responsibility of thinking for himself. When I visited Germany a number of years later, I heard people say with pride:

"Hitler thinks for me."

Far Horizons

ALTHOUGH I had looked on Europe as but a halting-place, eight years had passed. Sometimes I thought half of these years were thrown to the wind, and they the best years of my life, but at other times I knew I had gained as well as lost. I had learned to know myself and I had won back my health. I had broadened my knowledge, learned something of the German people and a great deal about India and Indians.

My alliance with Virendranath terminated early in 1928. To me he was not just an individual, but a political principle. For me he embodied the tragedy of a whole race. Had he been born English or American, I thought, his ability would have placed him among the great leaders of his age. Despite all this, I could not take up life with him again.

I was not to see Viren again until 1933. Much time and what seemed centuries of events had flowed past. Hitler was threatening and Viren had left Germany for the Soviet Union, where he was connected with the Academy of Sciences in Leningrad. Upon my arrival in Moscow he came to see me. He was at last growing old, his body thin and frail, his hair rapidly turning white. The desire to return to India obsessed him, but the British would trust him only if he were dust on a funeral pyre. What happened to him after that I do not know.

In an effort to free myself from him totally, I had spent a number of months of 1927 in Denmark and Czechoslovakia, where I wrote my first book, *Daughter of Earth*. This book was a desperate attempt to reorient my life. I returned to Berlin in 1928 to teach at the university, but as soon as vacation time came I left for France, where I completed plans to go first to China and then to India.

For two years previous to this, I had been studying Chinese history. The Chinese "Great Revolution" of 1922–27 had broken on the rocks of class warfare when the Kuomintang had split the national front and begun war on the Communists. Many middle-class Chinese revolutionaries had fled to Europe and the Soviet Union. I had made friends with a few of them and had edited a book by one. Virendranath had tried to unite all subjected Asiatic people behind the Chinese Revolution, and I had become involved. To the turmoil of German life was now added a new element, the Chinese Revolution; and at this time I attended Berlin meetings in which Chinese and Germans of different factions actually fought one another physically.

The League against Imperialism had been organized by the Communists, with Virendranath as one of its founders. The Indian delegation to its first Congress included Jawaharlal Nehru, and after the Congress in Brussels, Nehru came to Berlin, where I met him. He was a quiet, unspectacular man, totally unlike most Indian leaders. He was so modest and reserved that it was difficult to think of him as a political leader at all; yet he wielded tremendous influence over Indian youth. The Chinese Revolution had made a deep impression on him. Unlike China, India was unarmed. This major difference was a subject of constant conflict between the followers of Gandhi and the advocates of armed revolutionary struggle. Virendranath was an unrelenting advocate of armed struggle.

Returning to Germany from France in 1928, I halted in Frankfurt am Main, where I met the editors of the *Frankfurter Zeitung* and signed a contract to act as their special correspondent in China. I was to hold this position until shortly before Hitler came to power, after which that old liberal daily was taken over by the Nazis.

In leaving Germany I was venturing into the unknown, entering a responsible profession in which I had but little experience. Sometimes the thought of this new task frightened me. With conflicting emotions of relief and desolation I waved farewell to friends as my train pulled out of Berlin en route to China through the Soviet Union.

As I saw it in late 1928, Moscow was very different from the city I had visited for six months in 1921 as a member of the Indian delegation. In 1928 I stayed less than two months. On both occasions, however, I visited schools, hospitals, factories, the opera, theaters, and the homes of the *bezprizorni*, or homeless waifs. In 1928 I also visited some of the collective farms in the neighborhood of Moscow.

On my first visit in 1921, the "azure city" period of the Russian Revolution was coming to a close and the cold gray dawn of undramatic hard labor was beginning. At that time grim Red soldiers, clad in captured British clothing and carrying captured British and French guns, were pouring into Moscow from the southern front, where they had driven out the White armies financed by England and France.

The Volga famine was beginning, and I saw thousands of refugees sleeping in railway stations and empty churches. Typhus was decimating the Volga region. Herbert Hoover's relief organization was being organized and the Russians were suspicious. American intervention in the Soviet Union and Hoover's black record in Hungary led Russians to believe that, as in Hungary, Hoover would try to do with food what interventionist armies had failed to do by armed force.

In 1921 everyone was ragged, but filled with hope and enthusiasm. Men with holes in the seats of their pants would say: "Anyway, we're free." Once some friends of mine left Moscow for Germany, but the engine steamed away toward the east and it was hours before anyone realized that the passenger cars were still standing in the railway station. Almost no telephone worked, no lock locked, and no train ran on time.

In all, I visited the Soviet Union during three different periods. Through all these years I maintained an interest in the fate of the *bezprizorni*. In 1921 the Government had issued a manifesto concerning the rescue of these homeless children, and committees were formed to round them up, examine and sort them, and place them in homes. The fate of these children affected me deeply because of my own childhood.

The Soviet Government regarded all children as its wards. Years have now passed and I remember but faintly the individual dramas that were played out before the *bezprizorni* committees. A plainly-clad motherly woman of middle age, with ample hips and bosom, would often hold out her hands to a ragged, filthy little boy. The child would shrink back in fear. Carefully, deviously, the woman would talk and laugh with him, caress him, and slowly win him to her.

I went to a number of churches, cathedrals, and monasteries which had been fitted out as dormitories and schoolrooms for the children. Some buildings were being equipped with machinery and tools in order that the boys might be drawn into constructive and disciplined work. Any form of manhandling was forbidden, and the boys had their own self-government and tried any offending comrade.

In 1933-4, when I visited the Soviet Union for the third time, I was too ill to do much more than inquire about the fate of the *bezprizorni*. I learned that there were no longer any homeless children; and those who had once been waifs were men and women. Some were skilled workers or technicians, some university students, some officers or soldiers in the Red Army. Once, in a sanatorium in the Caucasus, I met a young agrarian economist, a graduate of Moscow University, who had been one of the 1921 waifs. In one of the Red Army rest homes I met two former *bezprizorni* who had become commanders. In the truest sense of the phrase, these men could say: The Soviet Union is my motherland.

Many of the foreign travelers were filled with a vitriolic hatred of the Soviet Union and would stare through the windows, calling attention to the poorly dressed people on the railway platforms. Though these foreigners had merely changed trains in Moscow, they felt that they had become authorities on Russian atrocities and tyranny. Certainly there had been many sad and tragic events during and after the Russian Revolution. But I never heard well-placed foreigners object to atrocities perpetrated by the White Guard armies against the Russian people, nor did they see anything wrong with the invasion of the Soviet Union by foreign armies during the Revolution.

For years there has remained deeply etched in my memory the scene that confronted me as I entered the Soviet Union in 1928. My train had passed through Poland and at railway stations I had watched fashionably dressed Polish ladies, painted and elegant, bid farewell to Polish officers in smart uniforms gaudy with gold braid. On a late wintry October day our train drew up at the Soviet-Polish frontier and I approached the customs station of the first socialist country. This building was rough-hewn out of great logs, and in the waning light it seemed to tower far into the sky and lose itself in the gloom. Before the entrance stood a tall Red Army soldier, his gray greatcoat reaching to the earth, his tall peaked cap with its red star shadowing his face. One end of his rifle rested on the earth and the fixed bayonet reached above his shoulder.

He stood as immovable as the powerful, rough-hewn building behind him. Beyond the scene stretched the gray, impenetrable darkness. Somewhere in that darkness I knew that people were struggling with the rudest forces of nature to build a new world of their own choosing, struggling alone and unaided. But always before the frontier station stood a guard, silent and watchful, facing the Western world. In such a position, I thought, had once stood the men who had founded my own country.

BOOK II

China, Past and Present

1928–1931

1928 ⌘ 1931

Into the Middle Ages

At the Soviet-Chinese frontier at Manchouli, Soviet porters helped us with our luggage. Silently they carried it into the customs station, where one of their representatives sat at a table and charged us a small sum for each piece. There was no asking for or accepting tips, no bowing and scraping. The system protected us and guarded the self-respect of the porters.

Our luggage stamped, we turned to face — the Middle Ages. Through the years I have never forgotten the frozen expression on the face of the dark-eyed Soviet railway man who stood watching the Chinese coolies take our luggage in charge.

A horde of these men, clothed in rags, scrambling and shouting, threw themselves on our bags and began fighting over each piece. Five or six fell upon my four suitcases and two struggled for my small typewriter — and their action seemed all the more debased because they were as tall and strong as the tallest Americans. Finally two of them carried off my typewriter, and before I could recover from shock, all of them began running with the luggage to the waiting train. Inside, six men crowded about me, holding out their hands and shouting for money. For a moment I was paralyzed, then began to pay them generously to get rid of them. A woman passenger kept warning me that if I overpaid they would demand more. I disregarded her; then the coolies were about me, shouting, shaking their fists, threatening.

A Chinese trainman came through the car, saw the scene, and with a shout began literally to kick the coolies down the aisle and off the train. Grasping their money, they ran like dogs.

I stood frozen. My face must have resembled that of the black-eyed Soviet worker who had watched the scene at the customs house. Perhaps his feeling had been what mine was now: here was humanity abandoned. The victims of every whim of misfortune, these men had grown to manhood like animals, without the slightest sense of responsibility toward each other or of human fellowship. When an opportunity for gain came, they battled one another like beasts, and the losers offered no protest. Here was "rugged individualism" and the "survival of the fittest" in its most primal form.

This scene became for me symptomatic of the social system of China, however disguised and decked out it might be. I saw it repeated in many other settings, often more polite, but always essentially the same — a life-and-death struggle in which the timid and weak went down before the ruthless and strong. Seeing it, I was forever saying to myself: "There, but for the grace of God, go I."

From the day I set foot on Chinese soil, I began gradually to realize that two paths lay before me. I could protect myself from the flood of abandoned humanity by building around myself a protective wall of coldness and indifference, even of hostility. I could learn to curse and strike out at those who molested me; or I could stand in the middle of the stream of life and let it strike me full force — risking robbery, disease, even death. For a long time I chose the latter way; then experience taught me to vary it by protecting myself to a certain extent. In my last years in China I again changed and took the stream full force.

Some people called me an idealist, others a fool; some called me both. Within my heart was some vague conviction that love and understanding begot love and understanding. For a long time I did not understand that most Chinese believe that all foreigners are rich. Nor did I realize how well dressed and well fed I seemed to the Chinese poor. To them I was nothing but a source of money. Once, when I fell while crossing a ditch in Peiping and lay unconscious, a crowd of Chinese, including a policeman, gathered around me, staring curiously — perhaps watching to see how a foreigner died. Not one offered to help, until by chance a student came by; he directed a ricksha coolie to take me to a hospital. Never had I felt so alone and deserted.

From that time on I began to seek out men and women who were socially aware, to wait in patience until they learned to trust me. Live apart from the Chinese people I would not. The road to an understanding of them and their country led only into their ranks; nor did there seem any other way for me to justify my own existence among them.

When I entered Manchuria in late December 1928, those three northeastern provinces of China were under the absolutist rule of Marshal Chang Hsueh-liang. He was called "Marshal" not because of experience or ability but because his father had been Marshal Chang Tso-lin, a bandit chieftain who had ruled Manchuria until the Japanese found him untrustworthy. They had killed the older man two years before. After that the struggle for the body and soul of his debauched young son began. On one side were the Japanese with their powerful grip on Manchuria; on the other the Kuomintang, the ruling nationalist party, striving to consolidate its hold on the entire land.

The Kuomintang had been formed by the father of the Chinese Republic, Dr. Sun Yat-sen, and as long as he lived it was a revolutionary party, based on a program of nationalism and independence, democracy, and the improvement of the condition of the people. In 1924 Dr. Sun had invited many Soviet advisers to Canton to help build a government and army that could overthrow the militarists. Under their guidance Army officers were trained, and the Kuomintang organized into a structure which resembled the Communist Party of the Soviet Union. Communists were admitted to it and for the first time in Chinese history peasants and workers were recognized as having equal rights with the middle and upper classes.

Yet everyone saw the handwriting on the wall. Millions of peasants and workers regarded the revised Kuomintang as the charter of their emancipation. The conservatives and moderates saw only that the masses were many and they few; and this they feared. Early in 1925 the great father of the Republic died. One year later a young military officer led his first abortive *Putsch* against the revolutionary Canton Government. His name was Chiang Kai-shek, and he had been one of Sun Yat-sen's followers. Dr. Sun had thought well enough of him to send him to Moscow to study, and for a time the Soviet advisers in China regarded him as the leading military man in the nationalist camp. But when Sun Yat-sen died, the cement that held the nationalist camp together began to crumble. Old class lines began to harden again and there was a fierce rivalry for the mantle that had fallen from the shoulders of the dead revolutionary leader. The three chief rivals were the Leftist, Wang Ching-wei, the extreme Right reactionary, Hu Han-min, and Chiang Kai-shek, the only military leader of the three and, by virtue of this fact, destined to become the most powerful. The canker of personal ambition for power seemed equal in each of them, and at one time or another all three had either lived or studied in Japan.

Chiang Kai-shek seemed to have a deep-rooted hatred of Soviet advisers. Just how much of this was real nationalism, how much was rivalry with Wang, who was then more closely linked with the Communists, and how much was the usual contempt for the masses, it seems impossible to say. Certainly Chiang's hatred seemed to concentrate on Michael Borodin, the chief Soviet adviser, who at that time exercised great power.

Despite the abortive 1926 *Putsch* led by Chiang Kai-shek, the breach in nationalist ranks was temporarily healed and General Chiang was appointed commander of the southern revolutionary army in the Northern Expedition of 1926-7 against the war-lords.

One year later, in April 1927, Shanghai Chinese bankers and factory-owners, aided by foreign bankers, offered General Chiang an initial loan of twenty-five million dollars if he would disarm and dissolve the trade unions and peasant leagues, purge the Kuomintang of Communists, and establish a new government in Nanking as rival to the one in Hankow, the city to which the revolutionary Canton Government had been moved.

Some said that Chiang Kai-shek walked the floor throughout the night before he made his final decision. Before him lay two roads: one was a revolution which would certainly be successful but would end in power for the people, the other pointed toward power for the owning classes, with himself as dictator. He chose the latter road, and the terror began on the night of April 11, 1927.

Thousands of factory workers and hundreds of intellectuals in Shanghai and other cities were slaughtered. There were no trials. In the interior, military governors, Army commanders, and landlords began killing peasants. Rivers of blood divided the earth of China. Foreign powers called it good and recognized the Government at Nanking as the only Government of China. Wang Ching-wei wavered, deserted Hankow, and fled to Europe, as did many other middle-class leaders. Madame Sun Yat-sen went abroad, refusing to lend her name to the Kuomintang.

Historical parallels are not always apt, yet it is significant that the German working class and intellectuals later went down like houses of cards before the Nazis, while the untrained, unarmed, unlettered Chinese workers and peasants resisted. Without outside help they began to fight — as they had fought to overthrow dynasty after dynasty.

Armed units of the Kuomintang Army, some of whose commanders were Communists or Communist-sympathizers, arose in July 1927 at Nanchang. After weeks of fighting in Kiangsi and Kwangtung Provinces they were all but wiped out. The workers and soldiers of Canton arose on December 11, but soon other armies, aided by foreign gunboats, defeated them and slaughtered thousands in the city. Under Chu Teh, a Kuomintang commander who had become a Communist, remnants fought their way back into the mountains of Kiangsi and soon a peasant-worker army led by Chu Teh and Mao Tze-tung, an intellectual of peasant origin, began to take form.

With infinite suffering, at colossal sacrifice, this new revolutionary army began to organize and train the people into the first Chinese Red Army of Workers and Peasants. For almost ten years it continued to grow and fight; in late 1934 it began its epic "Long March" to the far northwest, where in 1936–7 it helped weld together another united front, this time against the Japanese.

After the Nanking Government had been recognized by the foreign powers, the "purged" Kuomintang revised the "Three People's Principles" of the dead but still influential Sun Yat-sen. Nothing but nationalism now remained. The Chinese owning classes rejoiced at this, but the foreigners with special privileges did not. Much as in Germany, the common people wanted more than nationalism; one answer was some form of socialism. Landlordism held the peasants in virtual serfdom, and they could not advance until their bonds were broken. They needed the democratic rights of citizenship advocated by Sun Yat-sen. But Sun Yat-sen was dead and his body was claimed by the new Nanking Government. Many men who had been his mortal enemies now joined the Kuomintang and helped rule the country.

Such was the background of China as I saw it.

It was this Kuomintang that negotiated with Marshal Chang Hsueh-liang to bring Manchuria under the control of or into alliance with the Nanking Government. Marshal Chang was a war-lord, a supreme dictator, an opium-smoker and owner of concubines. But what Kuomintang member dared throw stones? The "Young Marshal" knew his Kuomintang. He agreed to raise the new national flag over Manchuria and place all foreign affairs in the hands of the Nanking Government. In return he received "presents" and was recognized as supreme ruler of Manchuria. In his domain he alone could appoint members of the Kuomintang.

He was a proud young war-lord, but conscious of his race. Unlike such war-lords as Chang Chung-chang in Shantung, he never received American consular officials while in bed with a concubine or with one perched on his knee. He could, however, halt his car on seeing a pretty woman, take

It was a bloody era in which workers, peasants and communists were beheaded in the streets.

Where child serfs in a Peking match factory slept.

her to his palace, and later return her to her family with a check in payment for use. Some families were proud of the royal touch.

I arrived in Harbin on New Year's Day 1929, just in time to witness the hoisting of the national flag over Manchuria. The national flag, incidentally, was produced by Chinese factories which had forced their workers to labor for twenty-four hours and then sold the flags at a handsome profit. The atmosphere was charged, for when the flag went up, the Japanese, having suffered a political defeat, became sullen and hostile. No one knew just when they would strike. Men talked in whispers, asking just how long it would take the Japanese to move troops into various parts of Manchuria. They were said to be in conference with Marshal Chang in Mukden, protesting and threatening, but he had replied that all foreign affairs were now in the hands of Nanking.

Would the Chinese fight? Some said they would, many said no. Most officials and military officers had bought their positions from the Government at Mukden, then used them to become rich. Some wanted only money, and they were in the pay of the Japanese. Others pined for such extra cash, but the Japanese found them useless. The Chief of Police of Harbin was a Japanese agent and, a few days before I arrived in that city, had opened fire on a public demonstration of students demanding the union of Manchuria with China proper. Many students had been wounded and a number killed. Manchuria reeked with corruption and treason.

Officials from two foreign consulates told me that the Japanese had lists of every Chinese official and officer, high and low, and knew just who could be bought and who not.

One of the first beggar cries that I heard in China was at Harbin: "Give! Give! May you become rich! May you become an official!" Sometimes the cry varied: "May you become rich! May you become a general!"

In Fu-jia-tien, the old Chinese section of Harbin, crowds of begging immigrant peasant women from Shantung and Hopei Provinces south of the Great Wall followed me through the streets. They had tucked their babies inside the front of their dirty padded jackets, and they threw themselves to their knees on the icy pavement before me, crying: "Give! May you become rich!"

When I passed on, they followed, crying, while a flock of children ran before me, falling on their knees and beating their heads on the ice, begging. I passed by; they followed and repeated their self-humiliation. To clear my path I would give again and again, only to find new crowds appearing from nowhere. I would take a ricksha, but they would cling to it, crying, and the puller would halt and wait for me to give. Only when my student guide drove them off with curses was I free of them.

I spent nearly three months in Manchuria, living in Chinese homes to which students took me. From foreign consular officials, Chinese railway officials, from students, publications, and every possible source, I sought to learn the extent of Japanese economic control and political power over railways, government machinery, investments in factories and land. Their tentacles reached into every cranny and they regarded every Chinese improvement as a menace. They operated through Chinese officials and Army officers, White Russian émigrés, and foreigners of every other nationality, including Americans.

My first series of articles were on "Japan's Mailed Fist in Manchuria." The *Frankfurter Zeitung* doubted their accuracy and did not publish them until Japan began the unheralded invasion of Manchuria on September 18, 1931.

The debasement and oppression of millions of the common people under feudal absolutism explain in part Japan's success in the final occupation of Manchuria. True, there was another side to this medal. There were Chinese patriots, among them officials, military men, and students, but they were few, and the students, regarded as "dangerous elements," were driven into secrecy.

There was indeed a gracious side to China: the life of those families which lived in spacious, sprawling homes, surrounded by high cement walls topped with broken glass.

White Russians stood on armed guard before the gates and in the watchtowers on the walls. These great homes sucked in wealth from the men who cultivated their estates, from timber workers in the great forests, from miners whose daily wage was less than twenty Chinese cents, and, in some cases, from the opium traffic.

The men and women who lived behind the walls of these "great family" homes regarded the poverty and suffering about them as only natural. It had always been so and would always be. Even students, more sensitive than others, took public scenes of brutality for granted, just as they took poverty and death. They would notice some cruel street scene only when I called attention to it. In this unawareness and indifference I saw how old and how deep was China's subjection.

One day a Chinese coolie, delivering laundry, passed me. From the ends of his shoulder-pole hung two baskets filled with newly washed clothing. The icy Siberian weather had coated his bushy eyebrows and the rag around his head with a frosty white sheen. Half-blinded by the cold, he slipped and fell, and his baskets flew out, scattering the clothing and striking a pedestrian. The pedestrian spewed curses at him, then passed on. Not one person paused — except a policeman. When the coolie saw him, he fell to his knees, threw up his arms over his head, and waited.

The policeman did not beat him. Instead he began to kick him, and with each kick the coolie was sent sprawling. He would rise to his knees time and again and with clasped hands plead for mercy. Crowds of people passed. They either did not see or merely gave an indifferent glance.

A number of times I exclaimed to my student interpreter: "This is the Middle Ages!"

The student beamed, perhaps proud that China should excel in anything.

On another occasion I heard the tramp of feet and the rumble of a cart. I looked back to see two lines of soldiers walking with the lithe grace of panthers, their breath rising about them in small clouds. Between the two columns rumbled a cart drawn by a shaggy Mongolian pony, and on it sat two prisoners with their hands bound behind them. They were filthy and their hair had grown long and matted. Behind each was a narrow board on which was written the name of the captive and the crime for which he was to be executed.

A curious crowd of men and boys ran after them. Outside Fu-jia-tien was an open space where prisoners were publicly beheaded before gawking mobs. The severed heads were often placed in baskets and hung up as a warning to others. Passers-by shrugged their shoulders. The victims were unlucky, they said. They had not succeeded in something or other.

After the cart had passed, my student guide, with the air of a man of the world, imparted a bit of information: "Over in Kirin, when bandits are beheaded, the relatives of men they have killed sometimes cut out their hearts and eat them."

Like the proverbial fool who walks in where angels fear to tread, I blundered in and out of offices and institutions, met all kinds of people openly or secretly, and asked such direct questions that those to whom I spoke were often struck dumb. Now and then a man would be so astonished that he would answer truthfully, then hastily backtrack. It was some time before I realized that China is a land of political secrecy and cunning and that few men asked or answered direct questions. They trusted no one.

One of my interviews with the president of the Chamber of Commerce was ironically amusing. I had learned that this man, like most of his colleagues, dealt in opium, and I had just visited an opium village in which there were long barracks filled with little opium-smoking cells. So I walked into the Chamber of Commerce and asked its president just how much opium was smoked in that village in, say, one week.

Dressed in his long blue fur-lined silk gown, he sat on the edge of his chair, his hands braced on his knees, and stared at me as a snake watches a bird. Recovering his composure, he graciously announced that it was an honor to meet a foreign lady who took an interest in Chinese affairs. My life must be bitter and I surely found the cold weather distressing. No, I replied, I liked the cold weather, but was interested in the opium traffic, of which I had so often read.

Did I enjoy good health, and did I like China? he asked. My health was excellent, I assured him. Had I seen the very old pagoda near the city? I had seen it, but was not interested in it as much as in opium. He smiled pleasantly and assured me that it had been an honor to make my acquaintance and he hoped I would call again, although he felt certain my important work would make that impossible. He rose and with elaborate courtesy bowed me out of the building, down the walk, and out of the gate!

After a few such interviews I began to learn Chinese tactics. Personal friendships, banquets, and endless hours of chatter might build up confidence and loosen men's tongues, but a direct question was met with blank stares followed by polite questions about my health. Incidentally, people who were asked such questions might well think of their health!

One day my student guide introduced me to a new aspect of this ancient world. I told him of an article which I had read in the Japanese-owned *Manchurian Daily News*. It had reported that twenty Japanese Communists, accused of organizing Chinese and Japanese railway workers and miners, had been arrested and taken to Dairen. But after that the subject had never been mentioned again. The student informed me that such arrests were quite common and that Manchurian prisons were filled with hundreds of Chinese and Korean nationalists accused of being Communists; Japanese prisoners were removed to Japan. Some prisoners died of sickness or torture and others were beheaded or shot, he said. But he refused to go with me to the Governor to ask for a permit to visit the prisons. If I did such a dangerous thing, he said, not only would I be suspected of being a Communist, but his own life would be in danger.

One day he took me to see some of the students who had been wounded in a demonstration. I found one convalescing in a small barren room in a barn-like apartment house. This building swarmed like a rabbit warren with poor people. Across the hall from the student was a little room occupied by Sano, a Japanese printer who spoke English. Shelves filled with books and pamphlets aroused my suspicion that he was a Japanese spy posing as a Communist. I had been in dozens of homes in north Manchuria, but no student kept any books besides texts in his room. One student had once showed me two copies of Gorky's novels bound as Confucian Classics, but even these he kept hidden.

I sat down near Sano's book-shelves and casually lifted out some of the volumes. A few concerned the Japanese peasant movement and their paper covers actually bore the sign of the hammer and sickle. I asked Sano about the twenty Japanese labor organizers who had been arrested and taken to Dairen. He turned an amiable but perfectly blank face toward me and, instead of answering, asked about the German Communist movement. I replied that I knew little about it beyond what I read in the press. Had I met any Japanese Communists in Moscow? he asked. I had met a Japanese playwright, but I told the printer I had met no one.

This futile sparring went on for some time and finally Sano and I bowed politely to each other and parted. A week later, however, my student guide told me that Sano had "run away" — he had really been a labor organizer. Japanese secret police had made inquiries about him at the newspaper on which he worked and he had immediately slipped out the back door and disappeared.

The conversation of men around me was often punctuated by this cryptic phrase: "He has run away." Chinese students, railway officials, clerks in foreign consulates, teachers and professors, and even members of the Kuomintang from Nanking, all had friends or relatives who were members of a great international brotherhood that seemed to be on the run. Once in Harbin I secretly met a representative of the Kuomintang from Nanking. He was a newspaper man, but even he was living in hiding and seemed to be poised, ready to run. He was anti-Communist and a nationalist, but only Marshal Chiang's official Kuomintang could exist in Manchuria. "It is very difficult," he kept telling me.

Soon I myself was drawn into this great international brotherhood of people who "ran away." A Chinese inspector on the Chinese Eastern Railway invited me to dinner one evening and began to tell a strange story. He had a friend, chief clerk in the American Consulate, he said, who had seen a confidential document from the British secret service informing the Consulate that I was not an American citizen, but a British subject, married to an Indian seditionist. My passport was false, the report had charged. I was to be summoned to the American Consulate and my passport taken from me. The clerk wanted to warn me to "run away."

I said the report was false and that I would go to the Consulate and tell them so.

"If you do that," the alarmed inspector cried, "the Consul General will suspect where you got the report and my friend will lose his job! He may even be suspected of being a Communist! You had better run away."

I talked about my civil rights, but the inspector insisted that nobody in Manchuria had ever heard of such things.

Though the charge against me was untrue, and though I was a correspondent, I decided to wait until I reached the American Embassy or some American consulate in China proper before I began to talk about civil rights. That same night the inspector and a student — my guide and interpreter — took my luggage to the railway station, checked it, and bought two tickets. Early next morning I left money on a table in my room and walked out. The student interpreter, who spoke both English and Japanese, was waiting for me. We slipped away. "When dining with the devil, use a long spoon," says an old Indian proverb.

A few days later as we drove through the Japanese and foreign settlements into the walled city of Mukden, where the Chinese population lived, our droshky-driver leaned back and shouted the latest news. Marshal Chang Hsueh-liang had just shot a General, and everyone was petrified with fear. Marshal Chang, it seemed, had invited some high officers to a banquet, beckoned General Yang Yu-ting, his chief military rival, into a side room, and shot him. He sent the body home to the General's family with a handsome check and a letter declaring that the corpse had been his best friend and that he had wept tears over it.

As a rule the huge steel-studded gates of Mukden were closed at midnight and opened at daybreak. After the latest shooting, however, they had been closed at eight each night and guards patrolled the wall and streets. Within a few days the city returned to normal, though people still talked in whispers.

We found refuge in a Chinese home within the shadow of the high walls surrounding Marshal Chang's palace. Life in Mukden was medieval. Watchmen with brass gongs told the hours of the silent night. Their voices, high and mournful, were swallowed up by the harsh cold, and no sound lingered. The world was wrapped in snow and, except for the two main thoroughfares, the city lay in white silence. Houses were encased in high walls which rose on either side of narrow streets. An occasional tree from some garden leaned over the streets, and sometimes a full moon, flowing through barren branches, left a delicate tracery on the earth.

From inside our walls we often heard the high voices of beggar women, peasant immigrants from famine-stricken regions within China, crying: "Give! May you be rich! May you be an official!" Then the night would strangle the cry.

In the evenings we would hire rickshas and drive to restaurants or the homes of friends. The soft-shod feet of the tall ricksha-pullers made not a sound. From afar came the beggars' cries and the bells or gongs of street venders.

Once we came out upon the main street just as a footbound woman, leading a child by the hand, slipped and fell. Her basket of meager provisions scattered about her. A crowd gathered and laughed uproariously. She sat perfectly still, looked about her, then began to "curse the street." She cursed the spirit of their mother's mother and their mother's mother's mother. She related tales of their incest and worse.

She worked them over and up and down until they lowered their heads and hurried away. At last she rose painfully on her "lily feet," gathered up her provisions, and hobbled away.

I visited Chinese people at night, and during the day went to factories, schools, the new Mukden arsenal, and other institutions. From Harbin I had written a Japanese woman friend in Tokyo for an introduction to Japanese in Manchuria. When the introduction came a new world was opened to me. As guest in the homes of Japanese, I learned of the deep contempt which the Japanese entertained for all Chinese and for all women. They talked of Chinese dirt, corruption, and cunning and of their concubines.

"Many Japanese women marry Chinese men," I reminded one professor.

"Yes," he answered bitterly, "because our women are obedient."

"Not all," I replied. "I was introduced to you by a modern Japanese woman."

His voice was withering: "We Japanese have no respect for such women!"

His wife gave me a timid look, then lowered her head.

Through these Japanese I visited Japanese factories, their Fushun mines, and their schools for Chinese. They objected to my Chinese interpreter, but I insisted that I did not like to travel alone. I instructed my interpreter not to indicate that he knew the Japanese language. If I left him in any factory while I went on, he was to talk, if possible, with the Chinese workers.

Almost all Chinese in Japanese mines or factories were forced to live in enclosed barracks or dormitories and were not permitted to leave them without a special pass. Few Chinese were interested enough in the lot of the workers to inquire about their living-conditions. Even students, generally suspected of being potential or actual Communists, had no contact with workers and thought of them as unimportant.

Like the factories, the great Fushun collieries maintained

the contract labor system, a disguised form of serfdom. This system operated in all Japanese factories in Manchuria and China, in many foreign and Chinese factories in China proper, in all mines, and all along the waterfronts. A labor contractor, working independently or for some rich man, would supply workers at perhaps twenty cents a day for a ten-, twelve-, or fourteen-hour work-day over a period of years. He would give the workers miserable food and shelter and perhaps five or ten cents a day. If it were a silk or cotton factory, he would contract for hundreds of village girls, paying their families thirty to fifty dollars for a period of years and the girls a few coppers a month. If workers fell ill from tuberculosis or heart ailments, the contractor dismissed them summarily. A contractor's only obligation was, if they died while on the job, to buy some sort of crude coffin and ship the bodies home.

Workers could not leave their barracks without permission, and if they ran away the police hunted them down and returned them to their owner. In later years I knew of cases in which the British police of the International Settlement in Shanghai arrested runaway girl laborers and returned them to their masters.

When I went through the Fushun mines and their barrack dormitories, I could not help exclaiming at the emaciated bodies of the miners. It was deep winter, yet their clothing was of thin cotton and so badly torn that the bare flesh was exposed. The Japanese glibly explained: "The miners squander their money in drinking, gambling, and prostitution. Most of them have syphilis. Our company maintains a medical clinic, but few go there."

The Japanese did indeed provide medical care and the Fushun mines even had a bath-house for workers. But medical care was not free except to men injured in mine disasters. A Japanese engineer was disconcerted when I told him that I knew the miners worked not eight hours, as he said, but ten, and that their pay was five cents a day, paid by the contractor. Miners were fined for indifference, lateness, slowness, absence from work for any reason, "damage," or "in-

The official figures of the Shanghai Municipal Council revealed that from 32,000 to 35,000 dead bodies were picked up in the streets of the city each year and buried in paupers' graves.

Four thousand workers, peasants, soldiers and students were mowed down in the counter-revolution which followed the Canton Commune, December 11, 1927.

subordination." At the end of each fortnight all were in debt to Chinese usurers. The mine always kept the first fortnight's wage as guarantee, and only if workers remained until the end of their contract and did not "agitate," try to form trade unions, or strike did they get the money which had been withheld.

"The contract system is merely an old Chinese custom," the Japanese told me.

The Mukden home in which I lived was torn by conflict between the old and the new. The family consisted of a father, his wife, and two sons, and two young grandchildren whose parents had died in the plague a few months before. We celebrated the Chinese New Year in this home — or rather we mourned it. Because of debt, the father and two sons had to leave the house and live with friends until New Year's Day. If debts were not paid before New Year's Eve, the creditors could not demand payment again until another year had passed.

Often I heard the loud, angry voices of the sons and their father. The old mother, who had borne many children but had lost all except the two sons, had grown ugly and hollow-breasted. She would sometimes turn her head away lest I see her eyes red with weeping. One quarrel developed because the father wanted to ask me for money to pay his debts. At the same time he was also planning to buy a concubine, a girl of sixteen, for seven hundred dollars. His rebellious sons threatened to leave home and join the Army.

The most ancient of Chinese teachings, filial piety, was crumbling before the onslaught of modern thought, and, in this case, of Christianity. Both sons were in high school, spoke English, and read modern books. The elder was a Christian and a nationalist, the younger a Christian and a Communist. They also quarreled with each other. The Communist son referred to Marshal Chang Hsueh-liang as a feudal war-lord who shot down anyone who displeased him. The elder son argued that the "Young Marshal" had succeeded in raising the national flag, was defying the Japanese by building railways and industries, enlarging the Mukden arsenal, and opening a modern military school to train young officers. When asked who could take the Young Marshal's place, the young Communist could not reply. The workers were not organized, even to fight the Japanese, and all students or Korean nationalists who worked against the Japanese were hunted down. The peasants were being cheated with worthless paper money and robbed by landlords, usurers, and officials.

At many a banquet table surrounded by officials I advocated trade unions as a method of opposing the Japanese. But Chinese, Japanese, and all foreigners were afraid of trade unions. Organized workers would demand high wages and shorter hours and turn into Communist bandits, they said.

When I left Mukden for Dairen and China proper, my student interpreter refused to go with me. Dairen was under the dictatorship of the Japanese, and every Chinese was watched. A student or two whom he had formerly known there had "run away." When I arrived at Dairen, two Japanese, each bowing politely and sucking in his breath, stepped forward to receive me and lead me to a car. "Friends" in Mukden had asked them to take me to the big Japanese hotel of the South Manchurian Railway. I went, registered — and surrendered my passport. When I set out to find several Japanese professors, the two Japanese were again waiting to escort me. Throughout my stay in Dairen they popped up everywhere and at all hours.

I tried to be as polite to them as they were to me, but never succeeded. I could not suck in my breath as they did, nor could I belch to show my appreciation of a good meal. Neither could I bow very low, because my notes and copies of my articles prevented me from doing so. I was impolite enough to carry these next to my skin instead of leaving them in my hotel for my escorts to read.

Despite their polite protests, I took a British coastal steamer from Dairen to Tientsin, instead of free passage on a Japanese vessel. When I told the Irish captain some of my Dairen experiences, he laughed and recalled an incident when he had made his first trip to Dairen. A Japanese quarantine officer had boarded his vessel, bowed very low, sucked in his breath, and announced:

"I am the plague."

"And roight he was!" laughed the Irish sea captain.

Patricians and Proletarians

THE CHINESE patricians liked to discuss the Chinese attitude toward death. Chinese philosophy, they said, had taught the people to accept death serenely. A German in Tientsin even told me that Chinese did not mind having their heads chopped off. "They are used to it," he said. I myself had seen a man dying in the street and a crowd gather, curious to see just how he died. Some sighed, their eyes sorrowful, but none tried to help. When I offered to call an ambulance, a friend of mine objected:

"If you do that, you must pay for the ambulance and cover the hospital bill and the burial expenses. If he recovers, you must support him. If you do not, he will die somewhere else."

In Tientsin I visited the outposts of death. A taxi took me to Nankai University to meet a group of professors. Leaving the well-paved streets of the foreign concessions, our car bounded along the rutted dirt road which the rains had turned into a quagmire. On the drab mud flats crouched many small mud and thatch villages. Here men made their last stand against death. Ragged, dirty children with small baskets picked at garbage heaps. In the fields and along the road were many grave-mounds from which the earth had fallen away, exposing the decaying coffins level with the earth. Frightened by the roar of our engine, curs leaped from the crumbling bones which they had been gnawing, and fled snarling into the fields.

The Nankai University patricians deplored this and hoped reforms would one day change such conditions. They were publishing a monthly magazine of agrarian and industrial research, and were later to publish a thick quarterly. They planned to take over a district or two somewhere in north China and introduce modern accounting, co-operative marketing, mass education, and medical clinics. Peiping doctors and professors were helping. They hoped these model districts would show how suffering could be alleviated if illegal or excessive taxes could be abolished and if the people were some time, somehow, aided in buying back the land they had lost to landlords and officials.

The patricians of Peiping were a group of men and a few women who had inherited the finest elements of Chinese culture and gleaned the best from the universities of America and England. Few were rich, most of them springing from landed gentry of moderate means. They were gracious, charming, and keen-witted. I saw the colleges and universities in which they taught, the scientific institutions they were trying to build, and that ancient city whose color, sound, and leisurely way of life they all loved. In other days it had been the center of the intellectual renaissance in which they had played so important a role. The city, like their minds, echoed the best in China's past. Though some had been influenced by Christian philosophy, few were Christians and all rejected the Christian idea that man is born evil. They spoke of science and education as the best means toward good ends. They resembled the patricians of ancient Greece; and like ancient Greece their society rested on the backs of men not far removed from slavery.

In China, as in classic Greece, "family women" never associated with men as friends or comrades. Only a few girl students dared become actresses, though many were learning to walk openly in the streets with men friends. In China, as in Greece, no man of education did physical labor. Theirs was the realm of intellect and they lost face by physical work.

In feminine fashion I challenged the Peiping patricians on the score of the backwardness of the wives of respectable men, on the concubine system, and on courtesans. Some asserted that courtesans were at least better than the prostitute system of the West. Worse, I insisted, for the West recognized prostitution as an evil; in China men's desires were absolute. A Chinese woman who dared take a lover could be "set aside" by her husband and family; the man never.

They spoke of the old family system in which the possession of concubines gave a man "face." The concubines were bought and could be sold or given away to subordinates. A poet who became my friend even asserted that concubines were the only opportunity for love that a man had. "Ridiculous!" I protested. "The concubine does not choose love — she is bought."

This poet had broken with the family system; like many other men he had refused the wife chosen by his family although she had been taken into his father's home as daughter-in-law. He himself had followed the modern way and married an actress; his family had not recognized the marriage and had refused to receive the new wife. Once he told me that he could love no woman over twenty who was not beautiful, did not have a willowy waist, or weighed more than a hundred pounds. Often when he and I sat in the teahouses, the restaurants, or the old Peiping theater I would ask him to select from the women around us those he considered beautiful.

"You choose empty, baby-faced women," I told him.

He was always sorry that I was a woman and that he could not smuggle me into an evening party at the home of some wealthy *hetæra*, mistress of one of his patrician friends. He himself had no courtesan mistress, but now and then let his gaze fall upon the wife of some other man.

Some modern men married educated women, but soon the family system devoured the wives. The wife ceased to keep abreast of her husband intellectually. While he sought love outside the home, she became merely the mother of his children. When I asked such a wife what she read, she answered: "Oh, you see, I graduated ten years ago and shortly afterwards married."

A few strong-minded modern women kept pace intellectually with their husbands. They were feminists of will and decision. Woe to the husband of such a woman if he tried to take a concubine or crept to a courtesan! When I listened to these women I wondered if the old custom of footbinding had not been simply a clever device to cripple women and keep them submissive.

For a time I was a companion of the patricians; and with a few I remained good friends. To them I was not man, woman, concubine, or courtesan. I was a foreigner who was no longer young, was not beautiful, earned her own living, and associated with men as an equal. Neither wifehood nor love was my profession.

Most of the patricians were humanists. Some, influenced by John Dewey, were pragmatists. Many, too, had been affected by Bertrand Russell's superlatively keen analyses of society and his crystal-clear atheism. They agreed with him, as I did, that if there had been no fear of death, there would have been no belief in immortality. (But they opposed his book on China because it praised China's evils and made the young people arrogant.)

In their pragmatism these patricians tended to distrust any movements that had not proved practicable. They approved American democracy, but questioned Russian Communism. I argued that the Soviet Union no less than America had had to chart a new course in history and, like Revolutionary America, was fighting for it against European opposition; but they asserted that Marxism was still only an experiment in the Soviet Union and had not proved itself. Many Chinese students believed in it, and some peasants and workers in southern China were fighting for it, but they themselves opposed it. Some insisted that there were no classes in China and that this idea had merely been invented by Marxists. One told me he thought the Chinese Communists should be given a province in which to experiment; if it proved practicable, other provinces might copy it. Science and education were the way to progress, they said; look what science had done in the West. I argued, of course, that Communists also used science and education.

One patrician, an interesting and thoughtful man, was an anthropologist who spent much time excavating ancient

Chinese settlements in the valley of "China's Sorrow," the Yellow River; buildings, utensils, works of art, oracle bones, and even cowrie shells, a form of money fashioned like the female genital organ — perhaps a relic of some ancient matriarchal system — were unearthed. This was valuable and precious, I admitted, but what about the present? The region in which they worked was the scene of wars, Yellow River floods, and famine. Millions of peasants had repeatedly been driven from their homes. For a bowl of noodles or rice they had sold their land to war-lords, landowners, or officials. Even their most essential possessions — primitive agricultural implements — had to be bartered in the market. Their sons poured into the armies to earn their rice; their wives and children were sold as servants, and their daughters as prostitutes or concubines. Driven by hunger, these peasants had stripped the land of all shrubs and trees, selling them as fuel in order that they themselves might eat. When the rains came, no plant was left to hold the water in the soil. "China's Sorrow" overflowed and desolated the land. Then had come the wind storms. The top soil had been whirled away in great clouds, and the desert had crept ever nearer. In some Chinese cities, one could walk on sand dunes that rose to the top of the city walls. Soon, I said, they too would become buried cities of the past.

"Why unearth dead cities now?" I asked. "Excavate them fifty years hence when the conditions that make more dead cities have been wiped out!"

Of course, that meant taking part in politics, and of course politics was corrupt and dangerous. Even if the patricians entered politics, they would merely be swallowed up, I was told. They must wait for better days, they said. But I wondered who could afford to wait.

In Peiping I visited a match factory. All but the foremen and a few men manning the engine were little children who had been bought from the peasants. Long lines of them, some hardly more than babies, stood twelve hours a day before trays filled with matches, their small hands working like lightning as they filled match-boxes. A foreman carrying a short stick walked back and forth along the aisles.

Each day the children were fed two meals of millet gruel and salt; sometimes there were a few bits of greens and sometimes a little lard. To keep warm they slept crowded close together on long *k'angs*, earthen platforms extending the length of barrack-like rooms and weakly heated by a coiling flue beneath. I asked about one child, covered by a thin quilt, lying on a *k'ang*. He had been sick for three days; no one knew why and there was no medical care. He would either live or die.

In China death moved about as bold as a lord. It found a home in the grisly poverty of peasant huts. It came in the form of tuberculosis or heart failure to miners and factory workers. It haunted the dreams of the rich, who armed themselves with foreign machine-guns to meet the threat of peasant rebellions such as had overthrown dynasty after dynasty. Foreigners living luxuriously in the port cities feared it in every advance made by China, whether through the nationalist Kuomintang or through a peasant revolution led by Communists.

Death walked arm in arm with poor students, but they braved it and thought only in terms of the social revolution. So I said to the patricians: "Your philosophy of death is false! The students do not accept it. Else why are they rebellious, searching the whole world for the way to a better life?"

In these degenerate days, argued the patricians, students were undisciplined and irresponsible, using school and university dormitories merely as centers of propaganda. How true this was I do not know. Certainly some students had become revolutionaries overnight. Was this not because they had no way of putting into practice what they learned? Forbidden by tradition to do physical labor, they were frail, delicate, almost a race apart. Despite this, many students, studying intensely, became critical and bitter, challenging death and intimidated neither by prowling spies nor by policemen's clubs.

Some patricians gave me a dinner one night, and I began

to understand why many foreigners loved Peiping, cultivated Chinese friends, and studied the language. We started for a restaurant that had in other days entertained nobility. Leaving the compound of the old Chinese house where I lived, I pulled the red-lacquered door behind me just as a coolie was passing. My fur coat seemed to awaken some childhood memory in him. With his face turned toward the wintry sky he broke into a lullaby about a tiger with a fierce fur skin but a tender heart beneath. Until he reached the corner he sang to a cold snowy world; then, surely, as did the whole leisure-loving Peiping populace, he halted in a crowd to laugh at a clown or juggler, a dancing bear, or perhaps some big swordsmen from Shantung performing in the streets.

My friends joined me. As we entered the old Chinese restaurant, waiters bawled until the open rafters trembled: "Eight guests arrived!"

Singsong girls were wailing, apparently running scales — and taking in all the flats as they passed — to the accompaniment of a screeching Chinese violin. The songs were from some Peiping opera. The singing mingled with the raised voices of men playing the finger drinking game — in which the loser must each time drain his cup dry. Their voices mingled with those of waiters bawling announcements of new guests. The noise must have warmed the heart of the restaurant-owner, for he kept smiling and bowing.

Several waiters brought open charcoal braziers to our room and others appeared with many small cups of various wines, one of them the cool, white, treacherous *bei-gar*. After my hosts had sampled the liquors, they gave their orders, and soon small pitchers of cold *bei-gar* and hot wine were brought in, along with platters of *hsiao chirh* — literally "small eats." Then came the manager, ever bowing and smiling, and behind him a column of waiters with the famous Peiping ducks, ready plucked, which we had seen hanging from the rafters as we entered. Our hosts felt the various ducks like connoisseurs, selected the best, and sent them away to be braised.

Meanwhile we sat about drinking from our ever full winecups, eating, laying down our chopsticks politely, and conversing. One short fat guest lifted his cup and cried: "Bottoms up!" That reminded him of a friend who had not quite mastered English, but wished to show off before some foreign guests. He had lifted his winecup and solemnly announced: "We will now show our bottoms!"

Once after a gale of laughter had subsided, one of my hosts exclaimed: "I repeat: There are no classes in China. Classes! Marxians invented the idea! My ricksha coolie and I can laugh and talk like old friends as he pulls me through the streets."

"Would you be his friend if you had to pull him through the street?" I interrupted. "Or if he revolted? You are friends only so long as he accepts his inferior position."

"*I also* am a proletarian. I work for my living," replied by table companion complacently.

One of my hosts lifted a heap of fried chicken livers on his chopsticks and placed them on my small plate. The poet who later on became my friend called for paper, brush, and ink and began to create a Chinese name for me. I objected to such a name as Beautiful Plum Blossom or Lotus Bud or Perfumed Brook. Finally he gave me the old Chinese family name of "Shih" and added the two syllables "mei ling." When I rejected the latter, he merely Latinized the name to "Shih Mei Di Li," which had no meaning at all; but because it had four syllables he called me a Mongol. My christening called for more wine and for a poem about the waves of the sea. I seemed to have responded with a song. It must have been "The Streets of Laredo," for that is the one song I really know. It was hailed as a work of classical art.

Then the duck! First we all sat and looked at it admiringly, assuring each other that it was a thing to see, then die. Our hosts shooks their heads deprecatingly, calling it most inferior. With a slight clatter we leveled our chopsticks on the table, then all plunged in together, lifting bits of the thin-sliced skin and flesh onto the fine pieces of unleavened pancake before us. We tapped them elegantly with a mixture of sauces, laid a baby onion on top, rolled the pancake up, and took a bite. We closed our eyes prayerfully for a second, then looked at our hosts gratefully, like beggars. The dams of sound split wide open after that. We drank and ate, pausing only to argue amiably about Chinese women and patricians and proletarians. The courses kept coming and the wine flowed.

When at last we rose to depart, a waiter went into the courtyard and bawled out the size of our tip, and as we went down the courtyard another waiter took up the cry. A third echoed it as we passed out. We were like an army of generals parading between columns of saluting privates. This gave us tremendous "face" and encouraged other guests to give generously. What a difference it makes if a waiter bawls out a tip of two dollars rather than ten cents!

We rode home in rickshas through the cold white streets, and someone behind me began to run scales in high falsetto about a prisoner who refused to be rescued because the prison was the prison of love. I took an oath that I would never, never leave Peiping, but would become a patrician myself even if it took all my life. This oath became mixed up with thoughts about my ricksha coolie silently running like a tired horse before me, his heaving breath interrupted by a rotten cough. Suddenly his broad shoulders began to remind me of my father's. I was a dog and the whole lot of us were dogs!

"Listen, you!" I screamed at my hosts in most unpatrician tones. "Get out and pull your ricksha coolie home! Let's all get out and pull our ricksha coolies home! Let's prove there are no classes in China!"

Fields of Life and Death

As my train roared southward from Peiping, I sat with my face pressed against the window of my compartment, staring at the great plains of the north. The whistle wailed inhumanly as we plunged onward into the hard white night. Graves, graves, graves, countless ancestral graves in countless ancestral fields! Always the presence of death! A few naked trees along the railway embankment . . . now and then the dark crenelated walls of some ancient city. . . . My heart filled with loneliness; I recalled the old Japanese "Wanderer's Song":

> The night is bitter cold,
> Our hearts are lonely.
> Like birds of passage we travel.
> Even through wind and snow,
> Still we must travel the long road.

Then Nanking, the Chinese capital: a few modern Chinese Government buildings, the beautiful structures of several mission universities, fine new villas under construction, and, beyond, the new Sun Yat-sen mausoleum, where the body of the founder of the Republic would soon be laid in uneasy rest. The blue and white mass of the tomb arose on the side of Purple Mountain like a glorified Standard Oil station, its garishness cast in high relief by the simple majesty of the near-by tomb of the founder of the Ming Dynasty.

The young Kuomintang official who had been sent to guide me seemed to embody all the bastard fusions of the Chinese Revolution. In a foreign business suit, he stood on the flat roof of the ancient Ming tomb and sang "The Spanish Cavalier." As he and I left the inn where I was staying, an automobile whirled by, crushing a dog under its wheels. When I gasped and halted, the young man exclaimed: "I'm surprised! I thought you a woman of the world!" We halted to hire rickshas, and the young fellow, whose name was Moh, chose two old men who were dressed in rags and looked like scarecrows. He then gave me some friendly advice concerning the selection of ricksha coolies: "Always take the older and poorer ones. They cannot afford to bargain very long and will always take less than the young coolies."

After visiting the tombs we went to the foot of the hill,

where we met Colonel J. L. Hwang, a huge bulky man, head of the new Officers' Moral Endeavor Association, who was to show me through the Central Military Academy and his association. Before leaving, Colonel Hwang took me through a small cottage still under construction.

"This house," he explained, "is being built for Madame Sun Yat-sen, the widow of the late Dr. Sun. She will live here near the tomb."

"Do you think Madame Sun will live here?" I asked.

"Oh, certainly! She is a member of the Central Committee of the party!"

"I thought she was in exile."

His manner and voice became offensively sarcastic. He asked if she was in Moscow — and where was Borodin?

Through my mind flashed the thought: "So this is the way they fight!" I answered that Madame Sun was in Germany, or so I had heard. But what remained with me always was the unscrupulousness of the remark. Colonel Hwang was one of the most trusted retainers of General and Madame Chiang Kai-shek; in fact, foreign journalists called him the "Grand Eunuch." My resentment had nothing to do with Madame Sun's personality, for I had never regarded her as sacred. Her ability and knowledge were said to be limited, but she was a woman of integrity and unblemished character. She had even gone into exile rather than permit her name to be misused by the Kuomintang. Both Chinese and Japanese of feudal outlook, I found, often used personal attacks to discredit either women or political movements.

Despite this episode and countless others like it, I sincerely sympathized with the Government's hope of freeing itself from the shackles of those unfair treaties into which China had once entered. I interviewed high officials, particularly those of the Ministry of Foreign Affairs, and tried to be scrupulously fair in my articles. At the same time I told officials over many a dinner table that I would not wish to see extraterritoriality abolished if it meant that I and other Americans might be subjected to their medieval laws and perhaps be thrown into their barbarous prisons.

When I first arrived in Nanking, the Kuomintang Congress was in session. No journalist, Chinese or foreign, was permitted to attend. After it was finished, the party handed out propaganda which it naïvely expected correspondents to cable abroad. There were some progressive nationalists in the Kuomintang, one of them Dr. T. V. Soong, the Minister of Finance, but they had little power. Somewhere in the heaps of propaganda literature I had read that the Kuomintang had 39,000 members. I asked an official if this referred to the whole country or only Nanking. He looked uneasy and answered evasively. The fact was that the Kuomintang had only 39,000 members out of a population of 450,000,000 people, that it had become, in other words, a small closed corporation of government officials and their subordinates. Even some of these despised its practices, yet remained members because they would not get positions otherwise.

On this, my first trip to Nanking, I still believed that the Kuomintang represented at least China's national interests. Its representatives talked of labor unions, but seemed to expect me to take their word that such unions existed. I asked to visit the unions. The young official given me as guide and interpreter first took me to a factory. The British manager refused to allow me to enter and merely instructed his comprador, a very oily and prosperous-looking Chinese, to talk to me. The Chinese simply asked me to take his word for factory conditions. After this travesty of a visit we went to a near-by building where we found a solitary man asleep with his head on the table. Apart from the table and two chairs, the only other things in the room were a teapot and two cups in front of the sleeper. This was the union office. When we awakened the man, he stood up sleepily and I saw a typical student who, judging by his evasive talk, seemed to have been sent to wait for me. He was utterly unable to answer any question — even as to the number of members of the union. When I asked how the weekly dues, deducted from the workers' wages, were spent, he made no attempt to answer.

I learned later that the trade-union fees were merely a tribute imposed on the workers by the Kuomintang. Its function was to collect money and prevent any workers' activity. Together with the factory-owners and compradors, it ferreted out discontented workers and branded them as Communists.

My guide seemed anxious to become friendly with me and I wondered why. I had once told him of my articles on the Japanese control of Manchuria and he had asked to take them home to read. Shortly after, a university professor congratulated him, in my presence, on the series of articles on Manchuria which he was publishing. After the wife of the professor read one to me, I asked Mr. Moh why he published my articles as his own. Completely unperturbed, he explained that he had no high family connections or friends in the Government, and consequently held so subordinate a position and received so low a salary that he could not marry. To be promoted, he must prove himself an authority on such a subject as Manchuria. Also, he explained, high officials, including the head of his department, entertained great respect for men with foreign connections. If I would help him, he pointed out, he could help me. Would I, for example, consider acting as an adviser to the Department of Labor? I said that I could not because as a foreign correspondent I had to keep free of official entanglements. He assured me that my name would never be mentioned and no one would know of the salary. "A number of other foreigners are listed as advisers," he explained, "some to the Ministry of Foreign Affairs. They all draw salaries from the Government."

When I still refused, he sadly observed that I was an idealist.

As he talked I recalled how he selected only ricksha coolies who could be easily underpaid and how callously he had reacted to the mangling of the dog. And then there was that remarkable episode on Confucian Street, where the prostitutes were kept. In an open space he and I had come upon a large tent roof under which about a hundred coolies and workers were squatting in total silence, listening to an old story-teller. I had halted, but Mr. Moh had objected nervously, saying that no respectable person associated with such low characters. Only when I insisted did he consent to remain. Soon I induced him to translate for me.

The story-teller was perhaps fifty years old and clad in a long dark gown and a small round skull-cap. He was telling an ancient tale of heroism and patriotism, and when his hero spoke philosophically, the story-teller sang. He held a pair of bamboo clap-sticks and clicked them softly together to maintain the rhythm of his tale. I was enthralled by the sheer beauty of his voice and the artistry of his delivery. Sometimes he laid aside the bamboo, took up two other sticks, and beat a rhythm on a small drum. Sometimes his voice and the drumming would rise to a crescendo; then they would drop again and he would resume his recital.

At last Mr. Moh's protests prevailed and we left. He began to lecture me on the proper way to act in China, the people to avoid and those to cultivate. I asked him who the story-teller was. Probably some useless creature, he answered, who had failed in the state examinations under the Manchu Dynasty and was compelled to earn his living by telling tales of the past. When I questioned him about his own amusements, he mentioned a number of trashy American movies. I was learning a great deal from Mr. Moh.

Soon afterwards we sat in the tea-room of an old Buddhist temple overlooking Lotus Lake and he confided to me the secrets of his past. He had formerly been much attracted to Communism, but after 1927, when such beliefs had become a crime, he had changed his "line." Only low characters remained Communists. Down in Kiangsi Province the Communists were organizing and arming peasants who could not even read and write and they were killing respectable people. Some workers and students also remained Communists, but the Government was weeding them out and killing them.

"Killing?" I asked. "Right here in the capital?"

"Of course," he replied indifferently. "If you want to see for yourself, I can take you."

I could only stare wonderingly into his bland eyes and smooth, weak face.

A few months later, in Shanghai, I again met Mr. Moh. He looked sleek and prosperous. He had become chief factory-inspector in the Chinese section of Shanghai and found the owners and managers most co-operative. At last he was going to be married.

"I think I have done as well as I could," he remarked thoughtfully. "The girl is a graduate of a missionary school, speaks English, and has good foreign connections. Her family is quite rich; it is a Christian family. I considered for a long time, but it seems the best I can do."

Through my mind ran the lines of an old Chinese poem written by Su Tung-po:

> Families, when a child is born,
> Wish it to be intelligent.
> I, through intelligence,
> Having wrecked my whole life,
> Only hope the child will prove
> Ignorant and stupid,
> Then he will crown a glorious career
> By becoming a Cabinet Minister.[1]

In search of what a Kuomintang official had referred to as important agrarian reforms, I went with two professors of Central University to an experimental station several hours' walking distance from Nanking. The professors had induced a landlord to allow them to experiment on his estate with some good American seeds, chemical fertilizer, and modern plows for deep plowing. Some twenty boys of primary-school age studied in the school connected with the experiment. They were all children of the landlord's family or of his friends. A crowd of ragged village children followed us curiously. None were in school. Their families were too poor to buy decent clothing. That was the agrarian reform!

[1] Translation by Arthur Waley.

On our return trip to Nanking, we halted in a village teahouse to rest. A number of shabby villagers congregated and I asked one of the professors to act as interpreter for me. I found that about half a dozen of them owned one or two *mou* of land (a *mou* is one sixth of an acre), but that the others were tenants or land laborers. Tenants paid fifty per cent of the crop as rent, and if the landlord's wife had another son, or if there was a funeral or a marriage, and at New Year's time they had to make additional presents. All peasants were in debt to the landlord, paying interest of three or more per cent a month if they could offer land, a draft animal, or agricultural implements as security. If they did not have these they could get no loans.

The villages were made up of disorderly mud huts fronted by open sewers. Almost every villager seemed to have a skin disease and the children had scabby heads and boils. On one side of the village pond women washed vegetables or dipped up water to be boiled for drinking; on the other side they scrubbed out their wooden night-soil buckets. The night-soil itself was used as fertilizer for the fields. On hot days the children swam in the pond. Everywhere in the fields lay the ancestral graves.

A few weeks later an agrarian research scholar who had come to Nanking to get official permission to make a survey of a certain district between Nanking and Shanghai invited me to accompany him. About a year before there had been an uprising in the district and forty peasants had been killed on the estate of the most powerful landlord.

We waited until the autumn harvest, then boarded a steam launch on the Grand Canal at Wusih and chugged northward. As luck would have it, the powerful landlord, Chu, was on board the launch. He was an unusually tall and formidable-looking man, wearing a long gray silk gown. He had an armed bodyguard wearing a khaki uniform.

Mr. Chu invited us to be his guests and we accepted. My scholar friend, a frail man with a cautious manner, remarked that if we refused we might as well not go to the region at all.

Gossiping freely, Mr. Chu told us he had left his elder son in Wusih to bring up some new American rifles and a machine-gun which he had just purchased in Shanghai. His younger son, a lad of eighteen, was a student in the Central University at Nanking, but was now home and had just been married to the daughter of a respectable Wusih silk merchant. He himself was the chief government official in his district, head of a Kuomintang branch, and commander of an armed force which he called the Volunteer Corps. He was therefore the political, military, and legal head of his territory — judge, jury, and executioner.

We reached his ancestral village, Chu Cha Li, and found a crowd of ragged villagers gathered along the bank. From the ranks of these came more armed guards who threw a protecting ring around us as we stepped ashore and moved down the narrow cobblestoned village street. The crowd followed in silence. As we left the village and moved into the countryside, my scholar friend and I dropped behind to talk to one of the guards. They were northern soldiers, the man said, brought here because they could not speak the local dialect and had no relatives among the local peasants. Two days before, they told us, the Chu family had arrested two peasants.

We approached a sprawling building of great size, three sides walled like a fortress, and the fourth moated by a pond. The building and pond were surrounded by a barricade of tangled barbed wire, inside of which were trenches. The doors of the building were pierced with loop-holes for rifles.

Passing into the main building, we found ourselves in a huge hall with a stone floor and with great red-lacquered pillars which supported heavy beams and a tiled roof. When servants lit the tall red candles, we saw that the entire hall was hung with rich crimson banners embroidered in gold. These were decorations for the younger son's wedding; they expressed wishes for long life, prosperity, happiness, and many sons.

The whole Chu joint family began to gather, together with the armed guards who lived within the building itself.

We sat down to tea and cakes, served with great formality by the head of the Chu clan. Meaningless conventional phrases were exchanged until I felt as though I were in the castle of some lord of the Middle Ages. Tea-time gradually melted into supper. My friend instructed me to conform to custom and ask to see the bride. The bridegroom was already with us, and soon the bride, a pretty young woman, older than her husband, obeyed our summons. We all rose and bowed and she sat down primly. I asked her about her educational work. Complacently she answered that all Chinese were inferior to foreigners and Chinese education was most inferior indeed. I could only stare at her in amazement.

My scholar friend instructed me to follow custom by toasting the bride and groom. We all rose, lifting our winecups, and I wished them long life and many sons. Just then I heard the clanking of chains from a dark corner of the great hall somewhere behind the crowd of people and soldiers. My friend had heard the sound, but his face was blank. No one turned to look.

The supper finished, we accompanied the married couple to their bedroom in an interior courtyard. The room was jammed with rich, brass-studded mahogany furniture. The young couple sat on the edge of the bed and served us tea and sliced pears while we congratulated them on their wedding presents. My friend told them that I had exclaimed at the remarkable beauty of the bride. I asked him afterwards not to lie any more than was necessary.

With relief we at last wandered out into the great hall. It was now empty save for a group of soldiers in a corner, and one of the Chu brothers, a tall, strong man in a long gown. Around his waist was a cartridge belt from which hung a Mauser automatic. My friend's assistant engaged this gentleman in conversation and finally maneuvered him out into the open, leaving my scholar friend and me to talk to the soldiers.

Utterly unlike the educated and ruling classes, the common people of China usually speak with the greatest frankness. The soldiers told us that the clanking we had heard while at supper had been caused by two more peasants who had been brought in as prisoners. Without hesitation they took us into a small room where the two men were held. They lay on rice straw with their hands and legs chained and the chains attached to an iron clamp in the wall. One peasant was of middle age, dark, thin, and sensitive-looking; the other a youth of about twenty with a bloated, unusually stupid face. They would answer none of our questions, and only stared up at us in silence. We left them, and the soldiers stood by with downcast faces. Outside it was night and the moon was full. The flat countryside lay silent, brooding. I felt that it somehow reflected my dark fears.

That night I was assigned to sleep in a room crowded with dark heavy furniture. There were two other beds in the room, one occupied by two girls of the Chu family, the other by a married couple. I got behind the curtains of my bed and removed only my coat, then lay down to a night of sleeplessness, my ears straining for every sound from the great hall. Sometimes I dozed off, my mind swarming with fantasies in which I moved stealthily to the great hall to unleash the prisoners . . . no, the soldiers were there. . . . I tried again and was on the roof removing tiles so that the prisoners could reach my hands . . . I lay flat to lift them up . . . they crept carefully along the tiled roof, dropped down the straight walls of the bastion, and crept through the brooding fields. . . .

With a jerk I sat up in bed, fully awake, then lay down again. The fantasies returned and again I awoke. And always fear was with me — fear of China, fear of human beings.

With the first faint streaks of dawn through the small square window high up in the prison-like wall of my room, I rose and made my way into the great hall. My friends and the armed Chu brother were there. Soldiers were leading the stupid peasant youth out of the little room into an adjoining courtyard. In the gray dawn I saw that the thin face of my scholar friend was drawn and pale. Neither he nor his assistant had slept.

On orders from the Chu brother, soldiers clapped steel

handcuffs on the wrists of the peasant youth, then tucked his hands up into his sleeves. A group of the guards and one of the Chu family, all now dressed in civilian clothing, their pistols hidden beneath their long gowns, drove the peasant before them. He stumbled as he walked.

"He will betray others!" I exclaimed to my friend, but he muttered: "They will find no one. Every peasant knows of the arrests. *They know everything.*"

"What will they do to that youth?" I cried desperately. "Where is the older man? Can you do nothing?"

"It is dangerous to try," was his answer. "We must do nothing to interfere with our survey. Make no sign. Today we are going to the villages."

During the day one of the Chu men led us from village to village. Armed soldiers walked before us and behind us. All villages were named after the Chu family; all land, all peasants belonged to it. The villages were groups of filthy hovels with earthen floors and walls. The beds were boards on which shoddy coverings lay piled in disarray. A few primitive agricultural implements were stacked in corners and a few broken clay cooking vessels lay on the floor. As we approached, unkempt women and girls hid in the dark huts. To them we were government officials, guests of their lord.

One old peasant brought a sheaf of rice and laid it on the earth before the Chu brother. Half-crouching, he pleaded for mercy because rust had ruined half his crop.

In a hard voice the Chu lord told us that these peasants were so dishonest that he had to station guards in the fields to superintend the harvests. If given a chance, they stole rice. A number of peasant men listened, standing upright, their arms crossed on their breasts. My friend tried to talk with them, but they stared silently at him, their level, unfathomable black eyes filled with hatred. He glanced meaningfully at me.

As soon as we were alone I exclaimed: "An army ought to march in, imprison the Chu family, and free the peasants!"

"Which army?" my friend asked.

I met the scholar in Shanghai a week later and said: "Last night I dined with some German business men and told them of the Chu family and the peasants. They criticized my attitude furiously. To hear them talk, you would think such an attitude as mine was their funeral!"

"It is!" my friend answered dryly.

He and his kind were revolutionary democrats I had stumbled upon, men who, like the patricians, had inherited the finest features of Chinese culture and added to it a gleaning of the best of the Western world. But unlike other patricians, they had placed their minds at the service of the people.

Terror in Shanghai

THE FACE of the young Y.M.C.A. librarian took on a pained expression when I said: "I wonder how many Chinese are 'rice Christians' — men who convert only to eat."

"There is no way of knowing," he replied. "Our secretaries seem to leap right into Government positions. Yesterday our secretary tiptoed around and gave us orders to go to the Assembly to pray because General Chiang Kai-shek had joined the Southern Methodist Church. He seemed scared."

"Many Chinese Christians scare me," I exclaimed, "whether Southern Methodist or not! When a Chinese business man adds Christianity to his equipment, it's a formidable combination. Piety, smiles, and handshakes combined with a business head are —"

Two young men entered and asked about books. The librarian closed the booklet which I had brought to him for translation. Its title was *The Gospel according to St. John*, but after a few pages of the Gospel it tapered off into "The Great Chinese Revolution." When the young men left, the librarian opened the booklet again and continued to translate chapter titles to me. It was a "forbidden book," perhaps published by the Communists, but bearing the name of a non-existent Christian Publication Society. The young librarian already had many such volumes, all with Christian or Confucian titles.

The librarian was a fountain of information. He gathered suppressed news from functionaries of the "Y," official friends, newspaper men, and from gossip in restaurants and tea-houses. He was not a Communist, but merely a young man concerned about the welfare of his people. If the Government offered anything of value, he read it, and if the Communists published anything beneficial to the people, he read that too.

One day the young librarian turned to me and asked: "Would you like to go down into the Yangtzepoo factory district to see workers' tenements? I could take you tomorrow. Many tenements are owned by the Catholic Church."

I consented eagerly and late the next afternoon I went to meet him at his home. He lived in one of the countless "semi-foreign" houses that disfigure Shanghai. These were long rows of connected buildings on lanes and alleyways off the main streets. The ground floor always had one square living-room with a small, dark kitchen and a totally dark, unventilated toilet. If a clerk reared in a missionary school lived there, there might be a worn volume of American *Popular Home Songs*, a hymnal, a moving-picture magazine, colored prints of the Grand Central Terminal in New York, or of a lady sitting on the edge of a fountain listening to a lover in knee breeches while a cupid with an arrow floated above.

Here in Shanghai was none of the spacious, leisurely charm of ancient Peiping, none of those beautiful, spreading buildings and colored tile roofs. For most Chinese, Shanghai was a shabby, barren city.

As I knocked at the librarian's door that afternoon, I was startled by a long-drawn-out "Sh-h-h-h!" from the window above and, glancing up, saw the face of the librarian. A few seconds later he opened the door and cautiously admitted me.

Without a word he motioned me up the stairs to the floor above. From a back window overlooking another row of small semi-foreign houses I looked down on a group of Chinese and foreign detectives hammering on a door. Faces appeared at all the windows up and down the lane, then withdrew into shadow again. The door across from us was opened by a tall thin man in a long gown. Two detectives lunged at him and others followed them into the room. A woman's voice screamed in terror, and we saw her, followed by the detectives, in the upper room directly across from us. She ran about wildly, then threw her arm against the wall and buried her head against it. The detectives ripped open the mattress and pillows and then searched the rest of the house. There was little to look for in that poor home, and within a few minutes they had finished. The street door of the house opened again and several of the detectives emerged with a tall thin man and the woman, both handcuffed. The woman's face was gray and the man's mouth was smeared with blood. Their thin bodies were outlined by their cotton gowns as they walked away.

Downstairs in the barren living-room the sister-in-law of the librarian exclaimed excitedly: "Some of the detectives have remained in the house to wait for friends of that couple. A girl friend of mine often goes there. I dare not go to warn her not to come. I might be arrested."

"I'll go," I offered. "They can't arrest an American for calling on a girl."

The woman sighed with relief and I memorized the name and address she gave me.

"She speaks good English," she cautioned, "so if detectives open the door, say you are looking for an English-teacher. Wait until I see if our lane is clear."

She ran upstairs and after a time whispered down that I should leave.

Once out on the main street, I meandered along, window-shopping until certain that no one was following. I then hailed a taxi and drove away, dismissed it at the center of the city, walked a block, took another, and dismissed it a short distance from my destination. As I walked through another lane of small semi-foreign houses, I wondered if detectives would open the door of the girl's house. My heart hammered as I knocked briskly. No answer. Then right above me a window opened cautiously. Glancing up, I saw the face of a beautiful girl with large black eyes and shingled hair.

"Come quickly!" I whispered.

There was the sound of running feet, and the door opened. I stepped inside and told her of the raid. Her gleaming eyes grew larger and she glanced at her bookcase. The mildest social novel might lead to imprisonment. Countless such young people were spending their entire youth behind prison walls.

"Give me anything you wish," I urged. "You can reach me through the friend who sent me."

Quickly she went to the bookcase and began to pull out books, among them a copy of Gorky's *Mother*. She ran upstairs and returned with some magazines wrapped in a package.

I walked back through the streets of this jungle city where detectives and gangsters hunted all men and women who entertained any thoughts other than the official ones. Within half an hour the girl would have moved her dwelling and would be warning all her friends. For, however strong the bond of family, friend, or comrade, torture might break it down. Those to whom the revolution had been only a romantic adventure or those Communist Party officials who had grown mercenary sometimes betrayed their comrades — even without torture. A few important Communist betrayers had even entered the Kuomintang secret service, afterwards known as the "Blue Shirts," and agents traveled in trains and busses, prowled through tea-houses and cheap restaurants, or went through prisons pointing out their former comrades. Others bought their lives by publishing "repentances." If any of these returned to their old haunts, suspicion hung over them, and often years could not dispel the shadow. To a Communist I once remarked:

"It seems you trust only the dead!"

"If we make betrayal easy, China is lost!" he answered.

"Your suspicion can also create betrayers. If you close your door, perhaps they will eventually enter the doors of the Blue Shirts."

"We have ways of knowing if a man has really escaped or not." Staring past me into space, he added: "The Kuomintang trusts no man who has once been a Communist, for if he has betrayed us, he can betray them. They also know that our ideas, once implanted in a man's mind, are never entirely eradicated."

"An unwilling tribute, isn't it?"

"Yes. There are a number of men in the Government who were once Communists. Some of them will always help us — not because they believe, but because they know the future belongs to us, and they want a kind of life insurance. But the secret service has killed many who have gone over to them. They suck all information from them and then dispose of them like squeezed-out oranges."

A young Chinese, Feng Da, acted as my secretary and translator. He read and clipped from the Chinese press, translated news into English, and built up my files. My files on the Chinese Red Army alone filled many cases but most of these were official reports. At the end of one six-month period I compiled official statistics and found that half a million Red soldiers had been reported slain, yet official releases still claimed that the Red Army consisted only of "bandit remnants" fleeing from their pursuers. Chu Teh, Commander-in-Chief of the Red Army, and Mao Tze-tung, Secretary General of the Communist Party, had been reported killed a dozen time. A month following their "deaths," new rewards would be placed on their heads.

I made a similar study of the execution of Communists or alleged Communists in various cities. Until 1932 the Chinese press published details and often pictures of mass executions of the victims. One report from Chungking burned itself into my memory. The provincial Governor had offered a reward of fifty dollars for any Communist captured or killed. Immediately the schools and universities were raided by soldiers, and students were shot down in the streets. Then the murderers claimed their rewards. I once laid a summary of such reports before Eugene Chen, who had been Foreign Minister of the Chinese Government until the middle of 1927. He was a harsh critic of the Government and he assured me that if he ever came to power again he would try to stop the Terror. When he rose to office in Canton in 1931, I went to him with a request that twelve sailors, arrested in Canton as trade-union organizers, should not be executed. He replied that the men had known what would happen to them if they engaged in such illegal activities and that he could do nothing.

Similarly, in the spring of 1931 I went to the American secretary of the foreign Y.M.C.A. and asked him to help prevent the extradition to the Chinese police of two foreign trade-union officials arrested in Shanghai. He refused, saying that I had never come to him on behalf of any Chinese. He asserted that his concern was the Chinese and that the rights of the poorest coolie were as sacred to him as those of any foreigner. I accepted his rebuke and a few months later went to him on behalf of five Chinese, three of them trade-union organizers, who had been arrested and would perhaps be killed. He replied:

"These men knew the law before they engaged in illegal activities. I can do nothing."

Like other foreign correspondents, I had to build up my own news sources and consequently maintained friendship with as many different types of Chinese and foreigners as I could. I liked the intellectual qualities of the scholar patricians and the outlook of a few newspaper men; but I particularly admired and respected the revolutionary democrats who came later to be known as the National Salvationists, and the Communists who, it seemed to me, embodied convictions and courage such as had characterized men of the French, American, and Russian Revolutions.

For the rest, there was a barrier between most foreigners and myself, and I rarely met men of my own profession. Of these, however, John B. Powell, American editor of the *China Weekly Review*, struck me as a man of much integrity. Since he disliked the Communists and believed in the Kuomintang, we often disagreed, but he was one American democrat who always defended my right to think and write as I wished. We shared a fear and hatred of British and Japanese policies in the Far East, and after the Japanese invasion, which threw us together on a common front, he published everything I sent him.

Years later when the Japanese began assassinating Chinese newspaper men, Mr. Powell organized his colleagues to bury them decently and with honor. Only after the Japanese occupied Shanghai in December 1941 did he cease his fearless defense of China. He had been on the Japanese blacklist for years and they soon arrested him, along with another American correspondent, Victor Keen.

Among my other acquaintances was a German pilot in the Eurasian Aviation Corporation. He was a neurotic man, inclined to mysticism, and I remained in touch with him only because he was a valuable source of news. Returning from trips to various inland cities, he would give me photographs he had taken and much information.

Again and again he declared that he saw no purpose in life. One afternoon, after a flight to Hankow, he entered my apartment and slumped into a chair. His face was pale and his lips were twitching. I poured him a glass of cognac and waited for some new outburst about the futility of existence. He tossed a package of films and prints into my lap. A few of the prints showed various stages in the beheading of a dozen Chinese Communists — that is, alleged Communists — on the square in front of the customs house in Hankow. A few showed the bodies of beheaded workers lying in the streets. One was of a very chic Chinese Army officer with a pistol in his hand; behind him towered the walls of a foreign factory, and at its base lay the bodies of a number of workers whom he had apparently just shot.

"I took all of these pictures with the exception of the one of the Army officer with the pistol," Kurt said. "The English factory-owner gave me that. I took the pictures of the mass beheadings from the windows of the customs house. The twelve men were naked to the waist and their hands were tied behind them. There were ropes around their necks and blood ran from the mouths of some of them. The police and soldiers were eager for the killing. They kicked the prisoners to their knees and pulled their heads forward by means of the ropes, while a fat executioner with a big sword chopped off their heads. The blood spurted out and some of it splashed on crowds of gaping Chinese, who stood with arms hanging limply at their sides."

"Did you protest?"

He continued without heeding: "One of the prisoners tumbled over and died before he was beheaded. A few were singing in high shrill voices. They sang the *Internationale*. When all were dead the police dipped faggot brooms in their blood and whirled them over the gawking crowd. The watchers ran like rabbits."

He retched, rose and went to the bathroom. When he returned, his face was very white.

"Look at this modern city, Kurt," I began excitedly. "Suppose you or I should tell people what we had seen — show those pictures to missionaries, business men, journalists, Y.M.C.A. secretaries. This city — look at it, with its paved streets, electric lights, great buildings —"

"For my part, I don't intend to get lynched for a pack of Chinese! I'm leaving this bloody country and going to Australia."

"Chinese are a species of animal to you, aren't they?"

Later that evening he told me that he had brought back some more pictures which had been taken from the air. This was forbidden by the Government, but he took them nevertheless.

"I've earned enough money on them to live in Australia like a human being until I find work," he explained.

I stared at him suspiciously, then asked: "Why do your bosses want pictures of Chinese territory?"

"I don't know or care!"

"You're being used as a spy against China!"

"China? How can you have any feeling for China? Just think of those pictures I brought you!"

"Nevertheless this country belongs to the Chinese people. You are helping their enemies."

"You're an illusionist!" he replied, and sat staring dejectedly into space.

Lu Hsün

ONE hot afternoon in the middle of 1930, two teachers, man and wife, called on me and made two requests: one, to contribute articles on India and money to a new magazine, *Ta Tao* (*The Great Way*), which was to be devoted to a study of subjected Asiatic peoples; the other, to rent a small foreign restaurant where a reception and dinner could be given to celebrate the fiftieth birthday of Lu Hsün. Lu Hsün was the great writer whom some Chinese called the "Gorky of China," but who, to my mind, was really its Voltaire.

The first request I granted readily, but the second was fraught with danger, because the hundred men and women who were to be invited represented the world of "dangerous thoughts." My friends assured me, however, that all guests would be invited by word of mouth only and sworn to silence, and that "sentries" would be posted at street intersections leading to the restaurant.

On the afternoon of the birthday celebration I stood with my two friends at the garden gate of a small Dutch restaurant in the French Concession. From our position we had a clear view of the long street by which the guests would come. At the street intersection before me I could see a Chinese in a long gown apparently waiting for a bus, while another sat on a near-by doorstep.

Lu Hsün, accompanied by his wife and small son, arrived early, and I met, for the first time, the man who became one of the most influential factors in my life during all my years in China. He was short and frail, and wore a cream-colored silk gown and soft Chinese shoes. He was bareheaded and his close-cropped hair stood up like a brush. In structure his face was like that of an average Chinese, yet it remains in my memory as the most eloquent face I have ever seen. A kind of living intelligence and awareness streamed from it. He spoke no English, but considerable German, and in that language we conversed. His manner, his speech, and his every gesture radiated the indefinable harmony and charm of a perfectly integrated personality. I suddenly felt as awkward and ungracious as a clod.

Almost immediately came the stream of guests, and Lu Hsün moved back into the garden. Repeatedly I turned to watch him, attracted by his thin hand raised in some gesture.

As the guests went by, my two friends explained that they included writers, artists, professors, students, actors, reporters, research scholars, and even two patricians. This last pair came not because they shared Lu Hsün's convictions, but to honor his integrity, courage, and scholarship.

It was a motley and exciting gathering — pioneers in an intellectual revolution. One group, poorly dressed and apparently half-starved, was pointed out as representing a new modern æsthetic theater trying to edge in social dramas between Wilde's *Salome* and *Lady Windermere's Fan*. A more prosperous-looking group proved to be Futan University students led by Professor Hung Sheng. They had produced some of Ibsen's plays and one or two written by their professor, who was also a director of one of the first Chinese motion-picture companies. A third dramatic group was made up of young Leftist actors, writers, and translators who had produced plays by Romain Rolland, Upton Sinclair, Gorky, and Remarque. Much later they produced *Carmen*, were raided by police after the third performance, arrested, and closed down. Detectives in the audience had not liked the last scene, in which Don José stabbed Carmen to death: as Carmen hurled her ring at her cast-off lover, she uttered words that reminded them of the split between the Communists and the Kuomintang!

From my place at the gate I now saw a number of people approaching. One tall, thin young man walked rapidly and kept glancing behind him; he was clearly a student, and as he passed, my friends whispered that he was editor of the *Shanghai Pao*, underground Communist paper which conducted a kind of journalistic guerrilla warfare in the city. Shortly after came one whose foreign suit was wrinkled and whose hair was wild and disheveled. He had just come from months in prison. He had been suspected of representing the Chinese Red Aid; the charge had been true, but money had proved stronger. His family had spent a fortune bribing his captors.

The garden was filled and no more guests came, but my friends and I still stood guard. When darkness began to fall, half of the guests left. Others took our place as sentries and we went inside the restaurant with the other guests.

After the dinner, speeches began and one of my friends translated for me. The Dutch restaurant-owner understood no Chinese, so he did not worry us, but the Chinese waiters stood listening intently. When the man with the wild hair made a report on prison conditions, we watched every move of the servants. After him came the editor of the *Shanghai Pao*, giving the first factual report I had so far heard on the rise of the Red Army and on the "harvest uprisings" of peasants who had fought the landlords and then poured into the Red Army like rivulets into an ever broadening river.

A short, heavy-set young woman with bobbed hair began to tell of the need for developing proletarian literature. She ended her address by appealing to Lu Hsün to become the protector and "master" of the new League of Left Writers and League of Left Artists, the initial groups which later became the Chinese Cultural Federation.

Throughout, Lu Hsün listened carefully, promptly turning his attention to new speakers, his forefinger all the while tracing the edge of his teacup. When all had finished, he rose and began to talk quietly, telling a story of the half-century of intellectual turmoil which had been his life — the story of China uprooted.

Born under the Manchu Dynasty into a poor scholarly village family, he had grown up in a feudal setting into which the first modern ideas preceding the 1911 revolution had seeped very slowly. Too poor to study in Western countries, he had gone to Japan, then sympathetic to the Chinese nationalist movement. He had studied modern medicine, but also read the first Japanese translations of the works of Tolstoy. Tolstoy had introduced him to social thought and to the power of modern literature.

He had returned to China to practice modern medicine, but, like many medical men of the Occident, soon realized that most sickness and disease are rooted in poverty and in the ignorance that goes with poverty. Only the rich could afford medical treatment. Influenced by classical Russian writers, he turned to literature as a weapon to combat feudal thought, began to write short stories in the style of the Russian classics, and gradually abandoned medicine altogether. During the Chinese intellectual renaissance he had been a professor of literature in Peking, the birthplace of the new thought.

In later years he had studied German and Russian and translated a number of Russian novels and essays. His purpose, he said, was to lay before Chinese youth the best of modern social literature. He had also begun to collect Western classical and modern paintings and specimens of the graphic arts, and had published a number of volumes for young artists.

He was now asked, he said, to lead a movement of proletarian literature, and some of his young friends were urging him to become a proletarian writer. It would be childish to pretend that he was a proletarian writer. His roots were in the village, in peasant and scholarly life. Nor did he believe that Chinese intellectual youth, with no experience of the life, hopes, and sufferings of workers and peasants, could — as yet — produce proletarian literature. Creative writing must spring from experience, not theory.

Despite this, he would continue to place the best of Western literature and art before Chinese youth. He was willing to help and guide youth, or, as they requested, to be their master. But protect them? Who could do that under a regime which called even the mildest social literature criminal? As "master," he urged educated youth to share the life of the workers and peasants, and draw their material from life, but study Western social literature and art for form.

As the meeting came to a close, one young man bent toward me and shook his head sadly:

"Disappointing, wasn't it? I mean Lu Hsün's attitude toward proletarian literature. It discourages youth."

My lifelong hostility to professional intellectuals sprang to life. Chinese intellectuals had never done physical labor and their writing was a profession divorced from experience. To them even the word "youth" meant students only, and toward workers and peasants they maintained a superior though sympathetic attitude. Much of the "proletarian literature" which they had created up to that time had been artificial, a weak imitation of the Russian.

To the young critic I replied that I agreed entirely with Lu Hsün.

My life became interlocked with that of Lu Hsün and with his closest colleague, Mao Tun, one of the better-known Chinese novelists. Together the three of us collected and published a volume of the etchings of Kaethe Kollwitz, the German folk-artist, and together we wrote, for the press of Occidental countries, most of the appeals against political reaction affecting Chinese intellectuals. Often Mao Tun and I would meet on some street corner and, after a careful scrutiny of the street on which Lu Hsün lived, enter his house and spend an evening with him. We would order dinner from a restaurant and spend hours in conversation. None of us was a Communist, but we all considered it an honor to aid and support men who were fighting and dying for the liberation of the poor.

Lu Hsün occupied the ancient position of honor, that of "teacher" or "master" to the young intellectuals of China.

There were many cliques among them, and each strove to win him to their side and their "line." He towered above them, refusing to be used by one or the other in their shifting alignments. He listened to all, discussed their problems, criticized their writing, encouraged them. And his name stood first in the magazines they published.

He often spoke to me of his plans for a historical novel based on his life, but the social reaction in which his country wallowed seemed to leave no time for this. So deep was his hatred of "the slaughter of the innocents" and the violation of men's rights that after a while he was using his pen only as a weapon — a veritable dagger it was — of political criticism.

Of all Chinese writers, he seemed the most intricately linked with Chinese history, literature and culture. It was almost impossible to translate into English some of his "political criticisms" because, unable to attack reaction openly, his writings were a mosaic of allusions to personalities, events, and ideas of the darkest periods of China's past. Every educated Chinese knew that he was comparing present tyranny with that of the past. Through these political criticisms ran rich streams of both Chinese and Western culture, couched in a style as fine as an etching. He introduced literary magazine after literary magazine to the public, only to see each suppressed. These introductions, compact and chaste, were flown like proud banners. To him, freedom of thought and expression was the essence of human achievement. So distinctive was his style that pseudonyms failed to shield him, and censors began to mutilate his articles until they often appeared senseless. Writers, editors, and artists associated with him began to disappear without trace; only his age and eminence protected him from arrest. For a number of years only the Left intellectuals of Japan were able to publish his unexpurgated writings. To Japanese intellectuals he was the best-known and most respected Chinese writer.

The disappearance or death of his followers acted like corrosive poison on Lu Hsün's body and mind, and he began to sicken. He sometimes grew so ill that he could not rise. He felt that his heart was failing and agreed to receive the best foreign doctor in Shanghai. After the examination the doctor took me aside and said that he was dying of tuberculosis and that only a prolonged rest in a cool, dry climate could halt the disease. The doctor added: "But of course he won't follow my advice. These old-fashioned, ignorant Chinese do not believe in modern medicine!"

Lu Hsün did not listen to the advice, but hardly because he was old-fashioned or ignorant. "You ask me to lie on my back for a year while others are fighting and dying?" he asked us accusingly. When we answered such objections, he reminded us of his poverty, but when we offered to collect the money needed, he still refused. Maxim Gorky invited him to the Soviet Union as his guest for a year, but he would not go. He said the Kuomintang would shriek to all China that he was receiving "Moscow gold."

"They say that anyway!" I argued.

"They dare not," he cried. "Everyone knows they lie! Anyway, China needs me. I cannot go."

We pleaded with him in vain. "Everyone cannot run away!" he said. "Someone must stand and fight."

Late in 1930 I went to the Philippines for a few weeks of rest. The night before I sailed, Lu Hsün and three young men writers called to spend the evening. One was a former teacher, Jou Shih, perhaps the most capable and beloved of Lu Hsün's pupils and friends. When I returned to Shanghai in March 1931 my secretary, Feng Da, met me with the news that twenty-four young writers, actors, and artists had been arrested and killed. On the night of February 21 they had been taken from prison, forced to dig their own graves, and shot. Some had been buried alive. One was Jou Shih.

I hurried to Lu Hsün's home and found him in his study, with his face dark and unshaven, his hair disheveled, cheeks sunken, and eyes gleaming with fever. His voice was filled with a terrible hatred.

"Here is an article I wrote that night," he said, giving me

a manuscript penned in his etching-like script. "I call it 'Written in Deep Night.' Have it translated into English and published abroad."

After he had explained its purport, I warned him that he would be killed if it was published.

"Does it matter?" he answered hotly. "Someone must speak!"

Before I went away, he and I prepared a manifesto to the intellectuals of the Western world on the slaughter of the writers and artists. I carried it to Mao Tun and he revised it and helped me translate it into English. As a result of it came the first foreign protest, from over fifty leading American writers, against the killing of Chinese writers. The Kuomintang was astounded to learn that the Western world disapproved!

Lu Hsün's article, "Written in Deep Night," was never published even abroad, and I have it with me still. Of all that I had read in China, it made the deepest impression on me. It was a passionate cry, written in one of the blackest nights in Chinese history. It began:

> One may pass a heap of paper ashes on the wild earth, or many carvings on a ruined wall, and never see them. Yet each is eloquent with love, mourning, or with wrath stronger than the human voice can express.

By the "heap of ashes on the wild earth" he referred to the Chinese funeral custom of burning paper for the souls of the dead. He then wrote of the woodcut *Sacrifice*, by Kaethe Kollwitz, which shows a gaunt mother holding out a dying baby — an offering of the common people to death — seeing in the babe a symbol of the twenty-four. His article continued:

> In China in the past a prisoner condemned to death was usually led through the busy thoroughfare, where he was permitted to shout *Yuen Wang*, to protest his innocence, abuse the judge, relate his own brave deeds, and show he had no fear of death. At the moment of execution bystanders would applaud, and the news of his courage

would spread. In my youth I thought this practice barbarous and cruel. Now it seems to me that rulers of past ages were courageous and confident of their power when they permitted this. The practice even seemed to contain some kindness, some benevolence, to the condemned man.

He then turned his daggers against the complacent Chu Tang, who, in an article in *Yu Chou Fang*, a magazine published by Dr. Lin Yu-tang, had had the temerity to observe that praise or sympathy for a condemned man might be a high ideal but was not good for society because it meant failure to recognize the victor. Lu Hsün answered him with bitter irony and then, speaking of the cruelty of the murder, wrote:

> Today when I am told of the death of a friend or a student, and learn that no one knows the details of how he died, I find that I grieve more deeply than when I learn all details of the killing. I can imagine the awful loneliness that overtakes one who is killed by butchers in a small dark room. When I first read the "Inferno" of Dante's *Divine Comedy*, I was amazed at its imagined cruelty. Now, with more experience, I see how moderate Dante's imagination was. It failed to reach the depth of the secret cruelty which is common today.

At the end he appended a letter which might have been lifted from the *Inferno*. It came from an eighteen-year-old prisoner who, with two other students, had been dragged from a Shanghai college and accused of Communism because they belonged to a group founded by Lu Hsün for the study of woodcuts. The evidence against them consisted of a woodcut of Lunacharsky. By a fantastic kind of reasoning, woodcuts were branded as Communistic. Fearing to arrest Lu Hsün, the Government had arrested his pupils.

The boy's letter from prison began with "Dear master" and related the tale of his Gethsemane from the day of his arrest until the night he had bribed a guard to deliver the letter to Lu Hsün. It told in particular of the torture of a peasant who had been accused of being a Red Army commander; he had had nails driven under his finger nails and had knelt in silence, his face like clay, with blood dripping from each finger.

"My dear master, when I think of him, ice grips my heart," cried the letter.

As Mao Tun and I translated this, he paused and said in a low voice: "It is indeed written in deep night."

"It is deep night," I said.

Southern Episodes

JUST as I arrived in Canton in the hot summer months of 1930, another General was killed by his bodyguard for the sake of the fifty Chinese dollars offered by a rival General. Such events had begun to strike me as sardonic. The Kwangtung Provincial Government was semi-independent, but in the hands of generals who took by violence what they considered their share in the loot of the south. They whirled around the city in bullet-proof cars with armed bodyguards standing on the running boards. Such was the spirit of the generals and of the officials whom they brought to power with them.

I interviewed them all and put no stock in what they said. They treated me magnificently, for foreign journalists seldom or never went south in the hot summer months. So I had a Government launch to myself, with an official guide to show me factories, paved roads, new waterworks, and the Sun Yat-sen Memorial Hall. For truth I depended on Chinese university professors, an occasional newspaper reporter or editor, teachers and writers, the German Consul in Canton — and on my own eyes and ears.

The real reason I went south in the hottest part of the year was to study the lot of the millions of "silk peasants" in a silk industry which was rapidly losing its American markets to Japanese magnates. But I did not wish to see the silk regions as a guest of the powerful Canton Silk Guild, for the Guild, after all, was like a big laughing Buddha, naked to the waist, his fat belly hanging over his pajama belt. At last I found a group of Lingnan Christian University professors who were engaged in research in the industry. One young expert was leaving for the Shuntek silk region for a six weeks' inspection tour. I went with him to the Canton Silk Guild, where he argued with a suspicious Guild official until given permission to travel on Guild river steamers and enter the region in which millions of peasants toiled. There the millionaires of the South Seas had erected many large filatures; the spinners were all young women.

Next day the young expert and I boarded a river steamer. Some twenty or thirty Guild merchants were the only other passengers. The steamers had armor plating and machine-guns to protect the merchants from "bandits." The "bandits," I learned, were peasants who took to the highway for a part of each year in order to earn a living.

I once calculated that if these "bandits" had attacked and captured our steamer, they would have secured enough food to feed a whole village for months. At meal times the merchants hunched over the tables, eating gargantuan meals and dropping the chicken bones on the floor. They talked of silk, money, markets, and of how much their firms were losing. The silk industry was indeed fighting for its life, but if there were losses, it clearly did not come out of the hides of these men. I pined a little for Jesse James.

My young escort was awed by these men, but when he spoke of the silk peasants or the girl filature workers, hostility and contempt crept into his voice. His particular hatred seemed to be the thousands of women spinners, and only with difficulty could I learn why. He told me that the women were notorious throughout China as Lesbians. They refused to marry, and if their families forced them, they merely bribed their husbands with a part of their wages and induced them to take concubines. The most such a married girl would do was bear one son; then she would return to the factory, refusing to live with her husband any longer.

The Government had just issued a decree forbidding women to escape from marriage by bribery, but the women ignored it.

"They're too rich — that's the root of the trouble!" my young escort explained. "They earn as much as eleven dollars a month, and become proud and contemptuous." He added that on this money they also supported parents, brothers and sisters, and grandparents. "They squander their money!" he cried. "I have never gone to a picture theater without seeing groups of them sitting together, holding hands."

Until 1927, when they were forbidden, there had been Communist cells and trade unions in the filatures, he charged, and now these despicable girls evaded the law by forming secret "Sister Societies." They had even dared strike for shorter hours and higher wages. Now and then two or three girls would commit suicide together because their families were forcing them to marry.

For weeks my escort and I went by foot or small boat from village to village, from market town to market town. The fierce sun beat down upon us until our clothing clung to our bodies like a surgeon's glove and the perspiration wilted our hat bands and our shoes. At night we took rooms in village inns or pitched our camp beds under mosquito nets in family temples. All the roads and paths were lined with half-naked peasants bending low under huge baskets of cocoons swung from the ends of bamboo poles. Market towns reeked with the cocoons and hanks of raw silk piled up to the rafters in the warehouses. Every village was a mass of trays on which the silkworms fed, tended night and day by gaunt careworn peasants who went about naked to the waist.

At first curiously, then with interest, my escort began to translate for me as I questioned the peasants on their life and work. Their homes were bare huts with earthen floors, and the bed was a board covered by an old mat and surrounded by a cotton cloth, once white, which served as a mosquito net. There was usually a small clay stove with a cooking utensil or two, a narrow bench, and sometimes an ancient, scarred table. For millions this was home. A few owned several mulberry trees — for wealth was reckoned in trees. But almost all had sold their cocoon crops in advance in order to get money or food. If the crop failed, they were the losers. Wherever we traveled the story was the same: the silk peasants were held in pawn by the merchants and were never free from debt.

Only as we neared big market towns, in which silk filatures belched forth the stench of cocoons, did we come upon better homes and fewer careworn faces. The daughters of such families were spinners. It was then that I began to see what industrialism, bad as it had seemed elsewhere, meant to the working girls. These were the only places in the whole country where the birth of a baby girl was an occasion for joy, for here girls were the main support of their families. Consciousness of their worth was reflected in their dignified independent bearing. I began to understand the charges that they were Lesbians. They could not but compare the dignity of their positions with the low position of married women. Their independence seemed a personal affront to officialdom.

The hatred of my escort for these girls became more marked when we visited the filatures. Long lines of them, clad in glossy black jackets and trousers, sat before boiling vats of cocoons, their parboiled fingers twinkling among the spinning filaments. Sometimes a remark passed along their lines set a whole mill laughing. The face of my escort would grow livid.

"They call me a running dog of the capitalists, and you a foreign devil of an imperialist! They are laughing at your clothing and your hair and eyes!" he explained.

One evening the two of us sat at the entrance of an old family temple in the empty stone halls of which we had pitched our netted camp cots. On the other side of the canal rose the high walls of a filature, which soon began pouring forth black-clad girl workers, each with her tin dinner pail. All wore wooden sandals which were fastened by a single leather strap across the toes and which clattered as they walked. Their glossy black hair was combed back and hung in a heavy braid to the waist. At the nape of the neck the braid was caught in red yarn, making a band two or three inches wide — a lovely splash of color.

As they streamed in long lines over the bridge arching the canal and past the temple entrance, I felt I had never seen more handsome women.

I urged my young escort to interpret for me, but he refused, saying he did not understand their dialect. He was so irritated that he rose and walked toward the town. When he was gone, I went down the steps. A group of girls gathered about me and stared. I offered them some of my malt candy. There was a flash of white teeth and exclamations in a sharp staccato dialect. They took the candy, began chewing, then examined my clothing and stared at my hair and eyes. I did the same with them and soon we were laughing at each other.

Two of them linked their arms in mine and began pulling me down the flagstone street. Others followed, chattering happily. We entered the home of one girl and were welcomed by her father and mother and two big-eyed little brothers. Behind them the small room was already filled with other girls and curious neighbors. A candle burned in the center of a square table surrounded by crowded benches. I was seated in the place of honor and served the conventional cup of tea.

Then a strange conversation began. Even had I known the most perfect Mandarin, I could not have understood these girls, for their speech was different from that spoken in any other part of the country. I had studied Chinese spasmodically — in Manchuria, in Peiping, in Shanghai — but each time, before I had more than begun, I had had to move on to new fields, and all that I had previously learned became almost useless. Shanghai had its own dialect, and what I had learned there aroused laughter in Peiping and was utterly useless in the south. Only missionaries and consular officials could afford to spend a year in the Peking Language School. Journalists had to be here, there, and everywhere.

I therefore talked with the filature girls in signs and gestures. Did I have any children, they asked, pointing to the children. No? Not married either? They seemed interested and surprised. In explanation I unclamped my fountain pen, took a notebook from my pocket, tried to make a show of thinking, looked them over critically, and began to write. There was great excitement.

A man standing near the door asked me something in Mandarin and I was able to understand him. I was an American, a reporter, he told the crowded room. Yes, I was an intellectual — but was once a worker. When he interpreted this, they seemed to find it very hard to believe.

Girls crowded the benches and others stood banked behind them. Using my few words of Mandarin and many gestures, I learned that some of them earned eight or nine dollars a month, a few eleven. They worked ten hours a day — not eight, as my escort had said. Once they had worked fourteen.

My language broke down, so I supplemented it with crude pictures in my notebook. How did they win the ten-hour day? I drew a sketch of a filature with a big fat man standing on top laughing, then a second picture of the same with the fat man weeping because a row of girls stood holding hands all around the mill. They chattered over these drawings, then a girl shouted two words and all of them began to demonstrate a strike. They crossed their arms, as though refusing to work, while some rested their elbows on the table and lowered their heads, as though refusing to move. They laughed, began to link hands, and drew me into this circle. We all stood holding hands in an unbroken line, laughing. Yes, that was how they got the ten-hour day!

As we stood there, one girl suddenly began to sing in a high sweet voice. Just as suddenly she halted. The whole room chanted an answer. Again and again she sang a question and they replied, while I stood, excited, made desperate by the fact that I could not understand.

The strange song ended and they began to demand something of me. They wanted a song! The *Marseillaise* came to mind, and I sang it. They shouted for more and I tried the *Internationale*, watching carefully for any reaction. They did not recognize it at all. So, I thought, it isn't true that these girls had Communist cells!

A slight commotion spread through the room, and I saw that a man stood in the doorway holding a flute in his hand. He put it to his lips and it began to murmur softly. Then the sound soared and the high sweet voice of the girl singer followed. She paused. The flute soared higher and a man's voice joined it. He was telling some tale, and when he paused, the girl's voice answered. It was surely some ballad, some ancient song of the people, for it had in it the universal quality of folk-music.

In this way I spent an evening with people whose tongue I could not speak, and when I returned to my temple, many went with me, one lighting our way with a swinging lantern. I passed through the silent stone courtyards to my room and my bed. And throughout the night the village watchman beat his brass gong, crying the hours. His gong sounded first from a distance, passed the temple wall, and receded again, saying to the world that all was well.

I lay thinking of ancient things . . . of the common humanity, the goodness and unity of the common people of all lands.

Shanghai Guerrilla Warfare

ONE late spring afternoon in 1931 I opened the *Shanghai Evening Post and Mercury*, an American daily, and found a double-columned center-of-the-page attack against me by a Mr. Woodhead, president of the British Residents' Association and one of the most reactionary British writers in the Far East.

The article was interesting, not because it concerned me, but because it was a perfect example of the "Shanghai mind." Even in a city and country where ruthless reaction rode roughshod over every man or woman who even mentioned such insidious ideas as the rights of man, it was a masterpiece of gutter journalism, attacking both my political and my personal life.

I might have ignored it had not my position already been made difficult by inquiries and attacks from official sources. A few months earlier I had been arrested by the Chinese police of Canton, acting upon a secret official document sent them by the British police of Shanghai; the document had charged that I was a Russian Bolshevik traveling on a false American passport. The police addressed me in Russian, which I did not understand, and then pocketed my passport. When the German Consul General intervened, the Chief of Police showed him the document from Shanghai. The American Consul General also saw it, but equivocated when I asked about it. While waiting for a reply from Washington concerning my citizenship, my Consul General asked me to give him the names of every Chinese I knew. When I replied that this was journalistically unethical and that I also considered it unethical for a consular official to act as an agent of the police, he was infuriated.

For weeks I lived under house arrest, with armed gendarmes wandering in and out of my apartment at will. If I went out, they followed, with murmuring crowds trailing behind me, apparently anticipating a Roman holiday. By the time Washington had verified my citizenship, I had fallen ill. My Irish sea-captain friend rescued me and took me back to Shanghai. I had to spend three months resting in the Philippines before I was in fighting trim again.

This Canton incident was really the setting of Woodhead's attack on me. In a succeeding article he brought up the case of a Chinese family of twelve which, he alleged, had been murdered by Communists and buried in a courtyard. The killing was said to have been an act of revenge against the head of the family, a leading Communist who had gone over to the Blue Shirts and betrayed dozens of his comrades.

The story had no meaning for me. Murder was an order of

the day in China. Anyone could get an enemy killed by paying a sum to thugs. Tu Yueh-seng, leader of the Green Gang of Shanghai, had accumulated a fortune from such work — not to mention the opium traffic and the "protection tribute" paid by every Chinese business house. Mr. Tu was the opium king of Shanghai and was referred to as the Czar of the French Concession. He and two other great gang leaders allied with him were called the "Big Three." The Green Gang often kidnapped recalcitrant wealthy Chinese and held them for ransom, and the chief Chinese detective of the International Settlement, who was connected with the gang, had grown very rich. At one time the gang poisoned a number of French officials at a banquet; when some of them died, the press called it "smallpox."

Nor could I be impressed by the attack upon my personal life. For years the British Chief of Police lived with the mistress of an upper-class brothel to which only white men able to pay "fifty dollars a shot" were admitted. This brothel mistress once had her picture taken with the Chief of Police and, grouped respectfully around them, the entire British police force. Incidentally, one such brothel mistress had a daughter studying in an exclusive finishing school in California.

I also recalled that when Mrs. Margaret Sanger once visited Shanghai, her crown of auburn hair had caused an elegantly dressed woman to approach her in a tea-room and ask her if she wished to earn a handsome sum of money, a fur coat, and other fine clothes. Margaret pretended interest. The elegant woman explained that the British fleet was coming in and Margaret was just the type for the Admiral.

Great as my sins might have been, I was not a member of the Green Gang or of the Shanghai police force, or at the disposal of the fleet. I refused to answer personal questions from any but my peers, and used my political reply to Woodhead's attack to expound unpopular views. Another vitriolic attack on me forced an American Marine officer to protest to the editors, and the paper declared the controversy closed.

A few days after this attack Feng Da, my secretary, came

with a mysterious warning to the effect that a Baltic German by the name of Karl Strauss, connected with the French and British police and the White Russians, was going to call on me. Strauss was referring to himself as the appointed representative of the International Red Aid, a Communist labor defense organization with headquarters in Berlin. He was said to be carrying two letters from Willi Muenzenberg, head of the Red Aid. I was not even a member, not to mention a functionary, of the Red Aid, and I doubted the story of the letters. Karl Strauss was known to many people as an international spy and such methods as these sounded too naïve.

Yet Strauss actually called a few days later. He was a short, thin man in his middle thirties; he had sandy hair and blue-gray eyes as hard as those of a snake. He presented letters which purported to put him in charge of the collection of Red Aid money, ostensibly for flood relief — which was childish. I said at once that I had nothing to do with the Red Aid or with Muenzenberg. Strauss replied:

"I want you to introduce me to your intellectual friends. I hear you know many who can help our movement."

Back of Strauss stood my leather walking-stick, leaded at one end — a weapon I now carried in self-protection. I went toward it. He turned and saw it, and without a word whirled and fled. I raced after him, shouting wildly.

He disappeared in a small cloud of flying leaves and dust.

That night I noticed that the big street light before my house was dark, and that a man, clearly a foreigner, stood behind it. I also saw that a new "art shop" had been opened in a building directly adjoining my motor driveway. White Russian men idled behind a few piles of paper, paint, and brushes. Then I saw two Chinese pass my house repeatedly. Experience enabled me to recognize these as members of the Green Gang. Notwithstanding the popular notion that "all Chinese and babies look alike," Chinese types are of course as distinct as those in any national group. And the Chinese thug is a very distinct type.

Then one morning my servant ran in from the kitchen,

crying: "Missy! One piece Chinese policeman in kitchen He want your letters. He say he take us to jail!"

I stalked into the kitchen, which was jointly used by three families, and found all the Chinese servants standing about. A Chinese in foreign clothing stopped talking as I entered. I ordered him out. His hard, cold face did not change expression, but he turned and went out. My servant gave notice and left at once. For two weeks two men friends took turns sleeping in my apartment, and I never went out without one or both as escort. The gangsters padded after us, never looking in our direction.

When it became plain that the gangsters and the White Russians were there to stay, I went to the American Court and told the special district attorney, Dr. George Sellett, the story. He rocked with laughter about Karl Strauss. He informed me that the Shanghai police had made three futile attempts to have me arrested. Since I lived in the French Concession, he advised me to write a letter to the French Consul General about the gangsters and the detectives.

I wrote a stinging letter. The next morning a lovely creature in white, with a blond waxed mustache and a dainty walking-stick, called on me. In a high, singing voice he introduced himself as representing the Political Department of the French police. This fairylike creature draped himself across a chair and sang out:

"Madame, I have called to tell you that the men you call spies and gangsters are unknown to us! I have come to offer you a good French detective to accompany you wherever you go. We desire only your comfort and safety."

"I need none of your detectives to protect me from your spies and thugs!" I exploded. "Please turn on the street light in front of my house and call off your dogs. If you don't I'll create an international scandal that will make the French Concession stink even more than it already does."

"Madame!! These are not our men. Nor does the French Concession stink!"

"Monsieur!! Those are your men, and the French Concession smells to high heaven of gangsters and opium and prostitution and White Russian thugs and whores!"

The fantastic creature rose on its hind legs, bowed, and cried: "Adieu! Madame, adieu!"

He walked off swaying elegantly, one hand on his hip.

To my amazement, the street light was turned on that night and the "art shop" folded up and vanished. The gangsters never reappeared. Once more I realized that as an American I had some protection. But the Chinese still had none.

Some time after this the Japanese *Nichi-Nichi* of Shanghai published an article about me. It was a truly amazing piece. According to it, I had been born in Michigan and educated at Ann Arbor. I spoke many languages perfectly, including Japanese, Chinese, and Russian. I was a member of the G.P.U. and made a specialty of sleeping with military men to worm their secrets out of them. This was easy, it declared, for I was young and beautiful and was a singer and dancer! I had been in Singapore spying on the British, in Java spying on the Dutch, in the Philippines spying on the Americans, and now I was in Shanghai spying on everyone!

Within a few days the *China Tribune*, Wang Ching-wei's English propaganda organ, published an article declaring that I had been a liar since childhood! As proof they quoted from my autobiography a story of how, when I was five years old, my mother whipped me because I told her that the wind carried stories on its back and that the red bird in our cherry tree also told me tales.

Before the ink on these stories was dry, a little German spy, Bernhard, apparently found himself in need of money; so he sat himself down and manufactured a "diary" of an alleged trip he had made into the Soviet regions of Kiangsi Province to attend a Soviet Congress. A foreign newspaper in Tientsin began to publish it. One diary entry "revealed" that I had gone to the Soviet Congress "with a group of Chinese students," taken a case of whisky with me, lived with students in the Soviet capital, and caroused drunkenly every night. When the Congress opened, it blithely continued, I had appeared stark naked on the platform, wearing only a red cap, and had sung the *Internationale*.

Such things as this may sound incredible to people living in an ordered society; they were commonplace in China. The "constituted authorities," both Chinese and foreign, accepted them. Some Chinese newspapers supported themselves by keeping a record of the secret lives of high officials, then threatening to publish the facts unless the victims paid up. As a rule they paid.

Chinese law read well on paper, but it was worth no more than its weight in bribes. For a penniless Chinese there was no justice at all, and Shanghai was filled with Chinese who sought protection under foreign law — although this, too, protected only a few. For a considerable period it protected the freedom of the press, but after the Blue Shirts established a censorship bureau in the International Settlement, even that protection disappeared.

Many upper-class intellectual Chinese campaigned ceaselessly for a "reign of law" within China. Among these were Dr. Lin Yu-tang and Dr. Hu Shih. Though Dr. Hu and I were often in disagreement, I have always recognized that he was one of the first Chinese leaders to urge the introduction into China of the Rights of Man.

BOOK III

Imperialism and the Revolution

1931 — 1936

BOOK III: IMPERIALISM AND THE REVOLUTION

1931 ~ 1936

March of Death

JAPAN's first step in the conquest of eastern Asia began in Mukden, Manchuria, on the night of September 18, 1931, when, without a declaration of war, Japanese troops blew up a stretch of railway and accused the Chinese of the crime. Before the night was finished, Mukden had been captured and Japanese troops had begun pouring into Manchuria from dozens of points. Henry Pu Yi, last degenerate scion of the Manchu Dynasty, which had ruled China from the downfall of the Mings to the foundation of the Republic in 1911, was kidnapped in Tientsin and spirited away to Manchuria, placed on a shabby throne, given a Japanese woman as wife, and told that he was Emperor of the new Empire of "Manchukuo." Ready-made Chinese traitors — the older and more unprincipled, the better — were placed in his Cabinet and Japanese "advisers" told them just when to talk and just when to keep their mouths shut. One of the few younger men who acquiesced was General Ma Chan-shan, and he was made Minister of War.

The Young Marshal, Chang Hsueh-liang, was at a theater in Peiping when he was notified of the incident; he did not leave. The Minister of Foreign Affairs was playing billiards and cultivating friendly relations with foreigners in the Nanking International Club. He was a pleasant, foolish man who had been put in his position, like many other officials, because of his ability to say yes. A million soldiers of the Central Government were busily engaged in trying to exterminate the Red Army in south China. A little thing like the occupation of China's three northeastern provinces was too unimportant for even one of them to be withdrawn for the defense of the nation. The League of Nations would put

Japan in its place, said the Central Government. People need not get excited and start shouting for war. China was unprepared for war, said Generalissimo Chiang Kai-shek — and continued to make war on the Red Army. Soon the Chinese representative was weeping before the League of Nations in Geneva while the Japanese representative watched him contemptuously, a big black cigar stuck in his face.

The Chinese Red Army and the Communist Party, which commanded it, appealed to the nation for the end of civil war and the formation of a united front to meet the danger of foreign invasion. Soon afterwards it issued a declaration of war against Japan. Its statements were suppressed, but managed to spread throughout the country, and the Japanese issued warnings to the Central Government that if the Red Army was not exterminated the Japanese would themselves do that job. Other foreigners in China agreed with those Chinese officials who declared that "the Japanese are only a skin disease, but the Communists are a disease of the heart." The Japanese, the foreigners said, would always respect private property, whereas the Communists threatened it. Furthermore, Japan needed room for its surplus population; given Manchuria, its demands for "living-space" would be satisfied. This had the further advantage of securing China against the infiltration of Communist ideas from the Soviet Union. Manchuria under the Japanese would be a bulwark against the Soviets.

When the League of Nations sent the Lytton Commission to China to "investigate" the Manchurian incident, the Americans and British could not agree on any policy and the Commission spent as much time studying British and American investments in China, and the "Red menace," as they spent in Manchuria. I never understood why such a commission was sent. Its presence seemed to indicate that news dispatches reporting the Japanese invasion were just Chinese fabrications. Japan's blueprint of world conquest, the *Tanaka Memorial*, which the Chinese had exposed, was branded by many foreigners as a Chinese fabrication, despite the fact that the occupation of Manchuria and then that of Mongolia were listed by that document as the first steps toward the occupation of all east Asia, the ousting of America from the Pacific, and finally world domination. The plan seemed fantastic. The white nations had ruled the world so long that they could not even imagine their power being challenged. Furthermore, the Japanese were men of color; they were runts. Much of what the people of America knew of them came from the romantic writings of Lafcadio Hearn or from *The Mikado*. Typical is *Madame Butterfly*, in which a Japanese woman is abandoned by her white lover and kills herself. It was sad but natural!

The Chinese people were not so foolish. They recognized the menace, and a boycott of everything Japanese spread through the country. The upsurge of hatred turned upon the policy of the Government, which tried to suppress every anti-Japanese organization while at the same time directing the wrath of the people against Marshal Chang Hsueh-liang, who was held responsible for the loss of Manchuria. The Young Marshal had received orders from the Central Government not to fight; in addition, he had declared his faith in the League of Nations. Fierce satires and cartoons were published about him; one declared that he was so annoyed with the Japanese that he had shaved off his mustache. He had followed up this desperate action by retiring to a mountain resort at Kuling, taking an ice-cream freezer with him, prepared to stick it out if it took months.

But up in Manchuria the bulk of the army of Marshal Chang Hsueh-liang disobeyed Government orders and fought. They were defeated and slowly driven southward through the Great Wall into China proper. General Ma Chan-shan, whom the Japanese had made Minister of War of their puppet "Manchukuo," used the period of his supposed treason to mobilize the troops of northern Manchuria. He then took the field as their leader and in the famous Battle of Nonni River lit a flame that swept all China. Because he received no support from the Central Government, he was soon driven across the border into the Soviet Union, but while he fought, the Chinese people regained their pride. The streets of Shanghai swarmed with students collecting money for him, and the names of Manchurian Army officers began to be honored by every Chinese, though their names could not be mentioned in the press. The Manchurian Volunteers and the Korean nationalists had also taken the field, and their number was increasing.

During a brief period a group of southern politicians, including Wang Ching-wei, used the Manchurian crisis to gain powerful posts in the Central Government. Like that of all Chinese politicians their power was judged by the number of armed men they controlled. These southern politicians controlled in part the famous 19th Route Army and it was soon withdrawn from the Kiangsi front, where it had been fighting the Red Army, to take up positions around Shanghai.

The 19th Route Army was a southern army known for its national consciousness and courage. While fighting the Red Army, it had learned not only the methods of guerrilla warfare, but much of that Army's social consciousness and anti-imperialist convictions. When the Japanese around Shanghai began to provoke their usual series of "incidents," they were arrested or shot down by the 19th Route Army, and war flared up again, this time around Shanghai. And again there was no declaration of war. I heard from officers of the 19th Route Army that Generalissimo Chiang Kai-shek telephoned General Tsai Ting-kai, field commander of their Army, not to fight the Japanese, but General Tsai refused to obey him. When some of the best Chinese divisions, trained by German military advisers, were dispatched to Shanghai, it was said that they had orders to disarm the 19th Route Army; instead they joined it. Once involved, the Government had no alternative but to support the struggle. Later those Nanking divisions, and not the 19th Route Army, were given credit for the defense of Shanghai, which was carried on with unparalleled heroism for three months.

In that campaign the patriotism of the people was established beyond doubt. Homes and schools were turned into hospitals; doctors, nurses, and students volunteered; and workers joined to fight or carry stretchers. Seven hundred workers took part with soldiers in the defense of the Woosung forts and held out for weeks against a combined land, sea, and air attack by the Japanese. They retreated only when outflanked, surrounded, and reduced to a few survivors.

This war gave me my first opportunity to learn at first hand something about Chinese soldiers, whom most foreigners regarded as mercenaries incapable of serious warfare. With a Cantonese interpreter I went through the hospitals and sat for hours talking with wounded soldiers about their lives and attitudes. Many of them were little more than boys, but most were seasoned fighters. Save for their speech, they might have been American farmers. Like the common people of China, they knew little of dissimulation and spoke their thoughts freely. They hated the Japanese, were anti-imperialist, and saw no sense to civil war. Though it was a crime to defend the Red Army, they spoke quite openly of the reforms which Communists had introduced among the peasant population of Kiangsi Province. They criticized their own officers and politicians, charging them with pocketing the wages of the soldiers. For the 19th Route Army had not been paid in four months. Right in the middle of the Shanghai fighting, Wounded Soldier Committees from the hospitals had demanded their back pay. Many of them had been arrested and taken from the hospitals to prison. The Chinese people and soldiers were poor, they said, but not the generals and politicians.

That China was poor no man would deny, but that both Chinese and foreign business men were making huge profits on arms and ammunition was just as undeniable. Chinese officials in charge of war supplies would not sign contracts with foreign firms until they had been paid high commissions. It was the foreign business men who exposed this, and such practices were eventually exposed in the American Congress. The names of the Chinese responsible for them were totally missing in the Chinese press.

I got a few sidelights on such matters from my many Chinese friends. One afternoon a Chinese woman friend called on me on her way to a tea party given by Mrs. Quo Tai-chi, wife of one of the highest Chinese officials. My friend was soliciting donations and recruiting volunteers for a hospital managed by Madame Sun Yat-sen which cared for a thousand wounded soldiers. I signed her list and gave a small donation. When she returned from the tea party she told me what she had seen. The guests were all wives and daughters of high officials and Army officers. One of these ladies appeared in a beautiful new gown, richly embroidered, wearing a new ring which the owner deprecated as paltry because it cost only seven hundred dollars. The women gambled at mah-jongg, losing or winning hundreds of dollars at each table. In the midst of their games my friend presented her appeal for donations. When the women saw that the first name on the list was my own and that I had given twenty dollars, they each gave twenty dollars, no more, no less. When my friend appealed for volunteers to work in the hospital, the women reminded her that they and their daughters were *ladies*, who could not be subjected to the rough talk of soldiers.

Not one volunteer came forth, but a few days later some of the ladies had their photographs taken as they went through the hospital distributing small bags of oranges and cigarettes. The soldiers had shouted at them:

"Go rape yourselves with your oranges! Pay us our back wages and we will buy our own oranges."

After three months of heroic fighting, which left the Chapei section of Shanghai in total ruin, Chinese and Japanese officials gathered in the British Consulate and signed an agreement. No one knew exactly what the secret clauses were, but that they existed every man suspected. In any case, Shanghai and the surrounding region were demilitarized and the Chinese agreed to suppress the anti-Japanese movement and to remove the 19th Route Army. Even the Chinese police force, which had turned its guns against the Japanese, was disbanded, and a special police force from Peiping, known to be more feudal and therefore more acceptable to the Japanese, was brought to Shanghai.

During the Shanghai war, foreigners prevailed upon the Japanese and China to call a truce for one day to permit the evacuation from Chapei of Chinese civilians — those who had survived the Japanese sword. Foreigners with special Japanese military passes were permitted to go into the battle zone to bring out people. I could not get a military pass, but the editor of the *Shanghai Evening Post and Mercury*, an American daily, agreed to take me if I cared to risk arrest. I decided to take the chance in an effort to find my friend the writer Lu Hsün. With a press sign on his car, and waving his military pass out of the window with one hand, my courageous editor friend swept at breakneck speed toward the Japanese barricades. While I sat breathless, we sped along the deserted road flanked by Japanese troops and were gone before they could lift a hand to inspect our passes. We reached the home of my friend and found it partially destroyed. I hammered on the doors and shouted in English and German, but no one answered. Marooned in their homes, many Chinese refused to respond to anyone, and some of them died of hunger rather than open their doors.

Failing in our mission, we again sped through the Japanese lines back into the International Settlement. Only when the war was over did I learn that Lu Hsün and his family had been rescued and hidden by Japanese friends.

During the fighting a number of my friends were murdered by the Japanese. I knew a returned student from America whose brother hid in a clothes basket when Japanese soldiers entered their home. After they had departed, my friend entered his brother's room, but the youth was gone and the room was splattered with blood. I asked two friendly Japanese newspaper men to find the brother. They went through all the concentration camps in which the Japanese Army held Chinese civilians.

Late one night — since no Japanese dared venture into the International Settlement by day — the newspaper men came to me. I had had one of my periodic heart attacks and was lying ill. One of my most unforgettable memories is of these two Japanese, collars turned up, hats pulled low over their eyes, clothes dirty and disheveled, and eyes bloodshot from days and nights of looking on horror, squatting by my bedside in total silence. When I asked the unnecessary question about my friend, one of them shook his head, but neither spoke. They must have sat in silence for half an hour. When they rose to go, one of them staggered from weariness. I proposed that they go into my living-room and sleep for a few hours on the couch. Without a word and without removing their overcoats, they dropped on the couch and were asleep almost before their heads touched it. I spent a sleepless night and at four in the morning awakened them. Before they left one of them said:

"It was horrible, horrible. But try to trust us. We will do all we can."

They went out and I never saw them again.

After the Shanghai truce was signed, the 19th Route Army asked to be transferred to north China, where the Japanese were preparing to invade the Province of Jehol. Instead, it was transferred to Fukien Province to the south, under orders to continue the war on the Red Army. Within a few months revolt flared within its ranks and for a few weeks its officers maintained a semi-independent Government which made a "non-aggression pact" with the Chinese Red Army. The Government moved soldiers against it, and when they began bombing Fukien cities, it surrendered. Some of its troops went over to the Red Army, and the rest were split up and scattered. Years later, in northwestern China, I met some of its officers, who had by then become staff officers of the Red Army. They had made the epic Long March with that Army.

The Chinese people writhed under the humiliation of defeat and impotence. Students who had demonstrated against the Japanese and demanded war were beaten in the streets and imprisoned. A 19th Route Army officer tried to kill Wang Ching-wei and other officials in Nanking; Wang Ching-wei went to Germany to recover and, after Hitler came to power, joined the Axis forces.

When, later, Italy copied Japanese technique and occupied Abyssinia, the resistance of the Abyssinians lit new fires of patriotism in the Chinese people. If little Abyssinia could fight a powerful invader so courageously, so could China, argued all Chinese patriots.

During the Abyssinian campaign I made another trip to north China and saw the confusion and despair that gripped the people. Students became hysterical and screamed as they talked, accusing their Government of selling out to the Japanese. Each week-end men and women students gathered by the hundreds in the Western Hills on what they called "picnics." I heard anti-Chinese foreigners accuse them of sexual debauchery. What they were really doing was practicing mountain-climbing and guerrilla warfare. Sticks were their weapons, and stones were their hand-grenades.

When I told officials that I could not understand why China could not fight as well as Abyssinia, one of them replied: "Oh, the Abyssinians are savages. If you step on a savage he will always fight. But we Chinese have an old culture and we love peace."

On the train from Peiping to Tientsin I witnessed the bitter fruits of appeasement, another aspect of the fearful distortion of the Chinese Revolution. The Chinese Government forbade anyone to ship silver money out of the country, but the Japanese sent armed men into north China to buy Chinese silver dollars with worthless paper currency and transport it to Mukden. Our train halted to allow hordes of these Japanese and Koreans to lug in heavy suitcases and sacks of silver dollars. They swarmed into every compartment and a gang of fifteen or twenty shoved me out of my seat. As I stood in the corridor, I watched a Chinese conductor come through the car, slide back the doors of each compartment, bow politely, and ask the gangsters whether they were comfortable. He dared not ask them for their tickets, for Japanese would not lower themselves by paying on Chinese trains.

When I told this story to a foreign friend who was very pro-Chinese, he answered:

"How can we expect individual Chinese to be braver than

their Government? The conductor would have been killed had he tried to collect fares."

Generalissimo Chiang Kai-shek was said to be anti-Japanese and preparing for war. I could see no signs of such preparation. What I could see was China's man-power, war materials, and national wealth being depleted in fratricidal fighting.

Friends in Germany had written me that the I.G. Farbenindustrie had bought up most of the shares in the *Frankfurter Zeitung*, the paper for which I was correspondent. I knew what to expect from my new employers because on three separate occasions the Chinese Government had requested the German Government to have me discharged. This paper, the oldest and most eminent liberal daily on the European continent, had weathered many reactionary movements in Germany, but the Nazi tide threatened not only its freedom of press but the lives of its owners. For, in addition to the "crime" of being erudite and liberal democrats, the publishers were Jewish. After mutual expressions of regret they gave me six months' notice, paid my salary for that period, and allowed our contract to lapse. A German, later one of Hitler's chief propagandists, was mentioned as my successor.

The Rights of Man

SOMETIMES leading Chinese intellectuals and I talked about the desperate necessity of introducing into China at least the fundamental liberties. Much we could not expect to achieve; but if we could gain some freedom of speech and press or a public trial for political prisoners, or, if we could halt the torture and secret slaughter of men or improve prison conditions, the gain would be precious.

Every leading Chinese scholar worthy of the name dwelt on these needs. One of the most impressive papers on this theme was written by Dr. Hu Shih, professor in Peking National University, and published in 1930 in a Shanghai literary magazine, the *Crescent Moon*, organ of a group of literary patricians. It presented sober and reasoned arguments for a "government of law" which would respect the rights of man.

Another liberal scholar, more volatile and critical, was Dr. Lin Yu-tang of Shanghai. He lectured and wrote on behalf of a system of law designed to take the place of the prevailing crass lawlessness. Unable, without endangering his life, to come out in the open in the fight for reform, Dr. Lin became a vitriolic satirist of officialdom, especially in "The Little Critic," a column which he conducted in a Chinese magazine published in English. Once I told him that he reminded me of Boccaccio, who, unable to make direct attacks on the power of the popes during the Italian Renaissance, satirized the immorality of individual priests and monks. In the scholastic hierarchy Dr. Lin Yu-tang occupied a place about half-way between Dr. Hu Shih and the revolutionary Lu Hsün. Lu Hsün charged that Dr. Lin's approach exercised a bad influence on youth because it led them to make humor out of political problems rather than face them. Lacking Dr. Lin's satirical genius, they wrote anemic, mediocre essays, jesting at frightful and bloody oppression.

Although more of an organizer and administrator — and politician — than a scholar, Mr. Yang Chien was also one of this group. Unlike the others, and despite his liberalism, he was a member of the Kuomintang. He was secretary general of the Academia Sinica, which numbered Dr. Hu, Dr. Lin, and scores of other scholars among its members. The president of the Academia was Dr. Tsai Yuan-pei, an old scholar, a humanitarian, and perhaps the most eminent of Chinese educators. In the middle of 1932 these scholars helped organize the first League of Civil Rights in China. Though members of the Kuomintang, Dr. Tsai Yuan-pei became president and Mr. Yang Chien secretary. Madame Sun Yat-sen was made chairman; Dr. Lin Yu-tang and Lu Hsün were on its executive committee. The only foreigners involved were Mr. Harold Isaacs — a young American newspaper man — and myself. Dr. Lin, Mr. Isaacs, and I were responsible for all publications and correspondence in the English language.

Our League took part in three campaigns for civil rights. The first was on behalf of a Chinese newspaper man arrested and secretly tortured to death in Chinkiang, near Shanghai. General Ku Chu-tung, Governor, lived in Chinkiang. This newspaper man had exposed the opium traffic and other corrupt practices with which General Ku was said to be connected. His murder aroused the Chinese press of Shanghai and it, together with our League, put up a valiant fight. We demanded a public investigation and the removal from office of General Ku.

General Ku issued a statement that the dead man had been a Communist; as "proof" he charged that five years before, in 1927, the man had tried to organize the ricksha coolies of Chinkiang. No Chinese newspaper outside the foreign concessions dared even mention the case, but the Shanghai Chinese press and our League pressed it vigorously.

General Ku invited our president and secretary to a dinner "to talk things over," and when they refused, the Blue Shirts of Nanking issued a secret warning to them to cease their activities. A Kuomintang committee secretly investigated the case, even exhuming the body of the dead man, but their findings were kept secret. Mr. Yang, who was an important Kuomintang member, told me that one of the legs of the dead man was found to be completely crushed.

By machinations beyond fathoming, the case was gradually smothered and soon became only a bitter memory. We had achieved nothing, and General Ku remained Governor.

Our League next attempted the public defense of five trade-union organizers accused of being Communists. We did not even demand a jury trial, for juries were unknown, and to have demanded one would have been like asking for the moon. Of the two lawyers who volunteered their services, one dropped out when he received a warning following the first hearing, and the other fled when Blue Shirts threatened to destroy his business and kill him. We failed again, totally and completely. Of the five prisoners, only one was saved. His mother, an influential Kuomintang member, secured his release.

The third case, in the spring of 1933, concerned the woman writer Ting Ling, a friend of mine. Along with another writer, Pan Nien, she had been kidnapped by Blue Shirts and spirited away to Nanking. Yang Chien, our secretary, took up this case with tremendous earnestness, issuing an appeal to the public.

A few days afterwards four Blue Shirts shot him dead on the steps of the Academia Sinica.

Our League for Civil Rights came to an inglorious end — vanquished by the Terror.

But the murder of Yang Chien, one of the best-known liberals, and the abduction of Ting Ling, a well-known writer, did become an international issue. Protests from American writers, women's groups, and intellectuals saved the life of Ting Ling, but Mr. Yang was dead.

Mr. Yang had been one of my friends. The revolutionary history of China, the influence of the intellectual renaissance, and study at Cornell University in America had made him a convinced democrat and patriot. He did not like the Communists personally, but he was opposed to the anti-Communist terror and to civil war. To him I owed much of my knowledge of old Chinese society and it had been he and the lyric poet Hsu Tze-moh who had often taken me to the old Peking drama. The three of us often called on friends, or went to some tea-house or temple to spend an evening in friendly talk. Mr. Yang's vivacious and witty conversation was among the few gay aspects of my life. My two friends spoke with amazing freedom of their own and their friends' love affairs and, to my continual delight, their spirited conversation was enlivened by vivid pictures of patricians harassed by love and irate marriage partners. Mr. Yang had had my book *Daughter of Earth* translated into Chinese and had introduced it to the public in his writings and lectures. But I sometimes noticed that he was more interested in my moral aberrations than in the social message of the book.

Mr. Hsu, the lyric poet, was killed in an airplane accident, and Yang Chien remained the first martyr to Chinese civil liberties. My friends were falling while I remained untouched; sometimes I felt as though I were living on the labor of others.

If I too paid my price, it seemed mild compared with that of the Chinese. After the German newspaper for which I corresponded terminated our contract, I was forced to live on my meager savings. I also started to work on a new book. The American Consulate seemed to know of my financial difficulties, for one day a consular official invited me to lunch and asked me to make confidential reports for him on the strength, activities, and program of the Chinese Communist Party. He brushed my refusal aside, pointing out that small reports day by day or as I came into possession of facts would be sufficient. He was too polite to suggest that I become a spy; instead, he asserted that our State Department should know the truth. To what end, I wondered. One consular official in China who had compiled an unprejudiced study of the Communist movement had been called a "Red" and was even ordered back to Washington for questioning. Other consular reports which I had read always referred to the Chinese Communists as "vermin."

As the consular official and I left the restaurant, we met one of his superiors on the street. Right before my face my host said to the other: "She says she knows nothing!"

The two men laughed.

I was determined that any facts which I gathered about the Chinese Revolution should be laid before the American public. That these would be incomplete and would be considered one-sided went without saying. Enough people were writing about the other side, and many were writing nothing else. I would write of the common people, the soldiers, and the intellectuals — of those who struggled for liberation from any form of oppression.

Motor Car No. 1469

ONE day in the spring of 1933 Li, a Chinese engineer, told me he was going to Peiping to meet representatives of the Manchurian Volunteers who were fighting the Japanese in the northeast. He planned to return to Manchuria with them. While in Peiping, he needed a safe place in which to live and asked me for help. I wrote a foreign friend asking him to meet Li at a certain foreign hotel.

Ten days passed and my foreign friend wrote that he had gone repeatedly to the meeting-place, but the engineer had not appeared. I was at once sure that Li had been arrested. I informed his wife, and she and all their friends immediately moved to new addresses. My address remained the only one he would know.

I was preparing to leave China for a sanatorium in the Soviet Union where I could receive treatment for a heart ailment. The night before I sailed, my telephone rang and I heard the voice of the engineer, tense with excitement. He told me that he had just got out of "the hospital" and wanted to see me at once.

While waiting for him, I wondered if he had returned as a spy. The reference to "the hospital" meant he had been arrested. Few men ever escaped from their captors; those who did were seldom trusted. But I felt instinctively that even though we had not been close friends I could trust this man fully. This instinct often guided me in my judgment of Chinese. It had caused me to dismiss Feng Da, my own secretary, and to look with distrust on his marriage with the woman writer Ting Ling.

When Li arrived, he was disheveled and agitated and his face showed marks of serious strain.

"I know you think I have come back a spy," he said, "but wait till you hear my story."

Sitting across the desk from me, and speaking in fluent English, he began:

"As my train neared Peiping, two men came up, seized me, and forced me to go with them. They said I was under arrest, but neither then nor later did they show any authority. I knew one of them. He was a former leader of the Communist Youth who went over to the Blue Shirts. He now helps kidnap his former comrades.

"These two men took me to a house in Peiping and ordered me to tell them where I was going and to give them the names and addresses of my comrades. I insisted that I had left the Communist Party months before and was now on my way to Manchuria to join the Volunteers. Of course that was as bad as being a Communist.

"Uncertain about me, they brought me back to Shanghai and said I would have to give the names and addresses of people I knew here. When we arrived, a detective in a motor car met us, and I noticed the license number was 1469. This detective was also an ex-Communist and is now a Blue Shirt detective.

"We drove to a small, dirty inn, the East Hung Chi, on the border of Nantao and the French Concession. It is a gangster den to which men and women are brought to be tortured until they say they are Communists. They are then turned over to the police."

"Why do they take them there instead of to the police?" I asked.

"I could not learn; I think perhaps they receive money for each Communist they capture, so they force people to say they are Communists. I saw many gangsters coming and going, and in some rooms they gambled and quarreled and fought. By their talk I knew they were the henchmen of Tu Yueh-seng, the gang leader whom Generalissimo Chiang appointed chief agent in Shanghai for suppressing Communists a year ago. Since then the whole underworld has been turned loose against us.

"Then the detectives unbound me and forced me to watch the torture of prisoners. A couple, man and wife, who looked like poor intellectuals, were surrounded by gangsters. The captives denied they were Communists. The detectives made me go up so they could see my face. They did not know me nor I them. To make them confess they put them on the airplane.

"The *airplane* is a kind of torture. They tied their hands behind them and then suspended them by their bound hands from a rope thrown over a beam. The woman fainted almost at once. A gangster took a wooden mallet and beat the chest of the man as he swung about. A man's chest becomes as tight as a drum when he hangs like that. The man cried horribly, blood began to gush from his mouth, and he lost consciousness. The gangsters took the couple down, carried them out, and brought in a man who was trying to fight them. They threw him on the floor and sat on his chest, thrust a rubber tube in his nostrils, and poured through it a filthy mixture which smelled like excrement and gasoline. His stomach bulged out. Then they sat on his stomach and the filth spurted out. They poured him full again and he vomited. When he lay very still they dragged him through a door.

"The detectives had forced me to look at him, and him at me. Of course he saw me standing with his torturers and perhaps thought me one of them."

"Wait a minute!" I interrupted. "Why were you not tortured like the others?"

"The Blue Shirts have adopted a new method with leading intellectuals," he replied bitterly. "They kill a worker or a peasant, for there is no way out for such men except the revolution. But the Blue Shirts know that an intellectual may waver, go over to them, and get a position in the Government or in the Blue Shirts. If we refuse to betray, they destroy us. They take us where other prisoners can recognize us, so that even if we manage to escape, none of our comrades will ever trust us again. Sometimes they make intellectuals accompany them through prisons in order that political prisoners may see them and never trust them again."

He turned back to his story.

"Under threat that they would treat me as they had treated the other prisoners, the detectives ordered me to write letters asking my friends to meet me in the Great Eastern Hotel in the International Settlement. Hoping to escape, I pretended to agree. I wrote two cards to false names and addresses; then they took me to the Great Eastern, hired a room adjoining mine, and locked my door.

"The first night they watched me closely and I could do nothing. The next night I heard them snoring. I crept to the window, intending to slide down the drain pipe to the street three stories below. Just as I put my leg out, I heard a noise, and, looking down, saw a man creeping *up* the drain pipe! He caught the window ledge just beneath mine, cautiously lifted the window, and then I realized he was a burglar. Before he could crawl into the room a woman screamed and he darted out and slid down the drain pipe. There was a great commotion — and I could not escape that night.

"No one came in answer to my cards, but I told the detectives it was because the man I once knew had probably moved or because no one would come to meet me anyway. They were very angry and took me back to their den and said they could convince me. Just as we entered, two gangsters were bringing in a good-looking, well-dressed man. We followed him right in and I was forced to confront him. I had never seen him. He was so scared that when they threatened to torture him, he began to betray his comrades.

"This miserable fellow sat down, trembling, and said that Ting Ling, the woman writer, was having a meeting that night at her home on Quinsan Road with two men writers who helped her edit a literary magazine. He insisted that Ting Ling was not a Communist, but nevertheless a Leftist."

"Wait!" I exclaimed. "Describe that man!"

He described my former secretary, Feng Da. I walked about the room in the deepest agitation, then turned to listen again.

"It was now dark," the engineer continued, "and the two Blue Shirt detectives and a chauffeur pushed me into that same motor car, No. 1469, and we drove to the address given by that coward. On the fourth floor the door was opened by a woman who must have been Ting Ling. She did not say a word, but turned very white when the chauffeur grabbed her and tied her with a rope, then forced her down the stairs.

"At the same time I was pushed into the room and saw two men, one tall and thin and one short and now very pale. Everything happened very quickly. The tall, thin man stood with his back to an open window, and when one of the detectives went toward him, he began to fight. But he was frail, and when the fight grew fierce, he whirled and threw himself through the window — down the four stories. The detective shouted, then ran fearfully out, to get the body — perhaps to avoid another kidnapping scandal in the foreign settlement.

"The shorter man in the room had also begun to fight and I picked up a stool and hit the detective on the head. As he staggered, I turned and fled down the stairs, along the street, and mingled with the crowds on Szechuen Road. I telephoned from a shop to my wife, but there was no answer. So I called you."

After a moment he added: "That is my story. Of course you will not believe me. No one could. It is too fantastic. But I swear that it's true."

We sat in silence. Finally he said: "Tell my wife what I have told you. I will stay in a cheap inn I know and she can have comrades watch me if she wishes."

"I know nothing of your wife or your comrades," I answered. "I collect stories, and yours is an interesting one."

Wearily he lowered his head and sat in silence. Yet I knew he was telling the truth, knew it as well as a mother knows whether her child is lying or not.

"Give me the name and address of your inn," I said.

After he had done so, he sat thinking for a time, then said: "Tell her this: one week from tonight, at this time, I will stand before the Buddhist temple on Bubbling Well Road, with a foreign newspaper in my left hand. If my comrades trust me, one should follow me as I walk away to a quiet street. He should approach me and ask if I have seen the four T'ang horses. I will reply that I have seen only three."

"And if they do not trust you?"

In a dead voice he answered: "Then let them do with me as they wish."

"I have no money at all," he continued. I gave him a few bills, and he left my apartment quickly.

Weeks later, in my room in a sanatorium in the Caucasus in the Soviet Union, I opened some late English-language newspapers from Shanghai. The earlier ones gave details of the assassination of my friend Yang Chien and the disappearance of Ting Ling and a man writer, Pan Nien. Not a word about the Blue Shirts or the man who had thrown himself from the window in Ting Ling's room.

The prominent position of Yang Chien had made necessary some explanation for his murder, and the French police had arrested two of his assailants, both wounded as they tried to escape. One had confessed before he died. The police announced that they were unable to reveal the men responsible for the murder "because this would involve the highest personalities in the Chinese Government."

Shortly after this, the startling headline: "Another Communist Outrage" caught my eye. It concerned the murder of a Chinese detective, a former Communist, who had "distinguished himself by hunting Communist bandits to their lairs." He and his chauffeur had been shot dead just as their car drew up before the Sweetheart, a brothel in an alleyway in the International Settlement. The police had refused to give out any information about it save to say they suspected Communist vengeance. The motor car was a large one and the license number, the report said, was 1469.

Two years later, after I had circled the globe, my doorbell in Shanghai rang, and when I opened it, the ghost of the engineer, Li, was leaning against the door-frame. His sick eyes stared at me from a gaunt and bloodless face. He trembled and his head wobbled from side to side as I led him into my guest room, undressed him, and put him to bed. He lay very still, like a man who has reached the point where he is ready to die. I called a doctor. The engineer had malaria, an enlarged heart, intestinal parasites, inflamed tonsils, decayed teeth, anemia.

For weeks he lay ill, staring at the ceiling above him, but when his health improved, he began to talk. First I asked him what had happened the night after he had left my house two years before.

"One week later," he said, "I stood before that Buddhist temple on Bubbling Well Road, and when I walked away a man followed. He came up and asked me:

" 'Have you seen the four T'ang horses?'

" 'Not four, but three,' " I answered. We talked and he arranged for my trip into Soviet Kiangsi, where the Central Committee of our party had moved. I went by coastal steamer to Swatow in the south, where I met a man who led me to a river boat. The boatman paid no attention to me, but took me to a distant village and delivered me to a man who guided me northward into the mountains of Fukien."

From Tingchow, in Fukien, Li had turned due west to Shuikin, the Soviet capital. He was examined by the Central Committee of his party, then put in charge of a Red Army arsenal near Shuikin. Since educated technical men were few, he was later asked to do almost everything from manufacturing war materials to constructing a soap and medicine factory for Red Army hospitals. His account covered every field of activity in the Soviet regions — medical work, education, administrative problems, mineral ores and vegetation, newspapers and books.

Part of his tale touched on the great military campaigns of the Kuomintang against the Red Army, and of the Battle at Kwanchang, in which the power of the Red Army had been shattered. In that one battle the Red Army lost four thousand men, and when it received orders to assemble for the Long March, it had to leave twenty thousand wounded behind. One hundred thousand men began that march in September 1934, but only the highest leaders knew what lay ahead. Of these he was one. He had buried his arsenal machinery and, with his staff of skilled workers, assembled as ordered. Then came the secret march through the cordon of Kuomintang troops. While the Kuomintang armies followed plans formulated by the German Reichswehr officer General von Seeckt, another foreigner, a German with the Chinese name of Li Teh, was responsible in the Red Army for the plan of positional fighting which resulted in defeat. His ideas had prevailed against those of Mao Tze-tung, general secretary of the Chinese Communist Party, an experienced guerrilla fighter. . . .

The engineer's story carried me along on a march and through a struggle such as history has seldom known — across mountains and rivers, in and out of battle, and by a thousand small and touching details into the lives of the common people. . . .

He told of the cruel cunning of the militarists:

"As our Army passed through northern Kwangsi mountains, officials beat gongs in the villages and cried that bandits were coming! The peasants fled. We marched through empty villages, but never molested a home. I fell ill with malaria, and along with a great many sick and wounded men fell behind the Army. We sometimes saw officials and policemen, thinking our Army had passed, return to the villages, burn or loot homes, and then, when the peasants returned, tell them that the crimes were the work of the Red Army. The people were turned against us."

He spoke of their treachery: "Soldiers or policemen would waylay our sick or wounded and shoot them down. Their detectives dressed themselves in clothing taken from our dead and then mingled with us as spies. I shot one man whom I saw do this."

And of the poverty of the peasants: "How poor are the people of Kweichow Province! I once went into a peasant hut and found an old woman cowering in a corner. She ran out, caught her only chicken, and fearfully offered it to me. When I paid her for it she wept. Thousands of poor men joined our Army."

He told of terrible betrayals: "When we reached northern Yunnan, a schoolteacher led the peasants to welcome us. This teacher had become a guerrilla commander, and because I was sick with malaria, our Army ordered me to remain behind as his political director. After the Army passed on and the Kuomintang Army approached, this teacher welcomed them as he had welcomed the Red Army! I had to flee for my life."

And of incredible extremes: "I moved on northward and met soldiers. They stripped me naked, taking even my eyeglasses. I came to a convent of Buddhist nuns; they gave me a robe and lent me seventy dollars to take me to Shanghai. I expected to die on the way. If your name had not been in the telephone book, I think I should have died, for all my friends are scattered."

Once he said: "From the time I left you that night over two years ago, I began to keep a diary for you, but when we left on the Long March I buried it with my machinery."

When he was once again able to travel, Li left for the Soviet Union for continued treatment and study. I never saw him again.

A wounded Red Army commander lived for a time in my home so that I might write down another epic covering nearly half a century of Chinese life. He was Chou Chien-ping, the commander of the Tenth Red Army Corps in its early days. This was when Fang Chih-ming, a chemical engineer, was political leader and organizer of the corps.

I never met Fang, yet of all the deaths of Red Army commanders, his execution in Nanchang in January 1933 affected me most deeply. Perhaps it was the hateful way a foreign newspaper correspondent, "Rex Driscoll," reported his execution that hit me so hard. I had never heard of Driscoll before and have not heard of him since. It may be that a missionary assumed the name for the purpose of publishing the reports. When Fang was captured in the battle that annihilated his small army, a wave of glee swept the ruling class, both foreign and Chinese. A tone of gloating runs through Driscoll's report, but the facts he recorded speak for themselves. Fang was placed inside an animal cage and paraded through the streets of Nanchang. People ridiculed him with the title of "King" because he sat proudly and with dignity inside the cage. When paraded before a mass meeting, he called to the people to arise and fight for liberation, and when taken out to be killed, he besought his executioners to join the revolution.

Chou told me his tales of Fang Chih-ming in a dry, matter-of-fact manner, but out of them there arose the figure of a great organizer whose loss China had ill been able to afford. Fang had exercised magic power over the common people because his every act was so plainly in their interest. He had organized primary schools and hospitals, agricultural exhibitions to improve the crops, a Red Army Training Academy, civilian night schools to end adult illiteracy, two large arsenals, and a Land Mine Bureau to take the place of the numberless home arsenals of the peasants.

Chou Chien-ping was a quiet, unassuming little man who had sprung from poor peasants in Kwangsi. His father had died when he was five and his mother had earned a living as a washwoman. He had joined the Army as a boy orderly at the age of ten and had risen to the rank of battalion commander. When he joined the Red Army, he took his entire battalion with him.

After leaving my home, Commander Chou went to the northwest to rejoin the Red Army. A few weeks later, at the age of forty-six, he died of smallpox.

Soviet Interlude

WHEN my health broke down again in 1933, I left China for the Soviet Union, where I remained for eleven months. Part of this time was spent in a sanatorium in Kislovodsk in the Caucasus, and the remainder in Moscow and Leningrad, where I completed my book *China's Red Army Marches*. Since my activities were restricted by my illness and by the work I had to do on my book, I was able to get only brief glimpses of Soviet life.

Once a watering-place for the Russian nobility, Kislovodsk had been turned into a city of rest homes where tens of thousands took free annual vacations. At that time there were fifty-nine of these homes, with eleven others under construction. The Red Army utilized two of these, the "learned professions" two, the textile workers' union one, and the miners' union one, a beautiful structure on a cliff overlooking magnificent mountain ranges.

After a few weeks I made the acquaintance of a Red Army officer and accompanied him on a visit to a rest home for commanders. It was early evening and hundreds of them stood in a garden where they had just seen a motion picture. They continued their military education during their vacations, with daily lectures and blackboard and moving-picture demonstrations. I was introduced to a commander, a professor from the Red Army Academy in Moscow. He spoke perfect English, and when he learned that I was an American, remarked that his life had once been saved by General Graves, commander of the American Expeditionary Army in Siberia during the Russian Revolution. In 1920 — I believe that was the date he gave — he had been editor of a newspaper in Vladivostok when the Japanese arrested him and eleven of his comrades. They were about to be executed when General Graves sent American troops and forced the Japanese to release them.

This professor told me that General Graves's book, *America's Siberian Adventure*, had been translated into Russian and published by the Red Army Publishing House. The Introduction to the book traced the history of American-Japanese relations in the Pacific and the conflict in their interests and policies. This conflict was reflected in General Graves's outspoken abhorrence of the Japanese and their White Russian puppets — to whom he always referred as butchers.

Under the system of socialized medical care, doctors and nurses made physical examinations of all arrivals in the health resort, and those needing medical or dental treatment received it without cost. The park and surrounding wooded hills were lined by winding paths, with numbered stations on the slopes. When a doctor said a patient could walk to the highest station, his cure was complete.

When I was at last allowed to go to the highest station, an American Indian friend — a student in the Academy of Science at Leningrad — accompanied me, and we walked over the wild, lonely mountain ranges. Wandering about, we came upon a solitary shepherd youth of about twenty, herding a large flock of sheep.

My friend could speak Russian, so we halted and asked the youth where he came from. His movements were so slow and thoughtful and his voice so unhurried that he seemed to be a part of the solitude. He said his collective sheep farm was in the valley far below us. Accepting the cigarette we offered, he sat down with us in a field of blue and yellow mountain flowers.

No, he said, he did not get very lonely in the hills because there were so many things to think and read about these days. He drew a paper-bound book from his pocket and said he was reading it for the second time. It was Tolstoy's *War and Peace*. Lenin, he quietly added, had considered Tolstoy the greatest Russian writer. Did we think the same? We talked about this for a few minutes and then he asked us what country we came from.

When we told him that we were Americans, he recalled that some of our countrymen had lectured at his farm. From them he had learned that there were twelve million unemployed in America. It had seemed almost unbelievable, he said — as many people as in the entire Caucasus — perhaps more. It was like a whole country having no way of earning a living. Looking compassionately at us with his very blue eyes, he remarked that it must be a great misfortune to be born an American.

"To think of having to ask a rich man for the right to live!" he remarked. "I'm very sorry for you."

"It's not so hot!" my friend agreed.

I wondered what would happen if the Soviet Union ever opened its doors to immigrants. Would millions of the poor pour into it as they had once poured into America? Certainly I had heard tales of political wrongdoing, but could my own country truly say that its politics were pure? Could one say it of French or English rule? No, not unless one chose to forget India, or to ignore the fact that the cruelties inflicted on the natives of French Indo-China were a byword in the Far East.

Limited as had been my visits to the Soviet Union, I was deeply impressed by what I had seen. Kislovodsk itself was but one of hundreds of rest and recreation resorts for those who labored. And everywhere great cities and industries had risen where none had been a few years before. Medicine had been successfully socialized, and education from grade school through universities was free. In such great metropolitan centers as Moscow and Leningrad cultural life was rich and varied. Books were issued in millions of copies and the great classics could be bought for a few kopeks a volume. Fine music and good theaters were widespread; the folk-life of the people flourished and at almost any hour one might see a crowd on a boulevard watching Red Army soldiers and civilians dancing folk-dances.

The life of the Red Army was particularly attractive: it had its own great theaters and publishing house, and its men, down to the last private, received the best educational and military training possible. I doubted if any army in the world surpassed it in such directions.

As I looked upon the Soviet scene, I constantly compared its swift and broad advance with conditions in China. China had developed a few of its roads and industries, but they constantly staggered under the burden of self-seeking private interests. It had built primary schools, but the children of the poor could not afford to attend them. Within its armies the corruption was notorious. China was bound by a thousand chains both internal and foreign; the people of the

Soviet Union labored under heavy burdens, but no one owned them, their land, or their industries. They were a proud, awakened people.

Yet I could not imagine spending my life outside of China; just why I could not say. Life in the Soviet Union would have been free and easy compared with life in China, and the income from the Russian editions of my books would have not only maintained me but even left a large surplus in the bank. But social and literary interests drew me irresistibly back to China. There, too, my friends lived and struggled.

But first I hoped to establish myself as the correspondent of some American publication and therefore decided to return to America. I left the Soviet Union in the spring of 1934, passed through central Europe, and set sail from France as a third-class passenger.

Once in New York, I tramped the streets of the city trying to find a position on some newspaper. I failed. One was willing, but when the editor asked if I thought there would be war in the Far East and I said yes, he replied that his paper could not publish articles with such a tendency. His paper, he said, stood for peace.

America was like a strange planet, and the friends of my youth, now middle-aged, seemed to be living and thinking much as they had lived and thought fifteen years before. On the west coast I visited my sister and my youngest brother, a veteran of the first World War. I had last seen my brother when he was a child, and he was now past thirty and had a wife and family. My sister was the principal of an elementary school. I had no place whatever in the life of either of them.

From my brother and sister I learned about my father, then a man in his seventies and as hale and hearty as any animal. He owned horses and chased women. The rest of the time he drank. Moved by a sense of filial duty, I had sometimes sent him money out of the royalties from my books. With these he bought gallon jugs of whisky, lined them up against a wall and went on a toot that lasted for weeks or months.

Two years later, when I was back in China, I was stricken with remorse on learning of his death. But the details in the letter which followed this announcement set my spirit at rest. On a hot summer's day in Oklahoma he had won sixteen bottles of beer in a poker game, and drunk them all. Then he up and died.

BOOK IV

The United Front and War

1936 — 1937

BOOK IV: THE UNITED FRONT AND WAR

1936 🕊 1937

Sian Incident

ONE evening in the spring of 1936 at the Shanghai home of my friend Lu Hsün I met a writer who had just come from the northwest as representative of the Chinese Red Army. He had made the epic Long March, that historic trek made by an entire army across twelve thousand miles of plains and rivers and mountains.

Every evening for weeks I sat with him, taking notes of his conversation. Though calm and factual, his recital was filled with pictures of incredible suffering and perseverance. Speaking of the long wanderings in the snows of eastern Tibet, he would say:

"Men grew so exhausted that when they squatted for natural functions, they were too weak to get up again. Thousands froze to death. For months we had only corn to eat, and many could not digest it. It passed through them. Others gathered it up, washed it, and ate it again — only to expel it once more. . . .

"When those of us who survived emerged at last on the plains of Kansu and saw our own native folk, we threw our arms about them, weeping and laughing. We were in rags or skins, or cloth primitively woven from sheep's wool. We were as gaunt as skeletons, and thousands of us were sick. The nights echoed with our coughing. Kansu was so poor that we often ate dogs, cats, and rats. Sometimes the women of the province hid in their huts because there was only one pair of trousers to a family and they were worn by the husband. Decades of wars, famines, drought, taxes, and merciless rents had stripped the people even of clothes. To the curse of destitution was added syphilis, spread by mercenary armies and the Mongols from the north. Many are sterile and there are places where no child under fifteen can be found."

This man told me how desperately medical supplies were needed, and thereafter two foreign doctors and I began to collect money and became, so to speak, medicine smugglers for the Red Army.

I had again become ill and after consultation with friends decided there was but one place where Blue Shirt gunmen were not a menace — the northwest under the Young Marshal, Chang Hsueh-liang. Many changes had taken place in the character of the Young Marshal since the time he had been a Manchurian war-lord. The occupation of Abyssinia had destroyed his admiration for Italian Fascism, and under the influence of young men on his staff, he had become a democrat. He had conquered the opium habit and was trying to rid himself of the feudal and militaristic influences of his youth. The National Salvation movement, banned in other parts of China, was protected in his territory, and despite protests from the Government he had permitted a National Salvation Congress to be held in Sian. Though under orders from the Government to continue the extermination of the Red Army after its arrival in the far northwest, neither he nor his troops relished fighting their own countrymen while the Japanese were occupying their native Manchuria and invading Suiyuan Province.

A Red Army representative, unofficially on the Young Marshal's staff, arranged for me to rest and work in a temple at Lintung, some fifteen miles from Sian. This was the center of the great northwestern region which had cradled the Chinese race, in which great dynasties had arisen out of the ruins of others and then had themselves decayed and been overthrown. There I hoped to regain my health and write another book.

The temple in which I lay had once been the pleasure place of Yang Kwei-fei, favorite concubine of Hsüan Tsung, an Emperor who had ruled from A.D. 847 to 859. Gazing at Yang Kwei-fei's pavilion, the lotus pond, the walks and bridges, I recalled a song which I had once heard an old Chinese musician play on his five-stringed lute. His music had filled the room like a small orchestra. It was the *Song of Unending Sorrow*, an ancient poem telling how the Emperor mourned for Lady Yang, whose spirit sent him a message of undying love from the enchanted isle where she dwelt among the immortals.

In such an atmosphere I read Chinese history and took up again my oft-interrupted study of Chinese. As my health improved I often wandered across country to the tomb of Ch'in Shih Huang Ti, who founded the Ch'in Dynasty in 255 B.C. and tried to destroy the feudal system of his time. His vigorous mind had thought in vast terms. It was he who began building the Great Wall to keep out the barbarians from the north, conscripting one man from each family of China for this work. Under his reign mighty irrigation works, Imperial highways, bridges, and cities were undertaken. Chang'an (the ancient name for Sian) had once been a city of colossal dimensions. Since the Confucian scholars were then — as they still are — the transmitters of feudal thought, Ch'in Shih Huang Ti had tried to destroy them and their works, burning all Confucian writings except those on agriculture, arboriculture, medicine, pharmacy, and divination. Near Lintung was a valley which was pointed out to me as the place where he had buried alive many recalcitrant Confucian scholars.

As Ch'in Shih Huang Ti grew old and soft in luxury, he turned to magic and sought the waters of immortality, which he heard were on the Blessed Isles somewhere in the eastern sea. It was recorded that he sent a fleet with three thousand young men and maidens, under a famous magician, to bring back some of this water. These youths are said to have colonized Japan — which was undoubtedly the worst thing they could have done.

The tomb of the Emperor rises from the plain beyond Lintung like a low mountain and beneath it, say historians, lies buried a palace filled with priceless art treasures of ancient China. The floors are of copper through which the rivers of China are traced in quicksilver, and the copper dome is graven with all that was known in ancient astronomy. Only the granite building that once armored the summit of the tomb had been removed — sold to an Englishman by a Chinese General in need of money.

Back in my temple at Lintung, I began work on my new book, pausing only when friends came from Sian to interrupt my loneliness and bring news. One of these friends was from the Red Army, and the news he brought was always disturbing. General Fu Tso-yi, Governor of Suiyuan Province, was fighting the Japanese, who were occupying Inner Mongolia in an effort to isolate China from the Soviet Union. The Japanese had also occupied Tsingtao in Shantung Province. Instead of fighting them, the Chinese Government had concentrated its most powerful Army, under General Hu Chung-nan, against the Red Army in the northwest. Ammunition dumps had been established on the roads leading up to this new theater of war, there had already been a number of fierce engagements, and General Hu had already suffered defeats. The commanders of the northern and northwestern armies had held a military conference to discuss the Government orders to surround and destroy the Red Army, but feudal inefficiency and conflicting interests had dissipated their efforts. Marshal Chang Hsueh-liang's Manchurian Army was more modern than most and his officers and men wanted to fight the Japanese.

Instead of an Anti-Red front, an Alliance of Anti-Japanese Armies of the northwest was taking form. It consisted of the Red Army, the Manchurian (Tungpei or Northeast) Army, and the Hsipei (Northwest) or 17th Route Army under General Yang Hu-chen. Delegates were negotiating with other armies to join the Alliance, and representatives of the semi-independent Province of Kwangsi in the far south had already arrived in Sian.

Hundreds of students from Peiping and Tientsin had gone into Marshal Chang's new Student Military Academy. Representatives of the Blue Shirts in Sian, led by a man known as Yeh Tao-kang, notified their chief of all these developments. When the Generalissimo accused Marshal Chang of harboring Communists in his academy, the Marshal replied that his only standard for judging students was their anti-Japanese sentiments. "I would advise you not to believe anything the Japanese tell you," he added.

One day in October 1936 three students who had just arrived in Sian were kidnapped by the Blue Shirts and imprisoned in Kuomintang headquarters. Marshal Chang sent troops who broke down the doors and released the students. Such incidents were warnings of an approaching storm.

Other news shattered my seclusion at this time. On October 20 a Chinese woman friend who lived in the temple — she was a gentle woman who seemed ignorant of political matters — came into my room and said dejectedly:

"We Chinese suffer many losses. Now we have suffered another — our great writer Lu Hsün is dead."

The news of my own father's death had reached me shortly before and I had felt regret and sorrow; the death of Lu Hsün came to me not only as a personal sorrow, but as a national tragedy. He had not lived aimlessly, nor had he given himself over to the search for wealth, power, or position. Of all Chinese intellectuals, he had wielded the greatest influence over educated youth. He embodied the common good, and the disease which killed him was fostered by sorrow and struggle. On death itself he had looked with contempt.

Only for the announcement of his death did the official censors lift the ban on his name. His funeral in Shanghai was memorable. Teachers and students left their classrooms, clerks their shops, workers their factories, and poor writers, artists, and actors came out of their hiding-places to follow his body. Madame Sun Yat-sen and her brother, Dr. T. V. Soong, were in the procession, and Dr. Soong helped lower the coffin to its last resting-place.

Lu Hsün was not a Communist, but the Communists honored his all-embracing culture and strength of spirit. In their center at Yenan they later founded the first Lu Hsün Library; I became the keeper of the seals of the foreign-language section and donated to it all the books I had collected in China. Later still the Communists established the Lu Hsün Art Academy, to which hundreds of educated youth journeyed from every part of the country to study under the best writers, artists, musicians, and actors. This was one academy which produced a living and militant art.

When Sian friends came out to Lintung on the day following Lu Hsün's death, even the temple manager, a business man without much imagination, came in and discussed Lu Hsün with them. As I listened to him and saw that even the owner of an isolated country temple knew of Lu Hsün's life and work, I asked myself: "What purpose did all the censorship serve?"

Other events interrupted work on my book. In late November I heard of another clash between the Young Marshal and Generalissimo Chiang. The Generalissimo had again accused Marshal Chang of failing to exterminate the Red Army, and the Young Marshal had replied:

"I and my officers and men have obeyed you faithfully for years, believing your promise to lead us against the Japanese. You have not done so. It is not too late. We now demand that you give us the right and opportunity to drive out the Japanese. In any case, I must tell you that I cannot control my army any longer."

A few days later a small group of young officers in the uniform of the Central Armies appeared at our temple at Lintung and ordered everyone to evacuate immediately. The temple was to be prepared as living-quarters for Generalissimo Chiang and his armed bodyguard, and as the seat of the Anti-Red Military Conference which was to start on December 7. All villages lying on the highway to Sian were also ordered evacuated.

I drove into Sian with my Chinese woman friend. The highway was choked by a great throng of people carrying their possessions on their backs or shoving them on wheelbarrows. Conscripted village men and boys were already at work repairing the road, filling up every small hole. The Anti-Red Military Conference was obviously not a popular event and the people were not being trusted: the empty villages along the highway were now occupied by detectives. Again I recalled the ancient past when powerful court cliques kowtowed and flattered emperors, pretending implicit obedience but in reality serving their own interests. Though I believed the Generalissimo to be a nationalist who loved power above all else, still I had never considered him the kind of leader to order every little rut in his path filled in. His court clique was certainly kowtowing.

I secured a small room in the Sian Guest House, the only modern hotel in the city, planning to return to the temple later. But within a few days the Guest House was filled with high officers of Generalissimo Chiang's staff and I learned that hundreds of Blue Shirts had established secret centers in many parts of the city. They were said to have machine-guns, rifles, and a secret radio station. Hsiao Li-tze, a former Communist leader, then the Generalissimo's private secretary, was Governor of the province, had his own armed guards in the city, and commanded the police. The Kuomintang branch, one of the most unpopular institutions in the region, was also armed.

When the military conference began in Lintung, the atmosphere of Sian became tense. Every day I heard reports that the Generalissimo was calling high Manchurian officers one by one, offering them money and position if they would transfer their allegiance from the Young Marshal to himself — which would mean their willingness to continue civil war. They replied that their homeland was occupied by an enemy invader, their families slaughtered, and their homes outraged; and then they proceeded to report back to the Young Marshal.

One morning my Red Army friend came to borrow my pistol and cartridges. There was proof, he said, that the Blue Shirts, aided by the Sian police, were planning an uprising that might result in wholesale slaughter.

On December 9, the anniversary of the anti-Japanese student movement which had begun in Peiping, thousands of Sian students and school children marched through the streets, singing national songs and distributing handbills urging national unity. They planned to petition Generalissimo Chiang to end the civil war and help General Fu Tso-yi fight the Japanese in Suiyuan. Under orders from the Governor, who received his instructions from the Generalissimo, the demonstration was attacked by the police, and two young boys, sons of Manchurian Army commanders, were wounded. The atmosphere of the city became ominous.

A few hours later a Blue Shirt, refusing to give his name or show any identification, came to demand my passport and residence visa and to ask why I had taken pictures of the student demonstration. I showed the visa, but replied that there was no law against taking pictures of students. He rushed off to the police captain who had given me the visa and, as I heard later, slapped the captain's face, tore the stripes from his uniform, and dismissed him from the service. Because the captain had referred him to the city government, which had ordered the visa, the Blue Shirt then stormed over to the city government offices; but here the officials told him to get out or be thrown out. Wild with fury, he returned to the hotel and declared that if the manager didn't throw me out he would do so himself and "settle with her once and for all"!

I reported these events to a Manchurian staff officer and the Red Army representative that night. They were furious. "Stay right here and defy the Blue Shirts!" they ordered. "If they attack you, it will become an international incident and expose them as having attacked a foreign friend of China while refusing to fire a shot at the Japanese!"

So I waited to become an international incident!

The next day the hotel manager received an ultimatum to throw me out within twenty-four hours. When I refused to go, the manager wailed that I would be killed.

I have never been able to learn all the details of what happened in Sian on the fateful night of the 11th of December 1936. What I did learn was that throughout that night

Marshal Chang, General Yang Hu-chen, and their high staff officers held a conference, and that at dawn a body of their troops, led by a young officer, Captain Sun, surrounded the temple at Lintung. Thirty of the Generalissimo's bodyguard and their commander, Chiang's nephew, were killed. The Generalissimo escaped in his nightshirt to a hill and hid behind a pile of stones, where Captain Sun found him. Chiang reminded Captain Sun that he was his Commander-in-Chief. Captain Sun told me later that he had kowtowed politely to Chiang and then replied: "You are also our prisoner."

Because the Generalissimo's feet were bruised by the rocks, Captain Sun carried him down the hill on his back and then delivered him to Marshal Chang and General Yang in Sian.

That night I had been unable to sleep and had wandered around my room fully dressed. I was standing at the window, watching the first streaks of dawn, when I heard the hammering of machine-guns and the bursts of rifle fire. "Well," I thought, "this is it! The Blue Shirts have started their uprising!" My heart almost stopped beating when I heard the sound of running feet within the hotel, then hoarse shouts and excited voices. Rifle-shots came from somewhere near by and then above the ominous cries and the crashing of doors rose the sound of splintering glass. The sounds were all those of danger and death. A woman screamed, men shouted, and automobile engines started up with a roar.

Rifle butts crashed against my door. Unwilling to help in my own murder, I backed into a corner just as three rifle-shots splintered the wood and the glass panel crashed and scattered. I heard shouts of "Japanese!" and thought in terror: "God! They're going to kill me under the pretense that I'm a Japanese!"

A soldier's head appeared through the door panel and stared wildly about. I recalled enough Chinese to say: "I'm not Japanese. I'm an American."

Someone pushed him and he tumbled into the room. A crowd of gray-lad soldiers, rifles ready, poured after him and then milled around confusedly. Some dashed into the bathroom, others jerked open the door of the clothes closet, and then all but two streamed out and began beating on the manager's door, which was next to mine.

The two soldiers left in my room began moving about. One suddenly thrust his rifle barrel into my stomach and pushed me back against the wall, while the other dumped everything out of my dressing-table. He filled his pockets with everything that struck his fancy — my eyeglasses, rolls of film, flashlight and batteries. He gathered up my woolen sweater and woolen underwear with particular exclamations of satisfaction.

The soldier pinning me to the wall reached out and flipped over the pillow on my bed. There lay my purse, with all my money. With cries of joy the two soldiers pounced on it and divided up the money. One took my fountain pen and one my pencil, then each clipped his trophy into his breast pocket. Finally each dragged a woolen blanket from the bed and disappeared down the hall.

Convinced that the marauders were interested only in loot, I staggered into my bathroom and bathed my face. Then I sat down and listened to the strange roar that filled the hotel and the surrounding city. I had read of soldiers running amok, and here I was living through such an incident. Curiosity overcame my fear and I peered cautiously into the hall, then into the room of the hotel manager, next door. Two big trunks were open and garments were scattered about. I called and a faint voice answered.

"They're only looting!" I called.

His face still white, the manager crawled out from under the bed and began clawing through his things. "They've taken my fur coat!" he wailed. "They've taken everything!"

Finally he peered out into the hall. "Now, don't be scared," he assured me. "I'll take care of this!"

He disappeared down the hall and was soon back, bringing with him a young officer who carried a cocked automatic and seemed half-crazed by the excitement. A soldier dashed past; the officer shouted an order and aimed his pistol at him. The soldier halted, returned, and stood at attention. The officer first rained curses on him and then threatened him with many kinds of torture if he allowed anyone to enter my room. The manager found a sheet of paper and a Chinese brush, and on this the officer wrote:

ANYONE WHO ENTERS THIS ROOM
WILL BE SHOT!

He signed it, and the manager, with the air of one who has done his work well, tacked it to my door. The moment the officer and the manager were out of sight, the soldier craned his neck into my room, walked over to where my clothes were heaped, and began rummaging in them. Nothing worth while there. . . . Then he caught a glimpse of my wrist watch. He reached out, grabbed my arm, tore the watch off — and disappeared down the hall!

I stood staring at the handsome sign, which no soldier would stop to read, which none could read even if he stopped, and which none would obey even if he could read.

Gradually the sound of shooting both in the city and in the hotel ebbed away and at last officers began driving the soldiers out into the open. With the manager I stood in the hotel doorway and watched a couple of young officers racing back and forth before a line of sullen-eyed soldiers in the yard, stripping bulging pockets of loot, piling garments on the earth. The manager blanched at the stream of invectives that poured from the mouths of the officers. I gathered from what they were saying that the female ancestors of the soldiers had led fairly colorful lives.

Above the sound of the telephone, which throughout had been ringing unheeded, we now heard the shouts of servants. The manager dashed away and returned crying:

"A man's bleeding to death in there! Do you know anything about first aid?"

I remembered an untouched suitcase under my bed and dug out my first-aid kit and ran down the hall. I found a short man with a small black mustache — he looked for all the world like a Japanese — lying on a bloody pillow. Examining him, the manager and I saw he was more frightened than hurt. A bullet had passed through the thin part of each cheek, but not a tooth was touched. Probably he had been shouting, his mouth wide open. While the manager made strong coffee, I cleaned the man up, applied dressings, then fed him coffee with a spoon. All the while he kept assuring us that he was not a Japanese.

After an ambulance had taken the man away, I noticed that the manager was dragging his trunks into my room.

"The soldiers may come again!" he explained. "You are a foreigner and your room is safer than mine. I won't charge you any rent."

A car rolled up and a group of young Manchurian officers took possession of the hotel. An officer who spoke English set up a table in the hall and then prepared to hear the complaints and claims of the guests. I made a list of my losses and was told that General Yang Hu-chen, in charge of the troops that had run amok, would reimburse me. (I never received a cent of compensation; three years later a man who had been on General Yang's staff told me that a sum of money had been sent me by a secretary, but the secretary had taken it for granted that all foreigners were rich and all Chinese poor.)

The young Manchurian officer gave me a copy of a proclamation. It contained the famous eight demands made during the Sian Incident: the formation of a National Defense Government representing all parties and groups; resistance to the Japanese; the release of all political prisoners, including seven National Salvation leaders, all of them professional men; the granting of free speech, press, assembly, and the right to organize; the abolition of all extraordinary decrees against the patriotic anti-Japanese movements; and an alliance with the countries favoring China's independence.

When I read this proclamation I forgot all about the looting. Whatever might come of this incident, I felt that China would never be the same again.

At this point I was called to the telephone. A military

friend had been telephoning for hours to tell me that this was not a Blue Shirt uprising. He was astounded to hear that the hotel had been looted. The city was in the hands of Marshal Chang and General Yang, he said, and the police station, Kuomintang headquarters, and Blue Shirt secret centers, with their radios and documents — including a blacklist — had been captured. Two imprisoned students had been found in one Blue Shirt center, and one hundred airplanes which had been sent to fight the Red Army had been confiscated. Generalissimo Chiang and Governor Hsiao Li-tze were in the city as Marshal Chang's prisoners, and all the ammunition dumps which General Hu Chung-nan's army had been prepared to use against the Red Army had been captured. Marshal Chang had issued a proclamation legalizing these actions, and there was to be a mass meeting the next day.

"Don't go out!" my friend warned. "Martial law has been declared and there are many dead and wounded in the streets."

"Wait," I cried. "Why can't I get a military pass to help care for the wounded?"

My friend talked with the Manchurian officer in the hotel, after which I had a pass, had slung my first-aid kit over my shoulder, and was on my way to the Baptist Hospital to get surgical dressings. I spent the day moving around the city, seeing to the wounded and sending them to hospitals.

The next afternoon witnessed the first of many great mass meetings, and on the 16th Marshal Chang spoke at one called by the National Salvation Union. He reviewed the record of Japanese invasion, the Government's actions, and his many controversies with the Generalissimo over a policy which, he pointed out, "had been a violation of the will of the people." Declared Marshal Chang:

"I wish to stand with all our armed comrades on the front line in the anti-Japanese war. The entire people must rise up and push forward in this struggle. If you are a laborer, give your labor; if you have money, give that. Let us mingle our blood in the defense of our country."

Sian was soon plastered with anti-Japanese posters. A specially trained political regiment of the Manchurian Army, along with representatives of the National Salvation and the Students' Unions, held small street meetings everywhere, and sent units to outlying villages to organize the arming and training of the peasants.

Political prisoners were released, among them three hundred captive Red Army soldiers, fifty-four Red Army women and thirty-three Red Army children. Of the released soldiers, nearly a hundred were sick with fever or had infected wounds. Although I knew only first-aid, I attempted to take care of them, trying meanwhile to secure hospital space for the worst cases and medical care for all. They lay on straw pallets in bare, ice-cold barracks; and only a few boasted thin cotton coverings. It was a week before a doctor took over my work. At last General Yang Hu-chen sent me two thousand dollars to buy blankets and food for them.

The Red Army soldiers were a revelation to me. They were from the Szechuen Red Army, all poor peasants between the ages of fifteen and fifty. They reminded me of descriptions in books about the Peasants' War in Germany. Their eyes were inflamed, many had no shoes at all, and their huge, peasant feet, scarred and bloody, had calluses an inch thick. When I first went among them, they stared at me suspiciously. To them I was a well-dressed "foreign devil."

On the day following the uprising, I was filled with a strange sense of watching history in the making. An airplane took off for the northwest, returned in the afternoon, slowly circled the city wall, and glided to the landing field. It brought the first representatives of the Red Army and the Central Committee of the Communist Party.

I met the Red Army representatives the day after their arrival in Sian. Nine years of civil war had passed, in which perhaps a million peasants, workers, and intellectuals had been killed, great wealth wasted, and war materials squandered. In some instances the whole family or even clan of a Red Army commander had been wiped out, the wives and sisters beheaded in the city streets. Yet when I talked with

Demonstrations of soldiers, civilians, and officials in the streets of Sian, demanding the end of civil war, and a united front against Japan. This is a peasant unit.

(left) After the war-orphans had been dressed in clean new uniforms and had been bathed and shaved, they began to get their first regular meals. (right) *Chu Teh, father of the Red Army.*

Chou En-lai, political director of the Red Army, and Yeh Chien-ying, its chief of staff, I felt that they had come not for vengeance, but to pave the way for a new era of unity.

A National Salvation newspaper appeared on the second day of the uprising, and in the next two weeks was followed by two other dailies and a student publication. Students and actors formed the first mobile theater to present plays to the troops and the people. To combat wild reports from the Nanking radio that Generalissimo Chiang had been killed, that the Red Army had occupied Sian, and that there was pillaging and rape, one of the newspaper editors began to make broadcasts in Chinese, while I undertook to make them in English. My broadcasts consisted of interviews with officials, military commanders, Red Army representatives, and National Salvation leaders and reports of developments in the northwest.

My talks annoyed the Nanking Government, and months later I heard from American newspaper correspondents that American consular officials in Nanking and Shanghai had even announced their determination to deport me. In an interview with the correspondent of the *New York Times* a Nanking spokesman declared that my talks "strongly advocated the united-front ideas and other projects conflicting with established Government policies." The spokesman said nothing about the American Y.M.C.A. secretary who was broadcasting wildly distorted reports from Nanking. I at least was telling the truth.

Dangerous news affecting the future of China began to reach us. The first of these reports concerned Wang Ching-wei, former political head of the Chinese Government and its ruling party. Wang Ching-wei had been living in Germany since a young officer of the 19th Route Army had tried to kill him. When Wang heard of the Sian Incident, he rushed to Berlin for a secret conference with Hitler, then took an airplane for China, obviously planning to take over the Government.

Japanese military commanders had also held secret conferences in north China and had warned the Central Government to crush the attempt of the northwestern armies to form a united front. General Ho Ying-ching, Minister of War, who for years had been an associate of Wang Ching-wei, began to mass troops at Tungkwan, the mountain pass leading to Shensi Province. Under the pretense that he was seeking the release of Generalissimo Chiang, he threatened civil war. I wrote a speech warning against civil war and before broadcasting it submitted it to Manchurian and Red Army representatives. In it I compared General Ho Ying-ching and his clique with Wu San-kwei, the Chinese General who betrayed the Ming Dynasty and allowed the Manchus to invade and subject China in the seventeenth century.

Marshal Chang Hsueh-liang talked each day with Generalissimo Chiang, urging the end of civil war and advising resistance to the nation's enemy. The Young Marshal had read the Generalissimo's diary and, I was told, was convinced that the Generalissmo really intended to resist the Japanese eventually. Soon Madame Chiang Kai-shek, Dr. T. V. Soong, her brother, and Tai Li, the sinister head of the Blue Shirts, arrived in Sian by plane to negotiate for the release of the Generalissimo and his staff.

In the meantime the official Soviet Russian newspaper, *Izvestia*, by publishing an article charging that the Sian Incident was a Japanese plot, virtually warned the Chinese Communists to release Generalissimo Chiang. Perhaps the Soviet Government considered Generalissimo Chiang preferable to Wang Ching-wei, who had openly allied himself with Hitler and Japan. But at that time a wave of cynical resentment against the Soviet Union swept through Sian.

The Generalissimo was secretly released on Christmas Day. The people knew nothing of this, and the authorities in Sian were apparently afraid to let them know. On the preceding day they deliberately circulated rumors that General Fu Tso-yi, heroic defender of Suiyuan, was arriving by plane on Christmas Day to join the Anti-Japanese Alliance. At the rumored hour the airdrome was black with people carrying banners to welcome him. A closed car drove up. Out stepped Marshal Chang. He was greeted with applause. Then Generalissimo Chiang and his party followed; only two or three recognized them and then hardly believed their eyes. The whole party entered the plane and took off. General Fu did not come, and the people were left milling about in confusion. When the truth became known, there was consternation. They realized that they had been drawn to the airdrome to give the Generalissmo the impression that they were there to honor him.

Within an hour a group of young Manchurian officers and National Salvation leaders were going from room to room in the hotel, complaining bitterly of the ruse. They stopped and said to me: "We have been betrayed! The Red Army induced the Young Marshal to release Chiang." One young officer contemptuously exclaimed: "The Young Marshal still has his head filled with stupid feudal ideas. Now he will never be free!"

Though the Central Government had threatened civil war only if the Generalissimo was not released, it continued for weeks afterwards to concentrate troops at Tungkwan. Fighting broke out at the mountain pass, and railroad stations on the way to Sian were bombed by planes. Faced with this menace, the Anti-Japanese Alliance held firm and prepared to fight. The high Manchurian officer who was left in charge by the Young Marshal carried on secret negotiations with General Ho Ying-ching, and other old officers began to undermine the Army from within. The young ones grew wild with fury, and demanded the release of Marshal Chang and the realization of his eight-point program of democracy and national resistance. The Red Army supported them in this and at the height of the Incident two Red Army corps threw a cordon around Sian, prepared, if the Minister of War persisted, for civil war.

Early in January, James Bertram, a New Zealander representing a London newspaper, arrived and began helping me broadcast, gather news, and address town and village mass meetings. When his voice was first heard over the air, propagandists in Nanking announced that a Russian Bolshevik was broadcasting from Sian.

Foreigners who believe that Chinese are passive, unemotional creatures would have revised their beliefs if they had seen the Manchurian Army. All its pent-up resentment over the Government's passivity in the face of the Japanese burst like bomb-shells in Sian. Its soldiers felt that they had become exiles from their homeland and were being used merely as mercenaries against their own countrymen. I watched two big demonstrations, one purely military, one civilian-military. The equipment displayed in the military review was pathetic. During the civilian-military demonstration I stood on the ancient drum tower in the center of the city and watched endless lines of marchers converging from every direction into a great throng that jammed the main boulevard. Long lines of peasants, carrying guns or spears, had come in from the country to participate.

The demonstration was led by mounted Manchurian cavalrymen wearing fur caps, with fur tails flying from the top, looking much like pictures of Daniel Boone. Manchurian infantrymen, as tall and strong as Americans, followed. I heard for the first time the Manchurian's nostalgic *Fight Back to Your Native Home* sung *en masse* by marching troops. Young officers led in the shouting of slogans; they would whirl about, leap high into the air, and shout with wild fury: "Down with the Japanese dwarf devils!" "Down with the Fascists!" "Release Marshal Chang!"

All those people's organizations which had once been barred, the unions of workers and of students, women, clerks, children, business men, marched. A huge cartoon showed Wang Ching-wei shaking hands with Hitler and branded him the "Running dog of the Fascists!" The strains of the forbidden *Volunteer Marching Song* floated militantly over the city.

Slowly Sian was crumbling. In Nanking, Marshal Chang allowed himself to be tried for capturing his Commander-in-Chief and was sentenced to prison. The sentence was immediately commuted, but Generalissimo Chiang took

him prisoner and held him in his home at Fenghwa. Years
have passed, but the Young Marshal still remains a prisoner. His fate has embittered all Manchurian patriots. His
army was dispersed and only a few of those who fought in
it are still alive.

The Sian Incident may have ended in a local defeat, but
it was nevertheless a national victory. Slowly and with
agonizing pain a United China was being born. Soon we
heard that Government troops were to occupy Sian. On
learning this news National Salvation leaders began to leave
for many parts of the country, for they knew that the Kuomintang would never grant civil liberties to the people.

Knowing that if I was caught in the city my fate would
be the same as that of any Chinese patriot, I started out of
the city on the morning of January 12. Sandbag barricades
had been thrown up around official buildings and at street
intersections. Slogans of liberation still shouted from the
walls, but the eight-point proclamation flapped sadly in the
winter wind.

I waited for four hours on the frozen road near the airdrome. At last a truck rolled up, a Red Army man sprang
out and ordered a man out of the seat next to the chauffeur,
and I clambered in. The truck was loaded with students,
each with a roll of bedding at his feet. Without a word we
drove away to the north — toward ancient Hsienyang, past
the Chou and Han tombs, toward Sanyuan and the Red
Army.

Men and Ideas

WE spent the night in a low mud inn. In the morning it was
bitter cold and the chauffeur had to build a small fire under
the engine to thaw it out. We roared through the ancient
city of Sanyuan, planning to have breakfast in the old, halfabandoned walled town of Tungli, the headquarters of the
First Red Army Corps under temporary commander Tso
Chuan.[1]

[1] Killed in action by the Japanese, July 1942.

At last we rolled up to the town, but the gate was too narrow for the truck and we had to climb out. A number of black-uniformed young soldiers began to gather, and to my surprise I saw among them my friend Ting Ling. She had been released from confinement in Nanking and had managed to make her way to the northwest and finally to the Red Army.

Many soldiers who had been practicing guerrilla tactics in the wheat-fields around the town came running to see the new arrivals from Sian. This was the first time that I had seen the Red Army *en masse*, and I looked around curiously. I was profoundly impressed by their faces. Instead of the depressed, empty expression characteristic of so many soldiers, their faces had something of the vital awareness that had been so pronounced in the great Lu Hsün.

When Ting Ling explained that I was a foreign friend, one of the soldiers turned and abruptly asked for the latest news from Spain! They spoke the sharp, staccato dialect of Kiangsi Province and I could hardly understand a word. Ting Ling explained to them that I was to speak at mass meetings, during which I would answer all questions. She tried to lead me away, but I would not allow this meeting to pass so casually. I stayed and began to ply the soldiers with questions.

Most were in their early twenties and had been in the Red Army for four, five, or six years; if they were twenty-five or thirty they had been Red Army soldiers for eight or more years and were called "old." There was not a man who had not been wounded, some as many as seven or eight times. Deprecatingly, one added: "But only twice seriously." Not one could recall how many battles they had fought; they laughed a little at this and remarked that there were too many to remember. Only two or three had ever been married, but the families of all were in Kiangsi Province and no one knew what had happened to them after the Kuomintang occupation. They spoke of the Kuomintang armies as "Whites." One said he did not know whether his father and two sisters were alive, for his sisters had short hair and had worked in a village soviet. "The Whites kill girls with short hair," he explained.

They waited for my questions, curious to hear what a foreigner was interested in. I told them I had long heard of their *Red Army Marching Song* and would like to hear it sung. They laughed a little, then one of them climbed into the truck, raised his arms, and counted *ee-ehr-san*, and on the third beat the men's voices rose in a song that stirred the blood with its revolutionary fervor.

The spell of ancient Chinese history was upon me, and after the soldiers had finished singing, I wandered, accompanied by my Peiping student interpreter and Ting Ling, through the magnificent Pompeii-like ruins of what had once been a center of great luxury. Carved stone monuments still stood before beautiful doorways leading into courtyards surrounded by empty apartments. Cobwebs hung from worm-eaten rafters and the decayed framework of filigreed windows. On the stone floors of these halls, now bitterly cold, the soldiers had arranged long, continuous pallets of wheat straw. These were their quarters.

One corner of the town was inhabited by peasants and small traders who lived in earthen huts. Near an old open-air theater, topped by a gorgeous, upcurving, gargoyled roof of colored tiles, stood a low hovel made of boards and rusty gasoline tins. Next to it an old man sold peanuts.

At ten o'clock, when the Army had its first meal of the day, Commander Tso Chuan and some of his staff found us squatting with a group of soldiers around a tin pan of boiled cabbage, our rice-bowls filled with steaming millet. The polished, diplomatic commander was shocked, for he still followed the time-honored Chinese custom of welcoming guests with a banquet. We rose at once and followed him to an open stone terrace on which stood a long table prepared for a banquet, and soon hot dishes began to arrive. I criticized banquets of this kind as a relic of feudalism. They smiled, perhaps thinking my protests the conventional politeness of a guest, but in the months that followed I made my conviction quite clear.

Tso Chuan was a suave but reticent intellectual, and his political director, a landlord's son who spoke perfect English, did most of the talking. This Red Army Corps had been stationed along the Great Wall when the Sian Incident occurred, but when civil war seemed imminent it had moved to this region. Many landlords had fled, first trying to create a panic by spreading rumors that bandits were coming. The peasants had no place to go and, in any event, did not heed their landlords. Despite the suppression of patriotic organizations and the total censorship of the press, students and other intellectuals had managed for years to set ideas circulating among the people. The peasants had therefore awaited the Red Army with interest — particularly after they were told that it might confiscate and distribute land.

Instead of confiscating land, the Red Army sent political workers into the villages and urged the people to form anti-Japanese associations of peasants, workers, merchants, students, women, and children. Since the inhabitants knew these were forbidden by the Government, they cautiously asked how long the Red Army would stay in their region. So organizational work was going slowly.

In the late afternoon Ting Ling and I spoke before two mass meetings, one of soldiers, and one of civilians from the town and near-by villages. This second meeting, held in a school building, resembled a country fair. Women had brought their babies and small children, who cried and whimpered, and since the place was packed, crowds of men gathered about the open windows and kept shouting: "We can't hear!"

The man who had formerly been the local magistrate presided at this meeting. He seemed an intelligent and patriotic man, but much given to the traditional and flowery phrases of outworn officialdom. In a fine flow of oratory he spoke of my wisdom, my travels, the countless books I had written, and the vast sums of money I had been paid. Despite all this, he said, I had come through snow and sleet, crossed rivers and mountains, to tell the Chinese people about the Japanese devils.

The people liked eloquence, but remained realists: one always praised guests, then forgot all about it. After the meeting many of them gathered to talk. The men tended to do all the talking while the women hovered shyly in the background. Finally we got rid of the men and, accompanied by a crowd of women and girls, went to our room in headquarters. Sitting on the beds, chairs, and chests and squatting on the floor, the women began to ask me all kinds of questions about myself. They wanted in particular to know why I wasn't married; this gave Ting Ling an opportunity to explain the emancipation of women, and to point out to them that they must organize a Woman's National Salvation Association and share the same rights and responsibilities as men in the fight against the Japanese.

The women were tremendously interested, and only when darkness began to fall did they leave. We bowed them out to the street gate and watched them walk away, holding hands and talking excitedly.

A few days later Ting Ling and I walked across country to a village where Ho Lung, commander of the Second Red Army Corps, had his headquarters. With us were a number of men belonging to a civilian delegation from the new Anti-Japanese Associations. Two were teachers, one a middle-aged intellectual-looking individual who talked volubly. Three were students, two were merchants, one a tinsmith from Sanyuan, and the others peasants. They carried silk banners of welcome which were to be presented to the various Red Army corps.

"Students have long known the Red Army's program and policy," the talkative teacher remarked, "and they have managed to pass their information along to the people. In fact, if the Government thinks one thing, the people always think the opposite. Many of my students have challenged their parents and gone to Yenan to join *Kang Da* (Resistance University). I myself have no prejudices against the Communists."

A small merchant, walking directly behind us, interrupted to add that even most of the merchants were anti-

Japanese and would soon return. He looked up at the teacher, laughed, and added: "Do you remember the night the Chamber of Commerce met? All the merchants had boarded up their shops and were ready to run away. Then two officers with red stars on their caps walked in and asked to speak. That meeting lasted until midnight. The next day people opened their shops and only a foolish few ran away. We merchants are tired of civil war. We sent a telegram telling the Generalissimo that if we had peace among ourselves we could drive out the Japanese."

The students were so eager and enthusiastic that once the teacher remarked to one of them:

"The revolution will be fought through only by the masses. You students are only the *voice* of the revolution, though some of you think you are the whole show!"

"Old people grow conservative!" a student chided.

Talking in this way, we reached Ho Lung's village headquarters. As we approached, a tall man with a black mustache and wearing a tall fur hat that accentuated his height came out of the building and waved. Ting Ling shouted: "Comrade Ho Lung, we have come!"

"Shades of the Taiping rebels!" I exclaimed to myself, for Ho Lung looked not like a Chinese, but like some old print of a mustachioed folk-tale Mongol or Central Asiatic. He was a man in his middle forties, but he walked with the lithe grace of a panther. As he drew near I saw that his dress seemed so strange and vari-colored because it was made up of the remnants of many uniforms. His jacket was of faded gray and his trousers black, the latter fitting so tightly that he appeared to be made up for some medieval drama. Above his blue cloth Chinese shoes white socks showed, and from his ankle to the knee was a splash of green — puttees wrapped tightly in a long leaf-like pattern. Something seemed missing from his uniform — oh yes, a blazing sash and a curved scimitar!

This was Ho Lung of fame and fable. A poor peasant of central China, he had been described as a local militarist, and even as a bandit. During the national revolution of

1925–7 his troops had been incorporated into the nationalist army and he had been made a regimental commander. He liked horses and armies, but titles interested him little; so he recruited some fifteen thousand men into his troop despite the fact that it was still called a "regiment." After the split in the nationalist forces, he had become commander of the powerful Second Red Army. This ever increasing force held large areas to the north and west of Hankow and had for years fought death to a standstill. He was illiterate and his army had not been so well trained politically as other Red armies. Hsiao Keh, an intellectual, now acted as his political director, and extensive political education was provided; but Hsiao Keh had been with him only three years.

For years Ho Lung had tried to join the Communist Party. Finally, after he had applied ten different times, he had been accepted. He could now read a little, but could not write. Of fighting, however, he knew enough, and his troops reflected his daredevil courage and self-assurance. Although now a Communist, he remained a member of one of the ancient peasant "Big Brother" secret societies, and bore its highest title — the "Double-headed Dragon." The title fitted him well.

One tale was told of a launch which he captured from one of the Kuomintang armies in the lake regions northwest of Hankow. He had called this his "navy" and had scooted over the lakes, directing guerrilla warfare. Men brightened up when they heard that Ho Lung was coming, for then they knew they would hear fine stories related with vigor and dash. An American doctor, Ma Hai-teh, who went to the Red Army when Edgar Snow visited the northwest, later told me many tales of Ho Lung in battle. "But he has a gentle, tender heart," Dr. Ma would insist, and tell a story of how Ho Lung walked into a medical station carrying a sick or wounded boy.

All the members of Ho Lung's immediate family had been killed in the revolution. Perhaps the most amazing was his sister, a woman of forty-nine who had commanded a Red

Army regiment and had fallen in battle. His last brother had died in a Shanghai prison. His wife, a schoolteacher, had been imprisoned at about the same time; nothing could bend or break her, and while in prison she had started literacy classes for poor imprisoned women.

Hsiao Keh, political director of Ho Lung's army corps, was also unlike any other Chinese I had ever seen. He was very thin and the movements of both his body and his mind were like lightning. All he needed to resemble some old Persian painting was a horse under him and a spear in his hand. I never saw Hsiao Keh in repose.

The civilian delegation from Sanyuan listened with delight to Ho Lung's many tales. He spoke with energy and many gestures, keeping the room in an uproar, but always remembering that he was a good Communist and ending with some political moral:

"Just think! If the Government had united with us and fought the Japanese when they first invaded Manchuria, it would now have two million more trained men. We need unity. There is no difficulty we cannot conquer!"

One morning, as he bent over his wash-basin making a great splash, I remarked on the courage of his imprisoned wife. He paused, then began splashing furiously. I glanced about and saw that everyone was grinning. The Peiping student said in a low voice: "He has another wife now in Yenan and they have a child. But his Shanghai wife has been released and is coming here."

"Just which wife is that?" one of the men asked innocently.

"Shut up, *tu-fei* (bandit)," Ho Lung growled.

A furious bantering began, with several men mentioning the names of women and others counting them on their fingers. Ho Lung wiped his face, turned to me, and in a solemn, gentle voice urged:

"Pay no attention to them! All that was before I adopted the new life."

A howl of derision rose on all sides.

Ho Lung's army had but recently come out of the "grass

lands" of Sikong and joined the main body of the Red Army from Kiangsi. Only a few had so far received new padded winter uniforms. The others were undernourished and clad in rags. When I went among them, I heard hollow coughing on all sides, for many were suffering from lung ailments. Their eyes were inflamed, but I could not tell whether it was trachoma or semi-starvation.

"As soon as we have our new winter uniforms, are rested, and have eaten, we shall be all well," Ho Lung once remarked sadly. I doubted this. Tuberculosis claimed too many victims in the Red Army.

It may have been their rags and illnesses that gave me the impression, but this Red Army Corps seemed very different from the Kiangsi men. When Ting Ling and I spoke at their meetings they seemed to have difficulty in understanding, and a political worker often halted to ask them whether they understood. He would repeat the idea, slowly. They listened hungrily. When they sang for us, their songs seemed strange and heavy, burdened with sorrow. Then I would think: "They are like men only recently risen from slavery."

Before I left the corps, Ho Lung asked me about my observations and suggestions. But they were already aware of all the deficiencies I could mention. The men needed warm clothing, good food, rest, and medical care. We discussed delousing, for typhus is epidemic in the northwest. But delousing stations were unknown and there was neither heat nor change of clothing. But many volunteers were entering the Army, and I proposed that a physical examination be given to keep out those who were syphilitic, for syphilis is also a scourge in the northwest. But there was no doctor in the Army able to identify syphilis except in its advanced stages. For its treatment they had nothing.

Chu Teh was Commander-in-Chief and chairman of the Revolutionary Military Council, but the commander of the Front Red Armies was the puritanical Peng Teh-hwei. Peng was Chu Teh's shadow and, some said, his military brains.

This austere leader was of lowly origin, but had received a fairly good education. During the Northern Expedition he had been a Kuomintang regimental commander in the nationalist army, but when the counter-revolution began, he had allied his regiment with the forces of Mao Tze-tung and Chu Teh. The latter had been beleaguered on Chingkanshan Mountain in western Kiangsi while organizing the first Workers' and Peasants' Red Army.

Many of the stories circulated in the Chinese revolutionary movement, as everywhere in China, were a mixture of rumor and fact and one was rarely able to tell which was which. One story was that when Peng Teh-hwei had first joined the Red Army, his wife publicly denounced him in order to save her life. The families of Red Army commanders were often killed, but despite this justification, Peng Teh-hwei had regarded his wife's action as unpardonable. After that, no woman had entered his life. Men said he was married to the revolution. However, he granted women respect and equality with men and demanded that his troops accept this principle as a basic aim of their struggle.

He lived the bitter life of the soldiers, ate their food, refused to give banquets, and rejected all comforts which they could not share. From many men I heard that his troops feared him, for he would tolerate none of the *ma-ma-hu-hu* (*mañana* or "do it tomorrow") habits that are characteristic of most pre-industrial civilizations. But they also respected and loved him, knowing that he imposed upon himself the same discipline and that he was a man of iron justice.

Ting Ling and I rode to a large village near the snow-covered mountain, Pei Wutienshan, where Peng had his headquarters. A small child was standing by his side, looking up, and he was listening as if deeply interested in its prattle.

He was of medium height, built like a stocky peasant, and perhaps in his middle thirties. He was ugly, but as he smiled in welcome his face was pleasant. His eyes were level and penetrating, his voice gruff.

When we arrived, he was ill. The Long March had left

him with gastric ulcers and in addition he had been kicked by a horse shortly before our arrival. But no one dared refer to his illness in his presence. Since all of them were anxious, they pushed me forward and I, innocent and unabashed, talked to him about his health. I also suffered from gastric ulcers and carried powders, milk, and soda crackers. I shared these with him, and because I was a guest he had to listen to my advice.

Because of his illness he spent much time in his headquarters, sitting before a brazier of glowing charcoal, and we often found him reading or working there. He always carried booklets or paper-bound books in his pocket. I never, incidentally, saw any literary trash in the Army or in its headquarters at Yenan. These men took the business of working for a new world as a matter of life and death. The political and military material which they read became reference- and text-books for the Political Department of the Army, whose business it was to impart the contents to the troops.

My many talks with Peng Teh-hwei and his staff took place near that charcoal brazier in his room. In the course of one interview Peng Teh-hwei said:

"The Kuomintang has spread all kinds of falsehoods about us. By their control of the press and the denial of civil rights to the people, they have contaminated the public mind and prevented us from placing facts before the country. They have said that we practiced free love, that we capture boys and maidens and use them for immoral purposes, that we have burned and robbed and slaughtered the peasants! They said we oppose Christians on the grounds of their faith.

"Now, I ask you: do you think we could have existed all these years if these things were true? It was the masses that gave us our strength. We represented their interests, drew all our man-power from them. The people are honest and upright and they could have exterminated us if we oppressed them.

"We are new in this region; some of us have been here less than two weeks, and yet I invite you to go wherever you will and ask the people about us. You will find that our soldiers live in the homes of the people like sons of the family. Our fighters are all from the masses and realize that they are the protectors and guides of the people. In the short time we have been here, twelve hundred young peasants and workers, and many students, have joined our Army. There are so many that we cannot get enough uniforms or guns for them. They know that our life is bitter and that their spending money will be only a dollar and a half a month — if we have the money."

His hoarse voice sank low and he watched me with level eyes. "You spoke at a peasant mass meeting yesterday," he said, "and you have been in the homes of the people. Tell me if you have heard complaints from one man, woman, or girl."

I said that I had heard only praise.

He stared into the charcoal brazier for some time, then continued: "Our peasants are unbelievably poor. But they are intelligent and their illiteracy is not their fault. Nor ours. They can be educated to realize that our main enemy is Japanese imperialism. Of course they do not want to bear the many heavy taxes and exorbitant rents, but they are still more unwilling to be slaves of the Japanese. Their basic needs must be satisfied so they will not have to drudge and worry all the time about food; then they can take part in the anti-Japanese movement.

"Generalissimo Chiang said that so long as there is hope for peace with the Japanese, he would work for peace. We do not hold that attitude toward the Japanese, but we hold it toward the Government — because the Kuomintang armies are Chinese. If the whole country is allowed to participate in the anti-Japanese movement and if all the people are imbued with knowledge and patriotism, even the poorest will give their labor — for they have nothing else to give — and the rich will give money to fight the enemy."

Our discussions were always of this sober nature. Of humor Peng had little and I never once heard him speak lightly. He might listen to light or aimless conversations, but, as his men said, he was "married to the revolution."

One evening I sat with him and his staff, our conversation roaming aimlessly. One man kept trying to tune in on the Nanking broadcast but, as usual, the radio only shrieked and sputtered. Ting Ling and Jen Pei-hsi, the political director, were discussing what they called "revolutionary romanticism," and from their conversation I learned that this term meant sexual promiscuity! They also jokingly called it "undisciplined guerrilla warfare." Ting Ling had given an account of Kollontay's book *Three Generations*, and Jen had quoted Lenin's famous opposition to the idea that sexual relations were no more important than a glass of water.

Peng listened in silence, one foot on the charcoal brazier, the other crossed over his knee. He kept trying to pull together a huge hole in the heel of his sock.

Jen Pei-hsi glanced at me and then announced: "Comrade Peng Teh-hwei does not believe in marriage. That is why he has gastric ulcers."

Peng grunted: "A lot of married people have gastric ulcers. You would make a bum doctor!"

He was about to add something else when the radio operator in the corner interrupted with a whoop of joy:

"Listen! It's Nanking! It's about us!"

In China the news broadcasters are women and their voices are high-pitched. Over the air came such a voice, saying: "The Red bandits are still occupying Sanyuan *hsien* (district). They are terrorizing the region, looting homes, murdering the peasants, raping women and girls. Thousands of people have fled."

I cried out in anger and disgust. Jen Pei-hsi laughed, imitated my exclamation, and then remarked: "They forgot to add that we have also captured a foreign woman."

"What can be done against such lies?" I asked.

It was Peng Teh-hwei's harsh voice that replied. "The only answer is our final victory!" he said.

Someone turned off the radio and there was a silence so acute that I glanced about the room curiously. The men all sat staring before them. Peng was looking deep into the charcoal brazier, and at the table Ting Ling leaned forward resting on her arms. The two candles in the room cast a faint glow on the rafters above and glinted on the legs of the table. The stillness was heavy, burdensome.

The Lion-Hearted

IN Yenan, which the Communists had just occupied as their main base and training center, the American doctor who had adopted the Mohammedan name of Ma Hai-teh took me to see Chu Teh, Commander-in-Chief of the Red Army since its earliest days.

"The fighters love him," said Dr. Ma. "He is their father and mother."

A short, strong figure in blue padded uniform rose from a table on which a candle burned, and I saw the Chu Teh to whom I had been referring in my writings for many years. Indeed, he looked like the father of the Red Army. He was well beyond fifty and his face was kind and lined with wrinkles. His generous mouth was now spread in a broad grin of welcome and he stretched out both hands to me. I flung my arms around his neck and kissed him on both cheeks. Dr. Ma also threw his arms around Chu Teh and kissed him resoundingly, then stood back to observe his handiwork.

We all laughed and I said to Chu Teh: "Let me take a look at you. For years I've heard you called a bandit whose head was worth twenty-five thousand dollars. And you are the man who has been declared dead a dozen times."

I walked around and around the stocky figure while Dr. Ma reached out and ran his hand over General Chu's shaved head, meanwhile uttering a long-drawn-out "Hum-m-m-m-m!" Our victim kept a sharp look-out.

After my personal inspection I turned to Chu Teh's work table, piled with military and political books, pads and pencils, and a heap of notepaper covered with scrawled notes.

"Those are the notes for a course on military science which I am giving in *Kang Da* (Resistance University)," Chu explained.

I turned and saw that one entire wall of the room, from rafters to the earthen floor below, was covered with a military map ringed with small red circles. Musing aloud, I said: "There are bandits and bandits. Those I knew in the cities were rather different. They wore foreign business suits, had polished desks, belonged to exclusive clubs, and read detective novels."

"A class distinction," laughed Chu Teh.

"Also," I added, "you are the liveliest corpse I have ever seen! I have brought you clippings from the Shanghai press announcing some of your deaths."

I drew the clippings from my pocket and he laughed heartily at one which was alleged to be a photogaph of him. Then we fell to talking about my plans and about his own work.

The chief task of the Communists, he said, was to re-educate the Red Army in the principles of the united front. Commanders were being called to Yenan by the hundreds. Since most of them were workers and peasants, it was not easy for them to learn the concepts of class collaboration.

Large numbers of students were also pouring into Yenan to study; there were so many of them and their problems were so different from those of the Army that a new "Northwestern Academy" (Shanpei), was being organized. All kinds of students were coming, including spies from the Blue Shirts and other political cliques. A group of ten had just been arrested for forming a "Free Love Club." The Trotskyites had sent three or four to intrigue against the united front, calling it a betrayal of the revolution. They had been examined and their ideas had appeared chaotic, without plan or purpose.

One of the chief problems, Chu Teh continued, was lack of teaching material — foreign military and political books, magazines, and newspapers. He himself needed German, Russian, and American military books, because the war with

Japan, he knew, would be entirely different from civil war. This was the origin of one of my chief occupations in Yenan in the months that followed — the building up of the new Lu Hsün library.

"Can you ride?" Chu Teh asked me that night, and when I said I could, we had a discussion about the beauty and character of horses which ended in his offering me a pony, one of twelve captured by Ho Lung's army from a rich landlord in Yunnan Province during the Long March. During the following week the General had a wooden Mongolian saddle padded for me with black and red cloth. The pony, which I called Yunnan, was a small edition of an Arabian steed, a beautiful stallion both wild and troublesome. His wildness got me into fights with a whole succession of muleteers.

Chu Teh asked me what I wished to write about. I was unsure at first, but as we talked that night and in the weeks that followed I gradually conceived the idea of writing his biography. I got to work on it, but it was an undertaking often interrupted by other work or by his visits to the front.

With my secretary interpreter, a former actress from Shanghai, I began to sound Chu Teh's earliest childhood memories. He had lived through more than fifty years of turbulent Chinese history and in his youth had been one of the earliest Kuomintang revolutionaries, who had helped overthrow the Manchu Dynasty. The revolution had degenerated into militarism and for a number of years he had been a militarist in Szechuen and Yunnan Provinces and, as was the custom, had smoked opium and taken concubines.

The ideas of the Chinese intellectual renaissance began to penetrate into these far southwestern provinces shortly before the end of the first World War. Chu Teh began to read, and joined a discussion club of intellectuals. So completely did the awakening of China influence him that, even though past forty, he gave up his old life, including opium and concubines, and headed for the coastal cities in search of the Communist leaders. They avoided him and he decided to go to Europe to study.

In Berlin he met the first small group of Chinese Communists, of whom Chou En-lai, son of a northern Mandarin family, was a member. He was permitted to join this group, and the one-time militarist became a humble typesetter for the first Chinese newspaper published in Germany. At the same time he studied under military specialists.

At the end of three years, in 1924, he returned to China to participate in the national revolution. When the split in nationalist ranks came, he was Chief of Police and director of a military training school in Nanchang on the Yangtze. With General Yeh Ting and Ho Lung and their Kuomintang divisions, he struck back at the counter-revolution, which had already slaughtered thousands of peasants.

He commanded a column of revolting Kuomintang troops that fought its way southward hoping to re-establish Canton as a revolutionary base. They were defeated near Swatow, but Chu Teh collected the survivors and led them into western Kiangsi, where, on the rolling, wooded mountain of Chingkanshan, they united with another stream of revolutionary troops and revolting peasants led by Mao Tze-tung. Here was founded the first Red Army, the first military-political training school, and the first arsenal. For years this Army was called the "Chu-Mao" Army. Mao Tze-tung had become the political leader while Chu Teh had always been the supreme military commander.

As Chu Teh told me of his life, he drew rough sketches of the marches and battles of the Red Army. It was against this army that the Nanking Government, purged of its revolutionaries, waged five powerful military campaigns. Chu Teh had also collected a mass of historical documents and maps and had added to them through the years — even on the twelve thousand miles of the Long March. We often discussed the necessity of preserving and using historical documents, and soon Chu organized the first research committee in Yenan to work on the history of the Chinese Revolution.

I had taken down the record of his life up to the year

1934 when, on July 7, 1937, the Japanese struck at Lukuochiao (Marco Polo Bridge) and the Sino-Japanese War began. Chu Teh started for the front and I was left with another unfinished book. I asked Mao Tze-tung which he thought more important for me to do — remain in Yenan and write Chu Teh's biography, or go to the front and write of the war.

Mao Tze-tung said: "This war is more important than past history."

So I stored my notebooks and prepared to go to the front.

The Army gave me permission to go, but while out riding one day my horse fell and I sustained back injuries which laid me up. I had to lie indoors watching the summer rains, which fell in torrents, sweeping away fields, mountainsides, and villages.

On the same memorable night that I first arrived in Yenan and met General Chu Teh, I was able to call on Mao Tze-tung, because he worked by night and slept by day. Calling on him at midnight, I pushed back a padded cotton drape across a door in a mountain cave, and stepped into a dark cavern. Directly in the center of this darkness stood a tall candle on a rough-hewn table. Its glow fell on piles of books and papers and touched the low earthen ceiling above. A man's figure was standing with one hand on the table; his face, turned toward the door, was in shadow. I saw a mass of dark clothing covered by a loose padded greatcoat. The section of earthen floor on which he stood was raised, accentuating his height, and the gloom of the cave, broken only by the solitary candle, lent a sinister beauty to the scene. It was like some ancient painting almost obliterated by time.

The tall, forbidding figure lumbered toward us and a high-pitched voice greeted us. Then two hands grasped mine; they were as long and sensitive as a woman's. Without speaking we stared at each other. His dark, inscrutable face was long, the forehead broad and high, the mouth feminine. Whatever else he might be, he was an æsthete. I was in fact repelled by the feminine in him and by the gloom of the setting. An instinctive hostility sprang up inside me and I became so occupied with trying to master it that I heard hardly a word of what followed.

What I now remember of Mao Tze-tung was the following months of precious friendship; they both confirmed and contradicted his inscrutability. The sinister quality I had at first felt so strongly in him proved to be a spiritual isolation. As Chu Teh was loved, Mao Tze-tung was respected. The few who came to know him best had affection for him, but his spirit dwelt within itself, isolating him.

Many tales had been told of him and, like General Chu Teh and many other Communist leaders, there had for years been a heavy price on his head. In him was none of the humility of Chu. Despite that feminine quality in him, he was as stubborn as a mule, and a steel rod of pride and determination ran through his nature. I had the impression that he would wait and watch for years, but eventually have his way.

Every other Communist leader might be compared with someone of another nationality or time, but not Mao Tze-tung. People said this was because he was purely Chinese and had never traveled or studied abroad. Neither had Peng Teh-hwei, Ho Lung, Lin Piao, nor other Red Army men, yet they all had their counterparts in other lands. Mao was known as the theoretician. But his theories were rooted in Chinese history and in experience on the battlefield. Most Chinese Communists think in terms of Marx, Engels, Lenin, and Stalin, and some take pride in their ability to quote chapter and verse of these or lecture on them for three or four hours. Mao could do this too, but seldom attempted it. His lectures at Kang Da and Shanpei, or before mass meetings, were like his conversations, based on Chinese life and history. Hundreds of the students who poured into Yenan had been accustomed to drawing their mental nourishment only from the Soviet Union or from a few writers of Germany or other countries. Mao, however, spoke to them of their own country and people, their native history and literature. He quoted from such novels as *Dream of the Red Chamber* or *All Men Are Brothers*. He knew the old poets and was a poet in his own right. His poetry had the quality of the old masters, but through it ran a clear stream of social and personal speculation.

His many books and pamphlets place him among the great revolutionary pamphleteers of all times. His *Protracted Warfare, The New Stage in the War,* and *New Democracy* have become landmarks in Chinese revolutionary thought, and in later years I found them in unheard-of places. Sometimes politicians, including violent anti-Communists, stole his military writings and presented them as their own.

Mao often came to the "cave" where I lived with my girl secretary, and the three of us would have a simple dinner and spend hours in conversation. Since he had never been out of China, he asked a thousand questions. We spoke of India; of literature; and once he asked me if I had ever loved any man, and why, and what love meant to me. Sometimes he quoted from old Chinese poets or recited some of his own poems. One of his poems was in memory of his first wife, who had been slain by the Kuomintang because she was his wife.

His humor was often sardonic and grim, as if it sprang from deep caverns of spiritual seclusion. I had the impression that there was a door to his being that had never been opened to anyone.

As a linguist he was as bad as myself. To supplement his Hunan dialect, he tried to learn Mandarin from my secretary and English from me. His efforts to learn English songs were a dismal failure, for his voice was a monotone. Pride prevented him from trying to dance. He had no rhythm in his being.

Once during a conference of high military commanders in Yenan I tried to teach a number of them how to dance. Their reactions were revealing. Chu Teh, who wished to learn everything on earth and never let pride prevent his trying, joined me in opening the demonstration. Chou En-lai followed, but he was like a man working out a problem in mathematics. Peng Teh-hwei was willing to watch, but would not move a leg; he was married to the revolution. Ho Lung, who was the very embodiment of rhythm, could hardly contain himself until he was cavorting across the floor, which was made of wobbly bricks. I acquired a very bad reputation among the women of Yenan, who thought I was corrupting the Army; so bad did it become that I once refused to give Chu Teh another dancing lesson. He rebuked me, saying: "I've fought feudalism all my life and I don't intend to stop now!" So I got up and, in the name of democracy, gave him another lesson.

But my entire time was not spent teaching tired Communists to dance. In fact, I had a few dozen occupations — I have always been a kind of tinker, attempting many things, proficient in few. In Yenan I continued to work on General Chu's biography; wrote articles and reports; took part in health activities; planted a flower and vegetable garden with imported seeds sent me by Edgar Snow and his wife; built up the foreign-language section of the Lu Hsün Library; distributed incoming periodicals to the various army corps and to educational institutions and leaders in Yenan; wrote to foreign correspondents in the port cities, urging them to visit Yenan and the Red Army; and chased rats.

My anti-rat campaign aroused only mild interest. People regarded rats as an inevitable part of nature. Yet plague is endemic in the northwest and periodic epidemics crept down from Mongolia, with the rat flea acting as carrier. Men agreed with me, but had little time save for military and political problems. The Japanese were, after all, more dangerous than the plague. Only years later did I read Hans Zinsser's *Rats, Lice and History*; I was entranced by the book, and especially about the way he sprang to the defense of the lowly louse.

Perhaps I was so fanatical in my anti-rat campaign because, upon my arrival in Yenan, I lived for a time in a stone house inhabited by many families of rats. Nightly they fought underneath my *k'ang* and on the rafters above. I kept a candle burning, but they grew accustomed to the light. I would awaken to see floor, table, and chairs shining with gray fur. I bought up all the rat-traps in Sian and wrote Edgar Snow and his wife to ship all they could from Peiping. I distributed them free in Yenan, but soon I found that they were being sold in the market!

Another activity engaged me: the Consul for the Spanish Republican Government in Shanghai kept me supplied with bundles of anti-Fascist posters which he had received from Madrid. These I distributed to the various Red Army corps at the front and at Yenan, so that the Northwest was perhaps the only region in China that echoed with the struggle of the Spanish Republic. In May of that year the entire region had demonstrations and meetings in support of Spain's struggle against Fascism.

Another of the unforgettable men I met at his time was Chou En-lai, vice-chairman of the Revolutionary Military Council and chief representative of the Communist Party and the Red Army in the united front negotiations with Generalissimo Chiang Kai-shek. He was above medium height, with a very handsome, unusually intelligent face and especially fine eyes. He sprang from the patrician class and had been educated in Nankai University in north China, in France, in Germany, and, for a short time, in the Soviet Union. He stood very straight, looked men directly in the eye, and always spoke with disarming frankness to foreigners and the highest Government officials as well as to members of his party. His knowledge and vision were all-embracing and his judgment free from sectarianism. If any worth-while measure such as the introduction of modern medical practice was necessary, it was Chou En-lai who signed the order and forced the measure through. For years afterwards he represented his party and army in the Central Government, winning the admiration and respect of such good foreign friends of China as General Joseph Stilwell, Major (later Colonel) Frank Dorn, and Sir Archibald Clark-Kerr, the British Ambassador.

It was said that Generalissimo and Madame Chiang respected Chou En-lai deeply, but from rumors which some Kuomintang members set adrift, it seemed the ruling group hoped to win him over from his party. They never succeeded, for he cared not at all for personal comfort, wealth, or power. The only other international figure with whom I could compare him was Jawaharlal Nehru, who possessed a similar combination of education, vision, and statesmanship. But Chou's convictions, like those of Nehru, relegated him to an inferior position in the affairs of his country. In his personal as in his public life he was modern and civilized. A lifelong love had bound him to Teng Ying-chou, one of the best-educated, most thoughtful and capable of Chinese women leaders.

In early April, during one of his trips to Yenan from Nanking, Chou talked with me about the negotiations for the united front. The basic problems of internal peace had been dealt with and civil war had ceased at last. But many problems still existed. In February the Red Army and the Communist Party had sent a lengthy official telegram to the Third Plenary Session of the Kuomintang, stating their conditions for the united front, and, without waiting for an agreement, began putting them into effect. This telegram offered to rename the Red Army and place it under command of the Central Military Council provided it was given the same treatment, equipment, and supplies as other armies and was permitted to retain its own political educational system. It demanded the introduction of democracy and civil rights throughout the country, the release of all political prisoners other than enemy agents, and the "liberation" of patriotic anti-Japanese organizations. It announced that in the interests of national unity the Communists had ceased confiscating land and were substituting the democratic system for the soviets.

Some of these demands were rejected by the Kuomintang. The most important question still unsettled, Chou En-lai said, was the introduction of democracy. Many leaders in Nanking and in the provinces realized that the granting of democratic rights to the people would end their own dictatorial privileges. One of the chief opponents of democracy and the united front was the Minister of War, General Ho Ying-ching. As late as the first week of April he ordered local national armies to attack the Red Army, and his orders to southern generals to fight the Red guerrillas in Kiangsi Province continued until Nanking, the capital, fell to the Japanese nearly a year later.

I asked Chou En-lai if Generalissimo Chiang was not responsible for all orders issued by the Minister of War. But the Communists were bending every effort to win Generalissimo Chiang to the united front, and the most any of them would admit was that the powerful cliques which surrounded the Generalissimo and treated him like a king might be using him for their own purposes.

I myself believed that if the Generalissimo had not approved of the actions of his Minister of War, he could have removed him.

Shortly after this talk with Chou En-lai, the first official delegation of military and political leaders from Nanking arrived in the northwest to review the Red Army and the administration in Yenan. From what I observed, not one of them could compare with the Communists in knowledge, capacity, culture, or vision. One leader of the delegation was a degenerate follower of Wang Ching-wei, who brought his own cook and physician with him. He suffered from syphilis in an advanced stage, and one night the leading doctors in Yenan were called out to help attend him.

Some of the other members of the delegation were of higher quality. One was an old Kuomintang leader who had long advocated peace and a united front. Some of his efforts to heal class wounds of the past were symbolic; these often amused foreigners, but they impressed the Chinese. Along with old Lin Pei-chu, a Communist leader and one of the earliest followers of Sun Yat-sen, the Kuomintang venerable once swept the grave of Hwang Ti, the first legendary leader of the Chinese race. This symbolized racial unity rising to meet national and racial danger.

After the visit of the delegation to Yenan, Mao Tze-tung

made a day-long report to Communist Party members on the progress of the united front and on the tasks of Communists. The concluding words of this report, according to my diary notes, were:

> Peace and democracy are the two conditions for the establishment of armed resistance to Japan. Our tasks are many, but the struggle for democracy is the main one at this stage. . . .
>
> Democracy is like rice, which we now get from Hankow — it takes time and costs money, and there are people who try to intercept it. Democracy is all the more difficult because it is intangible. If we underestimate its importance and if we slacken our efforts to secure it, armed resistance on a nation-wide scale, victory over Japan, and the recovery of our lost territory will be impossible.

News Blockade-Runners

A GROUP of us in Yenan, including Li Teh, the German, were discussing the methods by which the Chinese Government had for years controlled all Chinese organs of public opinion and, through censorship or bribery of foreign news agencies or correspondents, had determined what the peoples of the Western world should learn about China. That was why the Red Army had so long been called "bandits," "Communist bandits," "Red bandits," "vermin," and similar names.

"The Chinese press," I exclaimed, "is perhaps the most servile on earth. The West, at least, has had newspaper men willing to be pilloried or dragged through the streets for the sake of a free press."

"I will admit Chinese venality and servility," a Chinese friend declared, "but we also have had press martyrs. Do not forget Lu Hsün and his followers."

"Yes," I admitted, "and there is Samuel Chang. He's one nationalist liberal editor who fights as best he can. He was having a bitter time with the censors when I left Shanghai."

I dragged out one of my boxes, containing a file of documents going back to 1932 when Sam Chang had been director of the Department of Intelligence and Publicity in the Ministry of Foreign Affairs. Among them were the originals of four articles which he had written on the corruption of the press and which had been suppressed.

In his articles — as I told my friends that evening — he wrote that the Kuomintang had once been a progressive, revolutionary party, but when it rose to power, many politicians from the old Peking Government had joined its ranks and introduced the old Peking system of bribery of the press. One article dealt with two secret contracts between Reuter's, official British news agency, and the Publicity Department of the Kuomintang and the Ministry. In return for $10,000 a month from the Kuomintang and $3,000 a month from the Department of Intelligence and Publicity, Reuter's agreed to give "favorable publicity" to the Kuomintang. Sam Chang declared that these contracts, introduced during the Japanese invasion of Manchuria, were blackmail against China.

I laid before my friends photographs of contracts which proved Chang's charges; and then I added: "The Chinese Government has conferred the Order of the Brilliant Jade upon the head of Reuter's of London.

"And that's not all by half," I told them. "A Shanghai correspondent for one of the largest New York dailies was revealed by another newspaper man to be receiving a regular monthly bribe from the Kuomintang and was discharged. The man who exposed him and got his job is himself very friendly to the Japanese. Many such foreigners work for the Japanese, but mostly they are British and American, for Great Britain and America are the two most powerful countries which Japan must hold off until it is ready. Sometimes these harlots work openly, sometimes indirectly. An English editor came up from Hong Kong to take charge of the *Shanghai Times*, a daily partly owned by the Japanese. An Irishman in north China edits a paper for the Japanese. The *Far Eastern Review*, a large monthly magazine in Shanghai, has been financed by the Japanese since the Versailles Treaty. Its publisher, an American named George Bronson Rae, was an adviser to the Chinese delegation during the peace negotiations and became so angry because the Chinese rejected his proposals that he walked right across the street to the Yokohama Specie Bank and entered the service of the Japanese. Rae had left Donald, an Australian, as editor in Shanghai, but when Donald learned that the magazine was henceforth to be a Japanese organ, he walked out. It was some time before the publication could appear. George Bronson Rae thereafter quite openly appeared as a Japanese propaganda agent and as adviser to the puppet Government of Manchukuo. When he left for Washington to do propaganda for Manchukuo, George Sokolsky, another American, became editor of the magazine, and when Sokolsky left for America, an American named Charles Laval took over."

"Americans are well represented!" someone interrupted.

"Yes," I said. "But we also have other kinds of Americans. Take John B. Powell, editor of the *China Weekly Review*. Incidentally, Powell once asked Laval why he did the dirty work of the Japanese, and Laval replied: 'When you get as old as I am, you will take a hand in anybody's poker game.' "

Later I felt that my high estimate of Powell was borne out when the *Chicago Tribune* ousted him as its China correspondent, a position which he had held since 1928. The *Tribune* wrote him that it no longer considered Chinese news important. After that they retained only one correspondent in the Far East, Kimpei Sheba, a Japanese from Honolulu, who had his office in Japan. He alone covered the China-Japanese War for the *Tribune*.

To these Red Army men, I said: "I am convinced that some American and British correspondents in China would never have sent out those official Kuomintang reports against you had they had a ghost of a chance of getting the truth directly from you. If they could visit you now, they would write honestly."

They thought about it, then someone said: "Well, if any would come, we would welcome them."

This was the origin of my attempts to break the news blockade against the Red Army. I sent confidential invitations to about a dozen leading foreign editors and correspondents in Shanghai, warning them, of course, that they would have to run the gauntlet of Kuomintang troops and Blue Shirt detectives which guarded Sian. I instructed them to come to Sian in groups of three or four only, put up at the Sian Guest House on certain dates, and wait till a foreign woman bearing a card from me arranged for their transportation northward.

The invitation aroused almost every newspaper man who received it, and Shanghai buzzed with excitement. The editor of the leading British daily, the *North China Daily News*, was a liberal and was regarded as the dean of the foreign newspaper fraternity. I invited him to lead the first group. I had not reckoned, however, with the journalistic practice of seeking "scoops." I held such practices in contempt, for I did not consider great national movements publicity stunts. Down in Shanghai everyone who accepted the invitation wished to be the first to come.

But the Chinese Government learned of the preparations and warned the journalists that if they tried to visit the Communists, the Government would consider it an unfriendly act. The board of directors of the British daily thereupon ordered their editor to drop out. But the head of the United Press office instructed Earl Leaf, his north China representative, to leave Tientsin and proceed to Sian. Later John B. Powell and Victor Keen, a correspondent for the *New York Herald Tribune*, also decided to run the gauntlet.

The two correspondents went to the Shanghai airdrome on the appointed date and were in a plane when special police appeared and ordered them to get out. Powell decided it would be unwise to resist and, after an argument, returned home. But Keen asked the police to show him a copy of any Chinese law which he was violating. Since there was not even a regulation, he angrily took his seat in the plane and refused to budge. When he reached Sian, detectives followed him night and day. A certain foreign woman met him, presented a certain card to him — and Mr. Keen mysteriously disappeared. Shortly afterwards he turned up in Yenan.

But even before this, young, beautiful Nym Wales (Mrs. Edgar Snow) had arrived in Sian. A special guard of three detectives dogged her footsteps. She watched their habits and one dark night crawled out of her hotel window, leaving a little note telling the manager she would be back later! She remained three months in Yenan gathering material for a book.

The next to heave in sight was Earl Leaf of the United Press, coming from north China. By this time the Government detectives suspected every foreigner, and though Leaf interviewed Sian officials and missionaries, he also was trailed. Then he too mysteriously disappeared!

These were the first foreigners after Edgar Snow, Ma Haiteh (the American doctor), the German Li Teh, and myself to reach the forbidden land. The arrival of each was a tremendous event in Yenan. A few weeks later Dr. Owen Lattimore and a group of American scholars who were making a tour of all China came through in their own car. All the men and women in Yenan educational institutions, all research groups, and all Communist Party members were ordered out to hear them lecture on international affairs. Bathed in sunlight, Dr. Lattimore stood on the ancient stone platform before an old Confucian temple and lectured in English to an eager audience. I felt that the best minds of the West were at last reaching the advance guards of the Asiatic revolution.

The foreign newspaper men who reached Yenan felt remarkably at ease. None of the formality and dissimilation of official life existed among the Communists. Speaking of them, one newspaper man made a remark of a kind which I was later to hear again and again from other foreign correspondents. He said they were "not Chinese, but new men."

These newspaper men interviewed all and sundry, visited educational institutions, and at night attended the "Anti-Japanese Resistance Theater." They spent evenings in pleasant conversation with Communist leaders, and my own house often resounded with their laughter. I would send a note to Mao Tze-tung to come and chat and he would soon enter, bringing a sack of peanuts. The foreigners would then be asked for a song, and when they had done their best, the Chinese would sing or tell tales. Or they would all plunge into a discussion.

At the evening theatrical performances the audience would often stamp or clap in unison, demanding that the visiting foreigners entertain. We Americans are not a singing people; when Victor Keen was asked to sing he wanted to sink through the earth. But the audience would have none of it. I asked Vic if he knew any figures of the Virginia reel. He did, and he and I got on the stage and to the great delight of the audience put on an American folk-dance.

One of the first questions asked by visiting Americans was about the sex life of the Army. Red Army leaders explained that men had sex needs, but the Army tried to absorb the energies of the soldiers in military training and various cultural activities which continued from reveille to taps.

One day a visiting cameraman asked me: "Does the Red Army provide the soldiers with *French letters* to protect them from venereal disease?" It was a question which showed the deep gulf existing between these Red Army men and the men from America. The Red Army was so poor that it lacked even money for the essentials of existence; it had never heard of *French letters*. All Chinese women are married at an early age; a sex life for soldiers would automatically have meant the violation of married women. Violation of women was a criminal offense in the Army, and prostitution was forbidden. When I explained this to the cameraman, he looked at me with an expression of horror.

After the Japanese invasion began and I was at the front, a number of other foreigners broke the blockade and visited Yenan, but never without having great difficulty with the police of Sian. Even after the Red Army had become a part of the national defense system, newspaper men could not get Government permission to visit it. To break the blockade became an adventure and a challenge.

Journalists never returned from the Red Army without feeling that they had been among modern men, men much like themselves. They liked Mao Tze-tung tremendously and told bizarre tales of him. One such foreigner was a long, lean, titled Englishman whom Mao teased mercilessly, even offering to marry him off to some Chinese girl if he would remain in Yenan. When the Englishman returned to Hankow months later, he was a deep-dyed pink; and he could not get over Mao Tze-tung.

War

TRICKLING over the radio into Yenan on the morning of July 8, 1937 came the news that there had been another "incident" — this time at Lukuochiao (Marco Polo Bridge), some fifteen miles southwest of Peiping. The Japanese had been "maneuvering" around Peiping, and the Chinese had felt much as Americans would feel if the Japanese Army were conducting military maneuvers around New York or San Francisco. On the night of the 7th the Japanese pretended that one of their soldiers was "missing" and demanded the right to search the walled town of Wanping. The magistrate refused. By such methods the Japanese had filtered into five Chinese provinces and had forced the demilitarization of a part of Hopei Province.

Some time between midnight and the morning of July 8, fighting began between the Chinese 29th Route Army, commanded by General Sung Cheh-yuan, and the Japanese at Wanping and at Marco Polo Bridge.

Despite the fact that they were entirely outnumbered, having only 10,000 men against twice that number of Japanese troops, the 29th Route Army (once one of the armies of the Christian General, Feng Yu-hsiang) continued to fight. By the third week in July the Japanese had sent eight war-time divisions and two hundred airplanes inside the

Great Wall. Chinese casualties were appalling, including hundreds of students.

It was becoming clear that even if the Chinese Government were willing to consider this a "local incident" the Japanese were not, but were determined to conquer the country. In the mountain resort of Kuling, Generalissimo Chiang Kai-shek debated the alternatives of war or peace with his highest commanders and officials. Throughout Yenan and the whole northwest, students took the small, primitive maps published by Resistance University (*Kang Da*) and began holding small street meetings to explain the war to the civilian population. Groups of them sat in the streets, talking and explaining, their maps spread on the earth before them.

All China was ringing with voices demanding full military support of the 29th Route Army, and on July 17 Generalissimo Chiang broke his long silence, issuing his historic four-point statement telling the country that the final stage had come, that China would have to fight to the utmost or "perish forever."

When the Generalissimo's statement came over the air, bugles sounded and gongs clanged and the streets filled with people. I stood under the old town gate to watch long gray-blue columns of men and women march past. I have never been able to convey the impression they made upon me. They were grave, solemn. Not a breath of bravado was in them, yet they seemed dedicated to death — and to life. In them was a simple grandeur as fundamental and as undemonstrative as the earth. They belonged to China, they *were* China. As I watched them, my own life seemed but chaos.

In August 1937 the Red Army was finally reorganized into the Eighth Route Army and divisions began leaving for the northern front, the sector in which the Japanese were conquering strategic cities and passes — often with little effort. For weeks groups of Kang Da commanders had been hurriedly finishing their courses and starting southward through torrential rains, with packs on their backs. Each group's departure was like a knife in my heart, for my back injury made it impossible for me to accompany them. In mid-September I at last joined a group leaving for Sian. Intent on reaching the Sian missionary hospital and being X-rayed, I went part of the way on a bamboo stretcher which Mao Tze-tung gave me and part of the way rode my horse or walked. Reaching Sanyuan after ten days over terrible roads, I sent my pony ahead to Chu Teh at the front.

X-ray examination indicated that my injury was only muscular, painful but not dangerous, and the doctors strapped me up and told me to lie flat on a board as long as possible before I left for the front. For three weeks I lay in a small room in the Sian headquarters of the Eighth Route Army, watching the open courtyard beyond. That courtyard reflected the momentous changes taking place in China. Each train discharged groups of released political prisoners. Prison pallor still marked their faces, and many had tuberculosis, nervous disorders, or stomach ailments. They remained only long enough to take the next trucks for Yenan where they hoped to recover their health and enter either Kang Da or Shanpei.

It was the middle of October when two Chinese journalists, Chou Li-po and a Manchurian, Hsu Chuen, and I left by train for Tungkwan. There we alighted to take the narrow-gauge, single-line railway that led northward to Taiyuan, the provincial capital of Shansi Province. China was now fighting in earnest and all conversation centered on this one subject. As we passed through the streets toward the Yellow River, we saw in the distance a long procession carrying national banners, and the strains of their marching song came to us from afar.

Then, suddenly, the war was upon us. Our junk landed on the north bank of the river in front of the rambling mud town of Fenglingtohkow. This little town, in which we hoped to find lodgings for the night, was a mass of soldiers, civilians, carts, mules, horses, and street venders. As we walked up the mud paths toward the town, we saw on either side of us long rows of wounded soldiers lying on the earth.

There were hundreds of them swathed in dirty, bloody bandages, and some were unconscious. Repeatedly we paused to talk to them. Some had been wounded a month before and had made their way southward from village to village, occasionally getting a ride on some lumbering cart. Thousands had died en route and the lightly wounded, now in serious condition, were waiting to be transported across the river, where they could take trains east or west. There were no doctors, nurses, or attendants with them.

As we passed through these lines of suffering and dying men, I said to my companions: "Our first war reporting will be about the condition of the wounded. I will try to get foreign aid and volunteers."

My party found one small room. All the men lay close together on the *k'ang*, and my guards pitched my camp cot in the narrow space at the foot. The sight of the untended wounded left me sleepless, and in the darkness of the night I heard the Manchurian, Hsu Chuen, turn restlessly and sigh.

"Why can't you sleep?" I asked, and he answered: "It is the Manchurian cavalrymen! They set me thinking of my old parents in north Manchuria. I do not know if they are alive or dead. I shall perhaps never see them again."

I lay staring into the darkness, wondering how many millions of Chinese carried such sorrows in their hearts.

Next day we found places in a crowded box-car. Night found us still crawling slowly northward. Once we remained at a station for a long time. Hearing voices, I rose and went to the open door. The moon was at the full, and on the tracks before us was a long train of open flat cars loaded with hundreds of wounded men who sat or lay in every conceivable position.

We reached Taiyuan before dawn on the second day and walked to the local headquarters of the Eighth Route Army. While we were at breakfast the first enemy bombers came over and bombed the city. We went into dugouts beneath the building. There were similar dugouts throughout the city, the official ones being hundreds of feet deep and made of reinforced concrete.

For days we visited high military and medical officials, including the old Governor, General Yen Hsi-shan, his medical chief, and General Fu Tso-yi, who had lost most of his army in fighting the Japanese in Suiyuan Province.

It was not polite in those days to speak or write the truth about officials or military men. Nor is it today, when China fights for her life. Yet the lid is off civilization, and if we are to build a new world we must see all that is wrong with the old. I am convinced that China — and this applies to my own country too — would never have suffered such defeats or losses as it did if its Government had been truly revolutionary and democratic and had ruthlessly cleaned its ranks of appeasers and unenlightened men.

General Yen Hsi-shan, Governor of Shansi and commander of the Shansi Provincial Army, was not so consciously reactionary as some other generals and officials; he was merely somewhat the worse for age, and utterly ignorant of the youth, virility, and ruthlessness of the Japanese Army. He and almost all commanders of his army were much concerned with the industrial plants of the province, and many were landlords. Their soldiers were "old," unenlightened, and badly equipped — pathetic in their impotence. The Japanese knew all this well and later, as they advanced, tried to turn the chief ones into puppets by protecting their homes and property. They even threw a cordon of protecting troops around the home of Dr. H. H. Kung, Minister of Finance of the Central Government, in Taiyuan. Their knowledge of China was great. But to the credit of even the aged and unenlightened, no one went over to the Japanese.

The medical department of the Shansi Army was primitive. When I spoke to the Surgeon General about the possibility of organizing volunteer stretcher-bearers and first-aid workers, he became suspicious; the idea savored of dangerous popular movements. He could think only in terms of money. No man would carry the wounded from the battlefield unless paid for it, he said, and he was considering a system whereby anyone who brought in a wounded soldier would be paid.

The Surgeon General sent me by car to visit two of the five base hospitals in the city. There were sixteen hospitals in the province, but they were generally buildings where men lay on straw on the earthen floor. The one exception to this was the hospital for the severely wounded in Taiyuan. It was a model because its chief was a qualified surgeon who had come down from the Peking Union Medical College. His work-day was never less than eighteen hours. He had a staff of nineteen unqualified doctor assistants, eighteen unqualified male nurses, and twenty qualified women nurses. While I was there, 1,300 severely wounded men lay under his care. In September his hospital had received 5,000 cases, and all but the most severe had been evacuated southward by train. This hospital had only the essential surgical instruments, and no X-ray, sedative drugs, or anti-tetanus toxin. Blood transfusion was unheard of.

The only X-ray in the entire province was in the mission hospital; but this institution had taken in only thirty wounded men, all officers who could pay. I went to the mission hospital to have my back strapped again and to have one of my guards examined for tuberculosis. The woman doctor remarked that there were not many wounded soldiers coming from the front because the Chinese did not fight, but always fled before the Japanese. At the time we were trying to win the missionaries to the united front, so I swallowed my anger and made a soft reply, telling her of the hospitals I had seen.

Before leaving Taiyuan for the headquarters of the Eighth Route Army, I spent an entire night preparing a report on the wounded of the northwest. To this I appended an appeal for foreign medical aid to China and for the formation of foreign committees to secure such aid. This report I sent to John B. Powell in Shanghai and he broadcast it.

The Japanese had now advanced as far as Sinkow, a strong mountain pass some two hundred miles north of Taiyuan, and as far east as Shihchiachwan, the junction of the Peiping-Hankow and Chentai Railways. From the latter point, the Chentai Railway, a single-track narrow-gauge line, ran through a formidable mountain gorge up to Taiyuan. The Japanese were therefore advancing on Taiyuan from two directions. One of the ablest nationalist commanders, General Wei Li-hwang, was in command of all the Chinese forces on the Sinkow front, among them a number of good divisions of the Central Government. The Eighth Route Army was "sitting on the tail" of the Japanese and was on both their right and their left flanks, attacking transport and troop columns moving down from the front. My goal was the Eighth Route Army headquarters in the Wutai mountain range and in the rear of the enemy.

The Chinese battlefront now stretched thousands of miles. Far away in Shanghai and Nanking the best-trained Government Divisions, with the famous Kwangsi Provincial Army, were standing like a Great Wall of human flesh against the combined force of Japan's naval, army, and air power. Unlike the armies in our regions, they had no mountains to shield them.

One glimmer of light had penetrated the darkness of north China. This was the battle of Pinghsinkwan. A young Eighth Route commander, Lin Piao, had led a part of one division against the Japanese at Pinghsinkwan, a pass near the Great Wall in the Wutai Mountains. Informed that the Japanese were trying to break through at this point, Eighth Route units marched for two days and two nights to reach it. After a few hours' sleep Lin Piao sent flying columns far to the rear and against the flanks of the advancing enemy, holding one regiment at Pinghsinkwan to meet them head on. The flying columns occupied five towns which the Japanese were using as rear bases, and small guerrilla detachments used hillsides and mountains to harass the advancing columns.

Since they had met only weak Chinese resistance up to

then, the enemy had no protecting airplanes or tanks. They also had difficulty with those strange roads that characterize the loess terrain of the northwest — roads that have been worn into the earth as deep as ravines. The Eighth Route regiment at Pinghsinkwan placed machine-gun nests along these tunnel-like roads, while troops lay in wait on the cliffs above. They would let an enemy column advance, then open up on it with hand-grenades from above and machine-guns from below. When the battle ended on September 26, one brigade of the old Samurai 5th Japanese Division had been annihilated. The Eighth Route had wiped out brigade headquarters and captured military maps, documents, diaries, and great quantities of clothing, money, and provisions. In one of the captured Japanese diaries I read the line: "The Red Army gives me a headache."

The battle of Pinghsinkwan was important because it was the first time the Chinese combined mobile and guerrilla warfare against the Japanese, because the civilian population had been drawn into the fight, and because it proved that by using the techniques of a "people's war" even a poorly equipped Chinese force could defeat a fully equipped enemy. Months later, in Hankow, Lieutenant General Joseph W. Stilwell, then a Colonel, and an American military attaché spent half a day with me analyzing this battle.

Time and space lost their significance and days passed uncounted. But it was some time in the third week of October that the two Chinese newspaper men and I left Taiyuan on an Eighth Route Army truck and climbed toward the walled mountain town of Wutai. I had worked throughout the previous night and as the truck roared northward I began to fall asleep. The men warned me to keep awake because Japanese planes made a practice of attacking trucks at night, spotting them by their headlights. But I slept on: death had come to seem an unimportant accident. Once I awoke to see a column of trucks, bristling with soldiers, moving southward, accompanied by long columns of marching men and heavily laden horses and mules.

Our truck labored up the stony gorges into the Wutai mountains and finally brought us to the headquarters of the People's Mobilization Committee in Wutai. Young enthusiastic men in uniform ordered a meal for us, and soon the room was filled with civilians. The newspaper men and I were weary for lack of sleep, but the others seemed to think that one could sleep any time, while the chance to talk with journalists was an occasion. Furthermore, they said, Japanese planes bombed the town almost every day, thinking it the headquarters of the Eighth Route Army, and we ought therefore to get out before eight in the morning.

We spent most of the night talking about this "people's movement" in the enemy rear. The movement seemed to me like fresh water in a desert, because I had also spent considerable time with a People's Mobilization Committee in Taiyuan. The efforts of the Taiyuan committee had been frustrated by officials who thought of the war only as a conflict between armies. If the common people should be trained and armed, they thought, they would indeed fight the Japanese, but afterwards they might refuse to lay down their arms and return to pre-war conditions.

So the Taiyuan People's Mobilization Committee had had to pussyfoot around, trying to convince the authorities that mobilization would make them popular and consolidate their power. Grudgingly, cautiously, the authorities permitted the committee to hold meetings and explain the purpose of the war, but only to the people living in regions bordering the actual battlefield. This region did not even include Taiyuan, for the authorities did not believe that city would fall. General Yen, however, had been prevailed upon to form the "Dare to Die Corps" of students, and military training schools were being started in various parts of the province.

Here where the Eighth Route Army alone dared penetrate, mass organizers swarmed everywhere, forming anti-Japanese associations of peasants, students, merchants, women, and children. They were drawing the young men into guerrilla detachments and the older men into village self-defense corps. A number of these older men had been elected by the various anti-Japanese organizations as magistrates or lesser county officials in place of those who had fled before the Japanese advance.

Some time before dawn we at last lay down to sleep, but were soon awakened. We could already hear the roar of guns from the west. After inspecting the partly destroyed town, we began trudging along the paths and narrow roads into the mountains. It was a crisp, sunny autumn day, and on the road was an endless caravan of people. Only the distant roar of guns, and an occasional airplane passing over, gave one the feeling of war.

Around noon we arrived at a village in a broad golden valley and were assigned to a large room in a beautiful stone building which had curved, gargoyled roofs of colored tile. A grove of birch sheltered the village and across the valley arose other peaceful villages and clumps of trees. One was the headquarters of Chu Teh, and soon a guard came galloping up on my pony, Yunnan, with a message of welcome.

The building which we occupied was the headquarters of the Political Department of the Army, and the courtyards were filled with commanders and political workers. They were using captured Japanese overcoats and pistols and we ourselves soon began to live sumptuously on Japanese food.

Among the men I met here was a political worker returned from Laiyuan, a town in western Hopei Province, southwest of Peiping, which had just been recaptured from the Japanese. When Laiyuan fell to the Chinese, he told me, the puppet Government established by the Japanese had fled into an Italian Catholic mission. The priest had previously selected the men as puppet leaders, and had helped the Japanese collect food and establish their espionage system. The Eighth Route Army had knocked on the barred gates of the mission, but the priest had run up the Italian flag and shouted that the Chinese and Italian Governments still maintained diplomatic relations and that Italian property was therefore immune from search. The Eighth Route Army had telegraphed all this to Nanking, but no reply ever came.

Many similar incidents involving Italian priests and diplomatic officials occurred but nothing was done about them. When I asked the Eighth Route Army commanders why they did not break down the mission gates and take out the Chinese traitors, they said they dared not lest they be accused of attacking Christianity.

I remained a week in the Wutai Mountains. I spent one day with Chu Teh, who gave us a complete report of the fighting his army had done since it had penetrated the enemy rear. On other days my colleagues and I went into the hills to watch young civilians being trained for guerrilla warfare. One village was the headquarters of the People's Mobilization Committee and the whole village was a training base. Very little was being done to mobilize women, but in the following weeks trained women organizers and educators walked all the way from Yenan to start this work.

I was witnessing the birth of the powerful mass movement that later turned the Wutai mountain range into a powerful base of resistance. In time the region became a great educational, hospital, military, and political center in which thousands of men from four northern and northwestern provinces studied.

Suddenly the Eighth Route Army received orders to move its headquarters and one division to the Chentai Railway in order to help stem the Japanese advance, and on the following morning we began a memorable march southward over the mountain ranges to the railway.

Though marching rapidly and under danger of daily airraids, I saw in operation the comprehensive system that had brought the Red Army to birth and enabled it to live and grow. Groups of men, representing various departments of the Army, went in advance of us. When we reached a resting-place at night, chalked signs on trees and walls directed each department to its quarters, and when we reached our section of a town or village, we found even the words "newspaper men" written on a door. According to its size, each home gave one or more rooms to the Army. Strict Army rules concerning the treatment of the people enabled the troops to live like sons of the family.

Each evening the soldiers gathered to continue their education. A course of lectures on the history of Chinese-Japanese relations was just then being given in all units. And as soon as we arrived in any stopping-place we heard the beating of gongs and shouts of "Kai hwei! Kai hwei!" (Mass meeting!) calling everyone to a meeting where speeches were made about the war and the need for the people to participate. Organizers were always left behind to continue the same mobilization work I had witnessed in Wutaishan.

As we approached the Chentai Railway, we began to hear the ceaseless roar of artillery. The Japanese had broken through the pass near Shihchiachwan and were pushing forward. When airplanes droned toward us we scattered or, if in a village, took cover.

We were soon marching only at night; one morning we halted just ten *li* (three miles) from the railway. Many of the near-by villages had been bombed and were almost deserted, but we found quarters and slept all day through a heavy roar of guns. I awoke often to hear bombers passing over and held my breath while listening for the deadly scream of falling bombs. The planes passed and I went back to sleep.

We began marching again at midnight, planning to cross the railway before dawn. I had mailed my last diary notes at a large town the day before, and I wondered what their fate would be, for the most remarkable of all institutions is the Chinese post office. Mail-carriers work regularly through rain and storm, war and peace. They walk, push barrows, drive donkeys, travel by bicycle, cart, horse, camel, river junk, railway, airplane. They may be late, but only some major disaster halted the service in any region. We were in such a region and my reports were safer with the post office than with me. As we neared the Chentai Railway, I ceased writing altogether and destroyed every scrap of writing in my possession.

The first faint glow of dawn came and we still had not

crossed the railway. Our vanguard had lost the way, and when they at last found it, the dawn threatened us like a dangerous beast. Never have I hated the light so much. Repeatedly down the column came the desperate order: "Hurry! Hurry!"

At last we reached the railway, but had missed the crossing! We had to march along the track for thirty minutes until we found the road leading into the country to the south. Moving forward silently, desperately, the men would start to trot, then fall into a walk again, panting. They were heavily laden with guns and ammunition. Mangled bodies lay along the track, and once we passed the remnants of a retreating Army unit, exhausted, with the horror of war still on their green faces. We found a soldier in a dead sleep under a bridge and all our shouts failed to awaken him. From the east came an engine pulling laden freight cars. The whistle shrieked and we cleared the track as it roared past. In the cab window I saw the set, hard face of the Chinese engineer watching the track in front of him and sending out his warning. I thought of the heroism of all the railway men of China. Day by day, month by month, year in and year out, they had faced certain death, for the railways always were chief objectives. They remained the unknown, unsung heroes of China.

At last we found the road and with a sigh of relief turned south. In less than half an hour, while the main body of our troops were still on the tracks, the first enemy airplane came over. We crouched or fled into the fields and waited. The plane passed, observing nothing!

For the next ten days the Eighth Route Army fought a running battle all along the southern flank of the Chentai Railway. The Japanese columns came on and on; and weary Chinese armies, including our own, fought them, retreated, and then fought them again. Japanese bombers roared over us daily, sometimes hourly, but did not find our headquarters. One morning I went to headquarters to talk with Chu Teh, but found it surrounded by a few hundred armed civilians, many of them ragged, unwashed, barefooted. With them were women and children, one a solidly built old woman over sixty years of age, her white hair flying. They were miners and railway workers who, as the Japanese approached, took arms from a local arsenal, tore up the railway, and began fighting. Many had already been killed. Now they came to join the Eighth Route Army.

Throughout one long night a fierce battle raged just across the hills from us. We could hear the harsh symphony of hammering machine-guns, and Chu Teh's face was the color of clay. With the dawn the word "Victory" was flashed to us, and my newspaper colleagues and I were off, galloping over the hills to the battlefield.

We passed hundreds of laden horses and mules captured from the enemy. The entire valley leading to the south was a chaos of shouting men and stamping, kicking animals. Once we stopped dead in our tracks at the sight of columns of armed men pouring over a hill in our rear and coming straight for us. They wore Japanese overcoats, but their bodies and movements were Chinese, and they ran forward with shouts and laughter, their coats spreading out behind them like wings. Like an avalanche they poured past us, shouting, singing snatches of song, hailing us with joy. It was the division of the Eighth Route Army which had left the Wutai Mountains weeks before. In the midst of the clamor I heard my Chinese name shouted and an officer ran toward me. I greeted him with outspread arms. It was Chen Ken, a commander who had worked with me years before when he had come to Shanghai to get medical treatment for a wound.

Then he too was off down the valley toward the battlefield. Thereafter my colleagues and I wandered from village to village having strange experience after experience — talking with Japanese captives . . . rescuing a big case of Japanese money which someone was joyously distributing as souvenirs. . . .

The battle continued for days, and the divisional headquarters which we had joined, Lin Piao's, was right on the ridge of hills overlooking the valley through which the enemy was pouring. Enemy batteries blasted a way for them and enemy planes kept sweeping over us.

One night at dusk as I was standing on a summit, a column of Eighth Route Army soldiers came up out of a dark ravine, passed me, and disappeared down into the ravine through which the Japanese were pouring. Strong, hardened fighters, they walked swiftly, easily, without missing a step of their rhythmic march despite the fact that they were heavily laden with ammunition. Their feet were softshod and made not a sound in passing. A boy of thirteen or fourteen carrying a big Standard Oil tin filled with water ran after a soldier bending under a machine-gun. The boy's face was filled with excitement and the water splashed as he ran. That picture is etched in my memory. Was it the faces of men going to meet a powerful enemy or was it that spindly-legged little boy with the gasoline tin that so deeply affected me? The gasoline tin was the only contribution from my country to China which I saw on the northwestern front. But the enemy planes above us were American and their bombs were made of scrap iron and chemicals from America.

Approaching from the north and east, the Japanese took Taiyuan. We left one division along the Chentai Railway and, with Lin Piao's division, general headquarters moved to southern Shansi under orders to sit astride the railway running the length of the province.

Now we marched more leisurely, seldom making more than eighty or ninety *li* (twenty-five to thirty miles) a day. I learned to reckon distance by my weariness. Up to sixty *li* I was fresh, but after that each mile seemed to grow longer and longer. The earth was frozen, the rivers covered with a thin layer of ice, and the mountains were wrapped in snow. It was often so cold that I could ride for only a few moments and then had to walk. But there were also warm sunny days when joy flowed through us, and on such days we took advantage of the noon hour to rest, to visit other units of the Army, or to wander off to talk with villagers.

When the rain or the soft snow fell, turning the earth to

a mass of mud, we sometimes remained in one place for many days. Then the vicinity buzzed with meetings, conferences, and civilian training. We crossed the Luliang mountain range in a snowstorm that fell in thick white clouds and turned the paths into a mass of half-frozen mud through which we slithered and struggled, pulling our horses behind us. I had lice, and the freezing mud filled my shoes. I found a man having an appendicitis attack by the roadside, and lifted him into my saddle, where he rode, moaning. The snow fell, heavily laden men stumbled, and horses and donkeys had to be lifted to their feet and reloaded. Black crows flew down, shivering in the snow, and the very cap on my head became a burden.

Then I heard a flute play. It came out of the snowstorm like a clear, sparkling stream, telling tales of loveliness unspeakable. It played and played, leading us on through the white world to the mountain summit. Then I saw the dim figures of soldiers moving downward, and one of them had both hands lifted to a flute.

Down past the ancient walled town of Hungtung and on over the broad frozen flat countryside beyond. Midnight found us wandering aimlessly from village to village. In the early morning we reached the home of a landlord, saw our name on a door, and entered to find the whole family waiting for us with hot food and drink. We had marched some eighteen hours this day and night, but how many *li* I do not know. The Chinese are very realistic. When they march up a mountain, the *li* becomes longer; when they descend, it is considered shorter.

We remained for weeks in the Hungtung region. I rode here and there, buying, begging, and borrowing medical supplies. Eighth Route fighting units marched northward, northeast, and northwest to anticipate possible routes of enemy advance. New volunteers came in long lines to headquarters, and soon all the wheat-fields were black with them as they drilled and maneuvered. At night the villages were filled with soldiers sitting in classes. Enemy bombers plastered Hungtung, thinking we were there.

In late December two foreigners arrived. One of them was James Bertram, the young New Zealander whom I had met in Sian at the time Generalissimo Chiang had been captured. He carried a copy of Shakespeare's works, and the halo of Oxford culture hovered about his head. This loftiness irritated me. The other visitor was Captain Evans F. Carlson, Marine Intelligence officer in China.

When I heard that Carlson had arrived, I decided to give him a wide berth. My experience with American officials in China had not been enviable. Most of them thought of the Chinese as "Chinamen" who took in washing for a living; I didn't like their religion, so to speak. Because I regarded the Red Army as a revolutionary organization of the poor, some Americans considered me a glorified streetwalker; and after the Japanese invasion their women in particular had looked on me as a camp follower, a creature who lowered the prestige of the white race.

One day I was sitting on a mud bank watching two Army units in a basketball game when Chu Teh came up behind me and asked me to meet one of my countrymen.

"I've long wanted to meet you, Miss Smedley," Captain Carlson said.

"Well, now you've met me," I remarked, and turned back to the ball game.

Carlson was a very long, lanky man — so bony, in fact, that he looked loose. But when you went walking with him you found that he was as firm as the farmers of his native New England. There was an air of utter simplicity about him which I first thought must be a cunning disguise.

He had come to the Eighth Route Army to study guerrilla warfare from the point of view of the technician, but he had soon realized that guerrilla warfare is not merely a technical matter, but intricately bound up with a broad and deep political educational system designed to give men something to fight for, live for, and, if necessary, die for. He began studying this political system and was soon calling it "ethical indoctrination."

The arrival of a foreign military man aroused the driving

intellectual hunger of the Eighth Route Army commanders, and they called a conference to talk with him. This conference lasted for days and merged into an extended discussion of a hypothetical Japanese-American war — which the Chinese Communists considered inevitable. They spread large maps on a table and for hours their fingers wandered over it from Singapore to the Aleutian Islands. They took it for granted that Singapore would be the base from which American and British forces would operate. The Chinese believed that America had fortified Alaska and the Aleutian Islands against Japanese attack — they could not conceive that it could be otherwise, for until then the Chinese had entertained a high regard for American military sagacity.

The Chinese commanders held back nothing about their own methods of mobile and guerrilla warfare. They sketched battle scenes, explaining how they avoided frontal engagements with a powerfully equipped enemy but instead prepared the whole battle region to serve in the lines or right behind them; how they attacked the enemy's flanks and rear, cut up his columns and destroyed the segments, and disrupted his lines of communication. They told of their observations of the weak and strong points of the Japanese and of their own strength and weaknesses. Of the civilian population they said:

"We move about among the people as freely as fish swimming in the ocean. By organizing and training the people we automatically eliminate traitors. We rest in the hearts of the people."

The friendship between Captain Carlson and myself which began in those days eventually became one of the firmest of my life, welded in the fires of war. On Christmas Eve I went to Carlson's room, where we made coffee, ate peanuts, and talked. He was of Norwegian descent, the son of a Connecticut pastor, and had a profound strain of religious ethics running through his character. His principles were deeply rooted in early American Jeffersonian democracy; that must have been why he felt at home in the political and ethical atmosphere of the Eighth Route Army. For

Friends of Hankow days: Major Frank Dorn; General Chou En-lai, representing the Chinese Communists in the Chinese Government; the author; Lieutenant Colonel Evans F. Carlson; Mr. Robert Jarvis, American Consular official.

(left) Our beloved "Vinegar Joe," Lieutenant General Joseph F. Stilwell, of the American Army. (right) Lieutenant Colonel Evans F. Carlson, "Battle Hymn of the Republic."

similar reasons most American newspaper men who visited that Army felt that they had at last found a fountain of Chinese democracy. Captain Carlson's reaction toward the Eighth Route was such that it constantly reminded me of two lines in *The Battle Hymn of the Republic:*

Mine eyes have seen the glory of the coming of the Lord;
He is trampling out the vintage where the grapes of wrath
    are stored.

And I always thought of him when I heard the line —

"As He died to make men holy, let us die to make men free."

On this Christmas Eve he raised his enameled coffee cup and said: "Agnes, we are celebrating Christmas," and drank. I did the same, then we both ate peanuts. He placed his cup on the bed beside him, drew a mouth-organ from his pocket and first played and then sang the song of the United States Marines. He followed this with *Oh, How I Hate to Get Up in the Morning*. Then he laughed and drawled: "Aw, shucks! I remember when I first heard that thing!"

We both sang a few lines of some Negro spirituals, then tried *Silent Night, Holy Night*, but broke down because we couldn't remember the lines. Finally we stood up and sang *My Country, 'Tis of Thee*, a song I love.

From a musical viewpoint that Christmas Eve was hardly a roaring success. But the conversation was not so bad.

Ike IV (1954–57): The Failed Trout and War 199

an "AP associate poet," American newspaper men who visited
Chou An-lai till this day held at last found a fountain of
Chinese eloquence. Captain Carlson's reaction beyond the
Eighth Route was such that it constantly reminded me of
two lines of The Battle Hymn of the Republic:

Mine eyes have seen the glory of the coming of the Lord,
He is trampling out the vintage where the grapes of wrath
are stored.

And I always thought of him when I heard the line:

As He died to make men holy, let us die to make men free.

On this Christmas Eve he raised his enameled coffee cup
and said, "You know, we're having Christmas," and drank.
I did the same, then we both ate peanuts. He placed his cup
on the bed beside him, drew a pomegranate from his pocket
and just placed and then sang the song of the United States
Marines. He followed this with Oh, How I Hate to Get Up
in the Morning. Then he laughed and drank. "An
Ameishi," remembered when I first heard that thingy."

We both sang a few lines of some Negro spirituals, then
tried Silent Night, Holy Night but broke down because we
couldn't remember the lines. Finally, we stood up and sang
My Country 'Tis of Thee, a song I love.

From a musical viewpoint that Christmas Eve was hardly
a roaring success, but the conversation was not so bad.

BOOK V

The Last Days of Hankow

1938

Today I saw a Chinese peasant soldier die. In his death was embodied the death of a million men of China who have given their lives that their people might not be enslaved.

All that was known of him was told by another wounded man who had been in the same company with him. They had attacked a Japanese position. They did not know they were wounded until the battle was ended and they began to return to their headquarters. Then they could no longer walk. One foot of each man had been pierced by a sharp, spikelike piece of bamboo which the Japanese had driven into the earth around their defenses.

The man lay silently on his bed, and the only thing he ever said was that his name was Wu and that he was a peasant by occupation. Every line of his face and body was eloquent of anguish. He seemed to be thinking and thinking. He saw little that passed about him. His mind was centered on some thought beyond. The doctor said of him: "He cannot live. He is so undernourished that he has no resistance at all."

By noon of the third day he closed his eyes forever. As he had lived, so he died, humbly, causing no one trouble. The men on either side of him did not know he was dead until men came and carried away his body. Soon his lean form was laid in an unpainted wooden coffin and lowered into a slight depression on a hillside, and the coffin covered with earth. A narrow, unpainted board bearing his name, the date of his death, and the army in whose service he had died was put at his head. . . .

Soon the rains will soak into the grave, rotting the coffin

and the body, and slowly the mound will settle. Grass will creep over it, sinking deep roots. And then one day some poor peasant child gathering firewood will carry away the little headboard. . . .

It is easy to die in the limelight, knowing a nation will honor you, and your life will be used as a model. But this man Wu, and a million others like him, fight and die in obscurity. In the future free society of China they will have no share. . . . Did they know that when they picked up a rifle?

How ugly he was in death — and how beautiful! How tragically great the common men of China! Their country has offered them nothing but sorrow and hunger, cold and suffering. Still they offer their lives for it. They die by the thousands on deserted battlefields. Other thousands stagger to the rear, looking ruefully at their uncared-for wounds, their eyes searching the mountain paths and the highways, yearning for help that never comes.

Book V: The Last Days of Hankow

∽§ 1938 §∾

Cross-Currents in Hankow

The ten months from December 12, 1937 to October 25, 1938, during which Hankow was the real capital of China, were months as crowded as decades. Like the mighty Yangtze, which intersected the triple cities of Hankow, Hanyang, and Wuchang (generally referred to as Wuhan or merely as Hankow), the capital rolled and seethed, a vast maelstrom of national and international forces. Against the powerful current of the patriotism of soldiers, common people, and some officials flowed the counter-stream of treason, venality, indifference, espionage, and international intrigue.

The fall of Nanking on December 12 had made a break in a reactionary trend that was unmistakably Fascist, and through this breach had poured the democratic people's movement, expressing itself in strengthened mass organizations, publications, and celebrations. But as time went on, the reactionary elements began to consolidate their ranks again. Wang Ching-wei still held great power in the Government and his followers occupied strategic positions in Hankow and other cities. Peace with the Japanese, he argued with the Generalissimo, was better than the eventual victory of Communism. The Kuomintang banned all youth organizations and ordered all students into the semi-Fascist "San Min Chu I Youth Corps," which was modelled on similar organizations of Italian Fascists and German Nazis. Mr. Chen Li-fu, Minister of Education, lectured to university students, declaring that they were too valuable to be expended in war. Educated men were told to preserve themselves for post-war reconstruction. The Communists had founded their *New China Daily*, and though it preached only national resistance, secret gangs of Blue Shirts broke in at night and damaged its printing plant. Class warfare continued to rage; gentlemen did not take part — they hired gangsters.

I also had my own difficulties and conflicts, and the first of these was the problem of earning a living. My revolutionary reputation closed all doors to employment. Many people held the belief that because I had always fought the Terror and advocated civil rights for the people, I was a paid Communist agent. On the other hand the Communists believed that all foreigners automatically had means of earning not only a living but a luxurious living. So I was suspended in an economic void. For a time I was a house guest of the Reverend Logan Roots, Episcopal Bishop of Hankow, and his daughter, Frances. But that could not go on indefinitely. The only means I had of solving my economic problems was to take a monthly loan from a loyal friend, a Chinese engineer.

My first visit upon reaching the new capital had been with Nelson T. Johnson, American Ambassador, to whom I delivered a letter from Evans Carlson, then with the Eighth Route Army. I had no clothing except my uniform, and in this outfit I called on our Ambassador and talked with him about the war. He concluded an account of fighting in the lower Yangtze by remarking that "the Japanese threw everything except the kitchen sink at the Chinese."

At one point I remarked that if the Japanese conquered China with American war materials, they would then turn on America.

Mr. Johnson made a gesture of disapproval and said:

"By that time they will be too exhausted!"

Mr. Johnson was not popular with many Americans in China. They called him spineless, but because he was Ambassador they outwardly respected him. He wasn't to blame personally — he was merely the Far Eastern extension of the State Department. His remark to me about allowing the Japanese to exhaust themselves on the body of China, leaving us free, indicated the policy of all the imperialist powers — England, France, the Dutch East Indies, and ourselves.

There were a few real American and British democrats in the Far East who saw the criminal fallacy of such a policy. Some were respected because they held high position, but the rest of us were deemed visionaries or, at worst, Reds. I was regarded variously as an immoral woman, an idealist or a Red. That didn't worry me in the least. I always remembered that when people had complained to Lincoln that General U. S. Grant was drunk half the time, Lincoln replied that he wished his other generals would also get tight if they could produce the same results.

Colonel (now Lieutenant General) Joseph W. Stilwell, our military attaché in China, was different. He was tough, gruff, and battle-scarred, a direct and honest fighting man. He loved the Chinese soldiers, and his heart was filled with compassion for the wounded. I was forever running into him. Once he stopped on a street and demanded of me:

"What are you doing here?"

"Loading this truck with medicine. What are you doing?"

"I'm standing here watching you!" he said, scowling. "I'm also telling you that the warehouse of the International Red Cross Committee is jammed with a new shipment of medicine — including the new sulfa drugs. Go right down there this minute and demand some for the Army!"

Following his suggestion, I asked for some of the foreign drugs, but as usual was refused. The International Red Cross Committees of China had no connection with the International Red Cross of Geneva, but were merely local foreign committees, made up primarily of missionaries. They received all foreign relief supplies and distributed them as they wished, usually to Christian mission hospitals. The Chinese armies and the Chinese Red Cross got absolutely nothing, for most missionaries believed that all Chinese, particularly non-Christian Chinese, were dishonest. They also argued that America, Britain, and other nations were neutral in the war and that supplies from them should therefore not be given to Chinese armies. My viewpoint was that a wounded soldier is as much a non-combatant as, let us say, a civilian air-raid victim; and my blood boiled when

I heard foreigners talk of all Christians as honest and all non-Christians as dishonest.

Another American who was a good deal like Colonel Stilwell was Colonel (now Major General) Claire Chennault, one of the most striking personalities I ever met, but one whom I never came to know well. A reticent, gruff man with a pockmarked face, he seemed to live within himself. He was seldom seen in foreign circles; at that time I had not yet heard the story that he had been forced out of the American Army because of his belief in air power. I lunched with him one day in an almost deserted tea-room and felt irritated because I could not get at him, could not understand what lay behind that grave, appealing exterior. He remarked that he would like to get hold of Chinese mechanics because he thought that he could train them to be pilots in half the time it took to train gentlemen's sons who had studied philosophy and literature and did not like to get themselves dirty.

Colonel Stilwell was so pessimistic about the whole Far Eastern situation that some officers and officials called him "Vinegar Joe" — which I considered far better than being called spineless. He once remarked to me: "The Chinese soldier is one of the best fighters on earth. I would be proud to command such men."

The other military men, Major (later Colonel) Frank Dorn, and Evans F. Carlson, also realized the dangerous situation which was developing in China. Dorn was an artillery attaché who traveled broadly and appreciated China deeply. For some reason or other he was ordered back to America, just after he had been told to remain for another three years. I wondered why. I even proposed to him that he mutiny and if necessary riot in the streets in order to remain in China. He was a very handsome, well-bred West Point lad and so disciplined that he went home. Before he left we all gave him a fine send-off. I wrote a poem addressed to him in the grand manner and Art Steele of the *Chicago Daily News* read it in a deep and passionate voice. Even in my poem, however, I did not betray Dorn's secret: he was a novelist, a painter, and, if I'm not mistaken, a musician.

Soon my other friends began to desert Hankow. Evans F. Carlson had returned from the northwestern front and was ordered by the Navy Department to stop talking. He had been telling about guerrilla warfare and, of all things, talking about political and "ethical indoctrination" as a weapon in war-time. Perhaps the Navy suspected him of Buddhism. But Carlson was not a New Englander and an echo of the *Battle Hymn of the Republic* for nothing. Feeling that it was his duty to awaken the American people to the danger of Japan, he forthwith resigned from the Navy. Instead of talking mutiny to him, I urged him to consider the nature of the capitalist system, which has no use for men of principle. I was afraid he might starve in America, where money was the standard of success. I was proud to be his friend when he replied: "Don't talk to me about economic security! The only thing that matters is — am I *right*?"

Though few people could help liking Carlson, now and then I heard cynical remarks about him. "The poor sap," one correspondent said, "he believed everything the Eighth Route Army told him! He's got religion!" They brushed aside the fact that he had not merely been told things by the Eighth Route. He had seen and lived with that Army. Its methods of fighting and its political indoctrination (which he called "ethical") might be brushed aside by men who believed in nothing except their own personal success, but Carlson was not a man to be shaken by such cynics. He had not been educated at West Point or Annapolis, and did not shine in the endless round of cocktail, tea, dinner and card parties, ball games, races, or golf matches which constituted the life of most foreign naval officers in the Far East. He did, however, have a number of foreign friends, and Admiral Harry Yarnell, commander of the American Asiatic Fleet, seemed to respect him. I might add that he himself felt a deep admiration for Yarnell.

So Carlson prepared to leave Hankow. At the same time Freda Utley, the English woman journalist, who was also leaving, soon created a scandal in the Hong Kong Rotary

Club by attacking Englishmen who supplied Japan with war materials for use against China. The president of the Rotary Club afterwards publicly apologized for her "unsportsmanlike" conduct.

In those unorthodox days before Hankow fell, the Captain of the British Yangtze gunboat patrol invited me to lecture to British officers and sailors on the deck of his flagship. I took maps along and did my job, but wondered whether the British were awakening or I was slipping. The American Navy reassured me by refusing me the same courtesy, although they allowed their sailors to learn that I was giving a lecture at the Navy Y.M.C.A. and their officers invited me to the dullest tea I have ever sat through. It was a boring life they led, sitting forever on little boats on the Yangtze, watching the Japanese raid the city. Admiral Marquardt of the American Yangtze patrol once looked me over at lunch on his flagship and was astonished to find that I was not so old or unprepossessing as he had expected. Perhaps he thought good-looking or presentable women were always snatched up by marriage, while the ugly ones revenged themselves on society by becoming rebels with principles. Or was it his Annapolis training that made him say to me:

"Why on earth does a woman like you bury herself in that Godforsaken northwest with a ragged army? Were you in love with a Chinese general?"

"To tell you the truth," I began in a strangled voice, "I once fell in love with an Admiral. He turned me down and I went to the northwest to forget."

Annapolis spoke again: "Ah, my dear lady, you fell in love with the wrong Admiral!"

I have forgotten everything else about that luncheon though I think we had hot biscuits. I'm certain I carried on propaganda, for I always did that. I really hoped he would give me a big donation for medical supplies for the Chinese wounded, but he didn't. I judged men by their willingness to fork out money for the wounded. Those who did I remembered; those who didn't I forgot.

I had much more success with the new British Ambassador, Sir Archibald Clark-Kerr, who arrived in Hankow about that time. When he invited me to dinner, I borrowed a dinner dress from Frances Roots and went, expecting to meet some devil of a British imperialist. He didn't much resemble a devil, but he certainly had the charm of one. He was a lean, brown Scotchman with a keen, tough mind and a scintillating sense of humor. In some ways he reminded me of "Vinegar Joe," Colonel Chennault, and Captain Carlson. I liked such men.

Sir Archibald had invited four other guests to dinner, all men and all members of his staff, one of them a monocled military attaché who had the misfortune to look exactly like an American cartoon of an Englishman. This blasé gentleman said to me: "Chahmed, I'm sure! We met during the Sian Incident, I believe."

"Oh yes," I answered irritably, "you were up there spying on the Red Army."

"And you were spying on me!"

"Naturally!" I answered.

All the other guests maintained a polite silence until Sir Archibald laughed whimsically; then they all laughed whimsically.

The dinner was simple but elegant, with a lot of cutlery and glass, and my borrowed dinner dress made me feel like someone playing a role on a stage. Fortunately there was a war to talk about — though Sir Archibald needed nothing to make him talk. He was interested in guerrilla warfare and the mobilization and training of the common people. At the time I wondered if he was really the militant democrat he seemed or if he was merely a very clever diplomat. Eventually I came to the conclusion that he was a good Scotchman fallen among diplomats.

He began talking about the plan of Industrial Co-operatives of which Rewi Alley, the New Zealand humanitarian, was the originator. Apart from being the father of the co-operatives, Rewi Alley is one of the most truly civilized and tender-hearted of the men who walk this spinning ball of mud. If the Generalissimo and Madame Chiang would accept Alley's plan, Sir Archibald said, a powerful means would have been found to solve China's war-time economy, and the foundation of economic democracy would be laid. Someone spluttered that Rewi Alley seemed to be something of an illusionist chasing a will-o'-the-wisp. Curtly the Ambassador retorted that it might not be a bad idea if some other people would also chase a will-o'-the-wisp.

Sir Archibald soon laid Mr. Alley's plan for co-operatives before Generalissimo and Madame Chiang Kai-shek and pledged British relief funds to its support. It was accepted. Dr. Wong Wen-hao, China's most famous geologist, who was chairman of its National Resources Commission, was also deeply interested in the co-operatives. Mr. Alley therefore gave up his official position in Shanghai, where he had been a factory-inspector, and came up to Hankow to found an economic movement which developed into one of the most momentous in Chinese history.

Sir Archibald Clark-Kerr had far too much charm for any good use. His culture was broad and universal, he dabbled in painting and literature, and had begun to study the Chinese language. A friendship filled with gay humor, further enlivened by sums of money which he gave me for medical supplies, began between us in Hankow and was renewed in strange ways and places in later years. He made one of my New Year celebrations memorable by sending a case of foreign food, cigarettes, and other things to me through the Japanese lines. Like a good Scotchman he enclosed a bottle of old Scotch, some butter, a Christmas pudding, and directions for their preparation. The guerrillas thought the concoction atrocious.

Red Cross Pioneers

Hankow introduced me to the Chinese Red Cross Medical Corps and its famous founder and director, Dr. Lim. Thereafter much of my life was dominated by work for the wounded. It all came about in this way:

Upon arrival in the city, I went in search of a friend, Dr. B. Borcic, the noted Yugoslav public-health specialist who had for years been health adviser from the League of Nations to the Chinese Government. Like many other men of science, he possessed uncommon knowledge and had social and artistic interests far beyond his profession. He had socialist leanings, was deeply interested in music and the stage, and had married an opera singer to whom he was deeply attached. His friendship for me helped make my life bearable during the days of the pre-war Terror.

I found Dr. Borcic living in the Terminus Hotel. He was momentarily expecting two Chinese medical men, Dr. P. Z. King, who later became director of the National Health Administration, and Dr. Robert K. S. Lim, China's most eminent scientist, who had sacrificed his career and perhaps a Nobel Prize to organize Red Cross work in both the Peiping and Shanghai-Nanking areas. Dr. Borcic began telling me that now that Nanking had fallen to the enemy, Dr. Lim was planning to reorganize the Red Cross Medical Corps on entirely new lines. Dr. Lim wanted to create mobile medical units of fifteen men or so and attach them to the various field and base military hospitals of the Army, for there were very few qualified doctors in the Army Medical Administration.

I asked him what had happened to the big Red Cross hospital in Nanking. He stared at the blank wall for a moment and then said quietly: "Wiped out!" Hundreds of severely wounded soldiers who could not be evacuated had been left in Nanking in the care of Chinese doctors and nurses. Chinese and foreigners had still believed that the Japanese would honor international law and the Geneva Red Cross Convention. But when the Japanese Army occupied the city, they not only put to the sword some two hundred thousand civilians and unarmed soldiers, but fell upon the hospitals, slaughtering the wounded, the doctors, and the nurses. The gruesome story of the rape of Nanking was already common knowledge, for a number of diplomatic officials and foreign missionaries had remained in the city and watched the Japanese in action, and even taken photographs of them.

Some seven hundred Chinese Red Cross doctors, nurses, dressers, chauffeurs, and mechanics had reached Hankow; many others had been slaughtered en route. Of the ambulances and trucks which had left Nanking, only seventeen, with half a load of medicine, had reached Hankow.

The mass evacuation of Nanking had resulted in unparalleled disaster. Sometimes it became a fight for life not only against the Japanese, but against the Chinese. One Red Cross chauffeur with a truck of medical supplies had been stopped by a Chinese Army in retreat and ordered to give up his truck. The chauffeur cursed and bellowed; in the midst of the clash Japanese planes began to bomb them. The Army took shelter, but the chauffeur roared happily off toward the west— only to have his truck bombed out from under him a few hours later.

Now the Chinese Red Cross had to begin from scratch. The Soviet Union had sent $100,000 to the Chinese Red Cross board of directors in Shanghai, and Dr. Borcic was trying to get this money for Dr. Lim so that the first mobile medical units could be organized, equipped, and sent into the field.

As Dr. Borcic and I were talking, Dr. King and Dr. Lim entered. Dr. King was a tall, handsome man in a black Chungshan uniform; Dr. Lim was short and slight, and wore a gray cotton Red Cross uniform. Dr. Lim swung a chair around, straddled it, and began puffing at his pipe as he listened to Dr. Borcic report on the Anti-Epidemic Commission. These doctors intended to train masses of men in anti-epidemic work. Along with the National Health Administration and the Army Medical Administration of the Ministry of War, Dr. Lim was also planning to found the first War-time Emergency Medical Training School.

At this conference I first heard the name of another man who, like Dr. Lim, became my friend. He was Dr. Loo Chih-teh, then field inspector of military hospitals at the front but later Surgeon General of the Army Medical Administration. He was helping found the first Emergency Medical Training School. He was one of the gentlest and loveliest characters I have ever known. He had once studied under Dr. Lim in Peiping, then in an American Army medical academy, and finally in England. Like Dr. Lim he never became callous or indifferent to the lot of the wounded. I think it was this quality in them both that made me love them like brothers.

This conference in Dr. Borcic's room was not only historic for me personally, but it was historic for China. In such meetings the foundation for socialized medicine in China was being laid. This involved a vast organization and an educational system to meet the exigencies not only of war, but also of post-war conditions.

After that I began to meet medical men of every kind and soon found myself involved in the old conflict over socialized medicine. For years the leading medical men of China had campaigned for socialized medicine. They had been opposed by missionaries, who had first introduced modern medicine into China and whose hospitals had been powerful bases of Christian endeavor. Socialized medicine would rob these hospitals of their power. In fact, educational and medical progress in China for many years before the war had seriously impaired missionary activity, and many Christians abroad had begun to question the usefulness of missionary activity as a whole.

The war had inadvertently proved to be a kind of godsend to missionary institutions. The large sums of money and medical supplies donated by foreign peoples were controlled by International Red Cross Committees composed of local foreigners, chiefly missionaries, and missions became stations in which countless thousands of civilians found refuge from the Japanese. They were fed and housed, and Christianity was preached to them.

Dr. Lim, Dr. Loo Chih-teh, Dr. P. Z. King, and many other modern Chinese doctors were baptized Christians. But to them China was a battlefield of national liberation, not a battlefield of the Lord. They envisaged a future in which health and medical care would be the right of every Chinese.

I believe this was the basic reason that the Chinese Red Cross Medical Corps received no foreign medical supplies or funds for over two years after its organization.

Dr. Lim himself had a bitter struggle. For years thereafter I heard almost every conceivable charge brought against him by both Chinese and foreigners. One missionary on the International Red Cross Committee of Hankow sourly accused him of liking wine, woman, and song and of being unable to speak Chinese. Another alleged that he used to have all his clothing made in England and his shirts laundered in London. An ambitious Red Cross doctor, anxious to take his place after the Medical Corps became a powerful organization, accused him of dickering in secret with the Studebaker Corporation and of harboring Communists on his staff. I was said to be using the Medical Corps to get medical supplies for the Eighth Route Army.

A lesser man would have left China and gone to England or America where fellow scientists would have welcomed him and given him opportunities commensurate with his abilities. But he was a stubborn man and his patriotism was deeper than that of his detractors. He had given up a great career and an excellent income to accept the chaos of war, a maintenance allowance which did not even enable him to educate his two children, and the slanderous accusations of his inferiors.

Dr. Lim's friends called him "Bobby," and did so as if they loved him. He spoke fluent English with a slight Scotch accent, and through his low, soft voice I heard a warning metallic sound as if his nature was not all gentleness. Almost immediately I felt a quality in him which I later felt in Dr. Loo Chih-teh: it was a *Weltschmerz*, or world pain, which I have since come to associate with men in advance of their time. And the advanced medical men of China are indeed about two or three centuries ahead of the social and political conditions of the country.

Once drawn into the medical world of China, I was soon

floundering in despair at the hopeless lot of the wounded under the backward Army medical system. I shall never cease being grateful to Dr. Lim and Dr. Loo for the patience with which they explained and argued with me, trying to show me China's place in history. For China was and is in much the same state as was America during the War of Independence, and the lot of its wounded is similar to that of the Russian wounded of 1812 as pictured in Tolstoy's *War and Peace*, or the British wounded during the Crimean War when Florence Nightingale appeared on the scene. Not that China did not have a number of self-sacrificing medical men or a great many Florence Nightingales.

Over this problem of the Chinese wounded I used to torture myself through endless nights. Should I write the truth or should I throw a romantic veil over China's heroism? Sometimes I would say to myself: "Listen! If you write the facts, the neat little souls of Americans and Englishmen will be so shocked that they will give no money at all for relief; they will just go to another movie in which Love solves everything."

Then I would answer myself: "Think of the wounded soldiers. Did any government in history ever take one step forward unless under the lash of public criticism? If you soft-soap the Chinese Government, even when it is in difficulty, it will stagnate. Tell the truth, be hounded out of China if necessary. But be loyal to the soldiers who are giving their lives while you give little or nothing."

The pitiful lot of the Chinese wounded was due to the semi-feudal military system and a ruling class made up of venal landlords, merchants, and politicians. Some of these had been progressive men before they had come to power. They were not ignorant or backward about their own self-interest. They had known enough to build model villas — the Japanese now occupied them — which they had equipped with every modern convenience. They had money enough to satisfy every whim. Their sons and daughters studied in American and British universities, and after the war began some families fled to America.

So the ruling class knew well what a modern army medical system should be like. But the Chinese Government still paid each individual army a set sum of money each month, depending on the number in its ranks. With this money, each army was expected to buy its own food and clothing and arrange for its own transport. It was expected to use only *ten cents per man per month* to buy medical supplies. Since medical supplies and equipment had never been standardized, since the chief medical officer was unqualified, and since China had to import almost all its medicine, the medical chief bought what he thought best or what he could get. As the war progressed, he could get little or nothing and prices kept soaring. Only civilian refugees were entitled to foreign medical aid. Chinese soldiers could be wounded by war materials supplied to Japan by America and England, but were not entitled to medical supplies from these countries unless such supplies were bought by the Chinese Government on a purely commercial basis.

There were perhaps a dozen fairly well-qualified doctors in the entire Army Medical Service. But there were 20,000 unqualified men with the rank of medical officers, and 180,000 soldier nurses and attendants. The soldier nurses had been drawn from the Army and put into medical work because they were too weak or incompetent to fight. Their medical knowledge consisted of a few weeks of training in changing dressings. Like many of the medical officers, they did not know the cause or cure of infection and had never seen a splint or a modern sterilizer.

My instinctive reaction was horror and hostility toward the Army medical personnel. I retained this attitude until I saw these men in service at the front, doing whatever they could. They never deserted and they did not regard medical work as a dirty manual labor unworthy of them. Millions of sick and wounded men passed through their hands along the two-thousand-mile front, and if half of these wounded died, at least half lived because of their care.

One step out of this chaos was taken when, at the beginning of the war, the Ministry of War began organizing its own Army Medical Administration and establishing some four hundred dressing stations and field and base hospitals. The individual Army hospitals kept their own superficially ill and wounded, but surrendered the severe cases to these institutions.

After Dr. Loo Chih-teh became Surgeon General of the Army Medical Administration, he and Dr. Robert Lim began to introduce great changes. They began the first standardization of medical supplies that had ever been undertaken in China. They were the chief forces in founding the War-time Emergency Medical Training School in Changsha to retrain the entire Army medical personnel; and they prepared tons of sterilized first-aid dressings, with a morphine tablet enclosed in each, which the unqualified dressers at the front could apply without trouble. In such ways did they fight infection, the great danger at the front.

But their educational work was the most important thing they undertook. Since the Chinese Government refused to conscript educated men for military service, qualified doctors were seldom found in the armies. Thousands of them remained in the port cities or in Japanese-occupied regions, engaged in private practice or in missionary hospitals. Even had the entire ten thousand of them entered the Army, they still could not have solved its problems. So the Medical Training Schools drew batches of hundreds of medical officers from the field and base hospitals and the individual armies, gave them intensive basic training, and ordered them back to the front to start courses for their unqualified personnel.

The Japanese suffered their first great defeat at Taierchwang, north of Hsuchow in May 1938, and the Hankow population poured into the streets, wild with joy. Up to then China had been beaten into the dust, and this one battle, small though it was, inspired the entire nation. I met American military observers from the battlefield who told me that the northern Chinese armies, up to then regarded as feudal and backward, had fought with deathless heroism. One of these armies had been commanded by the same

General Chang Tze-chung who once had been called a traitor. Another was commanded by an old northern General who was so fat that his guards had to push him up a strategic hill. He panted and puffed, but once on top nothing on earth could dislodge him. He just stood there like an infuriated fat Buddha, and only when the retreat of the Chinese armies began did his guards help him down the hill and up another and still another.

At this time I joined the Red Cross Medical Corps as a publicity worker — a glorified name for beggar. The *Manchester Guardian* of England had just arranged for me to work as their special correspondent, sending them two mail articles a week — work which I continued until I left China in 1941. The honorarium they paid me enabled me to work without payment for the Medical Corps and even to make donations. My first articles were on the condition of the wounded and on the endless problems of the Army Medical Service and the Red Cross Medical Corps. I also wrote reports to organizations throughout the world begging for trucks and ambulances, gasoline, medical and surgical supplies.

Then came a day in Changsha when the Medical Corps had just two hundred gallons of gasoline left and no money to buy more. An American oil company had a supply and was anxious to sell it before Japanese bombers destroyed it. At this moment the Scottish Red Cross cabled Dr. Lim £750. He stood staring at the draft, and had he been a sentimental man he might have wept. Instead, he began figuring how much gasoline it would buy. I rushed off to the oil company and arranged the purchase. The oil man incidentally took the trouble to sneer at one of my articles in the *Manchester Guardian*, in which I had charged that by selling war materials to Japan, American and British business men were digging their own graves.

"Why shouldn't we sell to anyone who will pay?" the business man challenged. "We sell to you, don't we? Why not to the Japanese?"

Reprobate that I was, I felt that there was some small difference between the Red Cross Medical Corps and the Japanese war machine. I argued that any nation which permitted buying and selling to determine its foreign policy was heading for disaster. I quoted the *Tanaka Memorial* and advised the business man to read it, murmuring softly: "That is, if you can read."

In June 1938 Hsuchow fell to the enemy and the Chinese armies were in full retreat across all central China, taking up new positions in the great ring of mountain ranges that surrounded the three Hankow cities. The victorious Japanese were in hot pursuit, slaying the Chinese wounded and captured soldiers on the battlefield, wiping out Chinese towns and villages, and filling brothels with Chinese women. To stop them the Chinese blasted the Yellow River dikes, and the flood swept down and halted the Japanese, drowning tens of thousands of them. The Japanese sent up a cry of Chinese barbarity, and official Chinese propagandists began to accuse the Japanese of blowing up the dikes. I considered this foolish, recalling the Dutch, who had once broken their dikes, proudly saying: "Rather give Holland to the sea than to the Spaniards." Indeed, rather give China to the floods than to the Japanese!

The mountain ranges around Hankow became the last great natural barrier protecting central China. A wall of Chinese bodies stood across them, but this wall, after all, was only human flesh. The Japanese blasted their way forward and, to the south of the Yangtze, battered at the gates of Nanchang. If captured, Nanchang would menace not only Hankow, but Changsha.

Our few Red Cross units were shifted to hospitals on the most active fronts, but there was still no money to support them for more than a month or two. Dr. Lim asked me to help him induce wealthy Chinese to be responsible for one or more units for at least a year. Dr. T. V. Soong, who never failed to help every decent movement, "adopted" eleven, and Chinese in Java did likewise. I vainly hoped to induce the American Red Cross to be responsible for others. Once I asked Colonel Stilwell in Hankow to inspect the Emergency Medical Training School in Changsha and help me get money for it. He reviewed our first graduation class of a few hundred student men and women ambulance workers, after which he and Evans Carlson induced the American Consul General to contribute $6,000 (Chinese), all the money left in the American Red Cross funds. All the rest had been given to the International Red Cross Committee and was used to prepare an illusory "safety zone," which eventually kept nearly 400,000 Chinese in that doomed city. The "safety zone" was considered humanitarian, but I considered it nothing but a reservoir of labor for the foreign factories of Hankow and the Japanese war machine. I knew one foreign factory-owner who intended to put his workers in this zone, without cost to himself, and "after Japanese blood-lust had cooled," to put them to work again in a Japanese-controlled city.

In the meantime I continued working for the Medical Corps. Each month the leaders of Red Cross units in the field sent in reports, some of them dry and factual, but some the stuff from which epic dramas are made. One unit on the Kiangsi front told of a field hospital so primitive that when the unit first stopped in the doorway of the hospital, some of the wounded soldiers greeted it with bricks. The wounded hated the title "doctor" and at first accepted treatment sullenly.

For one week the unit labored eighteen hours a day, cleaning, preparing straw mattresses, organizing a nursing and sanitary system, building an operating-room and an operating-table, introducing special diets and, to the amazement of the wounded, baths. Before the week was ended, every wounded man who could hobble around was asking to help. There was not a man who was not humble with gratitude. Never again was a brick hurled at a unit.

The unit next organized training classes for the untrained hospital personnel, and these men were as grateful as the wounded had been. Only ten days had passed when a near-by town suffered a fearful air-raid, and half of the unit went off to care for the victims. Hardly a night passed without the doctors and nurses being called to attend women in labor in a large refugee station near the hospital. Eventually they had to take over the medical care of the station too. For two years this one unit remained in the field without once returning to the rear for a rest.

I went back and forth between Hankow and Changsha, which were filled with tens of thousands of sick and wounded men. Every path leading from the front was an endless line of stretcher-bearers, and of walking wounded and sick, some of whom crawled off beneath the bushes to die. Malaria was decimating the armies, and when Dr. Loo Chih-teh went up to the front, he always loaded his car with all the quinine he could find, halted columns of soldiers, and gave each a dozen tablets. Whole regiments would lie down during attacks, then rise and fight again and again. Telephone communications broke down in some places when the operators got "the shakes."

Every day I saw dust-covered Red Cross trucks and ambulances leave their mangled cargoes at hospitals and heard the drivers tell of the Japanese planes that machine-gunned and bombed Red Cross cars along the highways. Finally no wounded man would ride in any vehicle unless the Red Cross insignia on the roof had been blotted out with mud.

One day in Changsha I saw a Chinese woman doctor, her face gray and desperate, roll in from a front where she had led a unit of women doctors and nurses. They had been bombed out of three hospitals within two weeks and all their supplies and equipment had been destroyed. She had seen one Red Cross truck machine-gunned on the road ahead of her, and even caught a glimpse of the grinning face of the pilot in the cockpit above. By the time night fell, this woman was on her way back to the front with more supplies.

Another time I saw a young Chinese doctor, originally from Trinidad in the West Indies, drive in. He spoke only English, and we called him "Blimy." "Chief," he said to Dr. Lim, "look what the soldiers do to us!"

He produced a photograph which he had taken at the

front. A Red Cross ambulance stood on the road surrounded by hundreds of wounded men standing or lying down. It was loaded and the lightly wounded had clambered onto the roof. Some had even crowded into the chauffeur's seat. The driver was standing in front of them, his arms uplifted, pleading desperately. This was a not uncommon scene. Wounded men would lie down on the highway to prevent the trucks from leaving them behind.

Dr. Lim listened and said: "Poor devils!"

"Chief," Blimy pleaded, "I'm dead tired! I've performed exactly one thousand operations at the front. Can't I take a little rest?"

"I know, laddie," Dr. Lim replied. "But you're young and strong. The soldiers can't stop fighting. Go back, and as soon as possible I'll give you a rest."

Blimy said: "O.K., chief," and returned to the front.

Dr. Loo Chih-teh was then occupied with the organization of rest-feeding stations along all the routes from the front to the rear. He was constructing low bamboo sheds every ten miles and was trying to have young civilian men in each station to change dressings and prepare food for the walking sick and wounded. His plan also embraced civilian refugees, since they were suffering from malnutrition and from them the future soldiers must come. When I heard this plan, I went off immediately to the Chinese Y.M.C.A. in search of a young Christian war-worker, Liu Liang-moh. Mr. Liu listened and then returned with me to Red Cross headquarters. Within a week he and a group of young Y.M.C.A. men and women had taken over many stations on the route to the front.

I delivered to Liu Liang-moh many huge crates of prunes and raisins which had arrived from America. These had been nine months on the way and half of them were spoiled. The flat roof of the Y.M.C.A. was soon blanketed with prunes drying in the sun. I opened some cases myself and spent days throwing out the rotten fruit. To save the good ones, I conceived the idea of drying them in three portable delousing stations in Red Cross headquarters. When I had triumphantly finished this task, a young doctor came storming into our office one day, shouting:

"Three of our delousing stations are ruined! The holes in the metal trays are clogged with something sticky!"

"I deloused prunes in them for the rest-feeding stations of Dr. Loo," I explained.

"You deloused prunes!"

"Yes, sir," I admitted feebly.

But when the Y.M.C.A. workers rolled off to the front, their Red Cross trucks were stacked with cases of dried fruit for the sick and wounded, and gay banners nailed to the sides of the trucks announced that these were "comfort gifts from America to our national heroes."

Changsha was a vast military hospital packed with masses of wounded lying under every conceivable kind of shelter. Tens of thousands were without any but the most rudimentary care, for all but three Red Cross units were at the front. Boats, carts, and trucks began evacuating thousands from Changsha to make room for those pouring in. From Hankow alone forty thousand wounded were evacuated to the west in the last weeks before the city fell.

In the middle summer months, when the Yangtze Valley steamed with heat, the Red Cross Medical Corps gained one of its most valuable foreign volunteers. This was an English woman, Mrs. Hilda Selwyn-Clarke, wife of the Medical Director of the Hong Kong Government. We had long carried on a friendly correspondence; finally she came to Hankow by plane. She was a handsome woman with flaming chestnut hair and liquid brown eyes. Her husband's position in the Hong Kong Government gave her prestige and authority and to this she added a tremendous organizing ability gained in the labor movement of England. Her horror at conditions in the Chinese hospitals generated in her, not hostility, but an iron determination to use all her ability and influence on behalf of China.

She flew back to Hong Kong and founded the Foreign Auxiliary of the Chinese Red Cross which became the Hong

Kong agency for the Red Cross Medical Corps. She built up a network of international aid, and organized an intricate system for getting medical transport through the Japanese lines. She turned Chinese refugee stations in Hong Kong into centers of Red Cross activity where women and girls rolled bandages and made sheets and surgical aprons. She stood at her post until Hong Kong was attacked and then took her place among the medical workers defending Hong Kong to the last.

When the fate of Hankow was sealed, Dr. Lim welcomed my suggestion for evacuating educated youth from Hankow and recruiting them for the Red Cross Medical Corps. He placed me in charge of this — a charge which, like everything else in China, seemed filled with almost insoluble problems.

One report which I made at this time covered a conference I had with the American Consul General in which I had submitted a six-point program for American Red Cross aid to China. The first point asked for a liaison officer of the American Red Cross to be stationed in China to supervise American aid. Another asked that the American Red Cross supply trucks and gasoline and support seventeen mobile Chinese Red Cross medical units at the front. My report concluded:

"The American Consul-General considers these proposals very good and, following his suggestion, I am sending one copy to the American Red Cross in Washington D.C., and another to the new American Bureau for Medical Aid to China. American newspaper correspondents are supporting this plan."

The Vice-chairman of the American Red Cross in Washington eventually answered my six-point proposal with a letter which concluded with these words:

"The data you present is most interesting and appealing and we are, of course, sympathetic with the efforts you are making to bring relief to the wounded. However, the funds which the American Advisory Committee is handling were raised specifically for civilian relief, as you will note in the enclosed letter. . . ."

The Yangtze rose higher and higher and Hankow became a city of merciless contrasts. Patriots exploited all the resources of their being in defense of their country, while traitors bided their time, banqueting and whoring until they could form a puppet government for the enemy. The German military advisers were ordered home by Hitler, who acted on demands from the Japanese, and foreign embassies began to watch with eagle eyes to see if Soviet military advisers would take their places. Everyone began to spy on everyone else. A group of White Russians working for the Japanese were arrested; then they were permitted to leave for Hong Kong. The Italian Consulate was known to be in radio communication with the Japanese, and the chief of the Nazi Gestapo, posing as a free-lance journalist, came regularly from Shanghai, sat in on all press conferences, and interviewed officers.

Madame Chiang Kai-shek and her women followers were gathering thousands of war orphans from the war zone. One day I went into their headquarters just as another train-load of these ragged, lice-ridden, half-starved children were being brought in. Dozens of women were shaving their heads, bathing and feeding them, and dressing them in fresh blue denim overalls. Long lines of these little tots were then marched through the streets to waiting boats or junks which transported them to the west.

By order of Generalissimo Chiang, factories were being dismantled and carried or shipped to the rear, and Madame Chiang organized thousands of factory workers and their families for evacuation. Making use of these workers, Rewi Alley, the New Zealander, along with Chinese engineer colleagues, began building industrial co-operatives.

The aid-raids were a physical horror and, to me at least, a spiritual humiliation. Every day and every moonlit night we would hear the dreadful wail of sirens. Then the city would begin to drum with the sound of the feet of thousands trying to reach the two foreign concessions. Foreign banks, hotels, and business houses barred their doors lest the Chinese take refuge in them, dirty the floors, or perhaps steal something. The two or three great foreign warehouses which had been prepared by foreign firms as air-raid shelters were soon packed. Other thousands of Chinese men, women, and little children lay down against the cement walls or prostrated themselves along the river bank. I lived in a small foreign hotel in the French Concession which had broad halls and an enclosed garden; but the owner closed the steel gates and turned deaf ears to the pleas of Chinese mothers with babies in their arms. Even the Chinese coolie who pulled the landlady's ricksha was not permitted into the building. With his wife hovering near and his baby in his arms, he would cower beneath his pitiful ricksha.

I was often caught in the Chinese city, and would rush back to the foreign concession. Seeking shelter, I would go up to the door of some foreign bank. The men inside would open to me, but not to a Chinese.

After each raid the city was full of the mangled bodies of victims; sometimes I worked in a Chinese railway hospital where hundreds lay on the floors bleeding to death. People died under our hands. I found myself growing coldly impersonal — selecting soldiers and workers who had only minor injuries and could be most quickly restored to fighting condition.

Through the streets of the doomed city marched endless lines of grave-eyed soldiers. They were moving into the mountains to the east and north, where every town and village was a heap of ruins and the hills were strewn with the bodies of the unburied dead. Boats and junks tied up to the bund each day, and on their decks maimed men lay in their own blood and excrement — without a soul to care for them. Columns of the walking wounded made their slow, painful way through the streets in search of some designated hospital. They would walk a block or two, then sit or lie down on the pavements until able to go farther. Crowds pouring from moving-picture theaters would pass, some hardly glancing at the prostrate figures. Day after day I watched the theater crowds, and not one among them ever halted and offered to help.

Time and again I would commandeer rickshas and load them with the wounded, then storm into the office of the Surgeon General of the Army Medical Administration. In answer to my protests the old Surgeon General would throw up his hands and reply:

"I have no power. I can only obey orders from above; I can initiate nothing! I wish the Generalissimo would court-martial and shoot me! As it is, all I get is kicks. The only consolation I have is that I am being kicked by my countrymen instead of by the enemy!"

I had done my part in attempts to induce foreign medical volunteers to come to China and work under the same conditions and at the same pay as the Chinese. When the war began, Mao Tze-tung and I had appealed to Americans to send surgeons to the Eighth Route Army. Before I left the northwestern front, Chu Teh and I wrote to the Indian National Congress, asking it to send qualified doctors to serve all the Chinese armies.

A group of three medical workers came from America, including the well-known Canadian, Dr. Norman Bethune. We had to ask one to leave the country because he was drunk all the time. After many delays, Dr. Bethune, along with Dr. Richard Brown, a missionary volunteer, left for Wutaishan. In December 1939, just before his planned return to America, Dr. Bethune died of septicemia.

In the late summer before Hankow fell, the first group of five Indian surgeons, all members of the Indian National Congress, arrived in Hankow and joined the Red Cross Medical Corps. They were asked by the British Consul General to join the International Red Cross Committee instead. The Consul General explained that in this way they would always be kept supplied with anything they might need and would work in well-equipped missionary hospitals. As an additional inducement he told them that in case of capture by the Japanese, they would not — like the Chinese — be killed, for the Committee had reached an agreement to this effect with the Japanese. To these arguments Dr. Atal, leader of the Indian Medical Mission, replied: "All you say proves that our place is with the Chinese."

After serving in the military hospitals of Hankow, the Indian doctors evacuated with units of the Medical Corps to the west. In Chungking they met and talked with Generalissimo and Madame Chiang and other leaders, then left for the Eighth Route Army; two of them are still in charge of medical work among flying guerrilla columns in north China.

Jawaharlal Nehru was primarily responsible for the Medical Mission to China. When he formed the first China Medical Committee of the Indian National Congress, hundreds of men and women doctors and nurses registered as volunteers for China. The Congress had enough money to finance, equip, and supply only five men in its initial group. It had already initiated "China days" and called for the boycott of Japanese goods throughout India.

Since I was in charge of this Indian group, and kept the Congress informed of the progress of the war and of China's needs, I was able to see the sharp lines that divided the Indians from other foreign doctors. They were as political in outlook as they were scientific in training, and they came not only to serve the Chinese wounded, but to study a kind of warfare which they might one day be forced to use in India. They were not only Indian nationalists, but anti-Fascists with a strong socialist bent. They regarded every action of the British with suspicion, and repeatedly warned the Chinese that the British might betray them at any moment.

The only similarity between the Indians and other foreign doctors was their horror at conditions in military hospitals. They had been trained in Indian medical institutions, where their every need had been met, and as men of the middle class they had been accustomed to comfort, servants, and hospital attendants. They soon learned to accept the primitive conditions of China, though the older men returned to India after two years, leaving the younger ones to merge themselves completely with China's war of liberation.

The End of Hankow

THERE was not an hour of any day or night that death and destitution were not about us in Hankow — death in the ugly form of sickness and mangled bodies; and destitution so deep that life itself sometimes seemed a kind of disease. Over and beyond this death agony of a city hovered the supreme heroism of the armies — cast in high relief by treason in high places. Down in Shanghai the British Ambassador once told the Japanese that only the riff-raff of China would help them build their puppet "Central Government." The Japanese coolly answered that they were dealing with some of the highest officials in the Chinese Government — and mentioned the name of Wang Ching-wei.

Out of this confusion of death and life there began to grow the most unusual friendships I had ever known. Our small group of foreign correspondents who were friends of China, along with consular and military men of similar minds, and a few Chinese, drew close to each other, searching each other's hearts and minds for the best way of life for all humanity. Our old values seemed to vanish and we lost regard for material things, for no one knew whether there would be a tomorrow. We were like passengers on a ship foundering in a stormy sea who at last had found their humanity and clung to each other with that love that "passeth all understanding." In the tense atmosphere of war even poetry, song, and wit blossomed among us and a magical glow shone over our friendship.

Members of this group kept departing or returning from all fronts, and each reunion was a cause for celebration. We all worked without regard for time, and day and night became one to us. Often, when unable to endure my thoughts after going through an air-raid or seeing the endless lines of wounded soldiers pouring through the city, I would go at any hour to seek the comfort of these friends. Two or three of us would stand beneath the dark window of another friend of ours and clap. A sleepy head would be thrust out to ask: "What's up?" And we would call: "Conversation. Come down." Our friend would wrap a bathrobe around him and come down to sit in a garden and talk of things that seemed portentous.

Almost all foreign wives and children, and the wives and children of Chinese officials and the well-to-do, had been evacuated from Hankow. An occasional American woman, well groomed and wearing a hat, would arrive to write feature articles about women — it was amazing that American women had not advanced beyond that stage. A few serious foreign writers flew in and out in the course of gathering information: Edgar A. Mowrer and Vernon Bartlett from England, John and Frances Gunther from southeast Asia, and Edgar Snow from the Philippines. An English woman who had formerly worked for Spain arrived and became very indignant because a crowd had not met her at the airdrome. She insisted on emergency airplane reservations in case she should want to leave Hankow at a moment's notice, because, she explained to me, she was too important to be killed in China. Both then as before and later many freebooters in the journalistic and camera world arrived and used the China war as a background for their own personal glory. They were as filled with physical energy and as empty of ethics or social consciousness as, let us say, an American steel or oil magnate busily making a fortune by supplying Japan with war materials.

The Germans and Italians in Hankow flocked together. It was common knowledge not only that German correspondents were connected with the Gestapo, but that they exchanged information with the Japanese. The new Italian Ambassador to China did not even trouble to appear in Hankow or Chungking, but spent his time with the Japanese and their puppets along the coast, in Japan or in "Manchukuo." The French were a race apart, weak, degenerate, cynical; and their cruel and corrupt administration of Indo-China was a shocking byword in the Far East. A perfect representative of the decadent section of the British ruling class was one Gunboat Patrol officer whom I knew. He painted weak watercolors — of which he was very proud — talked sex, and was always exceedingly well preserved in alcohol. He once told me of his well-greased pathway through life from his little velvet-suit and golden-ringlet years through an expensive public school, until he landed, without any effort whatever, in the naval command. He had never had a struggle in his life, least of all with a thought. I asked him if he had not been bored stiff, but he insisted that he had found life delightful. When the Japanese occupied an important Chinese city, he did not resist, but in his best old-school-tie manner smilingly surrendered the British Concession to them.

The foreigners of Hankow had induced many Chinese and a few foreigners to pay for huge wooden gates leading into the former British Concession "to keep out the Japanese"! Shortly after the British Concession had been turned over to the Japanese, I heard Captain Stennes, an ex-Nazi and the chief of Generalissimo's Chiang's bodyguard, exclaim: "The British Empire is finished!"

The missionaries had their own pious circles. Though the Lutheran Guest House, which housed foreign correspondents and Red Cross workers, refused to rent me a room — saying I was immoral — I was often intimately involved with them because of their medical and relief work. The younger missionaries were progressive and divinely discontented, and some of them often in conflict with their elders. Such young people did not look on China merely as a "heathen land to be converted," but sympathized with it. However, I believe I have never, anywhere or in any profession, met more viciously reactionary or bigoted men than among some of the elderly foreign missionaries. Many of them supported Generalissimo and Madame Chiang Kai-shek for no other reason than that they were Christians through whom missionaries might eventually convert all China. Think of a church in each Chinese village, with jobs for every foreign and Chinese pastor and their families, and not an atheist in sight to keep alive a little spiritual integrity! I heard serious-minded foreign newspaper correspondents call one sinister, ambitious missionary the "Father Rasputin of China."

The attitude of Chinese and foreign Christians toward Pearl Buck was an interesting one. Among them she was noted not only for her books on China but because she had left her church, divorced a husband, and married a second time. As many political parties often attack former members, so the missionaries looked askance on Pearl Buck. They hinted that she would deteriorate, and when she obviously did not, they were much put out.

Many Chinese disliked Pearl Buck's books because she did not always show her characters dressed in their Sunday best. A Chinese colonel once announced to a friend of mine that Pearl Buck was "finished" because she wrote an article about the Eighth Route Army, calling it "Guns for China's Democracy." She was henceforth isolated from China, he declared, washed up. What nonsense! Such were the rumors that hateful people spread about Pearl Buck.

Like the moon that turned night into day and enabled the Japanese planes to bomb sleeping populations; like Wang Ching-wei, who negotiated with the approaching enemy; so did the Yangtze River turn traitor to the land of its birth. The mighty river rose higher and higher and enemy vessels of war blasted their way toward Hankow, preparing the way for their land troops.

In late September the National Military Council issued orders for the evacuation of Hankow. In the second week of October I left with Dr. Robert Lim and a woman Red Cross doctor, and five of us set up cots in Dr. Lim's small house in Changsha. After the fall of Hankow would come the fight for Changsha.

When the last Chinese trucks had left Hankow, Chinese

troops began blowing up the roads and bridges connecting that city with Changsha. As the last Chinese military groups left, they set off dynamite charges in all buildings in the old Japanese Concession. The city roared and trembled. The Chinese also planned to blast Japanese-owned buildings in other parts of the city, but foreigners went through and cut the fuses, determined to protect their property to the last. After all, China was not their country.

Every night we left our Red Cross headquarters in Changsha and reached home in time to hear the news broadcasts from Hong Kong. When Canton fell without a struggle in the middle of October, it was like a drink of bitter gall to the Chinese. On the night of October 25 we hovered around the radio and heard a voice say:

"Hankow fell to the Japanese today. Japanese warships anchored in the river. The Italian Consul General waited on the bund, and when the first naval officers landed, he shook hands and congratulated them on their victory. As Japanese troops marched through the city, White Russian and other dancing girls on Dump Street distributed cigarettes to them. Japanese soldiers began rounding up groups of Chinese, driving them before them to the river banks, where they pushed them in with their rifles and then shot those who struggled. . . ."

The voice went on and on, finally fading away. Dr. Lim was bending over the radio, his back to me, and from this position he did not move. As if turned to stone, Dr. Loo Chih-teh stood before the open window, staring into the night. On either side of me were two women doctors, Jean Chiang and Eva Ho Tung, their eyes fixed on the radio. There was an interminable silence in which I could almost hear the universe tick.

"What now?" Eva Ho Tung asked bitterly.

Slowly Dr. Lim straightened up and without turning, answered: "We will continue to fight. Our Army is not broken."

The silence lapped about us again. Then from the night I seemed to feel some approaching menace, but before I could speak, the long mournful wail of the air-raid siren sounded, sickening me. The lights went out, and through the darkness we heard the roar of the awakened city and the humming of trucks and cars rushing into the country. All of us went out on the veranda and stood with our hands on the railing, our faces turned in the direction of the throbbing menace.

We heard the planes circle, as if searching.

"They can find nothing," Dr. Lim said in a low voice.

Time and again they roared nearer, then faded away. We went to our rooms and lay talking until dawn, then rose and went to work again.

The Struggle Continues

THE AMBULANCE truck of the New Fourth Army, on which eight persons including myself were traveling, ground to an abrupt stop. We leaped out and fled into the hills, and as we fled, the droning black specks in the pallid eastern sky grew into roaring monsters. The Japanese pilots deliberately flew low, as if scoffing at us, mocking our impotence.

In how many ditches of China had I not prostrated myself before the god of Japanese imperialism — and American greed! Numberless air-raids had taught me no bravery. Each deathlike wail of a siren, each beating gong from a hillside, clanging bell, or staccato warning of a bugle, caused my heart to constrict.

Again the planes. But this time they droned on toward Changsha. It was October 29, 1938, and I was on my way to the enemy rear along the lower Yangtze. After Canton and Hankow had fallen, Generalissimo Chiang Kai-shek had called to all Chinese in the enemy rear to fight with every means in their power. The Japanese lines were now drawn out long and thin along the main routes of communication, and on their flanks and in their rear was a vast territory still in Chinese hands.

I had urged Dr. Lim to send medical workers and supplies to the enemy rear, but he had replied that we knew nothing of conditions there, nor whether medical units could function and be kept supplied. I therefore made arrangements to make a tour of investigation, combining my work for the *Manchester Guardian* with that of the Red Cross, to which I would send reports.

The highway along which we traveled eastward was in the active zone. Divisions of khaki-clad soldiers marched rapidly toward Nanchang, and groups of wounded poured in from the battlefield along the southern banks of the Yangtze. Armed sentries guarded the approaches to every town and village.

At the end of the first day we halted in a small village and put up at a primitive wayside inn. After a night made sleepless by mosquitoes and bedbugs, I rose at dawn and went outside to find a group of thirty wounded soldiers sitting or lying by the roadside. They had just come out of the no man's land along the Yangtze — a strip of territory fifty to one hundred miles in depth on both sides of the great river. There the Chinese armies were destroying all roads and paths that could be used by Japanese mechanized equipment. Chinese still fought there, but the walking wounded could not pass through in less than two weeks.

The thirty wounded soldiers were gaunt and weary, their wounds infected, their uniforms threadbare and faded from months of exposure. Some were barefoot, and their arms, legs, and feet were bound with bloody, dirty bandages which had not been changed for days. Since they had not yet entered a hospital, they had not received their ten-dollar wound bonus and only a few possessed enough money to buy even roasted chestnuts. Those able to hobble about were carrying cups of boiled water to their weaker comrades.

I hauled out some of the sterilized dressings and a case of supplies from our ambulance. Both the ambulance and the truck were loaded with supplies which I had collected for the New Fourth Army, the chief guerrilla army in the rear of the enemy along the lower Yangtze. To the Red Cross and people's contributions, I had added bales of face-towels, bolts of bandage cloth and gauze, and, out of my own funds, cases of soap and quinine. With the help of my secretary I set up a wayside dressing station and began caring for the thirty wounded soldiers.

At another point our engine balked and we halted near a small mud hut while the chauffeur tinkered with it. As usual, civilians gathered, asking for quinine. Malaria was a scourge affecting everyone. An old man came out and looked at our ambulance with its big Red Cross insignia and the inscription which announced that it came from the "Chinese Laundrymen's Union, Boston, Massachusetts, U.S.A."

"My daughter is very sick," the old man said humbly. "Can you give me medicine?"

I took my first-aid kit and went into the hut. It had two small, dark rooms; the only light came from the door. There was a board bed across trestles in each room, and in one there was also a crude, unpainted table and benches. In a corner was a small clay stove and three or four cooking pots. A few primitive agricultural implements stood against the mud wall.

In the inner room lay a girl under a pile of ragged padded quilts. After I had administered quinine and instructed the girl's old mother in its use, the aged couple placed a few peanuts and a tea-bowl of hot water before my secretary and me.

Around the head of the old lady was a cotton cloth draped like a bonnet and dyed with native herbs in a sort of batik pattern, and on her feet were colorful woven sandals. The peasants of Kiangsi, like those of Szechuen and Yunnan, have preserved a folk-art which sprouts even in the direst poverty. I recalled the beautiful sandals woven by the soldiers of the Eighth Route Army and wondered if any sons of this family were with that Army.

Through the open door I could see one of the many blockhouses which dotted the mountain tops or guarded the highways approaching all large towns. Relics of a decade of civil war and a fear of revolution, these forts were designed by the German General von Seeckt when he was chief military adviser to the Chinese Government. They were utterly useless against the Japanese, but if the enemy should capture them, they could be used against the badly equipped Chinese.

At last I was able to ask the old peasant couple if they had any sons.

"Four. Two are fighting in the Army." The old man waved a hand in the general direction of the Yangtze.

"And the other two?" I asked.

"We do not know," the old man answered after a pause.

I sipped the hot water and thought of this family, gutted of all its sons. . . . When the sons of the poor have saved China, the rich will return, I thought.

Nanchang was a city tensed like a bow string against the enemy. The Canton Army still stood at Tehan to the northwest, where it had fought for months. Each night heavily laden ammunition trucks groaned up toward the front and battalions of stretcher-bearers began bringing in the wounded. Four thousand wounded a week were pouring through the nine receiving stations of Nanchang. The severe cases were sorted out and carried to the field and base hospitals in the city or to the rear.

On the night of our arrival we found the city decorated brilliantly, and columns of singing soldiers, their weapons clanking, marching with fierce, measured tread: the city was celebrating the birthday of Generalissimo Chiang, who had just arrived for a military conference. But since the tentacles of the Japanese secret service reached everywhere, we had also arrived in time for devastating air-raids. In the two days and nights we remained in the city, Nanchang rocked with bombs that spared nothing. Each time we emerged we picked up chunks of bomb fragments which lay scattered about the courtyard and the frail dugout in which we had all taken shelter.

On the night of our arrival I crossed the street from the local office of the New Fourth Army where we were staying and, unannounced, entered one of the largest receiving stations for the wounded. I expected to find the usual cruelly primitive institution, but found instead one which heralded the dawn of a new spirit.

The halls of the four-storied building were spotless, and the walls were decorated with colorful posters, banners, and wall newspapers. Across one wall hung a red and white banner which read: *Millions of hearts with one mind.*

The building sheltered eight hundred wounded, each with a board bed, a mattress of rice straw, a pillow, sheet, padded quilt, and mosquito net. Watchful male nurses moved along the aisles.

Wandering unattended, we heard distant music and went toward it. In the middle of a huge ward sat two poorly dressed women folk-singers and a man with a Chinese violin such as one often heard in tea-houses. One of the women stared vacantly before her, pouring out her soul in some old song, and as we drew near we saw that she was blind. Some of the wounded were propped up, their eyes fixed in space; and so absorbed were they all that not one noticed our approach.

We wandered farther and came to a ward in which many men with minor wounds sat on the edge of their beds or walked about, talking and laughing with uniformed students. One of the students approached us and, speaking in English, introduced his group as a branch of the Kiangsi Anti-Enemy War Service Association, which, he explained, worked in the hospitals.

The superintendent of the receiving station found me some time around midnight, welcomed me enthusiastically, and began to explain his work. While we talked, the first lot of wounded arrived from the front. Members of the War-Time Service Corps welcomed the wounded as heroes and gave each new arrival a small cloth bag containing face-towel, soap, fruit, and cigarettes, talked with him, and offered to help in writing letters.

The following day, as soon as another dreadful air-raid was over, I went through smoking streets to the 109th Base

Hospital, where a Red Cross medical unit worked. The building had formerly been a school. Over the entrance stretched a long painting of men of every class marching in one direction. Beneath were the Chinese words: *Follow in the bloody footsteps of our martyrs. Avenge the death of our people.*

The Chinese, as I had long since learned, put their hearts into such slogans.

The hospital was organized much like the receiving station, and the same people's organization worked in it. Dr. Liu, the young superintendent, introduced two volunteers: an elderly woman and her eighteen-year-old daughter, both of them pious Christians. They purchased and directed the preparation and serving of food. At meal times they went from ward to ward, bending gently over beds to ask soldiers if the food was satisfactory. An atmosphere of kindliness and warmth permeated the hospital.

Dr. Liu told me that just as the last air-raid had begun, the Red Cross surgical unit had been performing a major operation, and even when the bombs fell about the building, they had not faltered. We donned white aprons and caps and entered the operating-room. A wounded man lay on the table, and at his head sat an American doctor administering an anesthetic. Over the wounded man bent the frail body of a Chinese woman surgeon, amputating a leg. Until they had finished, neither she nor her associates looked up; when she took off her mouth-mask, I saw that she was Dr. Ma, head of a volunteer unit of Chinese medical workers from Hong Kong. Dr. Ashland, another physician, was the only American volunteer in the Medical Corps. Without any fanfare he had arrived three months before, joined up, and left immediately for this front.

The doctors and nurses prepared rapidly for another operation. A young soldier was brought in on a stretcher. I bent over him and saw that blood was gushing from his mouth. His eyes, filled with the consciousness of death, looked up into mine.

As I left the hospital, I halted at the entrance, intending

to tell Dr. Liu what I felt about his hospital. No words came. I felt his hand tighten over mine and I lifted my other hand and placed it over his.

Two days later our party was whirling eastward again. Our truck and ambulance rolled nearer and nearer to one of the active Yangtze battlefields, and the highway became an endless procession of fresh troops moving up and exhausted troops retiring. We spent the next night in the ancient town of Kingtehchen, famous for its pottery for nearly a thousand years. Martial law ruled the town, for the front was just over the mountain ranges to the north, and agents of the Japanese, clad as monks, beggars, refugees, or business men, crawled through the country.

After the wounded in the poor local hospital, what interested me most in Kingtehchen were labor and social conditions, and of these the few owners and master potters of the great potteries who remained in the town spoke freely. They seemed utterly unconscious of the feudal nature of their industry. Little boys of seven or eight, they explained, were apprenticed to master potters, who housed and fed them. The owners paid the apprentices one dollar a month, through the master potter, who kept twenty cents of each dollar as "compensation for teaching the craft." With the remaining eighty cents the apprentice tried to meet all his needs.

A master potter might have ten to fifteen apprentices, who remained *jhay tso* — "confined by a belt" — until their families bought their freedom and they became master potters. Many boys remained *jhay tso* for ten or more years, and we talked with young men in their twenties who had mastered the craft years before but had not yet been able to buy their freedom. They could mold about two hundred pieces of pottery a day. The products of their labor were sold by the master potter to the firm.

Though the apprentices were a source of income to the master potter, it was not he who accumulated wealth. One master potter told us that in good years he had been able to earn eight hundred Chinese dollars a year, but since the war only twenty. It was the owner of the kilns who grew rich. The owner explained enthusiastically that, before the war, pottery was the most profitable investment in the country. He had a friend who had come from the north with only $2,000, but at the end of two years was able to show a profit of $200,000.

If an apprentice had a family, they might accumulate enough money, or secure a loan from a money-lender, which they would present to the master potter as a "gift." If it was accepted they gave a feast to the master, and the apprentice was at last freed. Free potters told us the greatest amount they could earn in a month was twelve dollars, but the usual wage was six.

I asked the owner of a number of kilns, whose finished products were displayed in a big shop, about the health of the apprentices. With something like amused pride, he explained that apprentices had almost every kind of disease — tuberculosis, malaria, and a variety of interesting intestinal diseases. They had no money to buy medicine, he added. As if displaying a choice exhibit, he called a young boy of ten and asked us to note how green the boy was from malaria. But even when sick, he concluded, the master potters, out of the goodness of their hearts, still fed them.

As we went through the plants, my mind swarmed with memories. During the early years of the civil wars, I recalled, the Chinese Red Army had occupied Kingtehchen. The Shanghai press had shrieked that the Communists had totally destroyed the famous Kingtehchen pottery works. Later I met one of the Red Army commanders, himself a former potter in Kingtehchen, who had taken part in the occupation.

The Red Army had many potters in its ranks, he said. Instead of destroying the kilns, it had allowed the owners to operate their kilns, but with many changes. The years of apprenticeship had been shortened, and during them both apprentices and master potters received regular wages from the owners. Joint committees of owners and potters managed the industry, and inspectors enforced the reforms. This system continued until the Red Army was driven out. The feudal system was then reinstated.

Before and after the Red Army occupation, potters and their families had small family shrines in their dark, unsanitary homes. Painted on the wall above each shrine was a mystic drawing, representing the spirit of the Red Army. In front of this the potters bowed in worship and burned incense.

Despite its feudalism, it was terrible to think of Kingtehchen falling into the hands of the Japanese. Here had lingered a precious cultural heritage. Here had been preserved the forms and designs of ancient China, some as delicate as moonlight shadows through a tree, and here was a rich, gorgeous folk-art drawn from all the mottled coloring of nature.

Leaving Kingtehchen, we sped onward to the east, up mountain ranges rich in autumn colors, alongside clear rivers and plunging waterfalls. Clouds floated past us in ghostly drifts. In the late afternoon we rolled down into ancient Kimen, home of the famous black tea of China.

BOOK VI

In Guerrilla Land

1938 — 1939

BOOK VI: IN GUERRILLA LAND

1938 ⁓ 1939

New Land

By November 9, 1939 I had entered the fringe of the guerrilla region along the southern shores of the lower Yangtze. A party of some twenty of us, including many students from Shanghai and printers and students from Hankow, floated on bamboo rafts down a river approaching the Yangtze. Shrouded by morning mists, the forests on the mountains on either side of us were dim and mysterious with shadows. Feathery bamboos waved ghostly arms, then vanished in the shifting mist, and melancholy oaks hung sadly over the stream as if gazing at their ancient reflections and sighing.

The scene might have been the first morning on earth. As the sun rose higher and higher, it drew the mists after it, the river glistened with joy and the mountains became a tangled mass of autumn magnificence. Tea plants stood in regimented columns, and small villages nestled behind fishermen's nets spangled with morning dew. Once we passed a white primary-school building, across the face of which were painted the words: *Down with dead education! Long live life education!* The rafts broke into cheers.

Narrow paths wound along the mountain sides, and a platoon of New Fourth Army guerrillas, our bodyguards, marched jauntily along them, shouting across the river to one another or to the soldiers who sat on the prow of each raft with rifles ready. No one in our party understood the guerrillas, for they spoke the Fukien dialect. Once I asked a man sitting on the raft behind me what they were singing. He told me it was the *Guerrilla Marching Song*, celebrating their comrades, the flying troops who "feared neither towering mountains nor deep waters." They sang that they had no food, no clothing, and no guns, but that they would capture these from the enemy. And when this song was finished they sang the *Youth Marching Song,* comparing China to a broken, storm-tossed boat which could be rescued only by its youth. Sometimes their voices would rise into a long-drawn out "Hai-h-h-h-h!"

The party on the rafts shouted and laughed. They were students, young and effervescent, some of them more revolutionary than the revolutionaries. Their gaiety made me feel old. I was weary from labor, strain, and conflict, and I had visited, as they had not, all the military hospitals on our route. Before my mind's eye moved an endless procession of soldiers bound for the front, endless lines returning wounded, and tens of thousands lying in primitive hospitals staffed by men incapable of carrying out the tasks imposed upon them by the war.

There was the field hospital in Taiping which I had visited the day before. Nearly a thousand men of the Fiftieth Army lay there, and among them a peasant boy of eight who had been shot by the enemy while guiding a Chinese column over the mountain paths near his village. He lay on his bed, playing with a paper bird and a kite which the soldiers had made for him. Dark memories harassed me and I dreaded traveling farther.

As we floated down the river, the first enemy bombers came over, following the stream up to Taiping. Again dread congealed my blood. Our boatmen thrust their poles deep into the river bottom and we came to a dead stop, waiting, wondering if the enemy might consider us worthy of their bombs. But they droned past.

When the river grew shallow, we landed and walked through sunny villages in fertile valleys. The lower Yangtze is a land rich in rice, tea, cotton, vegetables, silk, and, at this point, forests. On the higher mountain terraces wheat had been planted in beds, like vegetables, and each row was cultivated tenderly.

We halted to gaze through open doors where long bundles of straw hung from rafters; in the bundles silkworms were spinning their cocoons. On the earthen floors lay heaps of wax-tree branches which were rich with white beans bursting from their pods and which would soon be transformed into candles.

The land was rich, but the peasants poor. Stagnant, green slime bubbled in open gutters. The shadow of a decaying landlord-merchant economy hovered over the land.

From a dark interior came a woman's voice, raised in an ancient song of sorrow, connected with the building of the Great Wall. It was the softest of folk melodies. Three days before, a servant in an inn on the Yellow Mountain had taught me how to play it on his flat-stringed harp. New words had been composed for it, and it was now called the *Anti-Japanese Seasonal Song*. The first line of each stanza spoke of a season of the changing year, and then the lines that followed struck home with militant pledges of undying resistance to the foe.

Darkness found us again on the river. As we turned a bend, the soldier at the head of our raft gave the long weird cry of a night bird. A bugle answered. Then we heard the mingled sound of many voices and saw the flare of pine torches casting into relief a surging mass of military caps, faces, and shoulders. A tremendous shout of *"Hwang yin! Hwang yin!"* (Welcome! Welcome!) came from the shore. The cries blended with the *Volunteer's Marching Song*. I saw the slight figure of Dr. C. C. Sheng, Director of the Medical Service of the New Fourth Army, climbing over junks. I had met him in Hankow and had helped him collect money and medical supplies. As we stepped ashore, a path was cleared through the singing crowd and we were escorted to the Rear Base Hospital of the New Fourth Army.

Instead of the dark, dreary institutions which I had expected, the New Fourth Army had the beginnings of the first modern medical service of any Chinese army. The Rear Base Hospital for the severely wounded, like the field hospital near general headquarters some twenty-five miles nearer the Yangtze, had a system modeled on the best Western hospitals. Whenever medical workers and supplies permitted, the system was being extended to the fighting detachments in the field.

This medical service was the achievement of General Yeh Ting, commander of the New Fourth Army. He, along with Dr. Sheng, had first induced eleven qualified doctors and twenty trained nurses to join the Army. Finding it increasingly difficult to get more, they hoped to found a medical training school to train hundreds of educated youth as sanitary workers for the companies in the field.

This Rear Base Hospital, located in the village of Hsiao Hokuo, was also the supply center for the entire Army, some of whose fighting units were two or three weeks' marching distance down the Yangtze. The hospital wards and living-quarters of the staff were in great stone ancestral temples. Their exterior walls were painted to match the earth, the interiors whitewashed, and the earthen or stone floors sprinkled with lime. Carpenters and tinsmiths had modeled and constructed every conceivable kind of equipment for the wards, laboratory, dispensary, and operating-theater. They had constructed wooden boxes, each capable of carrying thirty pounds of medical supplies; a man could carry two, one slung at each end of a bamboo pole. Army trucks gathered empty gasoline tins along the highways of the rear, and from these the tinsmiths manufactured equipment, including containers for salves. For medicine which could not be transported in metal containers, carpenters had even manufactured bottles from bamboo.

This Army possessed the only X-ray and the only microscopes and autoclaves and had the only laboratory — with two trained technicians — in any army in China. Lacking equipment, the doctors had modeled an incubator and a pill-making machine and had them cast in the Army machine shop. Here was also the first delousing and bathing station.

In this Rear Base Hospital I found a medical library with reference volumes in English, German, Japanese, and Chinese, and copies of Chinese, British, and American medical journals, for which it subscribed. Its doctors knew of the latest medical discoveries, of vitamins and the sulfa drugs, and were avidly reading the experiences of doctors in the Spanish Republican Armies, as recorded in the *British Medical Journal*. The doctors were also writing and publishing pocket medical manuals and sending them to sanitary workers at the front.

Organically connected with the civilian population as it was, the New Fourth Army, like the Eighth Route, opened its medical service to civilians without charge. By December 1938 the two rear base hospitals had given treatment to 35,000 civilians. There was no other public medical service in the war zones of the lower Yangtze and most of its supplies had been donated by Chinese people's organizations, the Red Cross Medical Corps, and individuals.

The Political Department of the New Fourth Army permeated all branches of the Army and anti-Japanese people's organizations and constituted a kind of revolutionary educational system. This work extended to the Army hospitals; neither the Eighth Route nor the New Fourth Army surrendered any of their wounded to the hospitals of the Army Medical Administration of the Ministry of War. The chief reason was that they wished to prevent the disintegration of the Army's man-power and hoped to continue their revolutionary training.

It was this system, and the Marxian political theory in which it was rooted, that bred charges against these armies and, in later years, again brought the country to the brink of civil war. Charges that the armies did not fight were simply untrue; they fought the Japanese bravely, but rejected the Kuomintang political system.

However ardent my own desire to see China firmly united, and much as I disliked the intellectual arrogance of some individual Communists, still, had I had a son or brother, I would not have wished to see him at the mercy of most Kuomintang armies.

An unending variety of activities animated the New Fourth Army hospitals. Each day the Political Director read about the latest war news or interesting newspaper articles. Theatrical groups presented plays, and civilians, including outsiders like myself, delivered presents, made speeches, or sang.

Over the beds hung a series of cards, each displaying five ideograms. Illiterate men were expected to learn one card each day. Literate men were supplied with books and newspapers. The Political Director or his assistant often sat by the bedside of men unable to write and took down anything they wished to contribute to the wall newspaper — their fighting experiences, criticisms, thoughts, or the lines of some poem or song.

In the Rear Base Hospital I found a small boy of nine who always lay with his head covered. When he saw a foreign face he began to whimper and tremble. A nurse bent over him and said: "That is not a Japanese, but an American, a friend."

Two months previously, Japanese soldiers had raided this child's native village, murdered his father and elder brother, and raped and killed his mother. He had screamed and fought until a Japanese mauled him into unconsciousness. One of his legs had had to be amputated.

On a later visit to the Rear Base Hospital I saw this child again. He had been adopted by the Medical Service and spent half of each day in class; the rest of the time he prepared swabs, surgical dressings, and bandages. Three other small boys, also war orphans, did the same. This was one of the origins of the *hsiao kwey*, or "little devils," as they were affectionately called. They had no home but the Army, and were its future "cadres." They were trained from childhood in Marxian thought, and in them an entirely new element entered Chinese society.

Passing along the hospital aisles, I often turned to look at interesting faces. Once I halted, attracted by a swarthy face with an expression of chilled steel. It was that of a man named Chou Ping, twenty-three, who had been a Red guerrilla for five years before coming to the front against the Japanese. He was recovering from three wounds, but coolly remarked that he would soon be able to go back to the front.

Six weeks before, he said, he had been sent with a small

guerrilla unit to waylay enemy trucks along the motor highway south of Nanking. He and another man were sent out to scout while the others lay in ambush. He saw a solitary Japanese truck coming with only one armed guard. The truck slowed down at a hill and Chou Ping leaped into it from the rear and killed the guard. When the driver looked around, he felt a bayonet against his neck. At Chou's order he drove on, but just as they neared the guerrilla ambush, Chou looked behind to find three more enemy trucks bearing down upon them. He drove his bayonet through the chauffeur and leaped to the road as the fighting began. His comrades destroyed the enemy soldiers, took everything they could carry from the trucks, left the rest in flames, and, carrying Chou Ping with them, made off.

"How are the Japanese as fighters?" I asked the wounded men. An avalanche of opinions answered me:

"They're weak when caught in the open and unprepared."

"If they are behind defense works, with artillery, they are very brave! That shows they are really cowards. . . ."

"No need saying they're cowards! They are good fighters; but we are also good fighters. . . ."

"I say they're cowards, particularly at night! Even when we set off firecrackers in a gasoline tin, they fire into the darkness all night. . . ."

"Why do you set off firecrackers in gasoline tins?" I asked.

"To make the devils use up their ammunition! We do that until they get used to it and pay no attention to us. Then we attack. . . . Now they patrol the roads with armored cars at night. Each car has a searchlight that swings around."

"I was wounded while we were attacking a garrison," a man on another bed interrupted. "It was a railway station. Some of our comrades tore up the rails while we attacked the station. There were only a few buildings and all the Japanese were upstairs in one of them. I climbed on a roof and looked right in. I saw ten or fifteen devils, and they had Chinese girls with no clothes on. We were sorry for the girls, but we couldn't help it. We set fire to the building and hurled hand-grenades through the windows."

One night I addressed the convalescing wounded and the medical staff in the hospital club room. During my talk a soldier ran at me screaming: *"Jherben Kwei-tze!"* (Japanese devil!) and was almost on me before one of the doctors intercepted him. The man had gone insane after being wounded, but had seemed to regain his sanity. On the night of my speech, hearing a foreign voice, he came into the club room. Then something had snapped again.

In a village across the river from this hospital was an Army transport station with a small garrison. When I came to spend a day there, a conference was called, and again I learned that I was expected to be both a walking encyclopedia and a prophet. Among other things the men there wanted to know the attitude of the American public toward China, the general condition of different American political parties, the influence of the Hearst press on American public opinion, and the effect on American policy of the appointment of Dr. Hu Shih as the new Chinese Ambassador.

A number of buildings in the village were equipped as machine shops, where about two dozen men were hammering and turning wheels, or blowing bellows at a blacksmith's forge. This small arsenal was manned by trained arsenal workers from Shanghai and Hankow. They worked in a frenzy of concentration and were able to repair old rifles and manufacture one new rifle a day.

There was a hush-hush atmosphere about this place, and when I asked why, I was told that the authorities had refused the Army any guns to arm its new volunteers.

Even after the Japanese invasion of China proper began, I was told, warfare continued to be waged against the Red guerrillas in south China who had been left behind when the main body of the Red Army went on the Long March. While Japanese artillery and airplanes roared overhead, General Yeh Ting, a military commander of renown, urged Generalissimo Chiang Kai-shek to allow him to assemble and organize the Red guerrillas into an army for operation in the enemy rear. Generalissimo Chiang agreed and the

Communists assented. The name "New Fourth Army" was chosen because, in 1926–7, General Yeh had been one of the most brilliant vanguard commanders in the famous Fourth Army, or "Ironsides," which had swept all before it in the Northern Expedition from Canton to Hankow.

But when, in late 1937, the Red guerrillas had begun marching from seven different southern provinces to an assembly point in south Anhwei, provincial armies, officials, and landlords attempted to provoke clashes. Blockhouses were manned by local government troops or policemen, and trenches were thrown up along the routes of march. The guerrillas were under orders to fire no shot, but even as they marched against the Japanese, they stared into the muzzles of guns in the hands of their countrymen. Ragged, undernourished, many of them sick or maimed, they continued to march, often changing their route and moving at night to avoid conflict. Many "Red Army families" went with them. As in the days of civil war, local landlords and officials spread rumors among the people that bandits were coming. Such incidents rankled in the hearts of the guerrillas.

Some of the old guerrilla units had been scattered in inaccessible regions and had had to march three months before reaching their assembly point. At the end of two months 15,000 men from Fukien, Kiangsi, Chekiang, Hunan, Hupeh, Honan, and western Anhwei had been mustered, the majority in south Anhwei, others north of the Yangtze. Of these, 13,000 were admitted to the ranks of the New Fourth Army, which was divided into four detachments. One detachment, the Fourth, remained in its position north of the Yangtze to harass the enemy rear; the First, Second, and Third Detachments were south of the river, in the vicinity of Nanking, Wuhu, and Chinkiang, Japan's "sealed zone" of operation in the heart of China.

Government inspectors counted the guns of the newly organized Army and allotted to it the same amount of money, ammunition, and uniforms allowed other armies. But they were not given new weapons. When other Red guerrilla units finally reached the assembly point, or when civilian volunteers in the enemy rear poured into the Army, no funds for their maintenance were allotted. The Army had to stretch its original funds to cover all these. Unlike the national armies, however, the pay of fighters and commanders was kept on a more or less equal basis, fighters receiving $1.50 a month and officers from $2 to $4 (the latter being the pay of a regimental commander). Food and uniforms were provided by the Army, but out of their pay all men had to buy their own shoes or sandals, or such luxuries as shirts, underwear, toothbrushes, or soap. As a result, few owned shirts or underwear. The relatively good pay that might have been given to officers was spread out over the whole Army.

The Army's rapid recruitment of local civilians became a constant source of friction with the Government. To the Army's repeated appeals for more money, guns, and ammunition, the Government replied: "If we give you more money, you will not improve the condition of your soldiers, but merely enlarge your Army." The class struggle appeared in a new form: the Government did not wish the New Fourth Army to increase its strength and influence among the people. I had, in fact, already heard charges from many sources that though the Government wished the Communists to fight the Japanese, some of its leaders also hoped that the Communists would be wiped out in the process.

The small arsenal which I saw in the mountains of south Anhwei had thus been founded to manufacture and repair guns for new volunteers. Its existence was one of those many Chinese secrets about which people gossiped. Certainly the Blue Shirt secret service knew about it.

From all I had heard, the commander of this Army, General Yeh Ting, seemed to be a candid man who made no secret of the growing strength of his Army, and when accused of it, declared that only by the total mobilization and arming of the people could China be victorious.

General Yeh Ting had been an early Kuomintang follower of Dr. Sun Yat-sen and after a period of study in the Soviet Union had joined the Chinese Communist Party. To him the united front had seemed the salvation of China, but when the split came in 1927 and the Kuomintang began terrorism against the Communists, he had been one of the chief leaders in the revolt of the Kuomintang armies opposed to the Terror. After the failure of the Canton Commune in December 1927, in which he took part, but with which he disagreed, he resigned from the Communist Party and went abroad to study. He refused to help the Kuomintang and was hostile to its reactionary policy. When the Japanese invasion of Manchuria began in 1931, he returned to China in the hope of helping weld the united front once more. He failed, for the Kuomintang still fought against the Communists. General Yeh's voice was again heard only after the Japanese invasion of China proper in July 1937.

Yeh's record seemed clear enough, yet when I arrived at the New Fourth Army eight months after its formation, men avoided his name. One evening the Medical Director and some of the doctors asked to discuss their problems with me. These discussions added new complications to an already tangled pattern. General Yeh Ting, they said, had left the Army and had asked Generalissimo Chiang Kai-shek to relieve him of his command. Three medical workers had also left, and other qualified doctors and some of the nurses were planning to resign.

As a convinced leader of the united front, General Yeh was between two fires. On the one hand, the Government held him responsible for the Army, yet rejected his requests for funds and equipment to enable it to meet the ever growing Japanese offensive against it. On the other hand, the Communist leaders, particularly Vice-Commander Hsiang Ying, conducted intrigues which prevented Yeh from exercising any control over the Army.

A wall of suspicion had been built up against him and the new medical workers. He had resigned, but the Generalissimo had rejected his resignation and also his offer to organize another guerrilla army to fight the Japanese around Canton.

The new medical staff had introduced a complete system of records and statistics and regular hours, but this ran counter to the old *ma-ma-hu-hu* (*mañana*) habits of an army that sprang from the peasantry.

Another complaint of the new doctors was that men found incapable of any other service were sent to work in the hospitals, and "little devils," children as young as eight years of age, were expected to act as nurses and attendants. In addition, feeble-minded men or even epileptics were put in as servants, the theory being that if an epileptic had a fit, he should have it in the hospital.

I listened as the Medical Director explained that he hoped to create the first model medical service in any Chinese army. I shared his hopes and argued that every effort should be made to settle conflicts and preserve the service. I reminded them of the struggles of scientific pioneers in the Western world, some of whom had been called sorcerers and had been burned at the stake. Where else in China could they work, I asked them. In most other armies they would be forced into antiquated systems and would hold their positions only by kowtowing to generals and politicians. Such politicians usually said that China had enough men to go on fighting for years; and one Szechuen Army commander had even rejected the services of a Red Cross unit, refusing to "humor his troops."

A young doctor listening to me declared: "You argue like a Y.M.C.A. secretary!"

My final plea was that the doctors ask Vice-Commander Hsiang Ying, their chief opponent, to call a conference to hear their complaints and plans. The doctors listened and concurred. Only one doctor and a laboratory technician finally left the Army. The rest of us worked along the lines agreed upon. In the process I nearly broke my own political neck. But the Medical Service finally emerged victorious, Vice-Commander Hsiang issuing an Army order in support of the modern Medical Service, its organization and practices. And at my request the Red Cross Medical Corps sent two mobile units to aid it.

The first modern Army Medical Service of a Chinese Army was at last firmly established.

The "New Fourth"

THE HOURS grew small and the tea in our cups became cold as Vice-Commander Hsiang Ying and I talked. Like the members of his staff who had gathered to welcome us, he was a Communist who had passed all his adult life in the revolutionary movement. Some twenty years before, he had been a worker, had entered the labor movement, become a Communist, and finally one of the leaders in the party in China. All the education and training he possessed had been gained within its ranks. After the main body of the Red Army started on the Long March in late 1934, he had been put in command of the Red guerrillas remaining in Kiangsi.

He was now about forty, of medium height, and strongly built. The social-revolutionary movement had molded him into an austere, unyielding personality, a man who would adopt any method to reach his goal. His critics said that intrigue and craftiness had become a part of his nature.

I could not forget that Hsiang Ying had given an interview to a foreign writer whose wife had thereafter published an article charging that General Yeh Ting, commander of the New Fourth Army, had left the Communist Party in 1927 after marrying a rich Hong Kong woman. Another rumor spread at the time was that General Yeh had resigned from the New Fourth Army "because he was afraid to fight in the enemy rear." General Yeh Ting's reputation was, in fact, being assassinated by gossip. I happened to know that the highest Communist leaders in Yenan and Chungking were enraged by such rumors against him. The poison kept seeping through nevertheless.

There was another side to this medal. Hsiang Ying had been one of the leaders responsible for the kind of organization and training that had made the New Fourth Army the most effective and intellectually enlightened military force in the enemy rear.

On the night of our arrival he stood with four of us before a general headquarters military map which reached from the rafters to the floor. The massed red circles of Japanese garrisons in the New Fourth Army theater of operation made the map look like a face afflicted with smallpox. The Army and the Japanese seemed to be fighting right in each other's laps.

This theater of operations was a long narrow belt from fifty to seventy miles in depth along the southern bank of the lower Yangtze River Valley. The Japanese-patrolled Yangtze bounded it on the north, and through this area, which the Japanese called their "sealed zone," or base of operation, ran a network of motor highways, rivers, lakes, and canals — all an advantage to the enemy but a great disadvantage to the guerrillas. Around Nanking and Chinkiang this zone was a plain, barren of hills and trees and intersected by rivers, canals, lakes, and the Shanghai-Nanking railway — an area ideal for an invader equipped with airplanes and motorized equipment. The wooded hills and mountains did not begin until the other side of the Yangtze city of Wuhu near general headquarters.

When the New Fourth Army first moved into its theater of operation, the Japanese held undisputed sway. All Chinese resistance, save a few small groups of civilian guerrillas, had been destroyed; puppet governments and armies had been organized in every town and village; Japanese trucks and tanks bowled along the highways and Japanese boats along the rivers, lakes, and canals; and the Shanghai-Nanking railway operated under Japanese control.

In April 1938 a New Fourth Vanguard unit stole into this "sealed zone" one night and fanned out in small groups of two or three men, moving rapidly from village to village to investigate enemy positions, equipment, and activities. The civilian population welcomed them and secretly sheltered them. In a month all members of the Vanguard unit were back in general headquarters with their reports.

Fighting units then moved in. The "sealed zone" was turned into a bedlam, with guerrillas striking in a dozen places at once. At the same time political workers of the Army moved into the villages and began organizing the pop-

ulation into anti-Japanese associations. Right under the
nose of the enemy, short-term training schools were founded
in which civilians were taught methods of organization,
education, espionage, and sabotage.

When I arrived eight months later, the Army had fought
231 battles, captured 1,539 rifles, 32 light machine-guns, 4
heavy machine-guns, 48 sub-machine-guns, 50,000 rounds of
ammunition, 22,738 yen in Japanese bank-notes, radios,
horses, mules, banners, maps, and other enemy trophies.
They had destroyed some 200 enemy trucks and railway
cars, 13 miles of railway, 4 miles of highway, 95 bridges, and
13 miles of electric power lines. They had taken 38 Japanese
and 613 puppet troops prisoners and inflicted 3,253 casualties upon the enemy. Their own losses had been 243 killed
and 4,231 wounded.

In addition, the New Fourth, in co-operation with the
civilian population, had wiped out 3,000 bandits, whole armies of which had arisen in the period of Japanese depreda-
tions. Some of them had been paid by the Japanese to
harass the countryside.

After less than a year of warfare the New Fourth guerrillas had either wiped out or won over most of the conscripted puppet armies in the Japanese "sealed zone." Such
armies, along with the puppet governments they guarded,
could exist only within large walled towns, in which the
Japanese now had to maintain heavy garrisons. Enemy
trucks or boats could travel only with armed guards and had
to be heavily convoyed. Local civilian guerrillas who had
formerly fought under the slogan of "Kill Japanese, then
die," were taught by the New Fourth Army Training Camp
how to "kill Japanese and live." And some puppets considered it a form of life insurance to supply the guerrillas with
information about the enemy.

Hsiang Ying showed us a number of Japanese handbills
dropped by airplane throughout their "sealed zone." One
was a cartoon in four pictures. The first showed the dark
figures of guerrillas destroying a bridge at night while a little
Chinese boy watched at a distance; the next three showed

the little boy racing to a Japanese garrison to betray his countrymen; the last was the laughing face of the child as he waved a bank-note in the air.

Another handbill looked like a bank-note except that the reverse side explained the procedure of desertion; it urged guerrillas to bring their rifles, halt at least two hundred feet away from the Japanese garrison, and wave a white flag. Next all should lay their rifles on the earth, then, with arms uplifted, approach the Japanese sentry one by one to be searched for concealed weapons. After that a life of ease would be theirs!

I was told of a New Fourth company which had recently surrounded and occupied a market town south of Nanking in which traitors were preparing to welcome a Japanese garrison force. The captured puppet leaders were brought to mass public trial before the citizens of the town, condemned to death, and immediately shot by the New Fourth, while the puppet soldiers — conscripted peasants and former policemen — were sent to the rear for retraining. Among the witnesses brought against the puppet chiefs were twenty girls and young married women taken from a "consolation house" in which they had been locked to await the arrival of enemy troops. The chief puppet, president of the local Chamber of Commerce, had defended himself at the trial by declaring: "The trouble was that there were not enough prostitutes in the town."

The day following our arrival I was taken on an inspection tour of all departments of the Army. The chief institution was the Army Training Camp, in which some 1,400 men and more than a hundred women were studying. Groups of commanders and political workers were withdrawn from the fighting detachments every three months for retraining in military, political, and cultural subjects. Hundreds of men and women in every stage of education, including college graduates and artists, had left Shanghai and other cities, passed through the Japanese lines, and entered the camp.

Military commanders gave seventy per cent of their time

This looks like Chinese currency but is actually a Japanese leaflet which on its other face explains the procedure for deserting.

Another piece of typical Japanese propaganda. It purports to show how rich Chinese indulge in debauchery in Hongkong while the common people starve under the lash of national resistance.

to the study of military science, and thirty per cent to political and cultural subjects; those destined for political work reversed this proportion. The main political course was in the theory and tactics of the united front. Most of the old Red Army commanders were poor peasants and found it no easy task to learn that they should work as brothers with landlords and merchants, for even in the midst of military war, class war was being waged against them. High officials of the Government even objected to the existence of the training camp, calling it another Communist university.

Other political subjects taught in the camp included the history of the Chinese Revolution, general world history, and methods of mass mobilization. Under "cultural training" came reading, writing, and geography. A young woman graduate from a Peiping university soon introduced the first courses in natural sciences. Following the settling of conflicts with the Medical Service, qualified doctors and nurses lectured on physiology, anatomy, and personal hygiene. I initiated the latter courses by giving a general lecture on "National Resistance and Health" to the entire camp.

One point in my lecture touched upon an attitude which was not peculiar to the Chinese: some educated students entering the Army expressed contempt for those who took time off from the revolution to take a bath or keep themselves in good physical condition. "Petty bourgeois," they called such students. In my lecture I declared that I could see nothing revolutionary in the scabies which afflicted most of them and that even hardened Russian Bolsheviks took baths.

The reluctance to bathe, however, was more than an "intellectual attitude." All water had to be carried from distant streams and there was no way of heating it. Students did all their own work while studying, and arranging a bath was a major problem which only the hospitals had solved. Subsequently, I used some of my royalties from books and articles, together with money sent me by the British Ambassador, to build the first D.B.S. (delousing-bathing-scabies) treatment station in the Army. It was a large building designed by the medical workers: only stone, earth, and timber were used. Pipes were made from trunks of hollowed-out bamboo, with spray holes punched at regular intervals. The construction of this station constituted a minor anti-Japanese triumph and I was proud of it.

Japanese prisoners came under the charge of the Enemy Work Section of the Army. This section examined all captives, keeping a few younger ones, particularly workers or students, but turning over older men or officers to the headquarters of the Third War Zone. The Government paid for each captive. An enemy officer brought a large sum. The New Fourth had retained three captives, two of them fishermen and one a student, to help teach the Japanese language and prepare propaganda for clandestine distribution among Japanese troops.

The Japanese prisoners, dressed in Chinese uniforms, had never been in chains and moved about freely. When I inquired concerning their attitude, Ling Shih-fu said they were tired of the war and never tried to escape. In any event, if they tried to get away, they would be killed by civilians, who hunted Japanese as they would snakes. The three captives who taught Japanese had written and signed a joint letter to the soldiers of their former division, telling them about their life in the New Fourth and urging them to desert. The three thus became men without a country; only the world revolution could give them a home.

One room belonging to this department was filled with war trophies of every description, including many flags, two of which were used as window curtains. Also among the trophies were two mail sacks filled with letters to and from Japan and a pile of Japanese soldier diaries. One of these I translated into English with the help of my secretary and Ling Shih-fu. It was a voluminous record kept by a Corporal Nakamura and was a remarkable study in gradual brutalization. It began when the Corporal was unwillingly conscripted. After he was marched to the port of embarkation, he wrote theatrically of a drizzling rain: "Is this rain, or are these my tears?"

In September 1938, after months of killing, looting, and raping, he wrote from somewhere south of Nanking:

> Fine weather. At four this afternoon we were all ordered to Lukuochen. We seized the village and searched every house. We tried to capture the most interesting girls. The chase lasted for two hours. Niura shot one to death because it was her first time and she was ugly and was despised by the rest of us.

A number of entries spoke of the repeated destruction of a strategic bridge by the New Fourth Army and of the Japanese going daily to repair it. Once they caught a group of five civilians and tortured them to death. Some new Japanese recruits watched the torture with horror, and Nakamura wrote of them: "All new recruits are like this, but soon they will be doing the same things themselves."

In late September, Nakamura was again ordered to Lukuochen. This time the entire population had evacuated before them. The Corporal wrote: "If the people act like this, how can we maintain peace and order in east Asia?" On the night of October 1 the New Fourth Army killed Nakamura. His rifle number was 750508, gas mask No. 82056, bayonet No. 2296713, badge No. 62. His father was Nakamura Yekichi of 90 Chome, Omaricho 3, Omoriku, Tokyo.

A few days later I talked with two new Japanese captives, one a soldier, another a Lieutenant. The soldier had been captured while in the act of raping a woman and was in the headquarters hospital as a syphilis patient. With buck teeth and practically no chin, he looked like a fish and was actually as primitive as an animal. I marveled at the self-control of the Chinese.

The captured Lieutenant was a cold, hard man who had formerly been a policeman in Tokyo. He was brought to the hospital because of an infected insect bite. He told me he had been captured outside a Japanese garrison on the

Yangtze. Three of his soldiers had left the garrison one morning to go to a near-by village to "get some chickens." Night came, and when they did not return, the officer climbed a small hill and looked around. Suddenly hands grasped his legs and others throttled him and carried him away.

"Brave men do not fight like that!" he added contemptuously.

When I asked him what he thought of the war, he replied coldly: "I don't think; I obey orders."

My day's inspection of the New Fourth Army headquarters ended in a "military men's conference" at night. Hundreds of men executed guerrilla maneuvers in the mountains during the day and followed the Army practice of gathering afterwards for a discussion of their "weak points and strong points." Mutual criticism between commanders and men was encouraged, and at the conclusion a chairman summed up the findings.

Such were the Army's efforts to "drive forward this great age!"

Doctors Need "Teaching Material"

THE MEDICAL TRAINING SCHOOL of the New Fourth Army had finally opened and the first thirty-eight educated youths drawn from the Army Training Camp had enrolled. The doctors and the head nurse, Miss Yang, spent hours each day, even while pursuing their regular hospital duties, preparing and delivering lectures. They were in great need of "teaching material" — above all, a human skeleton. Three of them went in a delegation to staff headquarters to ask the Vice-Commander and the Political Director to permit them to use the bodies of soldiers who died in the hospitals for demonstrating to their classes. They also argued that they themselves wished to perform autopsies because a number of soldiers had died without any apparent reason.

The commanders were deeply interested, but said it could

not be done. Only when a scientific attitude had permeated the Army and the civilian population could autopsies be performed. Most of the soldiers were from the local villages, and if they or the people learned that bodies were being cut up in the hospital, a serious situation might develop. A mutilated man, moreover, would have no place in an after life. I myself had already heard of soldiers in other armies cutting off the noses or ears of the Japanese dead on the battlefield in order that these enemy souls might never find a resting-place.

Arguing with the commanders, one of the doctors said: "Today a student of mine denied that he had two bones in his lower arm. Another believed that he had two sets of intestines, one for big business, one for little business. It is difficult to teach theoretically."

"We will try to send you a dead Japanese from the battlefield," a commander answered. "The Army won't care what you do with that. But, as a rule, the Japanese carry away their dead."

One day a convoy of stretchers came in, and Dr. N. C. Gung, a high-strung, gifted surgeon with the hands and mind of an artist, performed five operations. One was an amputation from the hip. Dr. Chang, the only woman doctor in the enemy rear, assisted. She taught anatomy in the training school. After the amputation an attendant prepared to carry the leg away, but before he could do so, Dr. Chang was upon him, crying something about "teaching material." She rescued the leg, carved off the flesh, and finally put it in a gasoline tin filled with disinfectant.

Some time later everyone in the buildings was brought to his feet by a fearful growling and screaming in the courtyard. We rushed out to see a mongrel tugging and snarling at one end of the amputated leg, and Dr. Chang at the other end screaming at the top of her voice. We helped her drive off the dog, and then watched her carry off her treasure to the main hospital building and put it to boil in a delousing vat.

Later I saw the new radio set which the Medical Director

had just triumphantly brought through the Japanese lines from Shanghai. All the other receivers in the Army were telegraphic. So when the first sound of voices and music came over the air, crowds of astounded soldiers and civilians gathered. They looked all around the machine and were awe-struck. Finally a peasant woman nodded her head wisely and declared:

"It's one of those things called Science!"

The others looked respectfully from her to the machine. When they had looked and listened their fill, they departed, and I was alone in the hospital library. I turned the dial with a feeling that I was reaching out into infinity. The Japanese stations at Nanking and Shanghai came leaping at me, but I passed them by and turned farther. The chiming of a bell came through infinity and an English voice burst on me, saying: "This is London calling!"

I sat almost petrified. The voice announced Beethoven's Fifth Symphony, and as the concert began, all my buried feeling for the culture of the West welled up in me and tears filled my eyes. Just then a hand touched my shoulder, and glancing up I saw Dr. Chang, her face contorted with misery.

"My leg is ruined!" she cried, while the Fifth Symphony flooded the room. "I left it boiling in the delousing vat and the servant went to sleep. The water boiled away and the bone is ruined!"

Dr. Gung appeared in the doorway and he entered and listened to her tragedy. "Don't worry!" he consoled her. "I have a plan, but we must keep it secret. I'm going to dig up graves until I find a skeleton good enough for teaching material. Will you come along or are you afraid?"

Apparently Dr. Chang resented the imputation of femininity, for she tossed her head and answered proudly:

"I challenge you to socialist competition in skeleton-hunting. I will find my own cemetery!"

While the Fifth Symphony soared, they made a compact in body-snatching and left immediately to go their separate ways with spades, sacks, and flashlights.

Chinese coffins are placed on the surface of the earth and the soil is merely heaped over them. Robbery would be easy. After Dr. Gung had dug up eight graves and Dr. Chang five, we realized the meaning of infant mortality in China, for most of the graves turned out to be those of infants. In some graves the skeletons proved useless, having been decomposed by the soggy soil of the lower Yangtze. On one trip, Dr. Gung dug up the skeleton of a New Fourth Army soldier. The flesh was not yet decomposed, so Dr. Gung marked the grave with a small pile of stones, planning to rob it a year later if their search still proved fruitless.

One midnight as I worked over the radio news, Dr. Chang entered and beckoned to me mysteriously. I followed her into the courtyard. As if displaying stolen jewels, she opened a sack and pointed to a pile of bones.

"She was from my native town of Wusih and she died of tuberculosis," she said enthusiastically. "I could tell because the body had been wrapped and the orifices stuffed with silk wool. The people of Wusih think this prevents the disease from escaping."

At that moment Dr. Gung came in, his hands dirty from earth. He stared at Dr. Chang's pile of bones with the envious eye of a connoisseur who knows he is beaten.

"I won!" Dr. Chang crowed. "You owe me a dinner!"

A week later the skeleton was all set up and Dr. Chang led me to it. She had wired the bones together, then strung them up on a bamboo contrivance. Each bone bore a small label. The thing had ceased to be a skeleton; it had been transformed into a minor monument of man's will to knowledge. So we walked around it, calling admiring attention to its "strong points" and its "weak points."

Late one evening the promised Japanese cadaver was also delivered to the hospital. It was brought into the large "treatment room" of the out-patient department. With the men bearing it had come a young male nurse from the Third Detachment. His eyes were gleaming with interest.

"We got your orders to bring in a dead Japanese for the sake of science," he informed Dr. Chang. "I came along."

A messenger raced off to a near-by village to summon all the medical students. They soon hurried in, clad in white aprons, skull-caps, and mouth-masks, their notebooks in their hands. A thick layer of lime was spread on the earthen floor beneath the board on which the body lay, and around it a primitive amphitheater was created out of low stools, benches, and chairs. The gleaming acetylene lamp was brought in from the operating-room and hung from the rafters, and a row of big glass jars filled with alcohol were placed on a table to receive "specimens" for "teaching material."

I wonder if any scientists have ever lived through a more portentous moment or approached their task with greater enthusiasm. The medical students had previously studied only ordinary academic or military subjects. It had, moreover, been almost necessary to conscript them to get them into the Medical Training School.

Dr. Chang and Dr. Gung, their aprons gleaming white, stood behind the outstretched body, and Dr. Chang lifted her voice in the first medical demonstration given to a Chinese army. There was not even a rustle in the room.

As midnight neared, I left them for my radio work, but through the news broadcasts from far-away America, London, Berlin, and Bombay penetrated the voices of the doctors in the room beyond.

The Women Take a Hand

WHEN I first met old Mother Tsai, she had already emerged as a leader of the women in the valley. She was unusually tall for a "south Yangtze Valley" woman; her skin was brown, and the veins on her old hands stood out like ridges on a hillside. She was thin and hard, and when she spoke, her voice was firm and almost harsh. Her hair, touched with white, was drawn back from a high forehead and rolled in a knot at the nape of her neck. As a peasant woman and the mother of many sons, she had suffered bitterly all her life, but of this she never spoke. Her white cotton jacket was neatly buttoned up close around the neck and her dark cotton trousers always seemed to have just been washed. Though none of these people ever ironed their clothing, hers must somehow have been pressed beneath some weight. She was the embodiment of dignity and staunchness.

It was difficult to believe that she was sixty-eight, for she seemed much younger. She was, she told me, a widow with four children. Of her three sons, the two elder were in the New Fourth Army, and the younger, a boy of fifteen, helped her and her daughters-in-law till the fields.

Before the war, life in the villages had been drab and monotonous. But when the New Fourth Army had marched into the valley the year before, the world had seemed to enter with it. Many girl students had joined the Political Department of the Army; when they went knocking on the doors of the village women, the old world had crumbled. The ladies of the gentry had refused to receive them, sending their menfolk instead, and thus suggesting that the girls were prostitutes. But when the girls knocked on Mother Tsai's door, she looked into their eyes and knew they were not bad. She invited them in, placed bowls of tea before them, and called her daughters-in-law and neighbor women to come and sit with them. And in this way the Women's National Salvation Association was born in the valley. It grew until it had over a hundred members.

Mother Tsai's lean, tall figure could often be seen walking along the paths from village to village, urging women to join literacy classes, and attend discussion groups to learn what the war was about and how they could help. After the day's work was done, women could be seen sitting on their doorsteps, cutting out pieces of cloth and sewing. When I asked them what they were doing, they replied: "Making shoes for the Army."

More and more women took over the field work previously done by men. The younger men had joined the Army and the older men and boys helped in the fields or carried supplies to the battlefield and brought back the wounded. On every festival day members of the Women's Association would go to the hospital to "comfort the wounded" with gifts of food, sing songs, and talk with the soldiers. It was always Mother Tsai who delivered the speeches in the wards, telling the wounded that they were all her sons and the sons of the Women's Association. And she never closed a speech without telling them about women's rights, or urging them to induce their womenfolk to join the Association. Some men had never heard such talk before and they listened with respect. About such matters Chinese men everywhere seemed much more civilized and tolerant than Occidental men, and only a few ever opposed the new movement.

The women had become particularly confident after Army women had conducted classes. One of these classes covered Japanese espionage and sabotage methods in the war zones and it urged women to become the "eyes and ears of the Army," to combat defeatism, watch everywhere for spies or traitors, and boycott Japanese goods. One phrase covered all such activities: "Guarding the rear of our Army." After that they never just sat and listened while their menfolk dispensed wisdom; they took part in conversations, conducted propaganda about almost everything on earth, went to mass meetings, and questioned every stranger who passed through the valley about his family and his family's family down to the tenth generation.

Now and then a man rose to protest against the "new women." There was, for instance, the merchant Chang, who declared that when the women got going, they wore out men and exhausted horses. Mother Tsai was the worst of all, he said, and an idea in her head rattled like a pea in an empty gourd. She had become particularly obnoxious to him since she had discovered that he was buying up all the small white beans from the lah tree. The people made candles from these beans, but Chang had begun cornering them and selling them in Wuhu. Now, the city of Wuhu had been occupied by the Japanese, and the women soon wanted to know just why any person traded in it. How was it, they asked, that Merchant Chang could pass through the Japanese lines, month in and month out, without difficulty?

And why had the wax beans of the valley suddenly found such a big market? Perhaps the Japanese made oil from them! No one respected Merchant Chang anyway, for everyone knew that he had a hand in the valley's new opium-smoking den, where the village riff-raff and even some family men had begun squandering their money.

Mother Tsai one day walked straight into Chang's shop and put the question to him. With withering contempt, the merchant asked her if *she* wanted to buy his beans. This was not only an insult, but it mocked the poverty of the old lady and of every peasant family in the valley. Merchant Chang soon learned what it meant to despise the will of the people. Not a soul would buy or sell him anything, and when he passed through the streets people looked the other way. Once a little boy threw a stone after him and called out: "Traitor." And one day as he passed a farmhouse, he distinctly heard a dog being set on him.

At last Merchant Chang went in anger to the local government official. The official called in Mother Tsai for a friendly talk. The old lady went, but not alone. The entire membership of the Women's Association escorted her to the official's door, and her son, her daughters-in-law, and several relatives accompanied her right into his home. Other villagers trailed along and it looked as if the whole village was waiting outside the official's residence. The official himself was not a bad fellow. In fact, he was patriotic and liberal-minded. But when he saw the crowd, he became more liberal-minded than ever. He asked Mother Tsai to explain her talk with Chang, and she told him about the traffic with Wuhu and about the opium and gambling den. The opium, she pointed out, came from some corrupt officers in a provincial Chinese army farther to the west. There had never before been an opium-smoking den in the valley, and the Women's Association asked that it be closed down.

The official admitted the evil of opium and gambling, but said there was no law against either. A new opium-smoking law was expected soon; until then he urged the women to argue with the men "with love in their hearts."

Old Mother Tsai replied: "We women have already argued with love in our hearts. The men will not listen. They tell us to go back to our kitchens and not interfere in men's affairs."

Mother Tsai ended the interview by announcing to the amazed official: "We women have risen. We will not allow rich men to despise the will of the people."

Nor could the official do anything about Merchant Chang. There was no proof that he traded with the Japanese. True, he replied, men had seen him in the streets of Wuhu. But he might have slipped through the Japanese lines like other men. There was no law against this.

March 8 brought matters to a crisis. This was always celebrated throughout China as International Women's Day and the valley buzzed with preparation for a mass meeting in the great courtyard of an old ancestral temple. Men leaders had been invited to say a few words of greeting, but it was a woman's day. All the front seats in the temple courtyard were reserved for women, while soldiers, officers, and civilian men were invited to sit in the back. The faces and names of the women scientists, writers, and revolutionary leaders of many nations shouted at us from scores of posters. A number of them called on the women to "revive the spirit of Florence Nightingale."

On this morning Mother Tsai led the entire Women's National Salvation Association to the Army hospital to present gifts to the wounded. Before going to the wards, they called to present me with ten eggs and a chicken. Mother Tsai sat very straight and asked me to tell Western women how the women of China had struggled to emancipate themselves. "You," she said, "express the high spirit of womanhood by your willingness to eat bitterness with us." I was deeply affected by her tribute.

I went with the women to the hospital wards and watched them bring in great bamboo baskets filled with eggs, cakes and half a slaughtered hog. Their husbands proudly carried the gifts down the aisles for the wounded to see and exclaim over. And when this was done, all the women gathered and sang the *Consolation for the Wounded* song, telling the soldiers, "O men of honor," that they had "suffered the wounds of war for millions of women and children."

It was a beautiful and moving scene. After it was finished, I talked with Mother Tsai and her followers. They wished to know what else they could do to help the wounded, and I proposed that they make pillows and pillow-cases, embroidering each case with such slogans as "Hero of the Nation" or "Toward the Final Victory." They accepted the idea eagerly and I started the campaign with a donation of money for cloth and silk thread, assuring them that they must not thank me, that this was my fight as well as theirs.

The mass meeting that afternoon was a tremendous success. Mother Tsai had an attack of stage fright, but conquered her fear and went on to speak of women's rights and their part in the war. Before finishing, she announced that her Association was going to root out all evils in the valley, including gambling and opium and idleness. In concluding she revealed that news had just reached her that one of her own sons had been wounded at the front. It was an honor to be the mother of a man who had suffered in such a cause, she said, and it made her own duty so much the greater.

She was about to leave the stage, but halted to stare. For all the soldiers and commanders had risen and were holding their rifles high in the air. To the stirring strains of the *Volunteer Marching Song* the old lady moved slowly off the stage.

A few days later one of the Army doctors called me out to the out-patient clinic of the hospital, and to my amazement I found old Mother Tsai lying injured on a stretcher. As I bent over her, she began in a weak voice to tell me what had happened. It was all about the opium and gambling den, she said. The Women's Association had argued with the men to close it down, and when they had refused, she and the other women had stalked into the place and peremptorily ordered the men to go home. The ruffians had shouted abuse at them. Finally Mother Tsai had brought a big stick down across the table, scattering all the money and mah-jongg cubes around the room. Other women had started to follow suit, the men had fought them, and there had been a great row. Almost every woman had been beaten — Mother Tsai worst of all.

For days the valley was in an uproar. Fathers, husbands, and sons, soldiers and commanders stalked about in a fury. Mother Tsai's bed was surrounded by a crowd of women, every one of them with some sort of bruise, but all of them chattering happily. For the opium den had been closed down and Merchant Chang and every man who had beaten a woman had been jailed. "A great victory — a great victory," the women kept saying.

Old Mother Tsai appealed to me:

"Now, American comrade, write to the American Woman's National Salvation Association and tell them about this. Tell about our victory and tell them that without sacrifice there can be no victory."

I think my voice trembled a little as I said I would do that, but I sat thinking of American women — women well clad and well cared for, convinced by a thousand movies that "love" was the solution of all problems. I doubted whether many of them could appreciate the conditions under which Chinese women lived and struggled.

It was a few weeks before Mother Tsai was back on the field of battle. One day I glanced up from my desk and found her standing in the door, a small group of young women behind her — all smiling. I went outside with them and found men, women, and children carrying pillows. Each pillow-case was embroidered with flowers and birds, and across each stretched such a slogan as I had suggested. Later the women went from bed to bed, presenting each man with a pillow. The surprise and pleasure of the patients was payment enough.

There were too few pillows, however, for several wounded men had just come in, including two Japanese prisoners of war. Promising to make others for them, Mother Tsai induced two Chinese soldiers to surrender their pillows to these Japanese. With the presentation, she delivered a speech about the rights of women. The Japanese gazed up at her with amazed and embarrassed smiles.

"It's grand, simply grand," I exclaimed to a doctor. "The old lady has the Japanese on their backs, and they can't do a thing but lie there and listen to her talk about the equality of women. What a dose for them! Just what they deserved!"

The Story of a Farm

As the year 1938 drew to a close and the New Year came in and dragged along, the entire lower Yangtze River Valley writhed in agony. The Japanese drove wedges southward from the river, one to the west of us where the Fiftieth Chinese Army held firm, another twenty miles to our east against the mountain city of Nanling. For weeks it seemed that Nanling could not stand up under the bombardment and bombings. A division of the Fiftieth Army passed through our valley toward the beleaguered city, and other columns from the New Fourth Army moved swiftly by night to join their comrades along the shores of the Yangtze and to strike night and day at the enemy rear and flanks.

Towns and villages changed hands a dozen times, and the wounded came in endless lines. Thousands of civilians fled to the rear, finding food and shelter in Government refugee stations or begging from door to door and around the Army encampments. When villages were recaptured, civilians who had fallen into Japanese hands were sent in for treatment. They had been bayoneted, mauled with rifles, or torn by dumdum bullets, and some had had air injected under the skin of their chests so that they still lay panting in agony. Others were dying slowly from partial decapitation.

When the long-drawn-out struggle began, the Medical Director of the New Fourth Army made a flying trip to Shanghai to solicit money and medical supplies from Chinese and foreign organizations. I sent reports and appeals to the British Relief Fund and the Special Advisory Committee of the American Red Cross. The director soon returned, flushed with success, and at the same time handed me $2,000 in cash from the British Ambassador. Half of this sum I sent immediately to the Mass Movement Department of the New Fourth Army; the rest we kept for use in our valley.

By the time the lunar New Year dawned, the enemy had been driven back. As the roar of artillery grew fainter, the peasant refugees gathered up their belongings, seated their babies in baskets, and started back toward their homes. They felt it a disgrace, a violation of their dignity as men, to depend on public charity. Even the civilian wounded in the hospitals felt that men without homes and money had no rights — not even the right to moan in pain. Many refused to wait until their injuries healed, but hobbled out secretly at night, ashamed of their poverty.

But their homes lay in ruins. All farm animals and poultry had been killed, and every scrap of metal in agricultural implements and cooking utensils had been carried away. Many public granaries had been looted, and those that escaped had little rice left. Men cannot till the soil with their fingers, and some rice, moreover, had to be kept for seed.

I discussed with the New Fourth Army doctors how best to spend the thousand dollars we had left. Near the hospital stood an ancestral temple which housed fifteen peasant refugee families, and beyond it lay a stretch of unused land which the *chu* (local administrative area) official, who was also a landlord, offered to us rent-free. The doctors conceived a plan for a self-sufficient community. They drew up a list of needed agricultural implements and seeds, went to the temple, and laid the plan before the peasants. They told the refugees that the women (those without scabies) could earn money by washing hospital linen and clothing and preparing surgical dressings. Soldiers could teach some to weave sandals, bamboo baskets, mats, and fans, and the hospital would be responsible for the health of all.

The refugee women kept silent, as was the custom, and the men thought long before asking how much interest they would have to pay on the money. The doctors told them that there would be no interest, but that if they earned a profit, it should be used to help other refugees settle the land. The men listened skeptically, and one remarked that the land was rent-free only because the Army was in the region; if it moved away, the landlord would demand not only rent, but back rent. The doctors offered to get documentary guarantees from the *chu* official, but the peasants observed that documents meant nothing if the Army moved away. Nevertheless they decided that they could at least cultivate the land until that time came; after the devils were driven from the Yangtze River Valley, they could always return to their old homes.

When all had agreed to this, one of them said: "Your seeds and implements are too expensive. We can buy them cheaper. And why have you put down watermelon seed? Beans are better; watermelons only taste good."

The doctors were a little abashed at this. We had meant only to enliven our diet of rice, cabbage, and, occasionally, a little pork. But the peasants ate meat only at New Year's, and watermelons seemed to them rank luxury.

A young peasant listened thoughtfully to all this talk and then remarked that the fifteen families could farm more cheaply if all combined and later shared the crop. Together they would be able to afford a buffalo or two to help with the plowing. They could even buy pigs; and ducks would be cheaper than the chickens we had listed, because ducks matured quickly and after a time could feed themselves. They should also, he said, examine the soil to see just what crops could be planted. It was virgin rolling hills, and rice would be out of the question.

Feeling like ignoramuses, the doctors finally turned the whole plan over to the peasants, and next day a group of them walked over the hills, feeling the soil and shaking their heads. When they had finished, five of them came to the hospital. They had radically reduced our original financial estimates and announced that three groups of men were ready to leave next morning, one to bargain for agricultural implements in a market town to the south, another to buy the best seeds in Nanling, and the third to look for draft animals and pigs and arrange for a duck-dealer to hatch a thousand eggs. They could buy ducklings at five dollars per hundred.

They counted to the last copper the money we gave them, but said they needed no money to sleep in inns. Peasants always found shelter in the homes of other peasants. But they would each need ten cents a day for food.

By the end of a week they had established their own cooperative farm. Their women came to the hospital for examinations, and those free of scabies began making dressings and doing washing, while the others were put under treatment. The Army sent soldiers to teach sandal-weaving. The doctors left the farming to the men, but insisted on arranging a balanced diet for them. The men objected to the luxury of meat once a week, but the doctors had their way, and when they were gone, two of the doctors began to sketch designs for a model village, with a schoolroom for the children, a bathroom, and a common laundry-shed.

One of the younger peasant men, as strong as an ox and with a face that glowed with life, was elected farm manager, a task he combined with tilling. It was he who came striding across the hills for all negotiations with us.

When the time came to lay out the model village, dozens of people wandered slowly over the hills and finally selected a high, dry spot in the center of the land. We watched the village grow from mud bricks baking in the sun to the first thatched house. Where the mud bricks joined the thatch they left an open space through which the smoke from the open stoves could escape. They questioned our innovation of windows in the outside walls, but again we had our way.

The broad fields of beans, peas, squash, and sweet potatoes grew, and we introduced a few tomatoes, of which they knew nothing and which they disliked. When we explained the virtues of spinach they agreed. In our honor they even put in a watermelon patch. The mother buffalo had cost a deal of money because she was with calf, but we housed the animals in pens, refusing to allow them to sleep in the houses. Naked above the waist and below the knees, the men tilled the soil, and their bodies grew brown and strong and beautiful — and free from scabies. I conceived new theories about scabies and talked learnedly of "diet."

Ducklings arrived in huge bamboo baskets, and the old men and little boys built a large low mat shed near a pond, carpeted it with a thick layer of straw, and raised a mud embankment in which to exercise their charges before giving them their brief daily swims. Connected with the mat shed was a low sleeping-space for the older men, for when the ducklings were tiny the old men kept watch night and day to prevent them from piling up on one another to keep warm. With a long bamboo pole tipped with sprigs of long grass, the little creatures were scattered and herded about. Soon the ducklings grew into gangling creatures with long necks, and after a while they were old enough to be taken down to the flowing streams to feed themselves.

The "cultural" training of adults and the education of children were placed in the charge of a woman teacher sent by the Mass Movement Department of the Army. Soon we began talking of a weaving institute to be connected with the farm. While on a trip to the city of Kinghsien, I had found a number of refugee weavers who had said they could make their own looms for eight dollars apiece.

We approached the farmers about the weavers, and again they speculated long before speaking. They thought about the new houses that would be needed for the weavers, about money for the looms, and thread, and the maintenance of the weavers' families until the finished cloth could be sold. They also talked of spinning-wheels and of bringing in raw cotton from the Kinghsien region. It was a big undertaking as their practical minds organized it; and it was plain that I should have to write for more money.

The doctors and I thought of establishing other centers among refugees along the lower Yangtze, but trained organizers would be needed. There were 200,000 homeless refugees in the territory, but would the British Relief Fund and the Advisory Committee of the American Red Cross give the money? They gave vast sums to missionary workers although the missionaries only fed and housed the refugees. Chinese undertakings they seldom financed. I could hardly qualify as a missionary and my connection with the Chinese armies also disqualified me. I sent the usual appeals, and eventually a little more money came in. But the entire sum never exceeded five thousand Chinese dollars, and some of it had to be spent on gauze for the hospitals.

When not tilling the fields, the co-operative farmers found time to do a variety of work for the hospital or the Army. When there were battles, they selected their strongest men to carry ammunition up to the front and bring back the wounded; this earned them thirty cents a day. We saw that they had become the strongest civilians in the valley, able to carry loads farther than any. Thinking of the "new diets," our doctors smiled in satisfaction.

It was the co-operative farmers who built the delousing station for the hospital, constructed according to plan with mud bricks, iron rods, and bamboo. At the time I departed for new fields, just before the harvest, there was only eighty dollars left in the farm fund, but the new crops and the ducks were expected to bring in a considerable amount. The hospital had begun buying ducks to feed the wounded.

At that time, too, I wrote an account of the farm and sent it to the British Relief Fund in Shanghai. A year and a half later, when I reached Chungking, the British Ambassador sent his car for me. To me a century seemed to have elapsed, but the Ambassador had not forgotten and was still smiling about the farm. He asked me if I could use some more money for it, and I said I could.

Men in Transition: the Fiftieth Army

IN a drizzling rain in the middle of February 1939 Dr. Chang and I rode over the mountains to the west on a visit to the Fiftieth Army, whose commander, General Kwo Shuen-chi, had invited me to be his guest. I rode a captured

Japanese horse which was lanky and gaunt, shod only on one foot, and had the heaves.

As darkness began to gather, we entered the fighting zone of the Fiftieth Army and saw the shadowy forms of sentries guarding every pathway. Near an old stone bridge overhung by willows, a young commander hurried out and questioned my guards excitedly. He then darted to my side, snapped to attention, and shouted:

"Salute! I have the honor to represent General Kwo Shuen-chi and to escort you to our headquarters."

Near the bridge stood a guard of honor, a platoon of tall, handsome men who turned eager faces toward me. Accompanying them were special Szechuen sedan chairs, with carriers, and I dismounted and got into one. The young commander and the soldiers could not conceal their excitement, and again I realized what a tremendous thing it was for a Chinese army to have a foreign visitor. They fought in a world that not only had abandoned them, but supplied their enemy with the means for their destruction. They watched the skies for signs of international help, and to them I must have seemed like the first harbinger of spring.

The guard of honor separated, some going before, some after us, and from my sedan chair I watched the swift marching of those in front of me. Their proud carriage, their occasional swift glances toward me, aroused in me a deep sorrow that I was only an individual representing no one. How deeply I regretted that I heralded no spring for them!

Before a small village a mounted soldier rode out, saluted the young commander, and asked if the foreign friend had come. Then he wheeled and galloped away, the hoof-beats of his horse fading into the darkness. One hour later we neared the outskirts of a village, saw the fluttering light of pine torches, and heard a murmur of voices that sounded like a distant river. As we drew near I saw that thousands of soldiers and civilians were gathered on both sides of the road, including many officers clad in khaki and ladies in long gowns. A couple stepped forward. The man was in the prime of life, strongly built and with an exceedingly intelligent face. I stepped from the sedan chair, grasped his outstretched hand, and heard a deep warm voice saying:

"As commander of this Army I welcome you!"

"You honor me too much, General Kwo!"

Madame Kwo, a slight little woman in a gray cotton gown, with the face of an intellectual, took my hand and held it in hers, welcoming me with warm words. While the voices of those pushing to see me rose in crescendo, General Kwo Shuen-chi introduced the members of his staff and their wives. From this moment on I found myself in a perplexingly formal world.

The headquarters of the Fiftieth Army had just been bombed, but in preparation for our visit the village had been put in perfect order. Scores of villagers had been employed to sweep and clean the streets, and a small house had been prepared for us. This building had been cleaned and whitewashed and furnished with a few carved tables and chairs, arranged with the exquisite taste of old China. Two scrolls decorated the walls and on a polished carved table between them stood a large vase holding a single crooked branch of a flowering shrub. Two large, broad-leaved plantain trees, apparently dug out of some interior courtyard, had been planted in the small enclosure in front of our house. Broad leaves glistened against the white walls.

Everything breathed the elegance and fragrance of an old culture. Such an atmosphere could never have been created in the struggling, slogan-shouting hurly-burly of the New Fourth Army; nor could it have sprung from Christian China with its half-baked imitation of the West, its cultural offshoots of America's Bible Belt.

At the back of our small, lovely courtyard Dr. Chang found a new structure built especially for the occasion. It was a privy. Inside, two steps led up to the seat as to a throne. Around the opening was a gorgeous seat-pad made of purple and crimson cloth such as were once used to protect the useless bottoms of European dukes and duchesses. When I first saw this creation, I thought of the Duchess of Milan who had once asked Leonardo da Vinci to create a special design for her private night vessel.

Dr. Chang and I glanced cautiously about to see that no one was listening before we indulged in a little ribald laughter, but she hastened to add:

"It's feudal, yet it shows how much they welcome you."

The Szechuen armies were considered the most backward in China, and the Fiftieth Army was one of them. But the war had made great changes in it, and it was now a mixture in which the old and the new struggled for mastery. Instinctive racial patriotism and the most backward practices and concepts mingled with the highest principles of modern humanity and half-digested ideas of democracy and socialism. The war was teaching it to modernize — or perish.

General Kwo Shuen-chi represented the modern tendencies, and some of the younger officers followed him by forming study clubs and subscribing to magazines and books. He was one of the most progressive and social-minded of nationalist commanders, but was impeded at every step by reactionary and corrupt staff officers who spent their leisure in gambling and smoking opium or in mere lethargy. It was an open secret that the trucks of this Army carried opium from faraway Szechuen Province to the lower Yangtze River Valley; so that the local authorities had to fight not only the Japanese and their poisonous drugs, but also opium within. The traffic was secret and officers had built up their own avenues of distribution. The Magistrate of Kinghsien had previously told me that he dared not search Szechuen soldiers passing through his district lest his men be shot.

Up to the time I made this visit, my contact with the Fiftieth Army had been confined to its wounded and to one of its modern young officers. During battles the wounded of the Fiftieth Army had passed through the New Fourth Army valley. Many had been barefoot and in rags and all had still been wearing their thin summer uniforms. Those on the stretchers had lain trembling without a shred of covering, and the walking wounded had stumbled miserably along the paths and at night lain down like homeless dogs against the walls of village houses.

The New Fourth Army had taken them into its hospitals, and before they had left they had gone from ward to ward, bowing their thanks to the patients and doctors. In the emergency dressing station which New Fourth Army doctors had prepared for them, an officer of the old world had once lain on a stretcher and peremptorily ordered Dr. Chang to care for him before caring for the common soldiers. She had quietly ignored him, and when she had finally unbound the bandage on his hand, had found nothing but a slight scratch.

Yet these soldiers had fought for their country. In enemy offensives they and the New Fourth had fought side by side like brothers. As their blood flowed in a common stream, so did friendship begin to flow between them. Perhaps the ever increasing Fascist forces heard of this, for a new Political Director was sent from Chungking to redirect the thinking of the Fiftieth Army. After his arrival General Kwo's influence began to wane and a campaign against the New Fourth Army percolated through the Szechuen troops. General Kwo and some of his officers opposed this, but the Political Director was a power unto himself, responsible only to his superiors in Chungking. He could send any report he wished without their knowledge, and he had the right to see all their reports. His work seemed to be that of a super-spy.

On the night of our arrival we attended a banquet of welcome. Foreign food, dishes, silver, linen, and wineglasses had been brought in for the occasion, and there were even place-cards, delicately painted by the wives of the officers. According to foreign custom, men and women sat side by side down the length of the white table, and with the exception of Madame Kwo, who was dressed as usual, all the other women appeared in their finest silk gowns, jewels, and foreign high-heeled shoes.

Dr. Chang and I wore our usual uniforms. We had

washed and even pressed them for the occasion, but we seemed to throw a pall over the banquet and I felt like something the cat had dragged in. However, dignified little Dr. Chang bore herself like a queen and remarked afterwards that she was proud of the uniform of her country. To our surprise, our outfits shamed the women, and two days later they all appeared in bright new cotton uniforms like ours. Only Madame Kwo continued to wear her unpretentious gray gown.

The wives of the officers were educated women, some of them university graduates, for an officer in China can claim the most elegant. Despite all their kindliness and graciousness, I still could not help observing that they were healthy women who had studied in ease, married officers with property, then put their minds on ice. They did no work in the Army, but spent their days in idle gossip and mah-jongg gambling.

Only two of them seemed out of place. One was a pious young Christian girl, newly married, who had studied Western music in Shanghai. She moved like an unhappy ghost among the others and I never once saw her smile. The other was Madame Kwo herself. A university graduate and formerly a teacher, she had left her three children in Szechuen and for months had shared all the dangers of war with her husband. She was not a Christian, and she was an austere patriot and an enemy of extravagance, opium, gambling, and idleness. Some of the officers feared her more than they feared General Kwo. She seemed to be the Army's conscience. I also learned that she and General Kwo had borrowed money from their families in order to buy the necessary medical supplies for the Army.

Each day I went by sedan chair to visit the various departments of the Army, including its hospitals. The hospitals had been put in their best order for our visit — the whitewash was still damp on the walls. The medical officers and attendants were all unqualified and did not know even the origin of malaria or scientific methods for its cure. Little good it would have done them, in any case, for this Army had received only two thousand tablets of quinine for the preceding year — in a malarial region!

One morning General Kwo and some of his staff took me to the Army Training Camp, where two hundred non-commissioned officers and a hundred educated youth were studying. The educated youth were being trained as political workers. I was asked to speak on the attitude of foreign countries toward China, and on Japanese propaganda and espionage in America and England. From magazines sent me from Shanghai, I had accumulated considerable information on both subjects. I could not hide from these men who were fighting for their lives that countries other than their own also had traitors working for the Japanese, and I gave the names of Americans engaged in this work.

The lecture developed into a conference which lasted many hours. Some of the questions I could answer, some not. But what I did observe was that the training camp was another facet of modern China where men strove to know everything that could strengthen them in their struggle.

While this conference was going on, the roar of guns on the banks of the Yangtze could be heard from afar, for the Army was using its new artillery pieces on enemy shipping and positions. Once all talk ceased as we heard the roar of approaching bombers. The building was isolated in a broad valley, and instead of fleeing, we all sat and waited, each with his own ruminations on life and death. The planes passed over; we drew a deep breath and continued our conference.

On another morning the Army put on a sports tournament in which headquarters guards, General Kwo and some of his staff, and several women took part. The Army placed great emphasis on physical training, and General Kwo was an ardent tennis enthusiast. A tennis court, a basketball court, and a small track had been laid out, and to these sports they added old Chinese boxing and sword play. In the bright, crisp air it seemed that I had never seen more beautiful or swifter bodies. These troops were physically far superior to the New Fourth Army. Turning to General Kwo,

I asked him why he didn't issue a challenge to all the other armies along the lower Yangtze for a general sports tournament, adding that it would encourage physical development and fellowship.

He agreed, then hesitated and said: "I fear it would meet with political objections."

He meant of course the objections which political directors would have against the New Fourth Army. These directors existed for the purpose of preventing friendship between the Communist Army and the other forces.

Often we gathered to watch the presentation of modern patriotic plays by the Army's Front Service Corps of educated students. The plays were good and the acting excellent, for almost all Chinese are talented actors. One evening the staff officers put on an old Peking drama for which they had bought gorgeous costumes. General Kwo was a hearty man who enjoyed everything; and he enjoyed the old opera. But these operas were regarded with contempt by modern China because they taught the feudal virtues. It was characteristic that the officers should present the old feudal dramas, but educated youth only modern patriotic plays. Here again were the two sides of the Army medal.

Returning from the theater that night, Madame Kwo suddenly turned to her husband and asked: "Who paid for those costumes? Each one cost hundreds of dollars!"

"What's that? What's that?" exclaimed the startled General.

"It's a disgrace to spend money in this way when we are poor and are fighting for our lives!" Madame Kwo cried.

The astounded General had never given the subject a thought, but his ever watchful wife had. As they left us, Dr. Chang grimly declared that Madame Kwo ought to have been commander.

On another evening Dr. Chang happened to meet a brigade commander from the front and went with him to the home of the chief of staff. As soon as they stepped inside the door, as Dr. Chang told me later, the sickly, sweet fumes of opium struck them full in the face. In the large reception room staff officers and their wives, including the Political Director and his wife, sat around mah-jongg tables, with piles of bank-notes next to them. They turned to the newcomers and, without any consciousness of wrong, asked them to join. Dr. Chang replied that she did not know how, but remained to watch. Madame Kwo, who was looking for Dr. Chang, came in at that moment. She stood in the doorway like a thin, gray specter, speaking not a word. A whisper passed from table to table, then every man and woman rose and in total silence stared fearfully at her.

"Dr. Chang, I have been looking for you," she said in a strained voice. "I want to show you a fish-pond."

Dr. Chang went with her and they walked without speaking through the dark streets. On the outskirts of the village they found a pond, but could see nothing. The gray little figure still did not speak, but moved away and turned her back. Knowing that she was weeping silently, Dr. Chang went up and took her hand.

"Do not weep; I understand," she said softly. "There are two worlds in our country — the old and the new. You and General Kwo are the new, and I also."

Clasping hands, the two women returned to my room.

Later in the evening General Kwo himself dropped in and remained for many hours, and that evening is one of my most treasured memories. We talked not at all as a Chinese and a foreigner, nor as a military man and a civilian, but as two human beings who longed for a new, free, and progressive world. Again it seemed to me that China possessed some of the most intelligent, best-informed, and courageous men on earth.

Studying the statistics which I gathered in the Fiftieth Army, I learned that it had more dead than wounded. The explanation for this fearful condition was that this Army's relations with the common people were so bad that the people would not remain with it during battles to help evacuate the wounded to the rear. Its medical personnel were not only medically unqualified, but so backward politically that they sometimes fled from hospitals during enemy advances and left the wounded to get out as best they could. And despite the fact that everyone in China knew that a wounded Chinese soldier left on the battlefield was always killed off by the enemy, this Chinese Army seemed to have no system for getting the wounded off the field. So far as I knew, there had never yet been a case of one Chinese wounded soldier taken into a Japanese hospital for treatment. Because of this, the Army had suffered losses of eight thousand dead and three thousand hopelessly maimed.

In one of my evening conversations with General Kwo I told him a story I had heard of how one of his Army doctors on the Nanling front had fled, leaving a hospital full of wounded men to shift for itself. Nineteen of them had crawled into the hills, where they had paid peasants to carry them to a New Fourth Army hospital. The General sat up rigidly and asked me for dates and exact facts. Then Madame Kwo at once sent for the medical officer. I repeated the facts, but the officer made excuses and even lied. I noticed that he seemed to fear Madame Kwo in particular. Eventually, very much frightened, he backed out of the room with many bows. A silence followed, and then I said that I thought no individual could be held responsible for the low morale when the political education of a whole army was slack.

General Kwo and I talked that night of the necessity of having his medical officers trained in the Medical Training School in Changsha, and of the need for a branch of the school on the eastern front. It was entirely too difficult to transport men across the face of the continent for a few weeks' emergency training when they might be needed at any moment if the Japanese launched a new offensive.

Once I asked Madame Kwo why she did not enter the Army's medical service. She argued that she knew nothing of medicine. Neither did I, I pointed out, but we both knew a great deal about household order and cleanliness and we knew how many stretchers were needed and how much food. I had become convinced that a few good housewives in charge of Army hospitals would have saved more lives than many of the medical officers and their soldier-nurse assistants at the front. I could not see why the educated wives of the officers were not willing to give up their useless lives in headquarters and enter the medical service.

In the report to the Red Cross Medical Corps which I wrote from the Fiftieth Army, I urged Dr. Robert Lim to send urgently needed medical supplies. I also asked for pocket manuals for the medical personnel. Finally, at the request of General Kwo, I urged Dr. Lim to review the Army Medical Service and propose changes in it.

A telegram from the New Fourth Army asked me to return at once to meet a Red Cross medical inspector who had just arrived there. I therefore interrupted my visit to the Fiftieth Army to hurry back and report on my observations.

A year and a half later General Kwo was removed from command of the Fiftieth Army because he was too progressive to meet the approval of the Political Director. He and many of his younger officers in the field had tried to prevent their Army from turning its guns against the New Fourth Army and away from the foreign invader.

The Hoofs of the Japanese

It was late June when I approached the district town of Suencheng, south of Wuhu and southwest of Nanking. Five miles to the north was a strong Japanese position and, beyond it, other garrisons on the highway to the Yangtze. The motor highway along which my party and I walked was one of the many built by the Chinese Government in former years. From this point to the coast the region was one of the major battlefields of the country. Over it fierce battles had raged and were still periodically flaring up.

Suencheng city had changed hands many times, the last time shortly before I arrived, when the Japanese had looted public granaries and carried away from 200,000 to 300,000 *piculs* (1 *picul* equals a cwt.) of rice to Wuhu. In this occupation the Japanese had brought with them hundreds of degenerate Chinese from Wuhu, and a number of Japanese and Korean *ronins*. These jackals looted homes and carried everything to their masters, who permitted them to keep a percentage.

What the Japanese had not destroyed, their jackals had burned. The entire region was like a nightmare. The highway was strewn with broken, overturned trucks, artillery chassis, and ambulances with the Red Cross insignia still showing dimly on their sides. All along the road were bomb craters and trenches half-filled with water and littered with derelict trucks, dead mules, and pieces of artillery. Charred ruins which once had been villages dotted the highway. A few ragged people wandered like ghosts among the ruins, offering for sale a few peanuts or boiled water.

Darkness was falling and rain pouring down as we entered the outskirts of Suencheng. Out of the gathering gloom rose fire-blackened walls and piles of bricks, ruined motor trucks, broken wheels, rusting cannon. Against some of the walls people had built low hovels out of broken beams, rusty gasoline tins, and rags — shelters fit for goats. With the coming of darkness these poor souls had gone to sleep and across the low opening that served as a door had propped crooked branches of trees to keep out prowling mongrels.

A broad river flowed past the ancient crenelated walls of the old city. The two old stone bridges across it had been dynamited; one was totally destroyed, and we crossed the other on rickety boards which could be withdrawn whenever the Japanese advanced.

Before the war Suencheng had had a population of about a hundred thousand people, but tens of thousands had been killed in air-raids and only a few hundred remained. Along one side of a slippery cobble-stoned street were a number of low shops partly repaired and dimly lit by native candles or open lamp bowls filled with peanut oil. On this street was a building in which the nude bodies of a dozen Chinese civilian women had been found after the Japanese were driven out. The sign on the door-frame facing the street still read: "Consolation House of the Great Imperial Army."

Coming out on a main street, we saw a low gray stone building with the name of an American Methodist mission chiseled above the entrance. The walls and roofs still stood, but the windows were gone, and through the gaping hole where the door had been we saw that it had been totally gutted. This building had been used by the Japanese as a military court and through its portals Chinese captives had been taken for "examinations" designed to extract military information from them.

Directly across the street from this mission was an old well which, like many others, was filled with the dead bodies of Chinese soldiers and civilians. The waters of the city were contaminated and many people had died in a mysterious epidemic. The Army was filling up the wells and sealing them with cement. The cement over the one across from the mission was still damp. There was a wall behind it, and directly across it was sprawled a Japanese slogan in red paint: "For the New Order in East Asia."

I stared at the well and the sign, then into the dark interior of the mission, which now seemed peopled with the spirits of the dead. The ghosts of despots were stalking the earth again, and I recalled that the Japanese had often proudly harked back to Genghis Khan and had even tried to capture his grave in Inner Mongolia. The Chinese Government had removed his coffin to the interior.

The two-story inn in which we took rooms had once been an American oil station. The roof and front had been bombed away, but crudely repaired. From my room I could look through broad cracks onto the street below. There was absolutely nothing in my room but a couple of boards across saw-horses. A servant brought in a wash-pan of hot water, and when I looked at it suspiciously, assured me that all water was now carried from up river.

I unrolled my blanket on the boards and changed to my dry uniform. I had hardly finished when two Army officers were announced. One was a Colonel in the 108th Manchurian Division, which garrisoned the city and surrounding areas. Like many Manchurian Chinese, the two men were tall, personable, and exceedingly courteous. Hearing of my arrival, they said, they had come to welcome me. At the front a welcome always lights a warm flame within the heart. The front always seemed to be a land of impersonal love, somewhere beyond ordinary friendship or love; you always reach out to men dedicated to death — or to a struggle for life. The two men asked me if I could come at once and address their regimental training camp in a building a few streets away.

We had been planning to have supper, for we had eaten nothing except peanuts since morning and the journey through the heat and rain had been exhausting. They insisted that we be their guests, and after dining in their headquarters we went to the training camp. A hundred noncommissioned officers and about half that number of political workers studied in the institution. With their regimental officers they gathered in the dark courtyard, for lights were few and dangerous. As they marched in I saw a column of strong, broad-shouldered men and caught the dim outline of dark, grim faces.

There in the darkness I tried to deliver a message that would bring courage and conviction to men who must fight and perhaps fall. Brushing aside the confusion in my own country, where predatory greed and appeasement of Fascism sought to drown out the protesting voices of liberals and workers, I tried to conjure up a picture in which millions of common people and a few enlightened leaders like President Roosevelt, Senator Pittman, and Colonel Henry Stimson sympathized with and supported China. I told half-lies. I strung together isolated news reports of strikes by maritime workers in California, Canada, England, and Holland against the shipment of war materials to Japan; of a boycott of Japanese goods; and of organizations collecting money for China.

The next year and a half I lied like this to the soldiers and civilians in the war zones. Had I spoken the truth that night, my speech would have been a cry of suffering and warning that would have sounded something like this:

Brothers! I am a citizen of a country that is supplying your enemy with the means of killing you and your people. A few of us oppose this and are burdened with the shame of blood-guilt. But the industrialists of my country value profits above human lives, and most of my people consider you "Chinamen" who "take in washing for a living."

You may ask why this is, for, unlike you, my countrymen are literate and have civil rights which enable them to develop in almost any way they wish. If they choose to follow the carrot which their masters dangle before their noses, they can; or they can use their brains and fiercely reject it. The world lies at their feet, but to take it means study, struggle, and thought. We have had great teachers of human liberty, and the foundation of my country is revolutionary. Yet my people know less of the world than you, though you perhaps cannot read.

As I move among you, I am amazed at your magnanimity toward me, a citizen of a land that aids your enemy.

No, I did not speak like that. I lied to them because men fight best when inspired with hope. But I could not hide all the evil facts from men who might soon die. After I had spoken, out of the darkness came that song of homesickness that Manchurians always sing — *Fight Back to Your Native Home*. Then they marched away as they had come, like shadows out of darkness.

On that same day we climbed Pagoda Hill inside the city walls and looked down upon the sea of destruction which had once been a city. And this had been a city in which the old had been giving place to the new. There had been a network of new paved streets and avenues, an electric-light plant, modern public schools, and even a technical college. Beyond the city walls a modern suburb had grown up, a suburb which was now nothing but a mass of ruins. Japanese airplanes had followed the modern streets of the town and leveled almost every building to the earth. Acres and acres had not even a wall standing, and now groups of destitute people rummaged in the debris, picking out bits of iron, porcelain, locks, furniture, clothing, or shoes and placing them on sale along the ruined streets.

On the hill beside us towered an old pagoda, shattered but not destroyed. Empty gun emplacements were partially hidden by foliage, and the sides of the hill were a network of trenches. On the wall of the pagoda some Japanese had penciled the lines of a sentimental poem about the "beauty" of a destroyed city.

We walked to a far end of the city where, on a ridge of hills, three modern schools, one of them a technical college, had once echoed with the voices of youth. All the buildings had been bombed and many burned. Piles of half-consumed furniture still lay in the larger halls. In a few of the rooms, still intact, a primary school was in session and in others the Manchurian Division had started a new training school. When we appeared, teachers dismissed classes and the pupils streamed out, lined up, and sang patriotic songs.

At the foot of the ridge lay the campus and buildings of a former American missionary high school. Like the Chinese institutions they had been used by the Japanese as barracks. On their inside walls were penciled Japanese slogans and indecent words. In the corner of one room, near the floor, we found these Japanese lines:

> Fighting and death everywhere and now I am also wounded. China is limitless and we are like drops of water in an ocean. There is no purpose in this war. I shall never see my home again.

One morning the streets of Suencheng reverberated with marching feet. Troops mingled with strong, broad-backed armed civilians from near-by villages, and the entire population marched, singing and with guns clanking, to the public square. At the end of the square rose an ancient bell tower from which warnings were always sounded when planes approached. Repaired buildings and charred walls were decorated with banners and slogans in both English and Chinese. Here again was the eternal cry of the Manchurian soldiers: "Fight Back to Your Native Home."

As we passed along, two soldiers with paint buckets and brushes smiled at us. Just behind them was a new slogan, the paint still wet. It read: *Long live the "Manchester Guardian," voice of democracy.*

A small group of young women, members of the local Women's National Salvation Association, were giving the final touches to decorations as we climbed the ladder to the platform of the bell tower. They were educated women in their twenties, eager and intelligent and, on this occasion, glowing with pride that a woman had been the first reporter to come to the war zone along the lower Yangtze. Many men speakers were on the program that day, but in honor of our sex a woman introduced me. She rubbed the equality of women into the hide of every lowly man in that audience, repeatedly waving her hand in my direction and calling upon them to view this pillar of emancipated womanhood who dared what no man reporter dared!

The crowd gazed at me with deference. Indeed, they could do little more, for they were packed so tightly that they could only turn their eyes.

The situation was inspiring. Here we stood amidst the ruins of a city, its wells filled with corpses, and its people so poor they owned only the clothes on their backs. The enemy had a strong garrison just five miles to the north, their planes in Wuhu could reach us within a few minutes if they thought us worth their steel, and there was not one anti-aircraft gun to welcome them. Every creature standing before me was gambling with death. Yet men stood here speaking of the certainty of final victory and a woman insisted on the equality of the sexes.

Crossing the Yangtze

From my diary:

Night of August 26, 1939

Before another week is passed I shall have realized a dream of many months — to cross the broad Yangtze between the

Japanese positions and go into that vast hinterland of the enemy rear in central Anhwei Province. There are 15,000 guerrillas of the New Fourth Army there now, and one of the regular armies has penetrated into it. Today General Yeh Ting said it would be "like going through darkest Africa. It will take months and at the end will come Chungking."

August 31

Today at noon staff headquarters delivered a telegram from Jawaharlal Nehru, asking where and when he could meet me. He has just arrived from India. He is the guest of the Government and will certainly remain for months and visit all the fronts. I am anxious to see him. I have wired and asked if he can meet me four months hence at Laohokuo, the headquarters of the Fifth War Zone in Hupeh Province to the west. If he cannot, then I must again cross the Yangtze and try to get a truck for Chungking. For I wish to propose large-scale medical aid from India to China, and to suggest that he send Indian volunteers to be trained in guerrilla warfare.

I have been re-reading the autobiography which Nehru wrote in prison, and its spell is still upon me. I suppose all autobiographies find an echo in the hearts of many people, and the more universal they are, the more is this true. Many passages in Nehru's book resound in my own heart, for example —

> I have become a queer mixture of East and West, and out of place everywhere, at home nowhere. . . . I am a stranger and an alien in the West. . . . But in my own country also, sometimes, I have an exile's feeling.

I have been in China for ten years, and when I came it was to me only a possible gateway to India. But as China conquers most people, so has it conquered me. As Nehru dreams of visiting his azure lake in the Himalayas, so do I still dream of one day visiting India. Like him, I fear I may grow too old to carry out my original plan. . . . I have reviewed Nehru's book for the Army monthly *Kang Di*, and the Army has set a man to translating the entire book into Chinese for publication. . . . Tomorrow evening we begin marching toward the Yangtze. I shall visit the Governor at last. . . .

This was my last diary note south of the Yangtze. On the morning that we left, Vice-Commander Hsiang Ying told me with subdued excitement that the Soviet Union had just signed a Non-Aggression Pact with Nazi Germany, and added: "The whole international situation is changing."

That familiar phrase aroused my suspicions and worried me. It savored of the incantations with which men hypnotize themselves. Though I pretended to no political omniscience, I could not see wherein the "whole" international situation was changing. I accepted the Soviet-Nazi Pact as a temporary expedient, but never doubted for a moment that a Fascist war against the Soviet Union was inevitable. The Munich Pact the year before had been a barefaced attempt of British and French imperialists to drive Nazi armies eastward against the Soviet Union. The Soviet-Nazi Pact had been the Soviet reply — a desperate reply. Nevertheless, the Nazis and their Japanese allies still remained the most dangerous enemies of the Soviet Union and of all mankind. Underneath, the international situation remained unchanged.

In the following months I tried to keep track of international developments, but found this difficult. For over a year thereafter I saw no foreign publications, and only one Chinese newspaper that published world news. The only international change I heard of was the rise in various countries of deliberately inspired isolationist and peace movements. I read that powerful American isolationists had their base in Congress and that some of their leaders had been decorated by Hitler. The Communists of England, France, and America had also started "negotiated peace" movements with the "German people."

Chinese often asked me significant questions. One was whether the refusal of the American Congress to fortify

Guam was due to Japanese bribery; I thought it doubtful. Chinese Communists asked why the British workers had opposed universal conscription and I thought they refused to have human lives conscripted unless the wealth of the ruling class was conscripted. For a time the Chinese Communists called the second World War an imperialist war, but although the Soviet Union maintained a truce with Japan, the Chinese Communists never talked of a "negotiated peace" with the Japanese people; to have talked thus would have been like injecting a drug into the blood-stream of China. They knew that the chief enemies of mankind were the Nazis and the Japanese. Even though the Government was permeated with reactionaries, the Chinese Communists encouraged unity — at the same time urging broad social reforms that would inspire the people to stronger resistance against the enemy.

After eight months along the Yangtze River Valley I was venturing into what had seemed to me a vast no man's land — the area north of the Yangtze. Up to this time I had been with armies which could retreat to the rear if forced to do so. This would no longer be possible. The territory north of the great river was surrounded on three sides by the enemy: along the Yangtze on the south; along the Tientsin-Nanking railway on the east; and along the Hwei River and the Lunghai railway on the north. The Japanese also occupied a number of walled cities within reach of their main forces scattered along the railways and rivers. In addition, two or three motor highways intersected the region.

However, millions of Chinese still lived in this great territory and held all but the enemy fringes. The New Fourth Army commanded some 15,000 guerrillas, whose ranks were constantly increasing, but whose poverty was also very great.

The column of men with which I would go consisted of one hundred trained military and political workers, among the latter a small Front Service Corps of educated youth. We also would take the first medical unit to service the northern guerrillas: one qualified doctor, N. C. Gung, graduate of the Scotch missionary Mukden Medical College, four qualified women nurses, and ten educated students who had just finished a six-month course in the New Fourth Army Medical Training School.

Of all the men in our column, only four knew the route of march or when we would leave. On September 1 we were given orders to start, but to spread the rumor that we were going to the rear. At dusk a long line of carriers arrived, for the medical unit alone was taking enough supplies to last six months and the military and political units were carrying educational material and a printing press. Each person was ordered to strip his personal belongings to the barest essentials. I had a carrier for my typewriter, paper, camera, medical supplies, and light bedding, and the Army assigned a special officer to accompany me. I also had a special bodyguard, Tsai Loh, the same tough young guerrilla soldier who had accompanied me on other journeys up and down the Yangtze. As an "old Red Army man," Tsai Loh dearly loved dangerous and interesting ventures.

Since news that a foreigner was passing through the battle zone might reach the Japanese, I was supplied with a sedan chair in which I would have to sit completely covered up when passing through the villages. At dusk our medical unit with its carriers moved out. After an hour's march we waited in an isolated grove of trees for the others. They appeared almost immediately, led by Commander Feng Da-fee, a man who was not much over thirty and yet had formerly commanded troops of the Red Army. He had been dean of the training camp of the New Fourth Army and was now in charge of our entire column.

When all had assembled, Commander Feng called us to order and gave the first report on the exact situation in the region through which we were to pass. He painted no rosy picture. Before the night was finished, he said, we would be in a zone in which there was almost constant fighting. It was the safest time of the month to travel, for the moon did not rise until one or two in the morning, and as a rule the Japanese never ventured out at night, for guerrillas lurked everywhere.

Every precaution, he said, had been taken to keep our plans a secret. During the previous week the Army had sent civilian and plain-clothes military spies up and down the Yangtze and into Japanese-garrisoned towns to watch for any unusual Japanese activity. So far nothing remarkable had been noted. On the march there was to be no talking, no smoking or lighted matches, and no flashlights. Each was to follow the man directly ahead of him. The nights were dark; if the man ahead stepped up or down, the man behind should at once do likewise.

"*Tso-ba!*" ordered our commander, and we began to move out single-file along the narrow paths.

Two or three hours passed and then the head of the column whispered over his shoulder to the man behind him. This whisper spread down the line and we all immediately sat down on the path and rested. There was not a sound.

Ten minutes later another whispered order came. We rose and marched.

So we passed through the night and at dawn came to a small village. We were on a battlefield and in the growing light I could see the figures of civilian sentries, with guns, standing guard on the surrounding hills. We ate and lay down to sleep, resting secure in the hearts of the people.

In the late afternoon we rose, ate a meal of rice with a bowl of boiled cabbage and eggs, marched for an hour to an isolated spot, and halted to hear another report from our commander. There was nothing new. When passing through villages from now on, he said, we should take pains to be very quiet, lest we awaken the sleeping people. Our shoes were made of cloth, even to the soles, and made no sound, but even so we were asked to walk softly through villages.

We passed through the sleeping, silent villages and only now and then did we see the dark figure of some civilian standing guard on a path, his rifle showing above his shoulder. From the direction of the mud walls with their low thatched roofs we always heard sounds of sick men moaning. It was a malarial region, but the Army did not have the medicine or medical workers to care for all the people.

Once we came to a cross-road. A tall civilian, with a gun, stood in the shadow of a tree and whispered: "Turn to the left!"

Beyond this one command, and the whispered order to rest or march, no word was spoken throughout the night. Up winding mountain paths, down through valleys, and up mountain paths again, we made our way. We went so slowly along the dark paths that the dawn found us still on the road. We saw the peasants beginning to harvest their ripened grain along the mountain terraces and in the valleys. They harvested with sickles, then gathered huge bundles of the reaped grain in their hands and whipped the ripe heads into big open wooden bins in the fields. Some of their older men, armed with guns, moved along the hill-tops and some stood watch at the far end of the valleys.

On September 3, before crossing the Yangtze, we took our last rest in a deserted temple high in the mountains. Before going to sleep we ran up the highest peak and looked down on the gleaming river, ten miles away. We saw the black hulk of what seemed to be a cruiser nosing its way up river. To the west we could see a pall of smoke over the Japanese-occupied river port Tikang. Feng Da-fee pointed to two towns lying on the plain below us, about five miles from the shore of the Yangtze. "Those are the enemy garrison points," he said. "Tonight we will pass directly between them."

In the late afternoon we rose and, without eating, moved forward. The path was blocked by felled trees and we had to pick our painful way through the brush. We were in the Hung Hwang Shan mountains where the 1st Battalion, Third Detachment, New Fourth Army, had its headquarters. I remember sitting in the lovely, cool little courtyard of the commander, Chen Lin-hung. He and the vice-commander, Ma Chang-yien, had formerly been peasants and also commanders in the Tenth Red Army Corps, whose leader was the famous Fang Chi-ming, long since dead.

These two commanders with their chief of staff and a number of other men gathered to talk with us. They had thrown a *cordon sanitaire* around the village to prevent any news of our arrival from reaching the Japanese garrisons on the plain below.

I was in the midst of youth. With the exception of Feng Da-fee there was not a man in the courtyard over thirty years of age. They literally seethed with energy. They told us that they had laid an ambush for the Japanese the night before and wiped out many of them. As we ate they said:

"Our fighting is not guerrilla warfare, not mobile warfare, not positional warfare — it's just nothing at all! There are no more than a thousand enemy soldiers on the plain below. If all our troops were concentrated along the river and organized in small units for guerrilla and mobile warfare, we could clean out this region!"

As they began to discuss our crossing they spread a military map on the table, but we hardly needed a map, for we could see the plain below and even the distant Yangtze. When we would reach our port of embarkation, the Japanese at Tikang would be just twenty *li* (seven miles) to our west and their gunboat would be able to reach us in a few minutes. It would take forty-five minutes to cross the Yangtze. Our boats would be nearly half-way across before the enemy learned that we had left. Add fifteen minutes to that and we would be near the north shore. The troops along the shore would in the meantime have opened up with heavy machine-guns to divert them.

"As a rule it's just a little jaunt," said one of the commanders. "Our men like it."

A typical reaction to all this was that of Dr. Gung's personal orderly, Tsai Ban-tang. He was a poor peasant of about thirty years of age who had joined the Army a few months before. He had been a little afraid at first, but now he had caught the challenging spirit of the battalion and walked around proudly, laughing, snapping his fingers as if saying to the Japanese: "Come on, you bastards!"

I also remember vividly how Tsai Loh, my bodyguard, stood tall and straight by my side, watching as I wrote in my diary. I had given him my pistol to examine and put in order. Finishing, he said: "Come!" and I turned to put the diary in my attaché case. But I saw that Tsai had the case over his shoulder, for he was young and strong and always insisted on relieving me of every burden.

We left the courtyard and went to a small grove of trees, where I found a remarkable gathering. On one side was grouped the special company of armed fighters who were to escort us to the shore of the Yangtze, and sitting on the earth near us were all our own groups and the small army of carriers. The carriers were all testing their burdens. It was growing dark. Picking our way over the piles of luggage, we took our places with the medical unit. My secretary was already there, talking in a low voice with the others.

Commander Feng's voice came through the growing darkness: "Attention, comrades!" He then began a last-minute report. This morning, he said, a Japanese gunboat had anchored in front of the very village from which we must embark. Enemy launches had come ashore and the Japanese had searched all men, forcing them to remove their clothing, feeling their heads for the telltale creases left by a soldier's cap, and asking if they had seen or heard any soldiers. No one had heard anything. The gunboat had then moved off and anchored before Tikang. All this, however, was the ordinary terrorist practice of the enemy and we were not to consider it unusual. Reports from men sent up and down the river and into enemy garrisons showed no remarkable enemy activity.

He continued: "When we pass between the enemy garrison points on the plain below, do not waver if you hear fighting from either the right or the left, but march steadily forward. The same order applies when we reach the river. We have troops for ten miles up and down the Yangtze; they will fight and are under orders not to retreat. Our sentries will know every Japanese move, and if an enemy gunboat passes while we are on the shores of the river, we will wait until it has passed, then cross. In case anything serious happens, of course we must retreat and return here. The chief thing is to keep a cool head and obey orders. If you are separated from the rest of the group, there is always a way out if you keep cool. But when we are once out on the river there can be no retreat. . . .

"Some of you are sick with malaria and some have sore feet. Disregard this; summon all your strength and make a supreme effort tonight. We will not halt for long periods of rest. There must be no sound, no lights — and no coughing. Try to quiet the barking dogs. Carriers, test your burdens and stick grass in all places that squeak. All of you comrades with white face-towels should stick one end inside the back of your collars and let the end hang down so the man behind you can see it in the darkness. Soon we will be on the plain and will be able to see the paths better. Do not fall behind. Now I give you all ten minutes to make final preparations."

There was a rustling as the men made ready. Ten minutes passed and Commander Feng's voice rose through the darkness:

"Tso-ba!"

I saw the dark shadows of our armed escort split in two, one going in advance, one remaining to bring up the rear. Then the rest of us began to move out, a column of about five hundred men. I could hardly see, so I reached out and placed my arm on Tsai Loh's shoulder as we moved single-file down the long, winding mountain path.

As we approached a darkened sleeping village, a chorus of mongrels would begin to bark. They heralded the approach of our advance guards and continued to announce us until the last man had vanished. By that time our advance guards had reached another village, and the dogs there would begin. Nothing could quiet them.

On the path there was no sound save the faint pad-pad of soft-clad feet mingled with the low creaking of bamboo poles over the shoulders of our carriers. Often I could see nothing. But sometimes the clouds above us shifted and then by the bright light of the stars I could make out the dim, moving shadows of two or three men in front of me.

Once as we neared a village the whisper "Rest" came down the line. We dropped to the earth in silence. One carrier lay flat and tried to light his pipe, but hardly had the match begun to flame before a guard was on him, knocking the light from his hand.

As I sat there I saw beneath a clump of bushes a small temple to the Earth God with a bright new candle burning in its little alcove. The candle had just been lighted — a signal that all was well. My bodyguard put his mouth very close to my ear and whispered that we must now pass directly between the enemy positions.

Down the column came the whispered command: "March quickly!"

We rose and began to move quickly, sometimes dropping into a slow trot. Suddenly I saw two soldiers, each armed with a tommy-gun, running in the rice-fields on either side of me. They had been ordered to my side to protect me, no matter what happened.

Sometimes we crossed rolling, barren hills, and then we crouched low and ran, lest our dark figures be seen in outline by enemy sentries.

I heard the night birds, the wind through the trees; and when the clouds shifted, the stars above seemed never to have glowed so bright. Once far away on our left I heard a faint call, like the bellow of a buffalo calf. But it sounded three times and had something weird about it. Then, far to our right, I heard an answering call, and knew that guerrillas or civilians were giving us a signal — a signal that all was well. For no whispered command came down the line and no warning shot sounded in the night. Through me swept a great love for the Chinese and for their guerrilla and civilian patriots. I loved them with all my heart that night, for many men knew of our passing and yet all had kept the faith.

Again the whispered order "Rest" sent us dropping to the path, and Tsai Loh whispered joyously in my ear: "We've passed through the enemy garrison points!"

All the men began to punch and nudge one another happily. My resting-place was on the summit of a slope. Suddenly the flare of matches lit up the sides of a deep ditch in which the men were crouching. In a moment the glow of cigarette tips had crept down the whole slope. They were like fireflies drawn up in a long column and they clearly revealed the location of our entire detachment! Tsai Loh also saw. He gave an angry grunt, leaped into the dark rice-fields, and began running toward the rear. Soon I heard the soft padding of many feet. Our armed rear guard swept past, and as they ran down the slope I saw all the little fireflies disappear one by one.

After ten minutes we were on our feet and marching again. We approached a village, but to our surprise no dogs barked! Our column seemed to be slowing down and stopping. My section moved into the village street, and I could distinguish a long line of dark tables, each covered with dozens of bowls. The ghostly hands of men, women, and children were reaching out, offering us hot drinking water. Just as I reached out to take a bowl a dog began to bark wildly somewhere in the village. The figure of a little boy leaped from behind a table, sped across the street, and disappeared in the direction of the sound. There was a low strangling yelp, then silence again. I returned my rice-bowl to a shadowy hand, pressing it in silent thanks, and hurried to catch up with those ahead of me.

Nearing the mighty Yangtze, we came out on top of the high earthen dikes that hold back the river during the floods. Dark lagoons slumbered on either hand — breeding-places of the malarial mosquito. Then a traitor appeared: the red half-moon rose like a balloon over the mountains behind us and cast its ruddy glow across the white dikes and the dark lagoons. I could see a part of the long column in front of me. We cursed under our breath and began to hurry and even run. Our carriers dropped into a slow, rhythmical dog-trot, breathing heavily.

Suddenly a whispered command to halt fled down the column and in confusion and foreboding we came to a dead stop, crouching, listening, staring intently through the night.

Low voices began to murmur confusedly, and then above them came an angry command:

"*Bu yao tan hwa!*" (Stop talking!)

Tsai Loh was pointing, and following his finger I looked far down the dike ahead and saw a yellow blaze flare up inside the walls of the village, then die down suddenly, as if it were paper burning.

"March quickly!" came the whispered order, and again we hurried forward, knowing that all was well — all save the traitor moon.

I heard the thud of running feet, and again our rear guards sped past us. They fanned out and surrounded the village ahead of us. Their dark figures soon moved along the top of the village wall, rifles in hand, and some ran through the streets to stand in the shadow of houses, watching for any signal flares that might be sent up by traitors.

Down the dikes came a civilian in white jacket and trousers, sauntering along as if out for an evening's stroll. As he passed me, I lowered my head lest he see the face of a foreigner. Right behind me he halted and said: "Everything's in order!" and came sauntering back.

We did not enter the village, but halted in a depression on the shores of a tributary of the Yangtze. Here two great river junks lay creaking, their sails up and their gangplanks down and waiting. Our carriers ran up one plank, quickly and silently dropped their burdens into the open hold, and then ran down the other. Within a few minutes the junks were loaded. As we waited, I heard whispering and low talking. Tsai Loh took my arm and said: "Take this junk — it goes first!" My secretary and I ran up the plank, forgetting to bid Tsai Loh farewell. He was returning that night to the mountains, going back with our armed escort. Then I learned that those who took this first junk had a better chance of surviving: it would leave ten minutes before the other.

Many of our people were exhausted and two women nurses had been sick for hours with a malarial attack. Ignoring the danger, they all fell flat on the deck, closed their eyes, and slept like the dead. The great oar at the stern of our junk began to creak and we saw that we were pushing off. Soon we came out on the broad bosom of the Yangtze, blanketed in a silvery haze. A rolling and mighty river, it stretched before us like an ocean. At this point it was five miles wide as the crow flies, but actually seventy *li* (about twenty-three miles) from our place of embarkation to the village where we were to land.

We anxiously peered at the dark shore and disappearing buildings behind us. The half-moon was now high above, casting a long silvery path over the waters. Flaky clouds floated across its face. The wind blew strong and fresh and we cried out in joy as it bellied out the great ragged sails and sent us leaping forward. Our eyes scanned the mist, watchful for enemy gunboats; and we strained our ears for any sound of firing.

Suddenly the sails went limp and the boatmen began to tack back toward the receding shore! Fear seized us. Each minute seemed an eternity. Finally the boatmen turned the junk, the sail filled out again, and we sped on and on toward a long black line that gradually became a shore edged with trees. On our left was the low, sandy beach of an island where we would have landed had the enemy attacked. Two big junks were anchored near it. As we approached, one of our boatmen leaped up as if catapulted and bellowed furiously: "Who are you?"

"Who are you?" came back a contemptuous shout. Our boatman was infuriated. "Get out of here!" he yelled. A mocking laugh answered.

The second junk also challenged us, and this was more than our boatman could bear. He roared like an angry lion, demanding to know who they were and what they were doing out at night. A calm voice answered: "We're the Fanchang Guerrilla Inspection Unit. Who are you?"

All the fury left our boatman, and in a contemptuous voice he answered: "None of your business!"

I laughed. We were in a land in which the nights belonged to the Chinese.

As if he had not just been frothing with rage, our boatman began to talk of the enemy in a matter-of-fact voice:

"This morning the maggoty sons-of-incestuous-mothers came to our village and made us undress. They stripped me naked and felt my head for the crease of a soldier's cap and asked me: 'You Chinese soldier?' I told the *tze-tze* (louse) that I'd never seen a soldier! . . . I know a man who just came back from Wuhu. Before they let him enter, they stuck a needle in his arm and made him pay a dollar for it! They called it an injection against cholera, but of course they are liars. They certainly put poison in him."

"*Wang bah tan!*" he cursed vilely, and spat.

His picturesque references to the mothers of the Japanese eased the atmosphere and we all began to talk.

"What would you do if the Japanese should come?" my secretary asked me.

"Well, I have my pistol," I remember answering. "And if everything else should fail, there's always the Yangtze."

He agreed, for we all knew that the Japanese took no prisoners.

The trees on the north shore became clearer and, beyond them, buildings. Down the river shore we saw the dim figures of sentries, rifles on their backs. As our junks touched land we leaped over the sides and ran excitedly toward a crowd of people. The whole village was up, waiting for us. A man in a white jacket and trousers came forward, introducing himself as the *chu* official.

We walked into the village and sank to rest on a broad flat threshing-floor which gleamed white in the faint moonlight. A group gathered, put their heads together, and began singing the *Guerrilla Marching Song*. Ten minutes later the second junk landed and our commander, Feng Da-fee, congratulated us on our military discipline. We had done much better than he had expected.

We still had ten miles to walk to the home of a big landlord who, with his brothers and sons, led the "North Shore Guerrilla Detachment." Their ancestral home was the guer-

The whole population of towns and villages gathered in groves to avoid air-raids, and there I told them of millions of foreign friends who hoped for their victory.

South of Nanking I met a column of peasant guerrillas who had fought the Japanese since the war began.

rilla headquarters and was big enough to shelter all our column. We would spend a few days there.

It was a pleasure to be able to walk side by side with the men instead of in single file. The dike was high and broad and a fine road ran along its top. But we were too weary to reach the landlord's house, and Commander Feng decided that we should sleep the rest of the night in a hamlet four miles inland.

The village lay silent in sleep and only a few people came out to see what the noise was. Leaning against the houses in the public square was some harvesting equipment. We pulled down huge mats, drying-trays, and benches and unrolled our bedding on them. Some men climbed inside the wheat bins to sleep. I was one of the few who possessed a mosquito net. I hung this from the branches of a tree so that it would drape over me, but few of us could sleep, for the huge black mosquitoes that infest the north swarmed on all sides. The men built smudge fires of paper and leaves and kept moving about restlessly.

We rose at the first signs of dawn and prepared to march six miles to a place where we would get breakfast and perhaps some rest. To Dr. Gung, who walked by my side, I complained that I was weary, hot, damp, and sticky and that I never before had seen mosquitoes as big as birds!

On one side of the dike flowed a broad canal and on the other stretched fields of wheat, corn, and *kao-liang* (a kind of sorghum). We seemed to have left the rice lands behind. The south shore of the Yangtze had been semi-tropical; simply by crossing the river we seemed to have entered the temperate zone! Around me was the same kind of landscape which I had so often seen as far away as Peiping.

That was how we crossed the Yangtze.

BOOK VII

Through Central China

Late Autumn 1939

BOOK VII

Through Central China

Late Autumn 1879

Book VII: Through Central China

Late Autumn 1939

Commander Chang Yun-ee and the Fourth Detachment

I LOST track of time, but it must have been September 12 or 13 when we arrived at the headquarters of the Fourth Detachment of the New Fourth Army in central Anhwei Province. Dr. Gung and I had spent a part of each day doctoring people stricken with malaria. This scourge had spread over all China since the beginning of the war. Southern armies moving back and forth across the face of the country had carried it to the most inaccessible regions. We took some comfort from the fact that the Japanese also had malaria. But they also had a good medical service, and every Japanese doctor and nurse had been mobilized for the war.

As we approached guerrilla headquarters, we came out upon a wide plain, with groups of solidly built buildings and temples among overhanging trees. Beyond, to the north and west, rose the foothills of the Ta Pieh mountain ranges. The plain before us was famous as the place where, in the remote Three Kingdoms period, the villainous Tsao Tsao had assembled and trained his troops. It was now covered with people hurrying toward the village from every direction. Some were soldiers, some were civilians, but all lined up and began shouting slogans of welcome and singing the Vanguard Marching Song.

Chang Yun-ee,[1] Commander of the Fourth Detachment, and Lai Chuan-chu, his chief of staff, came out eagerly to welcome us. A bath which refreshed our weary bodies was followed by an excellent supper served on long tables in a courtyard overhung with climbing vines and shaded by tow-

[1] Killed in action by the Japanese in the summer of 1942.

ering willows. Reclining bamboo chairs were brought out and we lay back and spent another memorable evening in conversation.

Commander Chang Yun-ee was slight and short of build and wore a strange smile that was not exactly a smile. He was an intellectual, a onetime commander in the Kuomintang armies who had become a Communist and had been for a period of years Mao Tze-tung's chief of staff. He was a thoughtful and well-read man, from whom I constantly learned much that was new and stimulating.

I asked him for details of a story I had heard in south Anhwei. Its background was this: Before the war this Fourth Detachment, then called the Fourth Red Army, had fought on the borders of Anhwei and in the adjoining Hupeh and Honan Provinces. It had been called a "model Red Army" because of its guerrilla tactics and its organization and education of the common people. After it had suffered defeat in a series of fierce campaigns in 1933–4, its main force had evacuated and eventually joined the central body of the Red Army in the northwest (which became the Eighth Route). Guerrilla units had remained behind, however, fighting sporadically. In November 1937, after the national united front was firmly established, three thousand of them had assembled and became the Fourth Detachment of the New Fourth Army. Kao Ching-ting, a Communist, was then the commander. In May and June 1938, when the Japanese began their many-pronged offensive against Hankow, Generalissimo Chiang ordered the detachment to organize into two regiments and to strike at the rear of the enemy along the Tientsin-Nanking railway and along the highways in Anhwei.

Separated from the main body of the New Fourth Army by the Yangtze River, Kao Ching-ting soon developed into a local militarist. His head grew big with power, he took concubines, became corrupt, and arrested and killed anyone who opposed him. Medical supplies sent to him from general headquarters were sold to shopkeepers, but Commander Kao kept demanding more.

In the late winter of 1938 Commander Chang Yun-ee was sent from general headquarters to investigate Commander Kao and to reorganize the detachment for more efficient fighting. But Kao had built up a powerful clique of personal followers against whom Chang Yun-ee could do nothing. In May 1939 General Yeh Ting, Commander-in-Chief of the New Fourth Army, had crossed the Yangtze on a tour of inspection, but Kao had thrown special bodyguards around his headquarters and waited menacingly. Such was the background of this detachment.

I asked Commander Chang what happened after that. He smiled his strange smile and said that General Yeh, totally unarmed, had walked right through the cordon of Kao's bodyguards and said: "Commander Kao, I place you under arrest!" And to Commander Kao's utter stupefaction, his bodyguards had not fired a shot. General Yeh even brought him to public trial before his own soldiers. They voted for his death, and in June 1939 General Yeh ordered the sentence carried out.

Two of Commander Kao's concubines who lived near headquarters were both expecting children by him. They received a maintenance allowance from the Army — for it was felt that the fault was not theirs.

When I heard this story, my admiration for General Yeh Ting increased, and I remembered his stubborn mouth, his fearlessness, his vision, and his militant, vital culture.

This guerrilla detachment had recently captured a number of Chinese who had become Japanese spies. One was being held in headquarters. In the hope of saving his life, this fellow admitted that as a result of an investigation he had made of the general headquarters of the Army to the south of the river, the whole valley in which the headquarters was located had been bombed and over a hundred people killed and wounded. I had been in the very midst of that bombing and, lying in a shallow ditch, had watched with horror as the planes, flying low, tried to hit the hospital. The planes had even gone after a herd of draft buffalo, machine-gunning and killing sixteen of them.

The prisoner talked freely of a spy ring of which he was a member. These rings were organized in groups, each headed by a "big man," a Chinese landlord or merchant. The particular group to which the prisoner belonged had its center in Tunling, a town on the south shore near the Japanese garrison at Sunan. Ordinary spies were paid fifteen dollars a month, he said, but sometimes the "big men" paid poor men a dollar for each piece of military news they brought in. The poor men did not know for whom they were really working, and since their homes had been destroyed, they welcomed every cent that came their way.

In the evenings Commander Yang Yun-ee and members of his staff sat in the courtyard of the peasant home where I was staying. They talked of the economic origin of banditry and poverty, and of the great landlords of central Anhwei, some of whom owned thousands of acres of land. The landlords had fled far to the rear or to port cities under foreign protection, but had left agents behind to collect the same rents and the same usurious rates on loans as before the war. The puppet Governor of the province, appointed by the Japanese, was Ni Tao-liang, a big landlord who still made use of his feudal relations with his friends and tenants to organize puppet troops. There were now about five thousand of these in the province, commanded by relatives of the puppet leaders.

But the Japanese seldom trusted the conscripted puppet soldiers to fight the Chinese guerrillas, using them instead as garrison troops in occupied towns. The puppets were bad fighters and the guerrillas had already captured and disarmed hundreds of them. Bandit gangs were paid by the Japanese to disturb the countryside, and few people dared travel without the protection of troops. The puppet troops could be re-educated and taken into the guerrilla detachment, but the bandits seldom or never.

Japanese tactics in dealing with the people had become very cunning, said the commanders. When they had first invaded this province, they had burned villages and slaughtered the people, thinking to conquer by terror. No Chinese had been permitted to live within seven miles of the Tientsin-Nanking railway. But in recent months some smart Japanese intellectuals had thought up a "reconciliation" approach. Around the lunar New Year of 1939 they had begun to confiscate the land of landlords who had fled from the railway zone rather than become traitors; then the Japanese had divided this land among the peasants, given each villager ten cents as a New Year's present, and distributed candy and cakes to the children. They had even instructed Japanese soldiers not to rape the women and girls.

In confiscating and dividing the land the Japanese were parading around in the cast-off clothes, so to speak, of the old Red Army. They had also learned from the Chinese the value of slogans and had painted the walls with such pronouncements as "Peace and prosperity to China!" "Lay down your guns and take up the plow!" "Oppose the Communist bandits!" and "Oppose corrupt Government and support the reformed Government at Nanking!"

The Japanese even took a leaf from the book of the Chinese Red Cross Medical Corps and began to send out mobile medical units to vaccinate the people against smallpox, cholera, and typhoid and to treat them for other ailments.

But their appeasement tactics nearly always failed. Since they were essentially an army of conquest, everything they did was for their own protection and power; and their soldiers had tasted blood too long to respect orders. The Japanese soldiers, moreover, were poor men who wanted to send money and valuables home to their families. Unlike their officers, they got nothing from the drug and opium traffic, or from confiscated Chinese banks and industries; so they took ruthlessly from the people. The people were thus compelled to fight them. Every man knew the true face of the Japanese, and all their slogans, their candy and cakes, their feigned kindness to children and animals, could not hide it.

At reveille each morning the doctors and nurses moved out into the hills to conduct physical examinations of the troops. This was a new phase of the Chinese Revolution. The soldiers had never before had a physical examination, and the New Fourth Army was the first in China to introduce the system. The practice was not universal even here, and it was not yet possible to examine all new volunteers.

The examinations aroused tremendous excitement among the soldiers and the civilian population, and they spoke of it almost with reverence. Radio news of the arrival of the first medical unit had been sent to all the fighting units, and the first seven stretchers carrying wounded men had already arrived. A new hospital was being prepared in a village. When Dr. Gung told one wounded man that medical supplies would not arrive until the following day, the man answered: "It does not matter. Just to see a doctor makes me feel better."

On the fourth day, when the mass meetings of welcome were over, the women's conference a thing of the past, and the many interviews ended, I had time to accompany the medical unit on its rounds. The bugle awoke us at dawn and with the doctor and nurses I walked for an hour through murmuring bamboo forests to the temple which housed the training camp of the three central Anhwei guerrilla detachments. One hundred and eighty lower officers, and soldiers selected to become lesser commanders, were studying in this camp. There was a teaching staff of fifteen, and henceforth a new course — in hygiene — would be given by one of the women nurses.

By noon the physical examinations were finished and the results cursorily summarized. Of the students 100 per cent had trachoma, 20 per cent hernia, 30 per cent malaria, 20 per cent caries, 50 per cent scabies. There were many cases of intestinal disorders, and eight men had active tuberculosis. There was no venereal disease. This record was about the average for all the troops, and was perhaps the average for the civilian population from which the soldiers came.

I spent the afternoon talking with the training-camp students about their lives, ideas, studies, and fighting records. Most of them were former Red Army men and of these the majority were poor peasants. The rest were artisans. Most had already fought from eight to ten years. Some of those who had joined the Army after the Japanese invasion had been selected to study because of their fighting records. There was one intellectual, a student, destined to be a political director.

The men took me through their billets and classrooms. A large wall newspaper was pasted up in the main lecture hall, and the halls were hung with slogans like "Fight and study!" and "Consolidate the united front!" The billets were clean and orderly, but more barren than anything I had so far seen. Down the length of each room were rows of bare boards laid across saw-horses, and at the head lay each man's "blanket," neatly folded. This "blanket" consisted of a double layer of dark blue cotton cloth two yards long — this and nothing else for summer or winter. On wooden pegs above the "bed" hung each man's rifle and ammunition belt, and beneath it his *shubao*, or cloth kit bag. The "blanket," the *shubao*, the rifle, and the uniforms on their backs were the sole possessions of these guerrillas.

I asked to examine the contents of some of the *shubao*, and half a dozen were immediately placed before me. A typical one was that of Hu Chia-chen, a twenty-seven-year-old platoon commander. He had been a member of the old Red Army for seven years before the Japanese invasion, and then had fought continuously at the front until selected to study. He came from a poor peasant family which owned 1½ *mao* (3 *mao* make an acre) of land and had a debt of $300 (on which they paid an annual interest of 36 per cent). Hu had learned to read and write in the Red Army, had been wounded five times, and now had malaria.

His *shubao* contained one short piece of candle, half a tube of toothpaste, an old toothbrush, a scrap of soap carefully wrapped in a rag, one letter from his family written by a letter-writer, a seal, three pencils, thirteen books and pamphlets, six lecture notebooks, and copies of the Army newspaper (with passages marked). Of books he had *Protracted Warfare* and *The New Stage in the War*, both by

Mao Tze-tung, General Secretary of the Communist Party, and texts on strategy and tactics, military science, elements of social science and natural science. Of Army pamphlets he had *Political Work in the Puppet Armies, Work among the Enemy, Japanese Primer, Army Rules, Army Song Book, How to Write for the Wall Newspapers,* and *War-time Child Education.*

I asked Hu if he had learned the Japanese language. He knew many words and phrases and could shout slogans in Japanese, he said, but could not yet talk with captives.

He kept his lecture notes under three headings: military, political, cultural. Under "cultural" were such general subjects as reading and writing, arithmetic, geography, and natural science. The political and military lectures were exhaustively outlined. The lectures on guerrilla warfare included, for example, such subjects as the general principles of guerrilla warfare; where to carry on guerrilla warfare; tasks; reserves; guerrilla warfare and the people; how to destroy enemy communications; capture of enemy transports; espionage; supplies; education.

The sub-heads for political lectures included political work in the Army before, during, and after fighting; political work among the people in the war zone; different political parties and their principles; political work in the enemy Army; and the policies of the national united front. This same notebook also contained detailed notes on the economic, political, and cultural aggression of imperialist powers against China.

Under the title "Tasks of the Chinese Revolution" were treated such topics as the present situation, its peculiarities and problems; causes of tendencies to surrender and compromise; Japanese inducements to wavering elements; compromise and surrender as a road to death; why wavering elements are ready to surrender, but are determined to fight the Communists; and the future of the war of resistance. I noted that all of this was from the Marxist viewpoint.

I turned to the notebook on "cultural subjects," and opened to a lecture on natural science. Here there were notes on the sun, the earth, causes of weather, eclipses, tides, the planets, stars, the polar star and how to find it, comets, clouds, and so forth.

These kit bags with their contents showed what was perhaps typical of the system of education imparted by all the training camps of the New Fourth Army. It was the only education many of the men had ever received, and what they learned they were expected, with the help of the political directors, to teach their troops.

The study of natural science had only recently been introduced; it existed in no other army I visited. When I asked to talk with the science-teacher, a soldier brought him to me. I glanced up and then sat staring at the face above me. It was deformed and twisted, as if someone had tried to chop the head in two but had failed. A broad, deep, black scar started from the nose, ran across the cheek and jaw, down along the neck under the ear, and stopped just short of the spinal column in the back. The scar sprayed out on both sides as if the flesh had been torn by some jagged instrument, and the fractured jaw had thrown the mouth to one side.

The teacher stood in silence, waiting. Then I looked above the scar into his eyes and rose to my feet. They were as level as the eyes of death, and in them was an expression beyond all earthly things, beyond all pain and suffering.

From his twisted mouth came the slow but clear words:

"I also was a member of the Chinese Red Cross. That is why my face is deformed. The Japanese tried to chop off my head."

I gasped, finally recovered, and began asking questions, trying as gently as I could to draw his story from him. During the general retreat from Shanghai this teacher, Chang Yen, had been a member of a Red Cross first-aid unit that had established temporary dressing stations along the roads of retreat. On November 8 it established a station near Chinpu, south of Shanghai, below a hill on which stood a French Catholic mission and observatory. Near that place a company of Japanese had suddenly attacked the unit.

"Our ambulances," said Chang Yen, "had a red cross on each side and we all wore broad Red Cross arm-bands. We had no guns and could only run. The Japanese killed nine of us. Some Japanese rose up right in front of me and I saw a big sword with jagged teeth down one edge — such as the enemy uses to saw through barbed-wire entanglements."

Chang Yen paused, turned his head slowly, and stared into space.

"When I returned to consciousness," he continued after a moment, "I was lying in a little stream. I dipped up water and threw it over my face and it was bloody. I crawled up the bank, but could see no one. Our ambulances were partly burned, and dressings and medicine were scattered about. Then I saw a man's hand appear above a gravemound. When I raised my hand he came running and helped me dress my wound.

"This villager and others had hid in holes dug along the banks of the stream, covering the openings with branches and weeds. He carried me to a dugout and kept me there until one day he told me that the Catholic priest on the hill would cure me if I would permit. That night the priest came and he and the villager helped me up the hill, and I lay in the priest's home for three weeks. There were thirty other wounded men there, some soldiers, some civilians. Japanese soldiers sometimes came and asked to search for soldiers, but the old priest said it was his private home, and if they entered, there would be complications between France and Japan.

"After three weeks the priest gave me some clothing and money, and peasants led me over the battlefield into the interior. The villages were in ruins and only a few old people tried to hide in them. The decaying corpses of our soldiers and people lay everywhere. The air was sickening. After a number of weeks I reached south Anhwei and heard that the New Fourth Army was being formed to fight the enemy in the rear. I volunteered to fight as a soldier, but the Army said the soldiers needed knowledge. So I began to teach natural science because I had been a science-teacher at Woosung before the war."

When he had finished I asked leave to take his picture, explaining that it would be proof of his story.

"Proof?" he repeated in amazement. I explained that there were many people in foreign countries who did not believe such stories, who thought them fabricated. "Why shouldn't they believe?" he asked, still utterly baffled.

"I don't know," I answered feebly. "Perhaps people like to see and hear only pleasant things."

He lowered his eyes and kept silent and a feeling of shame flooded over me. With something like sarcasm he said I could take the picture. To keep him talking, I hurriedly asked how he liked Army life.

"Like it?" he answered. "I never thought of liking or disliking it — it has to be done. The only thing I don't like is the lack of teaching material. We have nothing, though I've written a small text-book and made a globe and a few things like that. If you could collect material for us, it would help." I promised, but it was over a year later, when I reached the far west, before I could fulfill the promise.

On the evening of September 18 Dr. Gung and I went to staff headquarters to bid Commander Chang Yun-ee farewell. I was leaving for Lihwang in reply to the Governor's invitation to visit the provincial capital. The commander, ill with malaria, sat up in bed and asked me what my observations had been in the training camp. It was by no means as good as the camp in general headquarters, he added, for it was new and lacked trained teachers.

I told the commander of the stories the men had related to me about battles with the Japanese and what they had seen of enemy strength and weaknesses. The Japanese were so well equipped, so well fed and clothed, they had said, that it took three Chinese to capture one Japanese, and even then they generally had to wound him. They accepted without complaint all the difficulties of their life: poor weapons, little ammunition, bad food and clothing, and the lack of medical workers and supplies. Instead, they talked of the ways they might overcome difficulties that would have appalled Western soldiers.

One soldier told how he had been wounded while attacking a Japanese motor convoy along a highway leading from the Yangtze port city of Anking. The soldier said that after supper one evening a civilian had come running with news of an approaching convoy. Immediately the soldier and many villagers had made for the highway and taken positions along the sloping banks. Soon they saw five enemy ammunition trucks approaching slowly, guarded by a cavalry unit of about fifty men. The guerrillas knew that horses could not be driven down the embankment. So they waited until the convoy was directly abreast of them and then attacked the horsemen with hand-grenades. The soldier said:

"I saw the drivers leap out and run wildly down the road, right among the plunging, falling, and screaming horses. Some horses dashed down the embankment and killed themselves and their riders. How many men we killed I do not know, but I counted twelve in our first attack and I saw others bleeding and slumped in their saddles. We captured six men, but all were wounded. We had to kill three of them because they would not stop shooting at us even after they were wounded.

Without delay the villagers had begun emptying the trucks. Even women and children came with carrying-poles. It was a tremendous haul, and afterwards the people brought grass and wood and set the trucks on fire. They stripped the Japanese dead of everything except bare uniforms and heavy leather shoes, which no guerrilla would wear because they were too heavy and made too much noise. When the fighting was ended, the guerrillas had twenty-two new rifles, a number of blankets, and five horses. Three of their own men had been killed and two wounded.

Commander Chang listened to the stories and once or twice wrote something on a note-pad. Then he asked me what I thought of the education itself. I told him I thought the teaching of political subjects and geography too abstract.

The men were learning the names of various foreign countries, but had no conception of their location on the globe. In particular, I said, they lacked a map. Some of the political training also seemed too theoretical. The Chinese intellectuals who taught such subjects often possessed nothing but book knowledge, and most of their concepts were based on the writings of foreign authors. But China itself also had a revolutionary history and great leaders. To me it seemed utterly artificial to hear slogans appropriate to the industrial development of the Soviet Union applied to under-developed China.

Commander Chang interrupted me and gave orders to his chief of staff to send to the training camp the only map of the world immediately available — that which hung in headquarters.

It was only a gesture, but behind it lay a great deal — the will to teach and to learn in spite of everything.

The Guerrilla Wounded

WE had walked since dawn — up jagged mountains, across the floor of valleys, along narrow paths where no animal could go. We rested in villages whose streets were bordered by open gutters filled with the green scum that bred disease, and where people came in crowds, pleading for medicine. Their bodies were a mass of scabies sores and the hair of the women was matted and wild. The heads of the children were covered with boils or the creeping ringworm that destroys even the roots of the hair. In the summer there had been cholera, and in the winter smallpox would come. And everywhere there was trachoma, malaria, dysentery.

Once we crossed a motor highway along which Japanese trucks dared to venture from time to time. In the afternoon we stood on the crest of a high mountain range and looked down on glory. Below us lay a natural basin of gold with a long azure lake reflecting the azure sky. Fields of ripe grain gleamed like liquid gold. A few small white villages, set in green foliage, sparkled like jewels, and above and about this vision towered black volcanic peaks.

"Our hospital is in that temple," one of our guards said, pointing.

An hour later we were walking through the basin toward the temple. It had roofs of colored tile and upturned corners and it was shadowed by ancient gnarled trees. On the paths in front of the temple stood lines of men in faded blue uniforms. Each man was waving a small triangular paper banner of welcome, and as we came in sight they began singing the guerrilla marching song. One of them came down the path to salute us. He saluted with his left hand, his right arm held rigidly against his breast, the fingers stiff and bent like the claws of a bird. His features were finely chiseled and sensitive, his black eyes eager, and the whole expression of his face had a strangely spiritual quality.

He led us up to the rows of men awaiting us, and as we came near I saw that most of them were crippled. Some were on crutches, some were without an arm or a leg, some had stiff legs or arms, and the bones of one man's leg had knit together at an angle. Almost all were maimed for life, yet almost all of them were in their early twenties. A good doctor could have prevented their deformities. Looking into their faces, I saw that they were anemic — obviously from undernourishment and suffering.

That evening I sat around a table with some of these men. Facing me was the man with the strangely beautiful face. In answer to my questions he told me that he was Chen Fang-chuen; he was twenty-six years old and had been in this Army since the fall of Nanking. Before joining the Army he had been a poor peasant, unable to read or write. Once in the Army, he had always been at the front and had been wounded three times. In the hospital he had found only other wounded men like himself and had been unable to learn. Now the wounded had some text-books and were asking one another about the words. They had tried to learn a few each day, but never knew whether they were right because there was no educated man among them.

"How did you get that stiff arm, and that hand?" I asked.

"One night in a drizzling rain," he began, "our commander said we were to attack the enemy coming from Hweiyuan. The news passed into our hearts and the hearts of the people so that we all forgot the bad weather. It was the 10th of August. Our commander said: 'Wherever we go, victory will follow. The enemy from Hweiyuan city has sent a column against us. With them they have a hundred puppet troops led by a traitor. They will have one heavy machine-gun and three light machine-guns, rifles, and hand-grenades. They think they can surround us before daybreak and attack us at dawn. But their movements are always slow. They will have to start marching at two or three in the morning. We must keep them marching all day in the heat before we give them a welcome. Now, tonight we and all the *lao pei hsing* (people) in Chungchuan will move to Sunyingtze. The Imperial Army will have to pardon us for not being here to receive them. They may feel poorly about that.'

"We all laughed.

"When the enemy came to Chungchuan next morning, there was not a shadow to greet them besides one very old man. They asked him about us, but he said he had never seen us and was so old that he couldn't remember if he had even heard of us. Then they marched on to Sunchaochuang, thinking they might surprise and exterminate us there. We were not there either, so they fired off their guns to make a big noise. They think that scares people. Some of the people then said that we were in another village farther on. It was noon and very hot before the devils reached that village. Sweat was running down their faces and they were tired, but they were ashamed to lose face by going back to Hweiyuan. So they marched on to another village, where they ordered everybody out to a meeting to hear one of them explain how the great Imperial Army had come to protect them from Communist bandits — that means us — and the party Army — that means the Kuomintang. As soon as they had protected the people, they said, they would withdraw.

"Well, the people made them welcome and some of them whispered, as if in secret, that we were at Neuwangmiao. Of course we were not, but when we were told that they were going there, we decided to give them a welcome.

"Our commander picked three of the best platoons, and I was in one of them. We took our three light machine-guns and found good positions along the path leading to Neuwangmiao. Many *lao pei hsing* came to carry away our wounded, and some had spears and big swords.

"The enemy soon came along. By that time they had been marching for about twelve hours. Our machine-guns went rat-a-tat-tat and many of the enemy fell. Some began to run, but some fought, and before long everybody was fighting except the devils who were carrying away the dead and wounded. They all began to retreat and we followed, and soon they began to leave their dead and wounded behind, though they try never to do that. We 'escorted' them for hours, right up to Hweiyuan, and by then there were not many of them left. I did not go so far, for I was wounded; but I heard all about it afterwards. Our Commander had said we ought to escort the devils right up to their barracks."

"That was a warm welcome and a very polite farewell," I remarked with admiration, and the men laughed.

"Now the lessons of this battle were many," the story-teller added, as if quoting from a text-book. "First, a guerrilla unit in a certain place should continue moving to new locations, particularly if close to the enemy. We did that. But our intelligence service was too slow; our reserves could not come up quickly enough to help us exterminate the enemy completely. That was a weakness. Third, after opening fire we did not charge quickly, and many of the enemy escaped. That was also a weakness. Those were the lessons we learned."

I asked him what kind of work he intended to do now that he could no longer fight. He wanted to go to the training camp and learn to do political work, or go into a transport station. "In a transport station," he explained, "I might see people coming and going. I'd like to learn how to work a radio and hear messages from the whole world. We don't learn much about the outside world up here. You are the first foreigner I have ever seen."

By this time the room was filled with men, some sitting on the floor, some on benches, some standing. Wherever I moved I touched someone. The candlelight flickered on interested, excited eyes. Instead of answering my question about his name, the man to whom I now turned asked: "Is it true that you have a machine that you can write on with all your fingers at once and that it goes very fast?"

My secretary brought my typewriter and I opened it and wrote. Gasps of astonishment resounded through the room and a voice asked how much the thing cost. When I told them the price in both American and Chinese money, they were staggered, and the man with the strikingly sensitive face cried out: "You are very rich!"

I denied this and even insisted that all Americans were not rich; but when I began to answer questions about how much money an American worker earned per day, one man interrupted: "Of course you mean five to ten dollars a *month!* You said a *day*." No, a day, I insisted and, ringed by gaping mouths, explained the cost of living and how much money was spent on food, rent, clothing, shoes, medicine, education, and so forth. They were amazed to know that workers' children went to school, not just for a year or two, but a number of years.

"Do the American workers have a Red Army?" one of the men asked, and when I said no, he wanted to know why not. I was soon engulfed by questions: What did an ocean liner and a factory look like? How fast did American trains travel? How did moving pictures work and what did they look like? What was a piano? I demonstrated my camera, after which it was passed from hand to hand and eye to eye. I drew maps; I talked about photographs; I discoursed on the origin and prevention of malaria, typhoid, dysentery, and cholera; I pointed out the virtues of democracy; I explained that the earth was round and that I once left China, visited the Soviet Union, Germany, France, and America, and then came back to China; I told them what I saw in the Soviet Union and in Hitler's Germany, and answered their questions about how the workers and peasants lived in these countries.

The hours passed, the table was covered with peanut shells, and our tea-bowls were filled time and again. Midnight came and passed and I said that all men should be in bed. They argued that I was the first foreigner that had ever come to them and that if I was rich enough to travel around the world, they could not see why I should want to come to the enemy rear. Then they asked me if I had children and why I was not married. When I explained that I had been married and divorced, and that I found life at the front and in the enemy rear far more interesting than anything else, the man with the striking face exclaimed admiringly: "You have the spirit of a Bolshevik!" I said: "No," but he said: "Yes!"

Then they asked me to sing some American songs. So I sang American songs and they sang some guerrilla songs, and finally I grew so weary that I turned to the man with the sensitive face and said that I had come to gather stories of the wounded, but it had been as hard as fighting a battle. He smiled and gallantly answered that if I would remain they would put me in their intelligence service; he felt certain I would make a very smart spy. I assured him that I would consider it an honor to spy on the Japanese, but that I really must go to bed. He regretted this, but said that there would be a big mass meeting the next morning and that they expected me to speak on the strength and weakness of both the Japanese and the Chinese. Would three hours be long enough for my speech, he asked; I assured him that it would be. Would I be expected to sing a song also, I asked him; and he assured me that I would.

He then serenely added that I also would be entertained at a dinner in the garrison and that the men expected me to speak on the international situation. There would be no time limit and there would be questions afterwards.

"My God!" I exclaimed. "I can well imagine." When my

secretary told him I had mentioned the name of God, the men all turned wide eyes on me and asked me if I was a Christian. To them Christianity meant missionaries, missionaries meant foreigners, and foreigners meant imperialists. When I replied that I was not a Christian, they asked me why not, and a sea of faces bent forward in happy anticipation of another long discussion. I said something about my need for a little rest, then dragged myself to the luxury of a board bed piled high with yellow rice straw, fresh and sweet. In my honor they had piled on a lot. Bending down to unwrap my puttees, I felt dizzy. At last I climbed up on the rice straw and sank back, saying to myself: "And you came to gather stories from the wounded! Fat chance!"

Kwangsi Base

FOR one week we walked westward through a sea of mountain ranges that rose ever nearer the sky. The midday sun burned us to a leathery brown and the nights cracked with cold. The autumn air was strong with the tangy odors of pine, birch, and chestnut, and sometimes we rested in bamboo thickets on grassy slopes spangled with bluebells and lavender autumn flowers. Clumps of maple flamed among the pines.

From the slopes we would descend into sunny valleys where newly-garnered corn turned threshing-floors to gold; and the sorghum-like kao-liang, from which the treacherous *bei-gar* was made, lay fermenting in bamboo baskets.

Sometimes it was difficult to realize that we were at war. I recalled the gory stories of a few foreign correspondents who had made flying trips to China. Two in particular had written of an "enemy rear" which they had never seen and had conjured up scenes of perpetual carnage. True, when the Japanese poured through this section in their mighty drive on Hankow, vast regions had witnessed such carnage. But the Japanese had never had the man-power to overrun and hold down this huge province with its thirty million people. Most large towns had been bombed, some were still bombed even now, and many villages had been raided and burned out, particularly those that lay in the line of the Japanese advance. Despite this terrorism, however, most of the province had by now been cleared of the enemy by the combined efforts of the powerful Kwangsi Army — the 21st Group — the New Fourth Army guerrillas, and a number of local guerrillas and *hsien* (county) militia. There were still fierce battles along the railways, rivers, and motor highways and in the large occupied cities on these routes of communication, but Chinese authority had been re-established almost to the very edge of occupied cities. In some cities the Japanese were almost prisoners, never daring to venture out except in strong columns and during the day.

Despite this, we never trusted the planes that sometimes roared above us, and always sought shelter under trees until they had passed. Some were in search of larger prey; others were transport planes plying between the far north and Yangtze cities.

I was looking forward eagerly to my first contacts with those Kwangsi armies which had left their native southwestern province when the war began and had thereafter fought on every major battlefield. The 21st Group Army had its base in the Ta Pieh mountain range in western Anhwei. Its Commander-in-Chief, General Liao Rei, was also Governor of the province and was known as a progressive administrator as well as an able military man.

I soon began to see signs of the many changes which had taken place under the General's administration. Once we came to a wooded valley in which five high schools had united to build a group of new bamboo and thatch barracks. Three such high-school centers with a school enrollment of nearly 15,000 students were located in safe retreats in the province.

During the Japanese advance on Hankow, 17,000 students and 500 teachers and their families had moved to far-western China. Thousands of other students, however, had remained behind to help the armies, guerrillas, and civilian population and were now pursuing their studies. In this center, students and teachers alike wore coarse green homespun uniforms like those of soldiers, and their lives were fashioned entirely after that of soldiers. With no maps, no scientific equipment, and only the few text-books that could be transported from the far west or could be printed in Lihwang, the teachers taught almost entirely from memory.

I had previously seen one of these high-school centers near Kinghsien, south of the Yangtze, and there was another farther north in Anhwei. The three institutions were the intellectual core of the new administrative and educational life which was being organized in the enemy rear. Certain graduates took competitive examinations, and the successful ones were sent to the universities or colleges of the far west as state scholars; but most students remained to become the future leaders of the province.

In the typical small town of Maotangchang (population 10,000) I made a brief study of the *pao-chia* (administrative) system which the provincial authorities were then reorganizing. As we entered the streets of the town we met a group of five students, three girls and two young men, who had recently come from the provincial capital, where they had been trained in the new Political-Military Training Camp. Two of the girls were teachers in the town's primary school and one was a teacher — and also the village head — in a near-by locality. The two young men were in charge of military and political training of a local Self-Defense Corps made up of fifty armed full-time men and thirty reserves, all peasants. As soon as the harvests were finished, the two men would begin training the thousand able-bodied men in the town.

The town leader, an educated man nearing thirty, called on me one evening and explained his work.

This *pao-chia* system had both harsh critics and heated defenders. When introduced by the Central Government in former years, it had been a powerful weapon against the Red Army, for by means of it every member of a group of ten families, or even of a hundred families, was held responsible if any one of them sheltered a Communist. Only in Kwangsi Province had the system served as a prelude to democracy — and even there all officials were appointed, not elected. When the Kwangsi Army became responsible for Anhwei and a Kwangsi General was appointed Governor, the Kwangsi system was introduced. Defenders of the system said that, in time, all lower officials would be elected, and eventually even the magistrates. But the ruling party, the Kuomintang, had, under one pretext or another, always postponed these first steps toward democracy.

The *hsien* (county) magistrates received their orders from the Governor and transmitted them to the administrative units under their control. Periodically the magistrate called a conference of town and village leaders in his headquarters to deliver and discuss Government orders. There was indeed some approach to democracy in such a lowly administrative unit as the town of Maotangchang itself: once a month there was a meeting attended by the heads of each group of one hundred families; this was called the *Pao* People's Conference. There was also a general monthly conference of the heads of each family. These conferences discussed national and local problems and were held responsible for the enforcement of Government orders.

Maotangchang maintained its own Self-Defense Corps, primary school, and air-raid sentries, and the merchants and gentry had formed a Buddhist "Red Swastika Society" to care for air-raid victims. There were two men in the town who were said to know something about first aid.

The town also had a Mass Movement Council of representatives from various anti-Japanese associations of merchants, peasants, women, youth, and children. These mass associations had first been organized throughout Anhwei by mobile units of the Kwangsi Student Army during the Japanese drive on Hsuchow in the previous year. This Student "Army" consisted of 300 uniformed young men and women trained in methods of mass mobilization and political work. The Mass Movement Council of Maotangchang called meetings on national holidays, conducted spring and winter sowing campaigns, led the movement for preparing winter garments for the soldiers, spied on the enemy, and popularized conscription.

The Provincial Government had just called for thirty conscripts from this town. The draft board — it consisted of seven members of the gentry — selected 140 men to draw lots. When the men left for camp the town gave one dollar to each as traveling expenses, the local merchants presented each with a face-towel, a toothbrush, and tooth-powder, and the whole town turned out to bid them farewell.

In a manner which would not offend, I remarked to the town head that I had heard many harsh charges brought against the conscription system and had in fact personally observed that the poor were conscripted, while the rich fled to safety, sent their sons or daughters abroad, or even got off with the payment of a few dollars. Yes, the young official answered in level tones, that was often true. When he had studied in Lihwang, the Governor had lectured against this form of corruption; since he had come to Maotangchang, nothing like this had happened.

Yet I could not believe that a draft board made up entirely of the gentry could make an honest selection of conscripts. I had heard that one rich man's son in the town had been conscripted, but when I investigated I found that he was actually the son of a peasant who happened to be well-to-do.

A few days later, high in the majestic Ta Pieh mountain ranges, we approached Liupiehtung, a large walled town near which the 21st Group Army maintained an artillery training camp. The town had been bombed a number of times, many had been killed, and the Japanese often sent in spies in the guise of merchants or refugees. Slogans and colored posters against Wang Ching-wei and other traitors screamed from every wall. Others indicated that we had definitely left the territory of the Communist New Fourth Army and had entered a realm in which other political ideas prevailed. Not that they were reactionary; everywhere, in fact, there were slogans like "Rich men give money, poor men give labor"; "Good treatment to families of anti-Japanese fighters"; "The Three People's Principles of Sun Yat-sen are the highest law of resistance and national reconstruction"; "Support national education and wipe out illiteracy." . . .

This whole region had once been the base of the old Chinese Soviet Government, guarded by the same New Fourth Army guerrillas whom I had but recently left. Along the approaches to the town towered huge stone blockhouses, relics of civil wars and at present occupied by Kwangsi soldiers, who now seemed to be interested only in the Japanese. The sentry at the town gate hailed my New Fourth Army bodyguard as brothers in uniform, but as I passed he stared in amazement at my blue eyes and shouted: *"Hu-chow!"* (Passport!). I presented my credentials and he began a conversation with our adjutant, speaking a dialect so strange that the two men repeated each phrase a dozen times. The adjutant explained that I was a foreign friend of China, an American. A number of other soldiers gathered, and an involved discussion of world affairs began. Eventually I learned that they were deciding whether or not anyone from a country that sold trucks and ammunition to the enemy had the right to enter Liupiehtung.

My defenders argued that I had nothing to do with selling trucks and ammunition to the Japanese, but that the "merchants" of my country "were ignorant and loved money." Finally they let us pass. As we moved into the town I heard one of the soldiers shouting to another down the street, and it was only a matter of seconds before my arrival was known to the entire town. We had no more than stepped into a dark little inn when a young officer appeared, bowed, asked for our passes, and then assured me that I was most welcome. He looked so smart and efficient, and his words were so unequivocal, that I saw my guerrilla guards draw themselves up proudly, trying to hide their shabbiness. Some of the buttons on their summer uniforms had long since disappeared, a number of them had malaria or ulcers of the feet and legs, and one had insisted on marching with us although he was on the verge of pneumonia. They had not received a cent of their dollar and a half monthly allowance, and in the previous month had been paid only fifty cents. In a town en route I had bought a pair of shoes for each, and though our adjutant had protested, the men did not. And each night I had doctored them for malaria or other ailments.

When I compared their condition with that of the short, tough Kwangsi soldiers about me, I had much food for thought. The Kwangsi troops were disciplined and well cared for, and though some undoubtedly had malaria, I detected no trachoma or scabies. It meant an army good in quality as well as quantity. Indeed, I soon learned that the Kwangsi armies had broken with Chinese tradition and bathed daily, summer or winter, and that some of them had habits much like those of the American Indian. As I watched them march through the streets of Liupiehtung that night, I was filled with a tremendous respect for them. Many were short little Annamese, of the same race as the people of Indo-China, some were racially mixed, and some showed clearly an ancient Chinese strain, albeit conditioned by the Kwangsi mountain region. They were fierce and strong, and as they marched, their rifles, ammunition belts, and machine-guns clanked. They marched in perfect unison and sang an anti-Japanese song so militantly that I felt certain it must be a prelude to immediate battle. Turning to the Kwangsi officer, I asked in a respectful voice if the men were marching out to fight. No, he replied, they were going to the movies! The Army was quite up to date, he continued, for the "Educational Moving Picture Working Unit" of the Central Government sent out a new motion-picture newsreel every two or three months!

I liked the idea of taking artillery to the movies. For years I had seen many American movies and Chinese imitations that had left me completely frustrated, without any way of revenging myself. I now realized that had I taken a heavy machine-gun or a trench mortar with me, I might have looked on with sweet patience, biding my time.

Despite all this, I did not go to the movies that night. We had walked seventy *li* (twenty-three miles) that day. Not only had we walked, but we had pushed and almost carried a decrepit horse and a little mule not much larger than a jack-rabbit. When they fell down, as they often did on the narrow mountain paths, we would lift them up and rearrange all our baggage on their backs. The horse was an utterly useless creature, but our guards dared not leave it behind because it belonged to the Army. I was certain that, on their way back, it would plunge into one of the bottomless caverns that yawned on every side.

After eating, I took a candle and went wearily to the board which was my bed. Somewhere a night watchman beat on hollow bamboo, telling the time. I could not sleep, and through my mind floated many shadowy memories. . . . I thought of the short steel-like Kwangsi mountain men outside. . . . Then I thought of a room in Hankow. The room had polished floors and polished tables and a Chinese vase filled with white flowers. Books lay about. And the room was filled with the music of Beethoven's Ninth Symphony. . . . There were many friends there . . . but that was their world, not mine. . . . And yet it was very beautiful. . . .

The next afternoon we stood in the Tientang mountain pass. Below us to the west and north lay a long, broad valley of incomparable beauty. The distant Shih, or Lihwang, River flowed through it, glimmering in the afternoon sun. This valley was our goal.

About us lay the Ta Pieh mountain range, its black, volcanic peaks gashing the light-blue sky. Winding over them was the narrow, spidery trail along which we had toiled. Once we crossed a broad motor road hewn out of the mountain side. It had been dynamited, and we had had to grope our way along a narrow ledge, clinging to the face of the cliff, while a deep gorge on our right seemed to plunge down into the bowels of the earth. Yet the Japanese Army had come up that same trail a year before, their airplanes blasting a way for them!

By the time the sun sank in the west, we had descended into the broad Lihwang Valley, center of the provisional war-time capital of Anhwei Province. On the outskirts of the village of Kupeichung, near which the 21st Group Army had its headquarters, we saw many new bamboo buildings with thatched roofs. Columns of blue-clad men and women singing national songs marched across a hard-packed drill ground, then squatted in groups around wooden buckets of rice and tin pans of steaming vegetables. Over the archway to the grounds was the sign: "Anhwei Student Army."

Two girls in soldier's uniforms came hurrying along the street, turned to look back, and then stopped to ask who I was. When I told them they insisted that I come into the Anhwei Student Army Headquarters. In an austere little office the girls introduced me to their director, Lieutenant General Ma Chi-ying.

Lieutenant General Ma Chi-ying was a graduate of America's West Point, class of 1924. Upon completing his studies he had returned to China and, although a Kwangtung Province man, had gone to Kwangsi and founded a training school for Army Officers. He was now Educational Director of the Anhwei Student Army, a body of 500 men and 100 girl high-school students, and of the Military Education Corps, in which 1,000 men were under training to become commanders of *hsien* militia and local guerrilla forces. He was also special adviser to Governor Liao Rei, and had the reputation of being one of the advanced leaders of youth in the province. I learned later that he was a son of one of the richest Hong Kong families and had at one time punctuated his military career with wild extravagances. Once he told me of a banquet he had given to the Crown Prince of Spain. It had lasted ten hours and there had been seven hundred courses.

Nevertheless, since the Japanese invasion he had been at the front. He spoke good English, but only the Cantonese dialect of Chinese. His fiancée, a girl student who spoke Mandarin and some English, was his interpreter.

The minute I reached Lihwang Valley, I entered a world of political intrigue in which the old order struggled against the new. Lieutenant General Ma told me at once that my old friend Chang Nai-chih, once a Shanghai banker, had waited for me for two months, but had had to leave.

Bluntly I said to General Ma: "So Chang Nai-chih has been driven out already!"

Just as bluntly he answered: "Yes, he was too honest and progressive. The 'C. C. Clique' will not welcome *you* either. But the Governor and the rest of us will!"

In Shanghai Chang Nai-chih had been one of the leading pre-war patriotic democrats. He had helped found the National Salvation Association, which had demanded that China resist the Japanese instead of fighting the Red Army. Because of this he had been one of seven patriotic professional men imprisoned by the Government for "endangering the Republic." Upon release after the outbreak of war he had gone to Kwangsi Province, the only place which welcomed democratic men. When Kwangsi generals were put in charge of Anhwei in 1938, they appointed him Finance Commissioner.

But shortly before I reached Lihwang, the reactionary group known as the "C. C. Clique" had gained control of the Kuomintang in Anhwei Province, and Chang Nai-chih had been one of their first victims. He had been driven out, and a new Financial Commissioner, with a retinue of personal followers, had been sent from Chungking to take his place. I soon learned that Lieutenant General Ma Chi-ying was also under fire from the "C. C. Clique."

As soon as I arrived and before I could catch my breath, Lieutenant General Ma instructed a student to summon the Student Army, and within five minutes I was standing on a platform in a large assembly hall, facing hundreds of applauding students, and listening to General Ma announcing: "Miss Smedley will now lecture on the second World War and how it affects our war of resistance."

We had walked over thirty miles that day and I was dog-tired and shaky. But these students also climbed mountains each day, and whenever they sat down to rest, they drew out their notebooks and waited for lectures from teachers. To avoid air-raids all classes were held in the hills. This was a nation at war.

So I spoke on the second World War as the beginning of the war against Fascism; and as I talked I longed for light and more light. I also wished that they had given me a few minutes to prepare!

The Anhwei Student Army, like its model, the famous Kwangsi Student Army, was made up of students who were taught the use of weapons and the elements of strategy and tactics, but whose main task was mass education and mobilization.

One hour after my lecture I stretched out on a board bed heaped with yellow straw, embarrassed because I was too weary to eat. A series of impressions like those in a movie reel flashed through my mind: our adjutant worrying because the room in the inn cost too much — fifty cents a night without food . . . General Ma giving me a tin of Shanghai cigarettes worth ten dollars by the time they reached Lihwang . . . he thought that the Governor's motor car, the only one in the province, would take me to the capital tomorrow, using gasoline that cost thirty dollars for a five-gallon tin. . . .

Anhwei: the Past vs. the Future

I LEANED back in the Governor's car feeling like a criminal. On the highway, half-way to Lihwang, we passed my bodyguard trudging along on foot and they looked solemnly at me as we sped past.

In Government headquarters we met the Governor, General Liao Rei, coming down the hall. Except for his unadorned uniform, he looked like some old Roman senator. In a dignified, courteous manner, but totally without pomp, he welcomed me and inquired about my well-being and needs, my journey, and my first impression of this base of resistance in the enemy rear. I said: "Your soldiers literally exude strength, health, and energy. They seem a race apart."

"We are a mountain people," he explained, and went on to say that baths, in winter or summer, seemed to prevent many diseases. Still, he said, he couldn't understand why they didn't suffer from malaria as much as the others. The Kwangsi troops were well fed, but even well-fed people got malaria.

The Governor told me there was a large field hospital and two receiving stations in the neighborhood. The hospital belonged to the Army Medical Service of the Ministry of War, but after the superintendent and business manager had been discovered "squeezing" money appropriated for food and coffins, the Governor had appointed a Kwangsi doctor as superintendent. I didn't ask him what he did with the offenders; Kwangsi men were quick on the trigger. The trouble with all such hospitals, he continued, was that they had to be very far from the fighting fronts or the Japanese would try to destroy them. The receiving stations were much nearer the front. None of them received the medical supplies they needed, and the Governor wanted me to support their requests for more medicine.

He watched me curiously, carefully considering each word I spoke. We drifted into talk about the two Kwangsi Army Groups, and in particular of the 21st, of which he was Commander-in-Chief. The major problem in the Shanghai-Nanking fighting, he said, had been the air and artillery superiority of the enemy; the fighting had resembled that in the first World War. Since that time the armies had learned night fighting and the use of camouflage. The mountains afforded natural protection. Defense works were now well camouflaged and the troops had learned guerrilla and mobile warfare. The Japanese still had the advantage of motorized equipment, but the Chinese tried to keep the roads destroyed. Since the fall of Hankow a year previously, his army alone had fought over two hundred guerrilla engagements.

Enemy "mopping-up" campaigns had been largely futile.

The 21st Group Army operated in western Anhwei and in eastern Hupeh Province, and regiments sometimes swept eastward down the Yangtze on special missions. Since the adoption of guerrilla warfare, enemy losses had become twice as heavy as Chinese.

When I asked him what had been their chief gains since the outbreak of war, he answered: "Battlefield education, which is very different from book theory. Our other chief gain is national consciousness. Our troops know that this is a life-and-death struggle for the entire country, not just for Kwangsi. They think it's an honor to fight, and if they don't have a chance to fight, they feel they've not done anything."

He spoke in an undemonstrative voice, as if he were weary or depressed. He was no more than fifty, but seemed much older.

The people, the Army, and the many new training schools of the Government were now scattered up and down the valley in huge new bamboo barracks. These structures were simple but excellently designed, some of them even beautiful. The outside walls were plastered with mud to blend with the earth, and the roofs were thatched, and sometimes camouflaged with branches or overgrown with vines. Many had been built under overhanging trees. In addition, caves had been dug deep in the mountain sides, and there was a telephone and radio warning system throughout the province. Air-raid sentries were stationed on mountains to give bugle calls or beat brass gongs in warning.

During my five weeks in Lihwang we had many alarms, but only one raid. This raid took place while I was in the field hospital. Those few who were able to walk went into the surrounding hills, but most remained where they were. They seemed beyond fear. With one of the doctors I went toward a shelter, but before we reached it the roar of the planes filled the air. Suddenly strength left me; I could not even walk and the doctor had to lift me into the shelter. The planes bombed a town just over the hill from us.

Liao Rei had been appointed Governor when Hankow had fallen eleven months before. At that time the Japanese occupied forty-one of the sixty-two *hsien* in the province and had shattered its economic and cultural life. This meant the destruction of almost a whole country, for Anhwei, with a population of 30,000,000, was a huge, rich province which lay in the middle of China as the heart lies in the body. In the ensuing eleven months the Japanese had been driven out of all but twenty *hsien*, and even in these they occupied only one or two walled cities. The Finance Department of the Government had built up an "Enemy Goods Inspection Bureau" in an attempt to blockade the goods of the enemy and prevent raw materials from reaching them. At the same time the Government promoted home industries, including spinning and weaving, paper-making, and match-manufacture. But these efforts were far too weak; enemy goods, disguised as Chinese or foreign, could be found everywhere.

On New Year's Day 1939 General Liao proclaimed his War-Time Political-Military Program, which had forty-two provisions for the emancipation, reorganization, administration, and education of the province. In carrying out this program he had the aid of experienced officials and military men from Kwangsi Province, and thousands of educated men and women, including hundreds sent by General Li Chung-ren, Commander-in-Chief of the Fifth War Zone.

The Anhwei Political-Military Training Camp, or School, with its seven branches, had turned out 4,000 men and women administrators by the time I arrived in Lihwang. It was planned to restaff every one of the 4,000 towns and villages, with their subdivisions (40,000 in all), with newly trained personnel. The different branches of the training camp, scattered up and down the valley, trained personnel for finance and accounting, agricultural co-operatives, primary schools, radio, and intelligence work. There was, in addition, a Citizens' Military Training Camp, the Anhwei Student Army Camp, which I had visited, the *Pao An Tui* (Peace Preservation Corps), and a Military Training Camp, in which 1,000 men were being trained as lower-ranking officers.

The task the province had undertaken was gigantic. Each reform might have to be defended by arms. Many officials were new and inexperienced and often without much basic education. The longer I remained in Lihwang, the more problems did I see growing out of the contest between the new and the old, between democracy and dictatorship, and sometimes between plain viciousness and ordinary human decency. These problems were not merely Chinese. They were international; for though Anhwei was a province in China's interior, it might have been a section of America or central Europe.

The provincial branch of the ruling party, the Kuomintang, often seemed to represent all that was dark and treacherous. It was numerically weak because it had long represented only the owning classes. Lacking popular support, it held power by dictatorial methods and intrigue. Its reactionary "C. C. Clique" was led by Chen Kuo-fu and by Chen Li-fu, Minister of Education in the Central Government. Mr. Chen had sent a small group of his followers to Anhwei to try to wrest power not only from the Communists in certain regions, but also from the Kwangsi Army. Chen had appointed a sleek, lynx-eyed gentleman, Fang Chi, to act as Commissioner of Education of Anhwei Province, and Fang Chi's first act had been to censor and ban progressive publications in all schools, including even the leading newspaper, the *Ta Pieh Shan Er Pao*, published by the People's Mobilization Committee of Lihwang under the guidance of the Governor.

The Governor was a thorn in the flesh of the "C. C. Clique," for he was liberal and progressive, a champion of youth and a firm worker for national unity. The "C. C. Clique" therefore joined forces with other reactionary elements, including a small group of staff officers and politicians connected with the Kwangsi Army and known as the "Hunan bureaucrats," a still smaller group of prominent Kwangsi politicians with personal ambitions, and three or four former Communist Party members. It was a weird mixture, typical of a civilization in transition and a nation in the throes of a war for survival.

The "Hunan bureaucrats" seemed to be particularly despised, yet they were among the most dangerous because they could exercise influence on the Governor through a concubine whom men politely called his "wife." Like many men of the older generation, General Liao had one foot in the past, one in the future. I was told that he had a wife and three concubines. One of the latter was with him in Lihwang. She was a native of Hunan Province, an illiterate but handsome, aggressive, and utterly unscrupulous woman. Men whispered that she used "bed-pillow influence" on behalf of her retainers. Her brother had become chief of General Liao's bodyguards, and one of her clique had become chief of staff of the 21st Group Army; the latter sat writing old *wen-li* poetry, which the "C. C. Clique" published in the local Kuomintang newspaper, side by side with endless attacks upon all educated youth as Communist or potentially Communist.

The Kuomintang and the "Hunan bureaucrats" had little in common save adherence to the old world and fear that the "new elements" would wrest power from them. They fought every democratic force and had, I was told, reinstated a number of local politicians who had been driven out by the Governor because of their connection with Wang Ching-wei.

The Governor stood between these groups, trying to reconcile conflicts, yet always managing to protect the democratic forces, the "new elements." It was, of course, still dangerous to be a "new element." When, soon after my arrival, I heard that this term had been applied to me, I knew that I would be in for it sooner or later.

The Kuomintang remained apart, housed in a small village where its leaders had started a party training class. I heard it referred to as a spy center against the "new elements." Though the party representatives consisted of a handful of men, none of whom had been elected, they had the right to sit in the Provincial Government and influence or even determine decisions. While returning from a lecture in a training camp one evening, a group of us had to step aside to allow a cavalcade to pass. We heard the clank of guns, and then a group of armed men, spread out fanwise, swept past, followed by carriers supporting a sedan chair in which sat the leader of the local Kuomintang. Another group of armed men brought up the rear.

One of our party exclaimed in disgust: "And such men would lead us!" I remarked that the man was perhaps sick, else why should he ride in a sedan chair?

"Not at all," someone answered furiously; "and what were the armed guards except a provocation?"

"Perhaps he's afraid someone will take a shot at him," another added; and I was convinced by his tone that he wished someone would.

I spent one day in the Finance and Accounting Department of the Government, talking with its leaders and lecturing in its training school. Two months had elapsed since Chang Nai-chi had been driven out of the province. The new commission and its retinue was still on the way, but the financial administration of the province was already breaking down and the Government was in arrears. The Governor had asked the Central Government for money, but it only kept telling him to balance his budget. So an air of depression hung over the Financial Department. Officials who had done good work knew they would soon be unemployed. They were men of all ages, in deadly earnest about the war and filled with revolutionary hopes and aims. There was deep pathos in their eager patriotism, in face of a future so uncertain.

The organization that suffered most from the attacks of the old elements was the People's Mobilization Committee, which the Governor had authorized and of which he was supreme director. The leader of this organization was Chang Pei-chuan, former professor in a university in Peiping and now chief editor of the *Ta Pieh Shan Er Pao*. Just before my arrival the organization had deeply offended the conservatives by holding a week's conference to discuss the meaning of democracy and the need for it. The organization had fourteen mobile "work corps" continually touring the province to mobilize and train civilians; it maintained three mobile dramatic corps; its members were sent to strengthen administrative organizations; and those older men and women who had been teachers before the war were instructors in the various training camps. It put out three magazines, the *Youth Monthly, Flood,* and the *Cultural Monthly,* published text-books, maps, and anti-Japanese posters, and had started an archive of war annals. Its Women's Committee had instituted night literacy classes for adults, and one group of them had founded and managed a spinning and weaving factory for refugees in a near-by town.

One afternoon and evening the Youth and Women's Committees gathered in a woman's conference with delegates from many parts of the province. I was the chief speaker, and because I was foreign I was expected to give an extensive report on the international women's movement. It was the most difficult lecture I had undertaken, for I had only fragmentary information on the subject. I did my best, but I knew that I was learning much more about the women of the interior of China than they were learning about foreign women. The room was packed with women, including many who were soon to have babies. Most of them were educated, but a number were peasants and workers. They had decorated the hall with banners carrying such slogans as *Unite all anti-Fascist forces of China with the women of the world!* and even one that hailed me as the *Mother of Chinese Wounded Soldiers!*

A group of war orphans, dressed in tiny military uniforms, had gathered wild flowers from the hills and presented them to me along with eloquent little messages to American children about the determination of Chinese children to struggle until China was free. The women refugees in the spinning and weaving factory had sent me two pairs of white cotton stockings, and the women of the Youth Committee had written a poem of welcome in which they declared that they had been trampled under men's feet for thousands of years, but foresaw a new dawn.

From these women I learned once again of the fearful handicaps under which Chinese women labored. Many said they would never marry until China was victorious, for family life imposed such burdens that married women could seldom take part in public affairs. This was a rare thing to hear, for marriage is considered the duty of every Chinese girl, and if they reject it the pressure put upon them by their families makes life a misery. Women beyond the age of twenty-five were considered "old," and after that age few thought they would ever have an opportunity to marry.

They told me that the masses of women were illiterate, untrained, without disciplined habits of thought, and still bound by feudal customs. In some villages in Anhwei there were still "baby-ponds" in which unwanted girl infants were drowned at birth. Girls were still affianced at a very early age, sent to their mothers-in-law to grow to maturity, and then married. The cruelty of mothers-in-law to "child brides" was a problem so universal that the Women's Committee often had to rescue little girls and keep them in their headquarters.

The secretary of the Women's Committee, Miss Chu Ching-hsia, an educated married woman in her middle twenties, once said to me:

"The Ta Pieh mountain range was once a soviet region in which women unbound their feet, cut their hair short, studied, and took part in public life. But now they have let their hair grow; women with short hair had been called Communists and killed by the Kuomintang armies. When we first went to them as organizers, we proposed that women cut their hair and take part in anti-Japanese organizations. They were afraid lest the Terror begin again.

"It is very strange. Most of these Chinese soviet women cannot read or write, yet they know all about capitalism and world affairs, and they speak very well before meetings. When we convinced them that they would not be killed if they took part in public life, they and the men of the villages were able to manage the local anti-Japanese associations without any help from us.

"We educated women find women's work very difficult. Our lives, habits, and standards of culture are so different from those of the country women that it is difficult to find contacts with them. So we have now brought a group of country women here for training.

"We have another strange problem. The soviets forbade forced marriages; men and women were allowed to marry from choice and neither side could pay a dowry. The Kuomintang called this 'free love.' But now, when the soviets no longer exist, some men lay claim to the women to whom they were affianced in childhood according to the old custom. Sometimes these women are stolen or taken by force from their homes. They may be widows whose husbands were killed in the civil wars or are now fighting in the Eighth Route or New Fourth Armies. But the childhood engagement is considered legally binding, and our Women's Committee is always having trouble forcing the men to return the stolen women to their homes."

General Lai Kang, Garrison Commander of Lihwang, one day told me what he had seen of conditions during a military expedition he had just made to Pochow, in the far north of Anhwei. In that region, he said, serfdom still reigned. All the men still wore the *queu*; the women had bound feet, and wore the costumes and dressed their hair in the style of the Manchu Dynasty. There were landlords there who owned 50,000 *mao* (over 16,600 acres) of land. The peasants were serfs or armed retainers, working for a bare subsistence, and their women were the landlord's household serfs.

"The people own not one single thing," said General Lai. "They do not know what China is and they do not care. Some of the landlords were Japanese agents; one Magistrate merely transferred his allegiance from China to Japan. I executed one Magistrate and many landlords. It was difficult to shoot the big landlords, for they had rifles and even machine-guns, and they could arm their serfs with them. In order to arrest one great landlord — he was the traitor Magistrate — I had a false air-raid alarm sounded, and when we all went into the caves, I arrested him, took him away, and shot him."

One evening in Lihwang, shortly after my arrival, the Theatrical Group presented two plays in the new "civic center," a unit which had a co-operative restaurant and hotel, a co-operative market, and an assembly hall accommodating five thousand people. The plays were written locally, and the theme of one was an episode in the city of Anking, formerly the provincial capital, but now occupied by the enemy. On the night of May 4, anniversary of the youth movement of China, the puppet troops inside Anking had opened the city gates and let in a regiment of Kwangsi troops. Fighting lasted all night and the Kwangsi troops, along with the puppets, withdrew at dawn to escape airplane bombing, but left behind a smashed Japanese garrison. One actor in the drama represented a Japanese staff officer who had been born and educated in China and was supposedly sympathetic to China.

When the performances were finished, I was asked to speak. Instead, I rose and suggested that the audience discuss the plays. My suggestion was opposed by an official who declared that the audience was too undeveloped to discuss them. The actors, still in their make-up, supported my idea and asked me to lead the discussion. Two of the playwrights offered to reply to criticism.

I spoke of the excellent acting, but objected to the idea of showing a Japanese staff officer as a friend of China. If he was a friend of China, why did he remain in the Japanese Army? The playwright replied that his Japanese character was drawn from life; that there really had been such a man in Anking during the May 4 fighting.

The dam had broken. A dozen men, some soldiers, some students in the various training camps, asked for the floor. They strode up the aisles, leaped to the stage, and told what they thought of the plays. And they talked intelligently. One soldier declared that one play was too filled with lofty talk which the common people could not understand. Still another pointed out that one of the plays showed a gang of Japanese and puppets having a feast and gabbing about the threat of guerrillas, but that the guerrillas never attacked and only the wife of the puppet leader had killed herself out of fear. No play, he declared violently, should ever show that treason *pays*. The guerrillas should have killed every low-down dog at the banquet table!

Ah, replied the playwright, was that reality? If the enemy was always lying dead on the stage, what was the use of continuing the war? Arouse the people by showing the facts!

Anhwei Intrigue

THE GOVERNOR'S difficulties were usually grave, but at least once the difficulty that confronted him was a ridiculous one. His concubine had hated Lieutenant General Ma for a long time because he was an undiplomatic man who openly campaigned against the concubine's Hunan "countrymen," as well as against the "C. C. Clique."

General Ma loved fine horses and, being wealthy, had bought a number of them, including one fine white steed. This he lent to a guerrilla commander going to the front. The commander sent the animal back to Lihwang by a *mafoo* (muleteer). The concubine saw it, and when the *mafoo* said he did not know to whom it belonged, she appropriated it and gave it to one of her retainers in the Army. One day General Ma saw his lost horse and asked the Governor, who was with him, to stop the car so that he might question the rider. The rider replied truthfully that he had received the animal from the Governor's wife through her brother, chief of the Governor's bodyguard.

The Governor grew pale with fury and returned to his headquarters to confront his brother-in-law. The young man admitted the circumstances, whereupon the Governor threatened to court-martial him if the offense was repeated. General Ma got his horse back and, if I know his character,

I suppose he rubbed in his triumph by continually riding the horse right under the concubine's nose. But the concubine and her brother bided their time.

This small thread wound itself in with the countless other conflicts that raged in the Kwangsi Army and among administrative officials. For instance, the old die-hard Commissioner of Civil Affairs, Chen Liang-Chu, had once branded Lieutenant General Ma a "Red" because he had entertained General Yeh Ting of the New Fourth Army, and because the Governor had thereafter begun paying the central Anhwei detachments of the New Fourth a subsidy of $20,000 a month. Chen Liang-chu, the Hunan bureaucrats, and the "C. C. Clique" had tried in vain to induce the Governor to withdraw this subsidy, but the Governor had argued that the New Fourth guerrillas were his countrymen fighting the Japanese, and he did not care what their political opinions were. At that time General Ma had been editor of the *Ta Pieh Shan Er Pao*, and the campaign against him had finally forced the Governor to advise him to resign. General Ma's defeat had never ceased to rankle. But opponents watched his every step, their knives ready. The young officer nevertheless continued to ride the white horse contemptuously, and even dubbed the Commissioner "old Chen *Pao-chia*" because Chen was a fanatical supporter of the *pao-chia* system and used it, General Ma said, merely to prevent the election of local officials.

A few hours' talk with "old Chen *Pao-chia*" made me realize that he was no mean opponent. He was a stocky middle-aged man with a small black mustache and beard, a big mouth, and two very conspicuous gold teeth, which he thought a mark of beauty. He was one of the most gifted intriguers in Lihwang and had raised the technique of vilifying enemies to a fine art. With his "wild" directness, General Ma was no match for this suave smiling gentleman. As Commissioner of Civil Affairs "old Chen *Pao-chia*" had appointed three leading Trotskyites as special commissioners in the very territory in which the Communist New Fourth Army operated. Chen called this "fighting fire with fire," for his special commissioners organized a clever network of espionage and rumor-mongering against the Communist guerrillas, and kept their chief in Lihwang informed of all they learned.

After a lengthy eulogy of the *pao-chia* system, old Chen told me how very difficult it was to introduce any reforms in the land system, and delicately suggested, by a species of reasoning too devious for me to follow, that I, as a foreigner, was perhaps personally responsible for the policy of imperialist aggression against China. As I was taking my leave, he remarked that General Ma was both charming and *broadminded!* He smiled, displaying his gold teeth. I decided that General Ma had better watch his step. And since I was living in his house at the request of the Governor, I knew, too, that anything that applied to General Ma might well apply to me.

In addition to all these intrigues, the Governor one day had to deal with a delegation of refugees who presented him with a long document accusing Fang Chi, the new Commissioner of Education and member of the "C. C. Clique" of "ten crimes," including corruption, nepotism, and reaction. Mr. Fang had formerly been in charge of refugee funds, and the delegation asked the Governor to bring him to public trial. Since the "C. C. Clique" was an arm of the ruling party, the Governor dared not do anything. But Lihwang seethed with rumors as the refugee delegation went from department to department; and one day they even presented me with a copy of their charges. It was an amazing document, one of the charges referring to Mr. Fang's loose life with a woman back in his Tokyo student days. China is four thousand years old and has a long memory.

Caught between a dozen fires, Governor Liao Rei one day had an apoplectic stroke. His concubine, who knew nothing about scientific medicine, first called in a number of old herb doctors, who proceeded to dose the prostrate man with new concoctions each day, hoping that at least one might work. The 21st Group Army had just acquired a new Medical Director, a well-trained graduate of the Rockefeller

Foundation's Peking Union Medical College, but the concubine would not allow him to see the Governor. Instead, when the herb doctors failed to produce any results, she remembered that General Ma possessed a "magic needle" given him by Buddhist priests of the sacred Omei Mountain in far Szechuen Province. The priests had taught the young officer the art of acupuncture, which enables the operator to reach the exact nerve center with each thrust of his needle.

Now, though General Ma had been educated at America's West Point, he believed in this remarkable needle, which, although it sometimes acted as a counter-irritant, was in general pure superstition. My host carried his precious needle around in a little velvet case, and I had repeatedly seen him use it, once on an old landlord, afflicted with syphilis, who had been brought into our cottage in a sedan chair.

When the Governor's concubine demanded that General Ma use the needle on the Governor, General Ma refused unless the concubine would sign a written statement declaring that, should the treatment fail, she would not hold him responsible for the Governor's death. The concubine refused, and charged that he wished the Governor to die. She added that he had urged the Anhwei Student Army in Lihwang to revolt and had encouraged some of them to desert and join the New Fourth Army. This was both true and untrue: the young officer had had something to do with the student unrest, but had sent some of them to a guerrilla army in the west, not to the New Fourth. And the Governor had been furious. The concubine didn't care a thing about the students, but she relished any charge against General Ma because he had humiliated her and her brother with the white horse.

Our cottage was filled with delegations of officers and officials urging General Ma to use his needle on the Governor. He stubbornly refused until the concubine should give him written absolution. The garrison commander, General Lai Kang, came and told him that the woman was whipping up a tide of resentment against him, but he replied that she was merely an illiterate concubine — which didn't help matters.

While all this was going on, the Governor lay in a dangerous coma. At last Kwangsi Army commanders ripped the matter out of the concubine's hands and called in their new Medical Director. He began a treatment which brought the Governor back to consciousness. But the Governor was sick at heart and kept murmuring: "Why is there no hope for Anhwei? Why is it that no one understands me?"

Feeling that he would die, he laboriously and pathetically dictated a last will and testament:

> I am a military man. I have been an Army Commander for a long time. After the war of resistance began I thought of nothing but how to give my life to the country and to destroy the enemy. Last year I was appointed chairman of this province. There was great disorder and the Japanese attacked us fiercely. I was very anxious and worked too hard. That caused my illness. But the enemy is still strong. Unless the Yangtze and the Hwei are cleaned out and defended, Lungsoh [Szechuen] cannot be protected and we will lose the Central Plains [ancient Han term for central China]. Unless the Ta Pieh region is strengthened, there will be no base to begin a counter-offensive. Our party, political, and military comrades must do their utmost to unite under the guidance of the Tsung Tsai [Generalissimo Chiang] to reconstruct Anhwei, revive China, and achieve eventual victory. In this way my unfinished task will be accomplished. I hope that my loyalty and difficulties can be explained in detail to General Li and General Pai.

The concubine grew impatient at the General's slow recovery and one day abruptly dismissed the Army physician and called back her three old herb doctors. Two days later she telephoned in a frenzy for the Medical Director. But it was too late. The Governor had contracted pneumonia. He died on the night of October 21.

One hour later, while my secretary and I were sitting at a table with General Ma and his fiancée, the door was flung open and the concubine's brother, with a number of armed guards, pistols in hand, rushed in and fell upon the General. I rose in horror, but the concubine's brother seized me and hurled me back in my chair.

General Ma was allowed to go to his room to change. From there we heard shouting and struggling. He tried, as we learned later, to telephone the garrison commander, but the telephone was knocked from his hands. He found his pistol, but it was snatched from him. Finally they carried him out in his bathrobe, literally hog-tied, and the whole group disappeared into the night.

We rushed to the telephone to call the garrison commander, but found the wires had been torn from the batteries. I connected them, and my secretary finally reached the commander. Later he came to our cottage and told us that he had sent out an alarm, and all the guards and General Ma had been taken to headquarters as prisoners of the Kwangsi Army. Ma was detained for a week, and then escorted out of the province under heavy guard, en route to Chungking. His fiancée went with him.

From that time on, Lihwang was in a state of perpetual alarm. "Old Chen *Pao-chia*" turned up as acting Governor and rumor had it that he might be appointed Governor. The members of the People's Mobilization Committee prepared for flight; some had already disappeared. But when the Governor's funeral was held on the 25th most of them turned up in force, along with all the troops and every official in the Government. The "C. C. Clique" marched with solemn faces, and the Hunan bureaucrats, although worried by the weakened position of the concubine, were also in line.

As I watched the funeral procession I noticed that every shop in the villages through which it would pass had set out a red-decked table on which burned candles and bundles of incense sticks. And everyone had a string of firecrackers to set off to keep devils from the casket. First came columns of Kwangsi soldiers marching four abreast, their soft-shod feet making no noise, their rifles pointing toward the ground in mourning. Behind me the sewing-machines in a tailor's shop buzzed noisily as if nothing was happening. Once I saw a whole column of soldiers laughing — someone had told a joke which had passed down the line! The pall-bearers, heads of departments, were hitched to the casket by long white paper ribbons. But the casket was carried by coolies.

The Governor had no children, so one lone man in white sackcloth walked directly behind the casket, and to my amazement I saw that it was the brother of the concubine. The concubine followed in a covered sedan chair. Right behind her walked the Medical Director; he had been ordered to stay near her in case she should faint. Twice I saw her brother turn to stare at me, and his face was so contorted by hatred that I realized he held me responsible for General Ma's escape.

Although I really should not have been, I was amazed by this funeral. It incorporated all that was old and feudal in China. There was the great palanquin, loaded with food, to accompany the soul of the dead man on its journey to the other world. And some of the marchers wore such gorgeous costumes that they looked like actors from the old stage. Over everything hung the fragrance of incense, and firecrackers spluttered along the entire line of march. When it was all over I heard several youths declare bitterly that the Government had appropriated twenty thousand dollars for the funeral, but that it had not cost more than a few hundred. The rest had "disappeared."

Immediately after the funeral Professor Chang Pei-chuan, leader of the People's Mobilization Committee, came to warn me that the Kuomintang had stationed secret agents along all paths leading to my cottage. Three girls from the Women's Committee came through the cordon to give me a similar warning and to say that they were leaving Lihwang. Many youths did not even return to their barracks after the funeral. Everyone urged me to leave. When a messenger slipped through with an invitation to rejoin the New Fourth Army, I decided to ask for a military pass.

Two days later a short, fat official appeared, sat down uneasily on the edge of a chair, and turned toward me a face so modest and humble that I suspected him of almost anything. He had been sent by the Government, he said, to inform me that there were floods on the route between Lihwang and the New Fourth Army and I could not possibly wade through. I did not mind wading through floods, I said. But, he protested, there was also an order from the Central Government prohibiting foreigners from visiting central Anhwei. When I asked to see the order, he shook his head sadly and said that it was secret! Then why reveal a secret order, I asked. He squirmed, murmuring that the Government was responsible for my safety; and when I assured him that I did not hold the Government responsible, he said he was very sad of heart. Why not go to other armies, he added brightly. Yes, I would do that, I said, but first I would send one telegram to the Red Cross Medical Corps informing them of my exact route of travel, and another to General Li Chung-ren, Commander-in-Chief of the Fifth War Zone, informing him that I was crossing central China to reach his headquarters.

The young man rose uneasily, purring something about my health, my bitter life, and my services to China. I almost laughed in his face.

On the heels of this man came another Government official, a friend of mine who had attended the conference before which my request for a military pass had come. He stalked in and asked: "What did that *jen tsai* (slave) tell you?"

I told him.

"A pack of lies!" he exclaimed. The head of the "C. C. Clique" had listened to my request and then merely declared: "She can't go!" Everyone else had sat in silence, not daring to utter a word.

The official asked me what I intended to do. Go across central China to the west, I said; to return to the New Fourth Army would not help that Army under present conditions. With a stony face he stared before him, then shook my hand and took his departure.

At dawn on the morning of October 28 a group of Lihwang Preservation Corps men were waiting to escort me to the west. As the garrison commander, who had been a friend of the Governor and of Lieutenant General Ma, said good-by, he shook his head sorrowfully and patted the big black mule which Governor Liao Rei had given me shortly before he died. After he was gone came a leader of the Theatrical Group, who raised his hands and exclaimed almost hysterically: "I know all that's being said and done, but still I believe we must try to work here as long as possible. There is still some hope!"

Finally Chang Pei-chuan, the young professor who represented the People's Mobilization Corps, came to *sung* me on my journey. He escorted me far beyond the outskirts of the town. As he bade me farewell he looked along the path leading into the mountains and asked: "Do you suppose anything would happen if I simply went with you right now?" I told him to look at the sergeant in charge of my armed escort. It was obvious that my friend would not get very far if he tried. From a hilltop I turned to look back. He still stood where we had left him.

Discord

I HAVE no heart to write of any of these events. It would be easier to write only of the courageous and magnificent side of China. Yet China is not just China, but a kind of little world where one can observe social forces that have their counterpart in every corner of the greater world itself.

One year after I left Lihwang I received a letter in western China from a doctor in the New Fourth Army informing me that the young professor, Chang Pei-chuan, and almost the entire People's Mobilization Committee of over a thousand educated men and women had made their way to the New Fourth Army. They had deserted in groups. The new Governor, General Li Ping-hsien, had not been a reactionary man, but had been sent to the province with instructions to prevent the spread of New Fourth Army influence. Educated youth had not been willing to work under the new conditions in Lihwang — had not been willing, among other things, to fight their own countrymen. They were not Communists, but the Communists left their doors wide open to them. So the youth of Lihwang continued their work — elsewhere. It seemed to me that even in their own interests the old order was stupid.

More: in mid-January 1941 all China was perturbed by the news that four thousand men and women of the Third Detachment of the New Fourth Army had been surrounded on the southern shores of the Yangtze by eighty thousand Government troops and annihilated. Women nurses and political workers had hanged themselves from the trees. Of the wounded soldiers I dared not think, for there is no fury like that of a ruling class whose power and property is threatened.

The news told us that General Yeh Ting, Commander of the New Fourth Army, had been wounded and taken prisoner and was to be court-martialed by General Ku Chu-tung, Commander-in-Chief of the Third War Zone. General Ku was the same man who had been responsible, as I have related, for the death of a newspaper man in Chinkiang in pre-war days. The reports said that Vice-Commander Hsiang Ying of the New Fourth Army had escaped, but was being sought for arrest. The Communists said he had been wounded, then killed.

Now I recalled what General Yeh Ting and I had once said to each other.

"Should civil war ever come," he had asked, "what will happen to such people as you and I, who are members neither of the Kuomintang nor of the Communist Party?"

"We might be the first to be killed," I had answered.

When these reports began to come through, the Chinese Government tried first to suppress and then to deny them. Within the Government's own ranks there was great conflict about such developments. General Ho Ying-ching, Minister of War, and General Pai Chung-hsi, vice chief of staff to the National Military Council, were held responsible for the orders that had led to the clash. I heard that when reports of the fighting reached Chungking, an order had gone out that firing should cease immediately, but that General Ku Chu-tung of the Third War Zone had not transmitted it. Once the news was out, however, the Government sought to justify the action as "military necessity."

The first official newspaper reports were wild and stupid. One charged that the New Fourth Army troops had revolted and attacked Government troops. Another charged that General Yeh Ting and the entire New Fourth Army had "plotted" to occupy first the great triangle lying between Nanking, Shanghai, and Hangchow, and then the towns of Chuyung and Tanyang, in order to use all of them as a base of operations against Chinese regular armies. In writing such reports, perhaps newspaper men knew that no one would trouble to analyze them or consult a map. Foreigners certainly would not. Had they done so, they would have seen that the Shanghai-Nanking-Hangchow triangle was occupied by the Japanese and was their main base of operations against central China. The towns of Chuyung and Tanyang were just south of Nanking and both were also fortified Japanese positions. If the New Fourth Army indeed "plotted" to occupy these places, then it was plotting to annihilate Japanese forces which had already defeated all the regular Chinese armies. I wondered why official newspapers had not charged that the New Fourth Army and General Yeh Ting had also "plotted" to occupy Nanking and Tokyo!

The position taken by the Communist armies was serious. The story that I gathered from many quarters was this: When the British had closed the Burma Road for three months in the middle of 1940, cutting China off from all military supplies, the Japanese had immediately offered China liberal peace terms. These terms remained a secret, but a Kwangsi Army commander told me that he had heard that the Japanese had offered to kick out chief puppet Wang Ching-wei and recognize Generalissimo Chiang Kai-shek as head of a semi-independent government. The Japanese offered to evacuate all their troops from central and south

China except for strategic coastal garrisons. But they demanded the right to hold all China north of the Yellow River. It was their demand for this territory that had first plunged China into war, and the Japanese had never given up their ambitions. North China was not merely a great source of food, and of coal, iron, and other raw materials, but the Japanese also wanted it as a base of operations against both China and the Soviet Union. It was also conceived of as a "sanitary" zone to prevent the spread of Communism from the Soviet Union into China. Yet it was this very territory which the Communist Eighth Route Army had occupied and in which it operated against the Japanese.

The closing of the Burma Road, the Japanese peace proposals, and eventually the order to the New Fourth Army to move north of the Yellow River, were regarded all the more suspiciously because the Eighth Route Army had been blockaded for many months by the powerful army of General Hu Chung-nan, a Chinese Blue Shirt. General Hu Chung-nan's army was said to consist of 500,000 of the best-equipped and best-fed troops in China. Though they were by no means pro-Japanese, the majority of them had not fired a shot at the Japanese since the Battle of Taierchwang in the spring of 1938. Instead, they had built three lines of fortifications in the rear of the Eighth Route Army. For over a year and a half the Eighth Route had been refused ammunition, money, or medical supplies from the Chinese Government. The Communists therefore saw that they faced a mortal enemy, the Japanese, on every front, while a powerful national enemy blockaded them from the rear.

The conflict with the New Fourth Army had developed because the Government ordered it to evacuate the lower Yangtze River Valley and move into the region to the north of the Yellow River. In this region there had been floods for months, so that the Eighth Route Army there had often been unable to feed its own troops. In early 1941 an Australian missionary nurse, Miss Kathleen Hall, had managed to penetrate the region and reach General Chu Teh's headquarters in Shansi Province. Miss Hall told me that she had seen vast areas which had been laid waste by the Japanese and other regions in which almost everyone had died from typhus or starvation. Even Miss Hall, with money to buy food, soon found her body swelling from beriberi. She had been forced to leave to save herself.

The New Fourth Army had finally agreed to move into this region, but had asked the Government to issue it winter uniforms, money to feed its troops, and ammunition to protect them en route. Its requests were rejected. The Communists therefore believed that the orders sprang from the Japanese peace proposals, which elements in the Chinese Government were always urging Generalissimo Chiang Kai-shek to accept.

Despite all these developments the First and Second Detachments of the New Fourth Army had obeyed the Government orders and percolated across the Yangtze from the territory east and west of Nanking. The Third Detachment, with its base hospitals filled with wounded, had remained in the same valley which it had always occupied. It was there that the detachment was finally attacked and decimated. After this tragedy reports came out that Wang Ching-wei's puppet armies had occupied a part of the territory evacuated by the New Fourth.

These events brought China to the verge of internal war. The Communists issued an ultimatum to the Central Government demanding the cessation of armed attacks on its troops, an apology for the destruction of the Third Detachment, compensation for the families of the dead, and the release of General Yeh Ting. They also asked that immediate steps be taken to introduce a democratic system which would give all parties a voice in the Government. Pending a settlement, the Communists began to appoint their own commanders, and all the New Fourth detachments, though declared disbanded by the Government, continued to fight as before. Instead of moving to the north of the Yellow River, they remained, and still remain, in central and eastern Anhwei and in the bordering north Kiangsu Province — areas which are at present erroneously shaded to indicate

Book VII (1939)   Through Central China   369

Japanese occupation. The Communists announced that they would continue to fight the Japanese and puppets, but would also defend themselves if attacked by Government troops.

The basic cause of all these conflicts must be sought in political and social forces, not in military conditions. The specter of civil war had never been laid, even after the Japanese invasion. The ruling class, primarily the landlords, viewed with terror the growth of the Eighth Route and New Fourth Armies because these mobilized, educated, and armed the common people. Landlords who had fled to the far west or to the port cities before the Japanese, saw their peasants in arms, standing their ground and fighting. Could such men be expected to lay down their guns after the war had ended and return to the old conditions? Certainly not!

Let it be clear that the Chinese Communists always declared that socialism could not be introduced until China had passed through the democratic stage. However, they never confused a private capitalism, with its tendency to concentrate economic power in the hands of a few, with democracy. They taught their troops and the people that all Chinese must unite and march forward together; and when they said forward they meant forward. That they made mistakes and were often as intransigent as Jesuits and capitalists cannot be denied. But as they preached, so did they practice. No men were more prepared to die for their convictions than they. Guns in their hands, they stood at the front with the people, and it was difficult to see just where their forces ended and the people began. Much later, in Chungking, I heard a high-placed official exclaim: "What amazes me is the number of Communist Party members who have been killed at the front."

Later on I was often to hear foreigners spreading rumors about "the arms smuggled to the Chinese Communists by the Soviet Union." I urged them merely to consult the map to see how completely the Eighth Route and New Fourth Armies were cut off from the outside world by vast distances, deserts, and blockading nationalist troops.

From early 1939 until it was attacked in 1941, the Soviet

Government supplied China with more arms, ammunition, and financial aid than did any other power or combination of powers. But such supplies were delivered directly to the Chinese Government, who saw to it that none reached the Communist armies. Had the Soviet Government ever attempted to furnish any individual Chinese army with supplies, it would have split China wide open. I doubt if even the most conservative Chinese official would dare charge that the Soviet Union supplied the Communists with anything. Incidentally, had the Soviets done so, the Communist armies would hardly have been in so sorry a state. Soviet military advisers replaced the Germans in China, but these advisers were pure military strategists, and not one was permitted to advise the Eighth Route or New Fourth Armies. There were no Soviet political workers of any kind in China, and the military advisers could talk only with the highest commanders of the national armies.

Until the conflict developed between the Communists and the Government, the Government furnished the former with money and ammunition; like all the armies of the country, however, the Communist forces had to furnish their own medical supplies out of these funds. After the conflict developed, even medical supplies bought in Hong Kong or contributed from abroad were not permitted to pass through to the Eighth Route sick and wounded. I did not fail to point out that this was a gross violation of international law.

Sometimes Government spokesmen charged that the Eighth Route and New Fourth Armies did not fight but merely sought to "stir up the people." The Japanese who fought those armies knew better. I saw dozens of hospitals filled with wounded Communist soldiers, but perhaps the Government thought there were too few. There would have been fewer still if these soldiers had possessed adequate arms and ammunition and if they had been fed well enough to resist sickness and disease. Once one of the highest Government officials was quoted as saying that if the Government gave the Communists more money, the latter would not improve the conditions of their troops but merely recruit still more. This was quite true; the Communists believed that unless all Chinese were armed, they would become slaves of the Japanese. Men with guns in their hands, they felt, learn how to talk back to aggressors.

A fierce light was thrown on these internal conflicts when General Chu Teh, Commander-in-Chief of the Communist Armies, issued a report to the nation on July 7, 1942. He prefaced it by stating that the Eighth Route had received no money or ammunition from the Government for three years! Despite this, he wrote, the Eighth Route and New Fourth Armies had in 1941–2 engaged more than twenty-four Japanese divisions, or 44 per cent of the total Japanese armed forces in China. In that same period the Eighth Route Army had suffered casualties of 23,034 dead and 40,813 wounded, the New Fourth 6,755 dead and 10,856 wounded. How fierce the fighting had been was indicated in the revelation that these armies had lost seventy-five of their highest officers.

General Chu estimated that in that year the Eighth Route had killed and wounded more than 24,000 Japanese and puppets. The two armies together had captured a total of 38,985, together with quantities of guns, ammunition, and other supplies. The New Fourth alone had taken 15,721 new rifles, 301 light and heavy machine-guns, and much other material, including clothing, food, and medicine. The Communists had literally lived off the Japanese.

When I read General Chu Teh's report to the nation, it seemed to me that behind his dull statistics glowed a thousand Marathons. The phrases of Leonidas at Thermopylæ seemed to pale before his concluding words.

"Victory will not come of itself, but can only be won by further sacrifices. We vow before our countrymen and the anti-Fascist peoples of the world that we will persist in our efforts to maintain and strengthen national unity under the leadership of Generalissimo Chiang. . . . We shall keep this vow until we have driven the Japanese across the Yalu River. We will co-operate with the Kuomintang and all other parties to build a democratic Republic, and with all freedom-loving peoples to build a new world. . . ."

In early January 1943 a small news item reported that the town and valley of Lihwang, Anhwei, where I had spent five weeks, had been overrun and for a short period occupied by the Japanese. How vividly I could recall that valley with its flowing river, its many new buildings, and those tens of thousands of men and women whose voices were the voices of new China! Again Anhwei seemed like a drop of water that reflected the whole world. I believed, and still believe, that the Japanese could never have occupied that mountain fastness had it not been weakened from within by political reaction. Men cannot triumph by guns alone.

Song of Desolation

THERE is a whole region of central China which I remember by a song of desolation in the night. It happened this way:

Leaving Lihwang, we moved westward through the towering Ta Pieh mountain range, ascending one summit only to find ourselves looking out on a sea of others. Drifting clouds caressed the black volcanic peaks, swept about us, and left us soaked.

Through sunny hours eagles floated lazily above us, and long wedges of wild geese flew southward, heralding the winter. The pine forests soughed as if in fear. The *lah*, or wax, tree blazed in red glory on the lower slopes. Its small, round white beans had burst their brown pods and gleamed among the red autumn foliage like spangles. And at intervals there were clumps of trees turning to bright cerise.

From earth's grandeur we would descend into squalid valley villages where poverty bred sickness and suffering. Here was cause and effect in graphic simplicity: the villages arose directly in the shadows of the landlords' mansion — indeed, they were its shadows. High walls with watchtowers, pierced by loop-holes, protected the mansion. The landlords had fled, leaving agents behind to collect the rents.

Near one village I saw two peasant men, barefoot and in rags, hitched to a plow held upright by a barefoot, ragged woman. Behind them walked another woman carrying a small basket and dropping bits of dried manure into the furrow.

For many years before the anti-Japanese war began, the border region of Anhwei, Hupeh, and Honan Provinces had been Soviet territory guarded by the Fourth Red Army Corps. Only after years of warfare had the Kuomintang armies been able to reduce it. How many people were killed no one will ever know, but the region was now sparsely populated, many villages were crumbling to dust, and old Red Army slogans on trees and wayside shrines were obliterated by whitewash.

The villages were so poor we could buy nothing to eat. One night we came into a large one and decided to sleep in an empty peasant hut. The floor was the usual packed earth, but the walls were crumbling and we could see the sky through the broken roof above. We bought two eggs, some rice and garlic, and after eating our meager meal we lay down on our piles of straw.

Only I was "rich" enough to afford a candle. When night fell, the people went to bed or sat in the darkness in front of their huts and talked in low voices. As I lay there thinking my painful thoughts, I suddenly heard voices singing in the night. First a man sang, then a woman answered, and the song went on and on. The music was as old as China; I did not know the words, but I felt that into these old ballads the people had woven their hopes and sorrows. There was something in it that moved me until I was sitting upright in my bed, listening intently, straining. It went on and on, a passion of desolation stretching back into time immemorial. . . . How many men had lived and died in this ancient land, and how abandoned! How desperate the sorrows of the people!

The ballad ended, the night closed in, and from the village came not a sound.

This song still returns to me whenever Honan Province is mentioned — that wide wheat plain where famine, flood, drought, banditry, and poverty are the constant companions of the people.

To my remark about this destitution, a young official once answered sadly: "Compared to north Honan, that is nothing. There the people have nothing at all."

In the western Ta Pieh mountain range we saw a slogan written in white paint along the walls of a landlord's mansion: *"The Army must love the people and the people must help the Army.* — Hwangchuan Youth Association." But we never met the writers. It was as if they had written the words, then fled. I recalled that while in Lihwang I had met three girl students who had come from the Hwangchuan Youth Association to study at the Anhwei base of resistance.

In the late evening of October 30 our armed escort delivered us in safety to the headquarters of the Magistrate of Shangchen, a ruined city on the fringe of a battlefield that runs the length of northern Hupeh and southern Honan Provinces. From Shangchen we could hear the roar of guns from an enemy garrison thirty miles to the south and from Macheng in Hupeh, the strongest Japanese position in the region. The Kwangsi Army had attacked this base and the Shangchen guerrilla detachment had been ordered there to help.

The Magistrate had gone to the front to command the guerrilla detachment. When I asked if I too might go, officials stared in consternation. It was too dangerous, they replied; Shangchen had been occupied by the Japanese for nine months, and they had been driven out only in May of this year. Once a city of 250,000, Shangchen now had a population of less than 5,000 and these lived in a perpetual state of preparedness for evacuation. Periodically the Japanese swept northward into south Honan in an attempt to exterminate the main Chinese armies.

In the absence of Magistrate Koo Ting, once a commander against the Red Army, I became the guest of the Chamber of Commerce and was given a room in its headquarters. There I met the town's leading merchants and officials. There were no mass organizations, for, my hosts explained, this was an old Red Army region and people's organizations were dangerous unless carefully organized and led. On the walls surrounding the Chamber of Commerce stretched two slogans: *Anyone who agitates the people or spreads rumors will be destroyed*, and *The chief virtues are obedience and filial piety*.

Mr. Ming Yao, local representative of the Kuomintang, was a young man with a face as cold and cruel as any I had ever seen. When I asked him about people's organizations, he listed the Chamber of Commerce; the *pao-chia* headquarters; the rice, wheat, and cotton merchants' guilds; the Barbers' Union with one hundred and twenty members, and the Carpenters' and Masons' Union with four hundred. He also said something about a primary school "outside the city" and some peasant associations.

When I asked to speak with representatives of the carpenters', masons', and barbers' groups, he replied that he was their representative and I could speak to him. When I asked in what villages the peasant associations were located, he grew vague and finally said that they were not fully organized — that he was thinking of organizing them, but that it would be difficult because this was an old Soviet region. The Kuomintang, he said, was planning to establish in Hwangchuan a training school for mass organizers. The Reds had held Shangchen and Hwangchuan for four years. To dislodge them the Government troops had had to burn down all the forests around them. Apparently forgetting this statement, he later declared bitterly that the Reds had themselves burned down all the forests. When I asked why they should want to do that, he answered: "The trees belonged to the landlords."

My host, the president of the Chamber of Commerce, was an older man who had once been captured by the Red Army and had been fined two thousand dollars as a reactionary. He had escaped to Hankow and returned after the Kuomintang Armies conquered the region. I did not ask him what he did then, for he belonged to the old world and in talking to such men I always felt as though I were wading through a swamp. He spoke pathetically of the lot of landlords, but said nothing about the peasants.

With my host I went through Shangchen. A strategic city lying at the base of the Ta Pieh mountain range, fierce battles had raged around it. Before the Japanese could capture it their planes had leveled almost every building, and when driven out in May, they had tried to burn down everything else.

The Shangchen authorities gave me an armed escort of fifteen men to take me to Hwangchuan, a large city to the northwest which had once been in the hands of the Japanese for three months. I had to postpone my trip for a few hours because a guerrilla detachment near Hwangchuan had just mutinied. They had not been paid for three months and, lacking political training, some had deserted to the Japanese, while others were now looting villages and waylaying travelers.

The motor highway along which we were to travel was the main "life line" of China north of the Yangtze. To prevent Japanese mechanized equipment from using it (China itself had no trucks or gasoline in this region), deep trenches extending far into the bordering wheat-fields had been dug across it. Along this route came an endless procession of carriers, wheelbarrows, donkeys, and mules, transporting war material to the armies of Honan and Anhwei, even to Shantung Province and to troops along the far eastern sea. It was a lucrative highway for either Japanese or bandits.

The only evidence of "people's mobilization" that I saw in Shangchen before I left was the way I got my two carriers. Because I had asked for men to help carry our bedding rolls, my typewriter, camera, films, and medical supplies, the authorities had sent armed men to the outskirts of the town, where they dragged two men from their beds at midnight, bound them, and brought them to me! The first I knew of this was when in the middle of the night I heard a scuffling of feet in the adjoining room. When I entered the room I found two ragged, barefoot peasants cowering in a corner. They were squat, broad-shouldered, and bare-headed, and their black eyes watched me in fear. Yet if I refused these men the authorities would merely round up others in the same way. When my secretary told the two peasants that we would pay them and give them good food, they merely drew back and watched him suspiciously.

When we halted in a town for rest a few hours later, one of the carriers escaped in the crowd; our sergeant went down the street to look for another. Meanwhile I noticed the other carrier watching me as I rummaged in a basket in which I had packed some additional food, cigarettes, and equipment for our journey. Everything that could be eaten or smoked had disappeared! In a cautious voice the carrier told me that during the morning the guards had eaten the food, taken the cigarettes, and searched everywhere for money.

It was then that I recalled that the sergeant of the guards had been asking if special troops were really coming to meet us, and that one little guard, a lad with an unusually intelligent face, had told my secretary that the guards were former bandits. To my secretary I remarked: "Since we've been looted in a small way in headquarters, on the road we may expect to be robbed in a big way."

Sure enough, when we were about an hour's distance out of town all the guards surrounded the sergeant and demanded that he pay them fifteen dollars each — their unpaid wages for three months. He offered each two dollars and a half and began writing their names in a notebook. They rejected the money. He went up to three dollars, then four, and finally five, after which he refused to bargain further. Sullenly they accepted the five dollars, but insisted that the little guard with the intelligent face read aloud everything written in the book.

We knew the issue was not yet settled. We continued on our way, wondering just when they would demand more money. We also tried to learn where the young guard had learned to read. He was wary, but when we started to talk about Shangchen and the old Red Army, he burst out: "Yes, the rich hated the Red Army, but the poor loved it. It was very good. It had clubs, singing groups, and things like that. I joined it when I was a child. That's where I learned to read and write."

One night we entered a medieval walled town perched on a hill. It had been bombed, looted by bandits, and left half-deserted; an air of decay and destitution hung over everything. We unrolled our bedding on a layer of wheat straw in a building whose entire front had been blasted away. Our two carriers had nothing but the rags on their bodies, and slept curled up against each other, their hands tucked into their sleeves. The nights had grown very cold and I gave them two of my thin woolen blankets, keeping one for myself. They assured me that they had no lice, but I was certain that they had. My secretary warned that they might run off with my blankets, but I declared that I would do the same if I were they.

Before turning in we wandered about trying to buy something to eat, and under a spreading oak found a small, lamp-lit stall where we could buy bread, dry garlic, and hot water. As we stood there, a group of uniformed men came down the street. They were all talking so eagerly and the faces of all of them were so alight with enthusiasm and interest that I stared at them. Suddenly one of them cried out my Chinese name and at once I realized that they were Eighth Route Army men. It turned out that they were on their way to the New Fourth in Anhwei to become commanders or political workers. They had walked across all north China accompanied by a young Englishman, George Hogg, a worker in the Chinese Industrial Co-operatives.

Since they had been sleeping in peasant homes and had not met officials, they saw everywhere only the reflections of that which they carried in their own hearts — victory. How wonderful everything was, they exclaimed. The war was going magnificently; the people were awakened, political prejudices stilled, victories everywhere! When we told them of our experiences their mouths fell open in bewilderment.

When they were gone and we had returned to our sleeping-quarters, I wrote of the great desolation that filled me. Up to this time I had been with men who had all tried, despite differences in political outlook, to think in terms of human progress. There had been dark moments and discords, but we all had had only one main desire — to free China and bring it forward. Now I seemed to have broken out of that charmed circle and into an ocean of darkness, poverty, and oppression. Along the highway I had found none of those slogans by which the Chinese express their hopes, no songs of conviction, no activity of the people. Sick and diseased people surrounded me everywhere, pleading for help — babies that had congenital syphilis — skin diseases — scabby heads — pus-filled eyes — ulcerous legs! Someone told me that there was a missionary hospital in Hwangchuan, but when I urged the people to go there for medical treatment, they replied in dull despair that the hospital charged money and they had none.

"What destitution, dirt, and disease!" I wrote. "I have used up half of my medicine, but there is no end. Only a gigantic transformation could end this misery!"

From a plateau on which a group of strong peasant men were drilling we looked down on Hwangchuan, a city that dated back to the ancient Chou Dynasty. The old inner city stood on a high hill, surrounded by a time-worn serrated wall washed by a river. I thought of Prague with its medieval Czech castle standing on a hill, the blue Moldau laving its feet. Behind us, far across the wheat plains, the faint blue contours of the Ta Pieh Mountains were shadows against the sky.

Suddenly people began running from the village across the wheat-fields. An air-raid! We fled into a cemetery and crouched between the grave-mounds, watching the skies. Out of the north came nine black specks. They grew larger and larger, roared over us, and on toward the south.

It was four in the afternoon when we crossed a bridge over a jade-green river and passed through the old walls. Directly over the gateway was the slogan: *Suppress Communists; they are connected with Russia!* Along the wall ran another: *Our heads may be cut off, but our hearts cannot be conquered.*

The inner city was under martial law. Climbing up and up the stone steps, we passed through three cordons of troops, each of which was searching all civilians. The Special Commission's headquarters on the summit was surrounded by another iron ring.

The Special Commissioner, Mai Ta-fu, was a young military man, a member of the Kuomintang who had formerly been aide-de-camp to General Cheng Chien, Commander-in-Chief of the First War Zone. He welcomed me to Hwang-chuan and ordered food for us. While we were waiting, he led us through his headquarters to a garden in the back, and we suddenly found ourselves in another world. Two bushes laden with blood-red roses perfumed a large, lovely garden. There was a weather-worn stone table with stone benches, and beyond that the low stone tomb of a prince of a dynasty that had ruled long before the time of Christ.

Commander Mai fitted into this picture. He was polished, exceedingly handsome, and elegantly dressed. With gracious dignity he began to discuss living-quarters for me. Because of the air-raids he suggested that I live in one of the three Christian missionary institutions in the town; they had their national flags painted on their roofs and so far had not been bombed. The Catholic mission, however, was suspect; an Italian priest had been driven out by the authorities because he had helped the Japanese during the occupation.

I did not wish to live in a mission. The missions were small foreign oases removed from the activity, thought, and struggle of the country. I preferred to take my chances with the Chinese. An adjutant was therefore sent into the city to look over the inns; he returned to report that they were too dirty. Finally I allowed Commander Mai to send a note to the American Lutheran Mission.

As a result I spent a few days in a comfortable American house eating American food and sleeping on a bed so soft that it kept me awake half the night. The room even had a picture of a cat playing a fiddle.

The missionary ladies were a Miss Patterson and a Miss Quello, both of Norwegian descent, the former a nurse and the latter an evangelist who had just returned from a two-week revival tour of the region to the north. I had entered a Lutheran Bible Belt that stretched across Honan.

Miss Patterson had seen so much of the dark side of China that she had grown cynical. She spoke of the deep-dyed materialism of the Chinese, of the corruption and banditry, but it seemed to me that her own reaction to this had been to become a hard-boiled business woman. Miss Quello was less biased, possessed a faculty for vivid description, and was more sympathetic toward China. On her last trip she had spent a night in a village from which the entire population had fled in fear of bandits. A military officer had warned her and the Chinese "Bible woman" with her to leave at once, but instead the two women had prayed, after which they had slept safely through the night. The next day the villagers had returned and she had conducted her usual Bible class and held a revival meeting. All her converts were old women, she said, and each time she returned they had forgotten all she had previously taught them. What interested me was the fact that most Christian converts were old people afraid of death. The young ones I had seen were largely "rice Christians." So far I had found no Christian soldiers.

In the visits I made to the military clinics in Hwangchuan, I found many sick and wounded men, but no medical supplies. They never sent their wounded to the missionary hospital, they said, because they could not afford to pay the registration fee and the fifty cents a day for a bed in the public ward. The Lutheran hospital was receiving free medical supplies from the International Red Cross Committee in Hankow, but refused to admit wounded soldiers free of charge. Miss Patterson argued that foreign medicine was for refugees only, that there were no refugees in the region, and that the armies had money enough to pay for their wounded if they wished, and that officers always had money. She maintained a small out-patient clinic to treat the very poor, but patients had to prove their destitution.

One day my secretary, who was living in the hospital, reported that a wounded soldier had been lying in front of the hospital for four hours, but was refused admission because he could not pay the eighty cents' registration fee and the fifty cents a day for a bed. I found this wounded man slowly bleeding to death on his stretcher. I paid the registration fee and the charges for one month's care; then I went in search of the hard-boiled Chinese Christian doctor and insisted that he care for the man at once. Because the money had been paid, the soldier was admitted.

When I informed Miss Patterson that I would have to report this case to the International Red Cross Committee and write about it, she rummaged among her papers and finally insisted upon returning my money. But no other soldier was admitted while I was there. The hospital suffered no loss for such a patient, since the International Red Cross Committee always paid his hospital fees. It seemed to me that missionary activity was sometimes just a kind of trade. Even though they were kind to me personally, I again regretted that I had to live in a mission home.

One afternoon, during an interview with Commander Mai Ta-fu, an air-raid alarm interrupted us and, along with the entire populace, we poured through or over the old walls and out of the city. The countryside beyond was a maze of narrow zigzag trenches and of holes just large enough for one person. I dived into one of these "fox-holes" and looked around. All around me were hundreds of heads sticking out of the earth, scanning the skies, each camouflaged with a little bunch of wheat straw or a branch.

Living on a hill-top, protected by troops, and with as much comfort as such a poor war zone could provide, perhaps Commander Mai did not see or did not care about the bitter lot of the people. As he talked to me I recalled that song of desolation in the night and knew that he could never sympathize with or even know the lot of the common people. To be a Chinese was not enough.

That evening I dined with the Commander, the Magistrate, and Major General Wang Chan-ping, Vice-Commander of the 7th Kwangsi Army, which held the front to the south. We stood before a huge military map and studied the Japanese and Chinese positions and they told of the changes they had observed since the war began.

I liked Major General Wang Chan-ping because he looked like a knot on a tree. He was a Kwangsi man, short and tough, with an ugly face, a shaven head and bow-legs. His eyes sparkled and his simple honesty was very appealing. He was the direct antithesis of the debonair, handsome Special Commissioner. He seemed to have no interest whatever in "keeping things as they are," and he judged victory not only by military standards, but also by the changing attitude of the people toward the enemy and toward their own armed forces. In the first part of the war, he said, the civilians always fled from their homes to far places, or ran in terror from one place to another; but now when the Japanese advanced they merely moved to some place near by and waited for them to be beaten back. If a few Japanese entered a village, the people did not flee, but killed them.

Man of God

OF all the missionaries in central China, I met none so remarkable as Dr. Skinsness, an American Lutheran of Norwegian descent. The slate-colored roofs of his hospital rising on a hill beyond Kioshan, a town south of Chumatien, could be seen for miles across the plains. Three different times Japanese bombers had come up from the south and had made special detours to bomb it. Thirteen American flags hung inside and outside its buildings, yet two of the structures had been destroyed and the others badly damaged.

Kioshan lay on the old Peiping-Hankow railway line — or rather on what had once been the railway. The nearest Japanese garrison was at Changtaikwan, twenty-five miles to the south, and south of that lay Sinyang, the main Japanese defense position above Hankow. North of Changtaikwan the Chinese had turned the railway bed into wheat-fields and had given the rails and girders to a group of railway workers who had set up a small foundry in Chumatien and were turning the steel into swords for the Chinese armies and guerrillas.

The Japanese were so close to Kioshan that their airplanes were able to be over the town within five minutes after the town bell clanged an alarm. There were four or five alarms each day and others on moonlit nights. For miles around the hospital there was no place to run for shelter, not even a tree or a bush. The planes therefore flew low enough to be able to spot and machine-gun anyone who fled from the hospital. So Dr. Skinsness, his wife, the two American women nurses, the newly trained Chinese women nurse attendants, and the patients just stood and took the bombings as they came.

I had become ill and the Magistrate of Kioshan sent a note to Dr. Skinsness asking if he could admit me to the hospital. I had already heard many tales of this doctor. One was that he was a Christian so grim that when he uttered the word "heathen" it sounded like a curse. Along with the Magistrate's letter I enclosed a note informing him that I was not a Christian and could not ask for help without informing him of this fact. In his answering note he invited me to come, and added: "You may not be a Christian. Well, I am!"

In his white apron, he followed his note down the hill and said he had room in his own home not only for me, but for my secretary. I went with something like trepidation. My secretary was even more reluctant, for he had begun to hate the missionaries for their too comfortable homes and lives.

But the home was not luxurious, though in that wilderness of poverty it might seem so to poor Chinese. It was a typical lower-middle-class American home, clean, orderly, and well cared for. The furnishings looked almost new, but had actually been brought from America twenty-four years before. With Norwegian thoroughness, every chair was kept repaired, oiled, and polished, and every hole in the carpets, couch cover, or window curtains darned. Only the big cracks in the walls and ceilings, caused by bombings, had not been repaired, because it seemed a waste of labor while the bombers kept coming over daily. From one of the nurses I soon learned that Dr. Skinsness and his wife had saved no money, and that their son and daughter were both working their way through school in Chicago, their son at Rush and their daughter tending a switchboard while studying to become a nurse.

The hospital had been equipped for eighty patients, but it now had one hundred and thirty, and had had as many as two hundred. It received medicine from the International Red Cross Committee in Hankow, but, unlike the hospital in Hwangchuan, gave it to anyone in need — to soldiers, refugees, civilians, and both the mission orphanage and the town's non-Christian orphanage. In addition, Dr. Skinsness bought medicine with the fees of patients who were able to pay, and at times gave surgical instruments and drugs to armies in need.

After the last severe bombings Dr. Skinsness's Chinese doctors and nurses had left, two of the women nurses going to an independent guerrilla detachment of the New Fourth Army which operated along the Peiping-Hankow railway. As the only doctor in charge, Dr. Skinsness was on call twenty-four hours a day. He was up at five or five thirty each morning and tried to perform operations before the air-raids began. He visited each patient in the morning and again in the evening, and for two hours in the morning and two in the afternoon he took personal charge of an outpatient clinic which served hundreds of civilians and soldiers. If patients could pay the ten-cent fee for examination, medicine, and treatment, well and good; it was not demanded, and no "means test" was used to establish the destitution of patients.

If there were five minutes during the day that could be spared, Dr. Skinsness spent it inspecting a dispensary that was being built, or directing the construction of new wooden bedsteads to take the place of those destroyed by bombs. In some of the wards men lay on mattresses on the floor, with just enough room for the doctor and a nurse to move between them.

In his life and work this missionary doctor was a grim, dour Christian. Often he spoke harshly, even fiercely, of his past experiences with "heathen" doctors, who, he said, had no compassion, no sense of honesty or duty. His iron conviction was that Christianity alone imbued men with these virtues. He used the word "heathen" precisely as Southern Americans use the word "nigger." But in his work with the sick and wounded I saw only a man dedicated to the service of mankind.

A fearful experience had had an unfortunate effect upon his attitude toward all Chinese. One day in early September of the year before, a high Army officer had brought his sick mother to the hospital for treatment and had quartered his bodyguards in a small building inside the mission compound. The old lady died and her body, protected by the guards, lay in the compound for a number of days. One night, after a hard day's labor, and while his wife was away in the mountains, Dr. Skinsness was awakened by a noise. He had one servant, a cook, who lived in a near-by cottage, but when he called, the cook did not answer. Instead four of the soldier guards, who had bound and gagged the cook, broke into the house and, waving guns and axes at him, demanded money. They drove him into his bedroom and snatched his watch, flashlight, and a small sum of money.

They demanded more money, but he declared that all he had was in the hospital safe. Then he remembered that he *did* have money in the house — five hundred dollars in silver which he kept hidden in the attic in case bandits or Japanese should ever loot the hospital. It was hospital money, saved from patients' fees over a period of many months, and he had planned to use it to buy more medicine. But as a Christian, he said, he could not lie, so he told the robbers of this money and went with them to the attic. Incidentally there was a large bomb-hole in the floor through which one of the robbers would have fallen if the doctor had not reached out and caught him.

The robbers took the five hundred dollars and then demanded more. They accused him of lying, and to make him tell the truth began to bore into his thigh with a pair of scissors. Blood spurted out and the doctor fell to the floor. At last the robbers decided to take him as he was, barefoot, in night clothes, and covered with blood, to the hospital. One of them dragged him to the garden gate, calling on the others to follow. But the others did not answer! They had fled into the darkness with the money. Determined not to be done out of his share, the robber released Dr. Skinsness, but shouted fiercely! "Stay here! If you move I'll kill you!" and disappeared.

The doctor decided that, since he might die anyway, he might as well die in flight. He stumbled down the hill and fell into the arms of a terrified night watchman inside the hospital. Although two men had to support him, Dr. Skinsness was on duty in the hospital the very next day.

High Army officers investigated the incident, but disclaimed any knowledge of the robbers. Bitterly Dr. Skinsness charged:

"They didn't even try! Not one man was punished. It was six months before the Government ordered the Army to return the five hundred dollars to me. Madame Chiang wrote a letter of regret over the incident and appreciation of my work in China. The Generalissimo ordered that the hospital be guarded by troops, and since then soldiers have been on duty night and day." He paused and then added: "But I bought police dogs."

While Dr. Skinsness was recovering from this experience, three enemy planes had another try at this hospital with its American flags flapping in the wind. One incendiary bomb splashed yellow chemicals over the buildings, but they failed to ignite; only one person on the hospital grounds was injured that day. Dr. Skinsness was convinced that God, in his mercy, had intervened.

Some missionaries believed and were preaching that God protected Christians but not heathens. Subsequently I heard some of them warn Chinese that if they took refuge in a Chinese temple they would be killed, but if they fled to a church God would protect them.

When Dr. Skinsness worked with the sick and wounded he was a modern scientist, but when he conducted prayer meetings for his small foreign staff, he became a fundamentalist. I was so much interested in his personality that I attended one prayer meeting. In it Dr. Skinsness preached on "casting out devils." He seemed to believe every period and comma in the Bible. What interested me most was the struggle he waged with himself. He humbly pleaded with God to wash from his soul all memory of his past sufferings. He knew, he said, that God did not protect people from harm and evil and, with his colleagues, he prayed for the calm faith to endure air-raids and everything else without fear. I jotted down one of his prayers in my diary. It ran:

> Merciful Father, protect the Chinese Red Cross Medical Corps, whose workers are ministering to sick and wounded soldiers on every front. Give them courage, O God, to continue their work, and lead them to Christ. Protect the guest within our gates who ministers to the sick and wounded, and give her courage to continue her work, and lead her to Christ. Guide the authorities in power to show no favoritism toward any army fighting for the country. Free China, O merciful Father, from the Japanese; bring it victory and peace, and teach the Japanese the error of their ways.

My Friend the Nun

ONE afternoon in November 1939, as we made our way toward Nanyang, rain began to fall steadily, and nightfall still found us on the road. My armed escort cursed vilely as they slipped and slid through the loess clay, and my big black mule skated around as if on ice. A thousand times we asked villagers: "How far to Nanyang?" Some said thirty-five *li*, some said fifty, some said twenty. And each changed his estimate almost immediately. It seemed to be a matter of whim, but none would admit he did not know.

Once I decided to send my guards back to Tangho. Bandits would not attack us in the pouring rain, nor were the Japanese near. But I changed my mind when we came to a village and stepped into a dark, dreary shed to order hot tea.

"How far is Nanyang?" we asked a mail-carrier, who had pushed his huge wheelbarrow, piled with mail sacks, under the shed.

"Thirty-five *li*," he answered. The ubiquitous postal workers of China inspired respect; they seemed to know everything. As the carrier answered, I caught sight of five soldiers sitting cross-legged on a *k'ang* with a small table in front of them. Even in the murky light I could see that they were indescribably dirty and that the towels tied about their heads were black. One of them was holding a small wine-pot over a little blue flame, and when it became hot, poured wine into tiny wine-cups before them. Before drinking they played the finger game, the loser of each deal emptying his glass. Their faces expressionless, they seemed like figures in a dream. The sight depressed me. Turning to the mail-carrier, I asked:

"Who are those soldiers?"

He studied them thoughtfully before answering: "They have no caps or arm badges, so they cannot be from any army. . . . They have guns behind them. . . ." He paused, looked around at my party, and added: "But I think you have enough guns to take care of yourselves."

I gave up all idea of sending my armed escort back to Tangho.

The cold rain continued drearily. It soaked through my padded winter overcoat and my padded uniform underneath. It soaked into our puttees and cloth shoes, and our caps became wet rags. My big mule continued to sprawl all over the place, and once he spread out in the mud like a daisy. I tried to walk, but the mud sucked the shoes off my feet and I had difficulty in finding them.

It was nearly ten at night when we approached Nanyang. A few miles to the south of the city we came upon a magnificent highway bordered by fine trees. This was one of the many beautiful motor roads which the Chinese Government had begun to construct before the war — and one of the developments which frightened the Japanese into attempting the conquest of China before it was too late. South of Nanyang a river had broadened into a lake, and with sighs of relief we pulled our animals up on the flat ferry that navigated it. Nanyang was a great military stronghold, and sentries challenged our every step. It had been bombed countless times and was badly damaged. But it is remarkable what punishment a locality can take without being destroyed. The populace was ordered into the country each morning, and returned around three or four each afternoon to conduct business. The whole town worked at night. Shops and restaurants were open and a vegetable market was in full swing. But many buildings along the street lay in ruins and at several points a whole block had been wiped out.

The Magistrate received me warmly and sent for some strong hot wine to brace us up. He began talking about the military preparations around the city. Since he slept through most of the day and worked all night, he was fresh and chipper and could have talked for hours. We had been on the road for more than eighteen hours, for the most part in a drenching rain, and we had eaten little since four in the morning.

But the hot wine soon began to put new life into us, and I even took out my diary and began to make notes of the

Magistrate's conversation. Once I looked up at him and to my surprise found that he had grown fully seven or eight feet tall and, what with his little black mustache, had begun to look like Charlie Chaplin. Cautiously I turned to look at his smooth-tongued secretary, but to my utter amazement this gentleman, sitting in the corner with his darkly clad arms braced on his knees and under the faint light from the open peanut-oil lamp, had a startling resemblance to a tom-cat. When he spoke he showed his teeth as if snarling and, without moving his head, rolled his eyes so that only the whites could be seen. As I looked at him I got the impression that he was speaking cautiously, as if he were literally filled to the brim with important secrets.

The Magistrate now began to stride about the room and seemed to be talking from somewhere near the ceiling.

"The bombings are not so very serious, and the Japanese raid us merely to make disturbances," he declared. "They can only hit civilians and market streets, for the Army is outside and the Government has moved to Loyang."

"My word!" I muttered in my best English accent.

"All the schools have moved to the country — primary, junior, and high school — eight thousand students in all," he went on. "And refugees — five thousand six hundred and twenty-two!" His voice sounded like the crack of doom. "All flood victims! We place them out in the homes of families able to support extra persons without cost. . . ."

Something or someone finally inspired the Magistrate with the idea that it might not hurt if I went to sleep for the rest of the night. But his headquarters was an armed camp and crowded — impossible! The inns were also impossible for they were in the center of the town and one did not have time to escape into the country before the bombers came. So I'd better stay in one of the missions.

Accompanied by the Magistrate's adjutant, we went out in the rain again, and after half an hour reached a Norwegian mission. But it had been bombed a few days before, had no roof, and was deserted. Farther on was a Catholic convent. We waded along the street toward it and began pounding on its heavy wooden gates. After an interminable interval a gateman's voice from far back in the courtyard fearfully asked who we were. We told him, but he repeated his question, asking where we came from, why, where we were going, and why we knocked at people's gates in the middle of the night. While the rain poured we answered these questions. He then asked us to wait.

Half an hour passed and still we waited. Suspecting that the gateman had gone back to bed, we were prepared to go in search of an inn when we heard the twittering of women's voices on the other side of the heavy gate. The adjutant told them who we were and asked, in the name of the Magistrate, that they put up an American lady.

"Oh, we cannot!" a faint voice answered. "We live like the Chinese and have no comforts that could possibly satisfy an American."

I answered that I was not used to comfort. We heard more twittering in Italian and then one of the voices said: "We live simply, but you are welcome."

When the heavy gates swung slowly backward, I saw that the entire trunk of a tree had been used as a bar. Inside, in the light of a storm lantern, stood a cluster of black-clad nuns with small, fluted black bonnets, looking at us in consternation. It seemed they still feared either bandits or Japanese. The eldest of them, a woman who, I later learned, was Mother Superior Erminia Malinverni, asked us to enter.

With much bustling about, the nuns led us into a reception room. After me came my secretary, the Magistrate's adjutant, and my three carriers — six drenched individuals, around each of whom small pools of rain-water were already forming. We arranged to have my secretary stay at the home of a priest. Leaving trails of water, everyone was at last on his way. I turned to my hostesses. Four or five of the ten nuns in the convent had come out, and one of these, a young woman by the name of Erminietta Cattaneo, spoke English. The room was of the long Chinese type, with stone floors, holy pictures and images on the walls, and in the center a long polished table bordered with chairs. Would this room be suitable, they asked.

When I told them I was accustomed to far less, to unrolling my bedding on tables, chests, boards, or earthen floors, they all began to flutter about, getting a bed ready for me. They brought in a camp cot and mattress, snow-white sheets, a soft pillow, and warm woolen blankets. One brought in a brazier of burning charcoal. When I slid out of my soaked garments, they wrapped me in one of the blankets and placed a covered tray before me. I lifted the snowy cloth and saw hot milk, toast, salami, golden honey, butter, and a pot of coffee! Oh earth, sweet earth!

"Would you like a bottle of wine with the salami?" asked the young nun, and she went on to explain that the Sisters made their own wine for the holy Mass. The convent was almost self-sufficient. It had cows, pigs, chickens, beehives, and grape arbors; the Sisters did their own cooking, washing, ironing, and scrubbing and made their own bread, butter, salami, cheese, and wine.

Some of the nuns were trained nurses, and Sister Erminietta was a trained laboratory technician; in addition she helped cook, wait on the table, and do the washing. This was the first missionary institution that I visited in which foreigners did physical labor. In fact, it was about the only time that I had seen any foreigner in China do any kind of physical labor.

As I ate they hovered about, gentle and shy, asking countless questions. When I went to my cot, they fluffed up the pillow, tucked in the blankets, and patted me.

"What luxury!" I exclaimed, running my hand over the crisp, spotless sheets.

Lying on my back, my eyes strayed beyond them to the walls and ceiling. The ceiling had been shattered, and two long, zigzag fissures ran down the wall. The paneless windows were boarded up.

"It's from air-raids," Sister Erminietta explained gravely. "They have not hit us yet, but many buildings around here have been destroyed. All our buildings are damaged and we are afraid the walls will cave in."

She said the convent had not been hit yet because they all prayed for protection. They also spread out a big Italian flag over their dugout and raised one over the buildings. On the corner of each flag they sewed a small cloth picture of Our Lady; this, they said, had saved them.

The minute each raid was ended, some of the Sisters went into the streets with first-aid kits and cared for the injured, while others remained in the clinic waiting for the victims to be brought in. They had a small ward with twenty beds, always full, and each day over a hundred people came to have dressings changed. In the days that followed I watched the nurses at work in their clinic. They were rapidly running out of many drugs, and of some essentials they had none at all.

"We are nurses, but must do the work of doctors," said one Sister. "We can do only minor operations; the serious ones are carried to the foreign hospitals in Laohokuo; but that is two whole days' journey from here."

Once a week the nuns went through the prison, doing medical and evangelical work. The prisoners were in shackles, and abscesses formed around the irons; they had no covering, and lay on straw on the prison floor. There were women prisoners with babies which had been born in prison. Three times a week some of the Sisters went outside the city to conduct a clinic for the poor. Speaking of this work, Sister Erminietta clasped her hands together and exclaimed: "Oh, never have I seen such skin diseases and head sores as in Honan! Such dreadful things are not in Italy! No, not even in England have I seen such things!"

At dawn the next morning I was awakened by chanting from the chapel across the courtyard; soon afterwards my door opened and Sister Erminietta, bright-eyed and smiling, brought in a basin of hot water and then a delicious foreign breakfast. During the night she had dried my outer garments and washed my shirt, socks, and face-towel.

I had at last reached a territory where I felt that articles for the *Manchester Guardian* and reports to the Red Cross Medical Corps had a chance of reaching their destination. There were a military field hospital in the city, a clinic of the *hsien*, a branch of the Buddhist Red Swastika Society, and a number of important schools. There were also the district militia, a guerrilla detachment, and, near by, General Tang En-po's forces, perhaps the most experienced and powerful group army in China. While I was there it was laying great emphasis on the education of its soldiers.

Sister Erminietta was a pretty young woman with big brown eyes in which the joyousness of youth and the gravity of experience struggled for mastery. Though she shared the pious life of the Convent, it was always difficult for me to reconcile her forthright speech and manner with the robes of a nun. I would look at her hands, as rough and healthy as a peasant's, and listen to her remark that the Sisters did physical labor in praise of God. To her, God seemed more or less like a neighbor. She was the daughter of a poor Italian peasant and had entered a Canossian convent at the age of sixteen; she repeatedly spoke of the last time she had seen her mother's face — from a train window — and of her sorrow when, in the previous year, she had received word of her death.

She justified and ardently defended the system by which the religious order had broken her will and destroyed all personal desire in order to make her a perfect servant of the Church. While a novice she had expressed a deep desire to go to China, of which she had read in missionary magazines in the convent. But because she had this desire, she had been sent to England — the last place on earth she wished to go. She accepted this as the most perfect way to serve God, and only after four years, when all hope of going to China had been crushed out of her, was she suddenly informed that she was to leave for China immediately.

Though the Catholics, like the Protestants, called the Chinese "heathens," the Catholics seemed to be more clever than the dry, sin-conscious Protestants. Like the Taoists and Buddhists, the Catholic churches had images, a colorful and mystic pageantry, chanting, and incense. I thought of the many Christian wayside shrines which I had seen in Europe — bloody repellent images of Jesus on the Cross. The small Chinese wayside shrines to *Tu Ti Kung-Kung*, the Earth God and his wife, which graced every village, seemed far more appealing.

Whenever a missionary mentioned the word "heathen" in my presence, I reminded him that I also was a "heathen," a remark that kept one missionary in Junan, Honan, on his knees for almost a week, praying for my soul. I carefully read the tracts he gave me, then urged him to show me something not based on the fear of death. He nearly passed out when I informed him that Jesus had been a social revolutionary who had been crucified because he fought the ruling class of his day, much as modern revolutionaries have done ever since. When my young friend the nun told me that the missionaries had given up home, family, and comfort to preach to the "heathen." I disagreed about the "comfort," and also reminded her that modern revolutionaries also give up home, family, and often life itself for their principles.

I cared not at all whether men and women were Christian or "heathen," provided they served mankind and did not try to prevent the emancipation of the poor. The Canossian Sisters knew nothing of such ideas, but they served the Chinese people without political motives — which their priests did not. I was not too much repelled when they presented me with a religious charm and urged me to wear it, and during air-raids to call upon Our Lady. But I preferred to depend on the Chinese armies.

After leaving Nanyang, I was able to send the Sisters considerable medicine and money to care for air-raid victims and wounded soldiers. On July 5, 1940 Sister Erminietta wrote me a letter of which the following are extracts:

> Sorrow is indeed the lot of every man here below, while waiting for a bliss to come. . . . Months ago many wounded and feverish soldiers were brought from the battlefield, and two of our nurses went to the military hos-

pital each day to help. I myself had the great pleasure of going with the Sisters sometimes. But one of the Sisters contracted typhus from the soldiers. Then the second Sister also came down with it. Meanwhile, on May 6th, Nanyang was badly bombed and the victims were over one hundred. On May 11th, while our two Sisters lay sick, a Japanese plane came and dropped two bombs right down on our Convent, a few yards off the room where the sick Sisters lay. . . .

We will remain here in spite of anything, ready to live or die with these poor brethren of ours, trusting that God in His Mercy will not only continue to protect us, but enable us to do the utmost to help those who suffer. . . .

In another letter, dated May 8, 1941, Sister Erminietta wrote:

Our news are something like last year, rather we had something worse because this time the Japanese actually occupied Nanyang after dreadful bombings of two days, with very short periods of rest. Fortunately the people had in the great majority left the city a few days before, dreading what might happen in such frightful events. A few days before the occupation one of our Sisters fell seriously sick, and so our Bishop, who resides in a village twelve *li* off at Kinkiakan, invited the Sisters to go over there. . . . But contrary to every supposition, the Japanese passed by there even before occupying Nanyang and of course the village was badly bombed. We took care of forty victims there but many more in Nanyang. A week later I too fell grievously sick so that I hardly escaped dying. A few days later another Sister also fell sick of a very dangerous disease which brought her to heaven. Now another Sister is affected with the same serious disease.

I forgot to tell you that in the bombing before the occupation some houses of ours have again been completely destroyed by incendiary balls. . . . The Japanese soon left Nanyang, but set fire to the city, which looked like a furnace. . . .

Dear friend, you are so kind to send money and medicine for us. No help can now reach us except by you whom God kindly inspires to help us. . . . On our part we will continue to do all we can to succor those who have recourse to us, since we came to China for nothing else than for this. I am sorry we have not received the typewriter ribbons you sent us but still hope for them. . . .

We like to remember you, how you arrived here on a rainy night, so dark, and we only feared that we could not give you something that might suit your taste. Instead you had no pretensions and were so glad for very little. How many things have taken place since then!

Rev. Mother and all the Sisters send you their love along with mine.

                    Sincerely yours,
                    Erminietta Cattaneo F.D.C.C.

BOOK VIII

Winter Offensive

1939 — 1940

BOOK VIII: WINTER OFFENSIVE

1939 ❧ 1940

Swords for the Japanese

"THE JAPANESE murderers were without a sword. America gave them the sword."

General Li Chung-ren, Commander-in-Chief of the Fifth War Zone, was speaking. After a day in his headquarters near Laohokuo, in Hupeh Province, I had asked him to give me a message to the American people. It was December 1, 1939. His message was this:

"China expects the United States to declare a total embargo on materials of war to Japan. I believe the American people are sympathetic to China and are especially opposed to indiscriminate Japanese bombings of defenseless cities. But their will is totally subordinated to the private profits of a few business men. This is a terrible thing. The Japanese murderers were without a sword. America gave them the sword."

We had talked through one whole day. First I interviewed him, then he interviewed me, after which we sailed out on the open sea of general discussion.

He was an unusually friendly man and astonishingly well informed. Ordinary in appearance, he might have been a citizen of almost any Western country. He was a Kwangsi man with a stormy military past and had the directness and frankness of most such military men.

His headquarters was located in two small houses in a tiny village outside Laohokuo. The mud walls had been papered with plain white paper manufactured by a local industrial co-operative, ceilings of unvarnished yellow boards had been put in, and the earthen floors covered with clean yellow matting. The large outer room was used for military conferences. A long table covered with blue cotton cloth extended down its length. On this rested a large, solitary, cream-colored vase holding the crooked stalk of a winter plant in blossom. One entire wall was covered by a white and black military map dotted with red circles and squares marking Japanese positions. The map added to the chaste beauty of the room.

General Li's combination office and living-room led off this conference room. It contained a narrow board bed, a desk piled with papers and documents, and a bookcase filled with books and magazines. Two easy chairs and several hard ones were scattered around a glowing charcoal fire in a polished brass brazier. On the wall hung an art photograph of his wife and two children. An atmosphere of harmony, even peace, permeated the two rooms. A loaf of bread, a jug of wine, and this small house. . . .

It was a little disconcerting to know that this pleasant and learned man commanded a vast war zone, and at Taierchwang had inflicted the first major military defeat the powerful Japanese Army had ever suffered. He talked much of world affairs, for, like all Chinese, he was deeply aware that China's struggle was linked with the struggle of all the peoples of the world. No people on earth except those of the Soviet Union have so much international awareness. General Li himself had just become a member of Colonel Henry L. Stimson's League against Aggression. He inquired about the fate of Evans F. Carlson, who had resigned from the Navy in order to tell the American people of China's struggle, and he asked why the United States did not cooperate with the Soviet Union in the Pacific. The termination of America's commercial treaty with Japan aroused some optimism in him that America's policy was changing. But he did not depend on this in estimating China's struggle.

Discussing the war, he said:

"We have traded space for time. We have prolonged the struggle, developed mobile and guerrilla warfare, organized the people, improved our administrative organs, and waged a war of attrition. Our man-power is limitless and national consciousness has increased with every inch of Japanese advance. Time and the human spirit are our allies. As a base Japan is very weak because almost all its war materials must come from abroad — chiefly from America. That is a terrible thing, for Japan is also the mortal enemy of America. . . . The Japanese know they have no future in China. They cannot give up what they have gained and they cannot evacuate. So they cry for a peace of surrender, and traitors like Wang Ching-wei and his followers — a gang of shameless opportunists and bureaucrats bought and paid for — echo them. Japan's cry for peace is like Hitler's after the Nazi occupation of Czechoslovakia and Poland — the cry of a bandit who talks of humanity after he has killed his victim."

Once he made a terrible remark:

"Now that the second World War has begun, American business men can sell war materials to Europe instead of Japan. So we expect a change in American policy toward the Far East."

During the afternoon I reported on my experiences and observations. He then told me that I could go up to the front during the coming Chinese winter offensive, and that when I was ready he would send me in his car to Fancheng in the south, where the 11th Group Kwangsi Army had its headquarters along the Han River (sometimes called the Hsiang River). He suggested that I visit the 173rd Division, commanded by Major General Chung Yi.

We saluted and parted. It had been one of the most impressive days I had had in China.

Before I left him, the General called my attention to the Korean Volunteer Unit in the Fifth War Zone, and I made arrangements to visit it.

Captain Li Yeh-hsing, leader of the small Korean Volunteer Unit in Laohokuo, introduced me to his four companions — one of them a woman — and said that five others were up at the front. Then he undertook to answer my many questions about his unit.

There were said to be around five hundred to a thousand Korean Volunteers in China at the time, all political workers in four different war zones. Since the Japanese had begun using Korean soldiers for the first time, the Volunteers were being transferred to the fronts on which such soldiers were used.

The Volunteers in Laohokuo had heavy duties. All enemy documents and broadcasts were turned over to them for study, analysis, and translation into Chinese. They were in charge of the clandestine distribution of handbills and pamphlets to Japanese troops at the front, and conducted the Japanese Language School which the Political Department of the Fifth War Zone had founded and in which two hundred Chinese were studying. Three hours each day they taught Japanese captives the background of the Sino-Japanese War, the Three People's Principles of Sun Yat-sen, social science, and the Chinese language.

Hu Wei-pei, one of the Volunteers, had just returned from the front lines and told me of the methods which he and his colleagues adopted to reach the Japanese. Peasants carried handbills into enemy-occupied regions and scattered them about. The Volunteers themselves crept up to Japanese positions at night and hung leaflets over the barbed-wire entanglements. They flew kites bearing anti-war slogans, tied bundles of leaflets around rocks and hurled them into Japanese positions, and sometimes used bows and arrows to shoot them in. In places where Chinese and Japanese trenches were close together, they sang anti-war songs or lectured in Japanese through megaphones.

Mr. Hu said that he once delivered speeches to Japanese soldiers for two nights in succession. On the third night an officer stuck his head above the enemy trenches and fiercely asked him who he was. Mr. Hu gave a Japanese name and address. "I chose a very stylish address in Tokyo," he explained. "I told the officer that he lied to his troops in saying that Chinese tortured Japanese captives to death, and I said the bullets used against China were the sweat and blood of the Japanese people."

"You are a traitor and a disgrace to the Great Imperial Army!" the Japanese officer bawled. "We will tear you limb from limb! Japan grows stronger and richer by the war!"

"Filthy liar! We know what lies you officers tell!" shouted Mr. Hu. A hail of bullets sang over him as he ducked back into the Chinese trench.

With a touch of poetic justice the Fifth War Zone authorities delivered all Japanese captives to the Korean Volunteers. In the previous three months the Volunteers had examined forty, kept three who were willing to be educated in anti-war work among the Japanese Army, and transferred the others to Chungking. I was introduced to the three Japanese prisoners and they asked me to look at some of their work. Ito, a former baseball champion, fancied himself a highly educated and cultured man. He had childishly daubed paint over three huge sheets of paper and called them Chinese war posters. I tried to show polite interest, but could not make head or tail of them. One poster was supposed to show a victorious Chinese soldier bayoneting a defeated Japanese. This was labelled "Victory." Staring at this creation, I knew he was a cheat, or worse. "Why don't you paint things in which you believe?" I asked. He stared at me in amazement, and the other two Japanese sat with blank faces and downcast eyes.

Before leaving, the three Japanese asked if they could have a talk with me about their personal problems, and though I could not understand what their motives were, I invited them and Captain Li to have tea with me the next afternoon at the Norwegian Mission Hospital, where I was staying. They came at the appointed time, but when the Chinese servants heard that some Japanese were in the garden, they were afraid to come out and, instead, stood staring out through the windows.

Matsui Katsutso, a worker from Tokyo, first stared at his hands, then turned his somber eyes on me and spoke in a depressed voice. They were prisoners of war, he said, and because they had helped the Chinese a little, they could never return home. The Chinese also did not trust them and they could not see what kind of future men in their position had.

Of course I could see no future for them either, for the war might continue for years. I asked them if they wanted the present Government in Japan, and if not, what kind they wanted. They had never thought at all about such matters until they were captured, they said. Itake, formerly an actor, said that no Japanese wanted to see his country suffer. He hadn't wanted the war and had fought only because compelled; he said he hoped for a government in which there would be no class discrimination and no rich men who owned everything. Yes, he admitted, the Koreans had taught him these ideas; he did not know whether men in his Army ever thought about such things; if they did, he had never heard of them.

The baseball champion said that he "used to just go to school and play baseball." After he had graduated from high school he had gone into business, but still had no "serious thoughts." He had hated the war, but felt he couldn't do anything about it. Now he had begun "to think about society," but was afraid the war would go on for years. He admitted that he used to think the Japanese would eventually be victorious. "Our Army is very strong," he said.

He talked about the danger to Japanese soldiers and his people, but not a word about the sufferings of the Chinese. Trying to keep my voice soft, I asked him if he could blame the Chinese for not trusting him. "Your Army kills prisoners and the wounded," I reminded him. "It rapes even little girls and old women. I've seen gray-haired children and insane pregnant women — thanks to your Army. The people call you *devils*."

Ito reacted violently. "It's because uneducated coolies became officers!" he declared. "Now our Government has given orders that no coolie can be an officer!"

Matsui and Itake lowered their eyes in embarrassment at this, but Ito stuck his heavy chin out at me stubbornly. Useless to talk with such a fellow, I thought, and, turning to Matsui, asked him what he thought about the future. "There is no hope unless we have a revolution in Japan," he said, but added: "If that takes place, what would happen to

the Japanese Army? The spy system is so strong that our
soldiers dare not say a word. If a man doesn't want to fight,
he can only commit suicide."

I asked the three Japanese why they didn't prepare for
leadership in the Army. In captivity they had a chance to do
this, and there were a few Japanese in Chungking, such as
Kadji, the writer, who were teaching Japanese captives just
such things. Matsui gave an incredulous grunt. "We are
simple men — we couldn't lead a revolution!"

"You can learn!" Captain Li replied, watching him curiously, and to Captain Li's encouragement I added my own,
telling the men that they were young and could afford to
spend even years in study. Men in Western countries had
done it, I told him; were they inferior to Western men?

Ito nearly exploded. Thrusting his jaw out at me again,
he informed me that the Japanese were not inferior to any
white man. Good, I replied, and then proposed that he try
to prove that he was not inferior to the many Japanese revolutionaries who had died in Japanese prisons. Those men
were inferior to no man, white or colored. "Carry on their
work," I challenged the three men. "If you don't, your Army
will go down in history as all murderers and rapists. Well,
I don't blame your Army alone — today a Chinese General
told me that you had no sword until my country gave you
one. So we are both criminals."

Captain Li, translating for us, began to speak in a low, passionate voice in Japanese, as if our words had released some
well of emotion within him. The Japanese sat staring at me.

The Co-operatives

WITHIN little more than a year the Chinese Industrial Co-
operatives had spread all over western China. Within half
that time — that is, by early December 1939 — Laohokuo
had six co-operatives doing spinning and weaving, one making paper, one producing improved spinning-machines, one
preparing chemicals for candles, soap, cotton, and gauze,

and three oil refineries. Six months later there were twenty-four co-operatives in the province, two of them managed by the Women's Committee of the Fifth War Zone.

One morning I went into a co-operative and found sixty refugees at work spinning, weaving, and operating stocking-knitting machines. This small institution was one of the most pleasant places I had come across in years. As I entered, the people were singing at their machines — the first time I had ever heard such a thing in China. The whole city had spent most of the night on its feet: it had had three air-raid alarms. But the workers seemed unaffected, for it had become a part of their existence. In the daytime most of the population slept in the country, returning in the late afternoon. But the co-operative worked through the day; its members did not even try to get away when alarms sounded.

The co-operative was both a family and a small self-governing republic. Its supervisory committee was elected by its members from their own ranks. Each month they all gathered to hear business reports, to discuss their work and economic and personal problems, and to suggest improvements. They worked eight hours a day, held union meetings, published their own wall newspaper, and attended night school. They even had their own theatrical group. No child under twelve was allowed to work; a co-operative primary school took care of them. Children and the aged were granted subsidies.

The average earnings of a co-operative member were fifteen dollars a month; if there was a profit it was divided according to the stock held by each member. The preceding month had produced a profit of $300, but the workers decided to set aside 20 per cent of it as savings, 10 per cent as reserve capital, 10 per cent for "public services" such as education and medical supplies, and 10 per cent for pensions or the relief of members. They had also just asked Industrial Co-operative Headquarters in Chungking for a long-term loan of $10,000, and if it was granted they expected to lay in a good stock of raw material and take in many more workers.

There was a long waiting list of refugees, many of them skilled workers, but some who needed training.

The institution had two experienced "high-salaried" specialists, both of them educated refugees. One, the manager, was paid $50 a month, and the other, treasurer and bookkeeper, $40. The manager disregarded hours and was on his feet constantly. He felt that this small factory was helping win the war. A small store in the front of the building sold goods, but he was planning to open a large one in the center of the town. This would cause some trouble with the large merchants, but the move was inevitable.

Some factory-owners and officials were saying that the co-operatives ruined the workers by making them proud and independent. Co-operatives were all right as a temporary war-time necessity, they declared, but after the war what? In the meantime the co-operative workers held fast and worked like mad. One weaver talked with me while his foot-operated shuttle flew without stopping. He had been a small Anhwei business man until ruined by the war, and had learned weaving in order to join the co-operative. Nothing would get him out of it now, he said. He could weave twenty yards of cloth a day.

Fifteen girls were operating stocking-knitting machines. They could knit five pairs a day, which were sold to the big stores at $5.60 a dozen. The retail price on the market was too high, said the manager, and the merchants had threatened to ask the Government to lower the blockade on Japanese goods if they did not lower the price.

One girl looked up and exclaimed: "I don't think the Government will do it! I should make the blockade more strict. We simply can't compete with cheap Japanese goods!"

"What we need is *more* co-operatives," another girl declared. "Then everybody will be better off."

I recalled the shy, inarticulate girls of pre-war days. These war-time co-operatives were producing a new kind of womanhood — indeed, a new kind of human being.

The manager, it is true, had his worries and doubts. He

thought productive work and relief work should not be mixed up. As it was now, the co-operatives sometimes lost money because they had so many unproductive children and old people to support. He thought only productive workers should be admitted and that they should be able to earn enough to support their families. And yet he knew, he said, that one of the main purposes of the co-operatives was to solve the refugee problem and to provide for all the people.

While we talked we heard the heart-sickening wail of an air-raid siren and the clanging of the bell in the near-by Catholic church tower. Workers lifted their heads and listened, and all singing and whistling stopped. The building was on the edge of the town, and the Catholic church flew the Italian flag, so the chances of being bombed were less than in the heart of the city. I looked through the street door and saw the children from the co-operative primary school marching in orderly file toward the church. But the machines in the little factory still hummed.

When the "urgent" sounded, everyone listened even more intently. Soon the roar of bombers rose above the whirring and clacking of the machinery.

"The sword again!" I thought with dread, recalling General Li's words. At last the roar passed and began to fade. But what about tonight — or tomorrow?

"*Tell Your Countrymen* —"

It was ten at night on December 6, 1939, and I was waiting in a small inn in Fancheng, central Hupeh Province, where I had been the guest of the Kwangsi 11th Group Army for a few days. Finally a young officer came in and said: "General Chung Yi is now free and is waiting near here."

He led my secretary and me along the dark, cobblestoned main street, past the ruins of bombed buildings, and into a deserted and partially demolished structure. We went up the rickety stairs to a large, hall-like room that somehow seemed peopled with the unseen presence of many men. There were many rough benches and chairs and three or four tables. The dust on the floor and window-sills had been disturbed, for the Chinese winter offensive was to start soon, and in this room, I knew, the fate of thousands of men had just been determined.

Close to a guttering candle on one of the tables lay an upturned military cap. In the dim light behind the table I saw a man in khaki. He was standing perfectly still, his face turned toward me, his black eyes appraising me. He was of medium height and quite young — I learned later that he was thirty-nine. The face was pleasant rather than handsome, and when he spoke, his deep voice was softly musical, with the faintest touch of wistfulness in it. I had heard such voices before and nearly always became friends with the men who possessed them.

This was my first meeting with Major General Chung Yi, commander of the iron 173rd Division of the 11th Group Army. We sat down at the table, the candle between us, and I felt as if I had known him always. He might have been saying: "As I told you before —"

On this evening he said something that others had said so often that it had come to sound like a phrase learned by rote. But when he said it, it seemed to spring from all that gave his life meaning. "We have our faith," he said. "Victory will not be easy, but we will fight until victorious. We have our faith — tell your countrymen. . . ."

Later, in his headquarters, he told me that he sprang from a poor landowning family of scholars of Hunan district, Kwangsi Province. His father had been a teacher, and he himself had studied with the intention of following the same profession. But the national revolutionary movement had aroused every conscious Chinese, and he had entered a military academy. When civil war between the Kuomintang and the Communists began in 1927, he had refused to take part, but had withdrawn and studied for a time in Japan, earning his living as a tutor. After leaving Japan he continued to teach in Shanghai until the Japanese invasion began, when he returned to active military duty. He had since fought on most of the major fronts. Since military men in China are promoted on the basis of merit rather than years of service, he was now a Major General. His division had covered many Chinese retreats, fighting rear-guard actions, and his force had been all but wiped out time and time again. In the last big Japanese offensive in May and June of that year, he had again lost most of his effectives, and was now training new recruits from Kwangsi.

At dawn the next morning my secretary and I, with General Chung Yi's secretary, stepped on a junk and were swept down the river Han to his headquarters. Once we anchored under some branches near the shore while enemy bombers passed overhead. We watched them circle, swoop, and bomb Fancheng and its ancient twin city across the river, Hsiangyang. There was an American Swedish missionary hospital there, already filled with air-raid victims, and now it would have more. Although it lay on the outskirts of the city and flew the American flag, that hospital had itself been bombed twice.

Major General Chung Yi met us before a building in the village where his general headquarters were located. He wore no cap, and his voice was again almost wistful as he said, by way of welcoming me, that I was the first foreign friend who had "cared enough for us to come to the front." Such friends were valuable, he added, because it took months to get publications to the front; what radios the armies had were only telegraphic.

He introduced me to a young man who spoke good English and had studied political science. Here again I touched threads of social conflict, for shortly before, I learned, many educated youth suspected of "dangerous thoughts" had been driven from the Fifth War Zone headquarters. Hearing of this "purge," General Chung had wired this young man to join his staff to help him study political science.

The vice-commander, a product of old China, began the breakfast by formally apologizing for the poor food, although the food was excellent. The conversation that followed continued for more than an hour, General Chung asking me of my travels and work and talking of the terrible condition of the wounded throughout the country. He had a number of fairly good physicians in his division, but their medical supplies were limited. After breakfast we retired to the General's room and talked for many hours. He walked restlessly about, speaking of his last campaign. His voice trembled and his eyes smoldered when he said: "I could hear the cries of the wounded, but could do nothing." The Japanese had used poison gas on one of his regiments.

I asked him what he thought would happen if the Japanese Army suffered great defeats.

"It's difficult to say," he answered. "Their morale is maintained by victories. Strategically it is dangerous for them to maintain a battle line from Suiyuan to Canton, but they do many things with an eye on their international position. I'm certain that their peace with the Soviet Union is but a temporary expedient and the time will come when the two countries will be at war. Then Japan will be defeated. But that will not happen yet. Japan has its eyes on the Dutch East Indies. That would make them independent of American oil and some other supplies."

He began to ask me penetrating questions about American policy and the extent of Japanese espionage and propaganda in America. He could not possibly understand, he said, why America should behave so foolishly — unless it hoped that both China and Japan would be so weakened by the war that they could be more easily exploited afterwards.

On another occasion three young officers shyly led me into their "club room" — a low mud and thatch hut. War books and magazines lay all around and the walls were lined with maps and banners, and prints of Madame Curie, Marconi, Pasteur, Lincoln, Washington, and many others. At one end hung the national and Kuomintang flags over large pictures of Dr. Sun Yat-sen and Generalissimo Chiang Kai-shek.

A number of young officers came to tell me of the way they trained the soldiers, and they soon led me to a building where some two hundred young "political soldiers" were waiting, notebooks and pencils ready; for this division had introduced a new system of training literate soldiers to act as political educators in the ranks. The regimental commander introduced me as a "foreign friend of China who cares enough for us to come to the front," and announced that I was to give them reports on conditions in the enemy rear.

One morning at dawn, when the hoarfrost glistened on the dry grass blades, I tried to shake the bitter cold from my body and mind and prepare for another lecture. General Chung Yi stood with me on a knoll and introduced me to his staff. I drew my padded greatcoat closer about my throat and spoke as best I could on the international situation. Afterwards we all went into headquarters, and the staff questioned me about events throughout the world, though they often knew far more than I. As we talked we sipped from bowls of hot weak wine in which soft eggs floated. This delicacy was served in my honor, for the division, like all the armies, served only two meals a day.

Soon a general review of the division began. A high military commission had arrived from Chungking to inspect the training and equipment of the armies that would take part in the winter offensive. By the time they reached our sector, the wide plains and barren plateaus appeared to have been transformed into a gigantic historical pageant. I seemed to be gazing on old canvases of the Napoleonic Wars. The troops marched or ran about or engaged in mock warfare, and everywhere there was the hollow sound of mortars, the hammering of machine-guns, and the crack of rifles. I did not even dream that within half a year most of these men would be dead.

When the review and maneuvers ended we returned to divisional headquarters and stood around long tables spread with food. The winter sun glinted on the red and gold insignia on the collars of the officers. As Major General Chung moved about, they congratulated him, for his was one of the best divisions in China. He listened thoughtfully, answered reticently. Sometimes he stopped to exchange a few words with me and I felt the melancholy that hovered around him.

On that evening there was a banquet spread over seven big tables in the great bamboo-thatched dining-hall. I sat between General Chung and one of the inspectors from Chungking; across from us was tall, strong General Mei, commander of the Eighty-fourth Army, of which the 173 Division was a part. The conversation remained formal and polite until the wine loosened tongues. Then everyone began to lift his wine-cup and appraise the maneuvers freely.

The formal vice-commander of the division rose from a table at the far end of the room, raised his wine-cup, and toasted me with an old poem. Following the custom, I arose and, cup in hand, replied with a few lines from a poem whose author I could not remember. The vice-commander recalled it and the tables broke into applause. Surely, I thought, no people were so gracious, none so magnificent as those willing to face death for the sake of all that they thought good in life.

When I sat down, General Chung lifted his cup, merely touching his lips to it, and said: "You put many Chinese men to shame."

"You also," I began, but faltered; for I saw that he had not spoken with traditional politeness, but from the heart. Would he say such a thing if he knew I was not brave, that I feared air-raids, and had said to myself a thousand times that I hated war, that I was not made for war? And he? I studied him as he sat turning his wine-cup around and around between his fingers, staring at it, unseeing. No, such a man as he was not made for war either. He belonged in a laboratory or on the platform of a university. But if he had followed his inclinations, there would be no laboratories, no universities at all.

He rose, the voices in the hall died away, and every man stood. He began speaking of the general review and of the coming offensive in which he would take part, and he pledged his division to the nation. When he had finished, there was a long silence before we all sat down again.

The high inspectors left for other armies, but the night maneuvers continued. I went out with Chung Yi and his staff, tramping along dark paths and through wheat-fields where sentries crouched in silence. There was no moon and only a faint light from the stars in the black heavens. The only sound was the tread of our feet. "Enemy searchlights!" Chung Yi shouted. The dark columns fell flat, motionless, their guns ready. We moved on and on until we were in position to watch soldiers creeping up around a sleeping village. Of course we captured all the enemy positions that night!

Afterwards the soldiers marched back singing the divisional song, the *Marseillaise* set to Chinese words, and the lines drifted fitfully back through the blackness. . . .

As I sat around those candlelit tables and chatted with my friends, it sometimes seemed that I was probing into the heart of China. Barriers of race and nationality vanished, and we were all human beings seeking a common goal. Chung Yi asked me again if I thought that America, England, and France really wished China to be victorious. The British surely feared the effects of a Chinese victory on the people of India, and the French were terrified about Indo-China. I agreed, believing that if China was not conquered and made Fascist, it would be the spearhead of oppressed Asiatic peoples. But I was convinced that the common people of the various countries would sympathize with China if they only knew the truth.

Once again Chung Yi began to speak of the doubts and worries that troubled him, and somehow I knew what they were even before he had finished speaking. We talked of Japan's ceaseless movement toward the oil and other supplies of the Dutch East Indies. Did I think America would renew its commercial treaty with Japan rather than allow Japan to buy all its oil from the Dutch East Indies? I thought it might. Were not American business men evading the "moral embargo" on war materials to Japan? I felt certain they were. Once he asked if I thought China should adopt the capitalist system, even though it dispossessed and starved millions and led to war and more war. I wondered. Speaking half to himself, he continued: "Men are afraid of life. They heap up wealth to make themselves and their children secure; but then there is only insecurity."

Just where had he and I talked before, I sometimes wondered. Something haunted me, like a half-forgotten melody. Afterwards lying on my yellow straw bed in the darkness, I would listen to the night sounds and think for the thousandth time of the spiritual bonds that are formed at the front, intangible, but so much stronger than steel or flesh.

On the night before I was to accompany one of Chung Yi's commanders to a regiment nearer the battlefield, we gathered for a final dinner. The flickering candles glinted on the small porcelain wine-cups and on the little pots of *bei-gar* and warm rice wine. I had made arrangements to return and join the division when it was ordered up, for I wished to write a story of it from the very beginning to the very end of a battle. Thinking of the fierce way his troops fought, Chung Yi had hesitated, then said he would welcome me with all his heart. That evening we spoke little of politics and more of poets and novelists, of artists and the theater. We told tales and drank to everything on earth. I toasted soldiers and officers who fought and died for "a civilization in which they would have no share," and Chung Yi lifted his cup to "brave and learned women." To this I protested, insisting that I was neither brave nor learned, but merely "historically curious." Laughing, the table drank to "historical curiosity."

How varied was the conversation that night! Once, I remember, a young Mohammedan officer began boasting of the power of the Koran, saying he knew a man who had died but whose corpse had grown soft again when the Koran was placed on it! Then someone had changed the subject, declaring that the three best things in life were an American house, a Japanese wife, and Chinese food. I informed the young man that he liked the Japanese wife because she was the most servile on earth. Chung Yi listened to this and added to it by asking me if I had seen, near Sian, a famous archway to a wife who waited for eighteen years while her husband, a General, was at the front. She sank into dire poverty, but remained faithful to him. What did I think of such a woman, he asked, watching me from the corner of his eye. Before I could reply, the vice-commander declared that the story was a tribute to the virtues of Chinese womanhood. This was remarkable, I declared, but what had the General done during those eighteen years, and where might I find even one archway to a faithful husband?

A young poet rose and said elegantly: "I drink to archways to faithful generals!" then laughed and dropped back into his chair.

Soon most of them had forgotten me and were arguing in loud voices with one another.

But Chung Yi bent forward and asked: "What would a modern woman have done during those eighteen years?" and I countered: "What does a modern general do?" The vice-commander seemed shocked at our levity, but we bent forward, laughing at each other across the flickering candles.

Next morning at dawn Chung Yi walked down to the river bank with us. We stood in silence for a moment and then I said: "When you are ordered to the front, let me know and I will return to your division and write about it."

"I will welcome you," he said. Then he opened his hand and in the palm I saw a small jade ring.

"This was given me by people who came to the front," he said. "It is of little value, but it is a symbol of hope and faith. Take it."

I could not speak.

We lingered at the river, then led our horses onto the ferry and crossed. Beyond, we rode up a hill toward a village. Chung Yi still stood on the other bank, alone. I turned my horse and lifted my hand. He raised his arm and kept it lifted until the walls of the village cut us off.

The pockmarked Colonel riding by my side cried out something and we all broke into a wild gallop and swept down the frozen highway toward the front.

Lieutenant General Chung Yi (in front of the banner); the older man to his right was the Vice-Commander. Nearest the camera was the young intellectual invited by General Chung to help him study. This was the breakfast of welcome to me. All of these men were killed in action.

General Cheng Su-yuan, Commander of the 124th Division of the 22nd Group Army, and his Chief-of-staff. For hours we talked across the candle light. It was Christmas Eve, 1939.

The reception given me by the 519th Regiment of Chung Yi's division cheered me greatly. The regimental commander, Colonel Yang Chang-chen was my host, but the whole regiment took a hand in welcoming me. Colonel Yang looked like a boulder worn and pitted by many summer's rains. The soldiers loved and trusted him, saying of him that he was "cold-minded but warm-hearted, and born without a sense of fear." Sometimes I saw him pat a sentry on the shoulder and ask him how things were going with him; the soldier would snap to attention with a grin, say that things were fine, and ask him how he liked the cold weather.

"When I joined the Army, I was just sixteen," Colonel Yang once said in answer to a question. "I am now an old man of thirty-four — the oldest in the regiment."

He was also the most inarticulate and I had to drag his words from him. "My family were poor peasants," he told me. "When I left home, they wrapped twenty cents in a piece of red paper and told me to use it carefully to buy food. Instead of joining the Army, my aunt told me to go out and get rich in the foreign way. I said: 'Nonsense — I will serve my country!' but she said: 'A plague on your country!' No, I never married. I was so ugly that no girl would have me. They called me 'Pockmarked Yang,' and said I looked like a cook. So I was a soldier for many years. When the Japanese invasion began I was a battalion commander. After the Shanghai battle we fought for Hsuchow, covering the retreat. We fought throughout central China and defended Hankow. Now we are a regiment."

I never worked harder in my life than in that first week in the 519th Regiment. There were lectures at the training camp for political soldiers, talks with men in the barracks, and a thousand tales of battle. Approximately eighty per cent of the soldiers were peasants, ten per cent workers, ten per cent students. All were between twenty and thirty years old. More than seventy per cent were illiterate, but they apologized, saying that most of them were new recruits and had just started their competition in reading and writing. "Come back later," they said.

At night I sat around open campfires with the young officers and they told me tales of battles. As we talked the leaping fire flickered on a long slogan on the wall behind them: *Weld the Army into iron.* But I noticed that one young officer never smiled or laughed, sitting with somber, downcast eyes; once when he looked into my face it seemed he was searching for something, something lost long ago when there was no war. He was like a ghost at the campfire, and from something Colonel Yang once said, I understood why. This group, he said, had once been the 131st Division — nothing was left of it but one regiment, and most of that was made up of new recruits.

"We lost so many commanders that the Army had to make me regimental commander," Colonel Yang added. No one contradicted him, for everyone had been promoted in this way. Their training had been on the battlefield.

One officer told me that in the first months of the war no quarter was given to enemy soldiers who threw up their hands. The news had spread through all China that thousands of unarmed Chinese had been slaughtered in Nanking, and with them the wounded soldiers who could not be moved. When Colonel Yang saw Japanese who cried for mercy his voice became high and he screamed: "Sha-h-h-h-h-h!" and his men fell on them, leaving not one alive.

The vice-commander, Guo Ping, had been a student and poet when the war began. He was the correspondent for a Kwangsi newspaper, but could seldom find time to write. He was twenty-five, he said, and had been mentioned for merit by the Government for having taken command of a company and helped cover the retreat of the whole Army after the fall of Hsuchow. The 131st Division had fought the rear-guard action, evacuating civilians from every village as the enemy advanced.

And yet when I asked Guo Ping to tell me some story of heroism, he said at first that he couldn't think of one! Hesitantly he mentioned several incidents: another vice-commander, Liu Shih-li, had once led his company against a convoy of Japanese trucks, wiped it out, killed a high Japanese staff officer, and taken valuable documents. The Japanese had many of their women with them, and they too had been killed. Commander Liu had also once held four strategic villages for one hour while the enemy closed in, killing half of the defenders and wounding Liu twice. When their job was done, Liu had ordered those few of his men who remained alive to retreat; he himself had brought up the rear with a wounded messenger, killing seven more Japanese who tried to capture them.

Guo Ping and the Political Director of the regiment helped the political soldiers publish a monthly front magazine, *Pei Yen*, or *White Bayonet*. This magazine had been born in the trenches while the regiment had held a sector for six months. It printed stories, poems, songs, and essays written by the soldiers. From its pages I culled extracts from soldiers' diaries. One began:

> A few stars shine in the sky, the wind moans, and it is very cold. We march through silent mountains. Not even a dog barks. No cock crows. There is no human voice. All things have fled. When we came we did not expect this.
>
> We will defend Shuihsien. We must take and hold Highland #1752. We pass farmhouses, climb a low hill, scatter and cover the hill, and wait for the command. Then bullets sing out. "Pih-pah! Pih-pah! Pih-pah!" everywhere. Our small field pieces roll along with a great noise. Smoke is over everything and the whole hill seems to be moving. After an hour the sun comes up as red as if it were drunk. The bugle calls for attack and our white bayonets are on the end of our rifles. We lift ourselves and rush forward. The machine-guns and field guns sound very bitter. "Sha! Sha!" We kill and go like a storm over Highland #1752. The bodies of the enemy cover the earth, and their blood turns the withered grass red. It is very slippery.
>
> Finished, we stand in line. I look down my line and see that it is very short. Twenty of our company have died. Lung Yu-an, our vice-commander, has been wounded and

our company commander killed. Another company commander and two battalion vice-commanders have been wounded and taken to the hospital.

Another soldier wrote more volubly:

After breakfast the day comes. The morning sun shines in our positions. It brightens us up. Lao Tso sits on a rock and sings "Nanyang Kwang" [a Peiping opera aria]. He has a coarse voice and I feel miserable when I hear him, but cannot stop him.

Suddenly I remember that the Kwangsi Student Army will come up to the front today to lecture to us. I take out my knife and mirror and begin scraping and pulling the hairs out of my chin. Lao Tso keeps on bawling at me. "What are you up to?" he asks.

"The Kwangsi Student Army will come today and maybe there will be a girl who will think of me if I clean my chin."

"I'd rather think of ——," he says.

Lao Tso is a *wang-bah-tan* who thinks of such things. He is really rotten. When the Fancheng-Hsiangyang Comfort Delegation came last time, he stared at the women like a hungry dog at wild geese.

"You are just a *wang-bah-tan!*" I tell him. He does not care and merely starts growling out a song again and I keep on feeling miserable. I take my water bottle and wet my chin and pull out all the hairs. . . .

Well, this afternoon the Kwangsi Student Army came. There were seven or eight men and women, all young, and the men keep their hair about two inches long. They all dress as we do, but have no guns. They wear leather caps and red badges. A boy and girl came to our position. They were about the same age and I wondered if they were man and wife. The man called us their *Lao-san* [countrymen] and said they were Kwangsi people like us. We told them that Kwangsi people are not the only *Lao-san*, but that everyone in the country now is *Lao-san*.

They gave us a lecture about our families in Kwangsi.

Kweilin has been often bombed, they said, but not very much damage done. The Government has ordered that the families of military men be given 300 pounds of free rice. Our families cannot be taxed or conscripted for labor. We should not worry, they said, for our families are well taken care of.

That Lao Tso sat gawking at the woman all the time. He made us all sick. Once he said to the man student: "I have no young wife. What have you got to say to that?"

"That does not matter," said the man. "If you come home victorious it will be an honor for a girl to marry you."

Lao Tso answered: "It's miserable because I am ugly and I don't sit around scraping the hairs off my chin."

The girl student laughed and said that if he returned a hero from the war he could marry the most beautiful woman. Lao Tso only said: "Huh!"

When the students left, we all laughed at Lao Tso, but he told us to —— ourselves. I hate to sit around for days listening to Lao Tso sing. It would be better to have to capture one of the enemy's big guns.

In the following weeks and months on the central China battlefield, I wondered why no news came from Major General Chung Yi's division. Yet in all the confusion, how could a letter have reached me? Often I asked about the division, and people said this and that. Someone had heard that it had moved to the central front in the Ta Hung mountain range, but could not be certain. No one knew just where it was. The winter passed and spring came, and I had traveled I did not know how many hundreds of miles, walking a great part of the way, lecturing to soldiers, speaking at civilian mass meetings, working over the wounded — with the roar of artillery and the droning of enemy planes haunting us day and night. In April a recurrent illness, complicated by malaria, forced me to go to a missionary hospital at Ichang in the rear, and when I did not recover, to continue on to Chungking.

One day while I was there, a young poet, Loh Fan, who had been with me on the central front, crossed the Yangtze River and came to see me. He brought a letter which had been forwarded and re-forwarded. It was written by Chung Yi in English, despite the fact that he did not handle the language easily. The letter was dated in early February. His division, he wrote, would be on the Chunghsiang front and I should meet him there. The last lines worried me, for they were like a farewell. "You are a writer," he wrote. "You must always tell your countrymen that we will fight to the death until victorious. Do not forget."

I suggested that Loh Fan wait a little while and we would go back together. But malaria is a merciless affliction, and between relapses I could do no more than lecture, raffle off my front-line trophies, and buy medical supplies with the proceeds. I sent off supplies to many armies, including a number of cases to Chung Yi's division, and induced the Women's International Club of Chungking to adopt the 173rd Division and make surgical dressings for it.

Then one day Loh Fan came to me again and said that Chung Yi's division had been annihilated and that General Chung himself was either dead or captured. I protested, calling it just another rumor. I did not believe it at all, yet it touched me like an icy wind.

Loh Fan went away again. When he returned he brought a Kwangsi officer with him. I listened to them as in a dream. The Japanese had come with planes, tanks, and motor trucks across the north Hupeh wheat-fields. Chung Yi's division had again tried to cover a Chinese retreat. It had stood with its back to the Tang River and tried a counter-encirclement of the enemy. On May 9, 1940, at the village of Ts'uan Tai Chen, even his headquarters had been surrounded. Fifty-four men and a number of women from the Political Department had been killed in fierce fighting. Along with two guards Chung Yi had escaped into the fields. At last, to prevent capture, he had turned his pistol against himself.

A guard who managed to escape had paid a peasant to go to the wheat-field when the enemy passed on, find his commander, and bury him. Later General Chung's brother had gone to Laohokuo and then to the battlefield. He had disinterred Chung Yi's body and now it had been brought to Chungking for state burial. Soldiers marched to muffled drums, and Generalissimo Chiang conferred posthumous honors upon the dead. . . .

On the night of the funeral I watched the pattern of trees against the dim sky beyond my window. The night was as black and brooding as my own spirit. Over and over again I lived through the battle in which Chung Yi had died. I kept seeing him as he had stood by the riverside, his hand uplifted in farewell and his voice saying something . . . yes, "It is a symbol of hope and faith." I saw the enemy planes and tanks and trucks coming on and on — steel death from my own country; and my whole being overflowed with a bitterness like gall. I saw the foe fall upon the headquarters near the river Tang, and I saw the fire of defiance blaze from every window and every ditch and far and wide over the wheat-fields; I heard the firing die slowly away and I saw Chung Yi run into the wheat-fields and turn his pistol against his own heart. The vision seemed like a vision of all China, of the whole world, and my mind became a pool of despair. I despised myself for not having returned to the 173rd Division to be slain with my friend by the weapons from my own country.

Weeks passed. One day two letters came from the central China front. One was an official-looking document written in the bold hand of General Moh Hsu-chi, Commander-in-Chief of the Eighty-fourth (of which the 173rd Division had been a part). The commander informed me in detail of how Chung Yi had "gloriously sacrificed" himself. The other was from the remnants of the 173rd Division, which was being again replenished and trained. The division asked me to contribute my memories of Chung Yi for a new book to be published by the Kwangsi Army. A hundred times I tried to write, but for many months I could not bear even to recall those terrible events.

In the autumn of that year I found myself in Chung Yi's

native Kwangsi Province. I met and talked with his brother and then I went out to the hills beyond Kweilin and stood alone by his tomb. It seemed utterly unreal. Only my memories were real — my memories and the jade ring on my finger, and his face across the great plains of China.

His face across the plains of China . . . and in the shadows behind it soldiers crouching and running, marching and singing . . . men in a candlelit room chatting gravely and gaily. . . . And Chung Yi's voice murmuring across a great distance: "We have our faith — tell your countrymen."

Winter Soldiers in Hupeh

WHEN I arrived in the Hupeh field headquarters of the 22nd Group Army — a Szechuen Army — in late December, the Chinese winter offensive was already in full swing. The Fifth and Ninth War Zones had received orders from Generalissimo Chiang to open their offensives simultaneously. For months thereafter we lived under the ceaseless roar of artillery and the zooming of planes. The very earth trembled.

The Chinese left-wing armies in north Hupeh were commanded by the famous northern general Sun Lien-chung, and the right wing by another noted northerner, General Chang Tze-chung. General Sun's field headquarters were in the Tungpeh mountain range near the main Japanese position at Sinyang. He had demolition units along the Peiping-Hankow railway, and one of his divisions was trying to clean the Japanese out of their northernmost position, Changtaikwan (not far from Dr. Skinsness's hospital in Kioshan). We had received news that the Japanese in that sector had already begun to use poison gas. The 22nd Group Army did not possess steel helmets, not to speak of gas masks.

The Szechuen Army in our sector was attacking the outer defense lines of the mighty semicircle of Japanese troops protecting Hankow. The main Japanese position was at Shuihsien, from which city they had thrust out tentacles in all directions and had, in particular, fortified six strategic mountain tops directly in front of us. The Szechuen Army had driven long wedges between these enemy bases in an attempt to isolate, surround, and destroy them.

The Chinese hoped to destroy the enemy's ring of outer defenses. They also dreamed of taking Hankow, but they all knew that with their equipment they could hardly do more than weaken the Japanese. They knew that if they captured an enemy position, they could not hold it without air power; and there was not one Chinese plane at the front. Japanese reconnoitering planes and bombers came over, selected their targets at leisure, and dumped their loads. On the six fortified mountain positions in our sector alone, the Japanese had thirty-eight short-range field pieces. The 22nd Group Army had just received two field guns from Chungking, but shells for them had to be transported by men or mules — and the distance from Fancheng, on the Han River, was ten days to two weeks by human or animal transport.

As we rode down from the city of Tsaoyang, an Army adjutant kept chattering like a shallow brook. "The Soviet military adviser attached to our Army is a strange man!" he declared brightly. "He's a humanitarian. He will not ride in a sedan chair, and he walks his horse up a hill. After every thirty *li* [about ten miles] he walks in order to give his horse a rest! If it rains, he helps the soldiers build defenses, even though the mud pours into his boots. . . . The Eighth Route Army is made up of Communists. They represent imperialism, and they only fight the Japanese because the Government pays them clothes and money. . . ."

"Where did you get such ideas?" I interrupted.

"From the Political Director," he answered.

I tried to explain to him what nonsense he had been taught.

The Szechuen armies had the reputation of being the most feudal and backward in China, and the conduct of most of them justified it. But the 22nd Group Army had become a strange mixture of old and new attitudes. The Commander, General Sun Chen, with whom I had spent considerable time in Tsaoyang, was a scholarly man who seemed to be saddened and oppressed by the reputation and condition of his army. On the whole, his troops were illiterate. They came from the poverty-stricken farms of Szechuen, where they, their fathers, and their fathers' fathers had been looted by feudal generals and politician-landlords. Since the war they had become imbued with national consciousness, and I saw them fight proudly and bravely, giving their lives for a country that had given them nothing. It is not easy to be proud and brave in China.

Along the highway leading from Tsaoyang long lines of lumbering ox-carts, wheelbarrows, human carriers, and an occasional pack-horse or mule moved toward the front loaded with military supplies and with huge piles of new padded winter uniforms.

As we rode toward the battlefield, I wondered if any spot on earth could be more dreary and depressing. It was winter and the half-frozen plains were gray and dour. In the distance rose the blue Tungpeh Mountains, which the peasants, in their poverty, kept stripped of trees. Right under our eyes the less severely wounded and the sick stumbled along the highway. In the convoys of stretchers some of the wounded lay in their summer uniforms, shivering in the cold; in some instances the bearers had taken off their own padded coats and covered the wounded. Unlike the soldiers, the bearers had undershirts.

In the villages where the bearers halted to rest and give their charges a drink, the civilians charged a copper for boiled water. It was not heartlessness; firewood cost money — a great deal of money — and the people were desperately poor. Compassion? In China any man who gives to another must give from his own skin.

The carts in the van of each convoy were filled with wan-faced wounded men trying to withstand the jolting; in the rear came the carts piled with the corpses of those who had died on the way. The shoes had been taken from their feet, for the living need shoes, while the dead do not. The feet of the dead were the coarse, calloused feet of poor peasants. Streaks of blood had dried on them and some were mangled.

Somehow these feet affected me deeply, for they told tales of a lifetime of bitter toil and sorrow.

Once as we drew abreast of one of these ox-cart convoys, a white-faced soldier with a bandaged arm appealed to us, crying: "If I ride farther, I shall die! I cannot endure it any longer!"

There were no splints at the front, and the man's arm had merely been set in a sling. I helped him on my horse and led him to a dressing station a mile and a half off the highway. There, to our amazement, a qualified doctor in a white apron came out and took charge in a gentle but efficient manner. The doctor had one qualified assistant, also in a white apron, and a group of fifteen soldier dressers. Tenderly and patiently these men led the wounded into clean, well-organized village rooms, changed their dressings with the utmost care, and gave them a meal, which even included some pork. Nowhere else had I seen a white apron; and even here there were no sheets, pillows, soap, or toilet paper, and the splints were made out of boards from discarded boxes.

As I helped with the wounded, I thought of the qualified Chinese doctors in Shanghai and Hong Kong who continued their private practices, at best giving a monthly sum to the Chinese Red Cross. Only two hundred of them had joined the Red Cross Medical Corps and a few hundred others the Public Health Administration. Sometimes I despised not only these doctors but the Government, which still refused to conscript them. Generalissimo Chiang Kai-shek had been quoted as saying: "The doctors have let me down!" The doctors had let down more than Chiang Kai-shek — they had let down an entire land.

The armies were not to blame for the lack of medical staffs. They had scoured the earth for qualified doctors and had even advertised in Chinese newspapers at the port cities. Despite this I had read one letter in which a doctor in the Chinese Air Force wrote a fellow physician urging him to come to the rear and get a job in the Chinese Air Force, because a flier was "of more value than ten thousand common soldiers," and because, incidentally, salaries in the Air

Force were very good, the work was light, and there was plenty of time to read!

One morning at dawn I stood by the roadside and watched thousands of gray-clad soldiers and laden pack-animals moving up to the battlefield to relieve men who had been fighting for two days and two nights without rest. They were solemn-eyed men marching in grim silence, trying to get out of the broad valley before the enemy planes came over. Their marching feet threw up a dense cloud of dust, and through this swirling dust came the first stretcher-bearers bringing in those who had been wounded in the night's fighting. The bearers panted as they moved forward in their slow trot. The wounded lay with their faces turned to the gray, wintry skies. A few were covered with captured Japanese blankets or overcoats, and here and there a captured Japanese flag fluttered from a stretcher. Some lay peacefully, still under the influence of morphine tablets given them by regimental dressers on the battlefield. Like the Spartans, they were being brought in on their shields.

At such a moment I felt nothing less than love for Surgeon General Loo Chih-teh and Dr. Robert Lim, for it was they who had prepared the tons of compressed, sterilized dressings, each with a morphine tablet in it. This development in the Army Medical Service had taken place in the last year and was the greatest single factor combating infection and death from shock. Despite all they had seen, neither Dr. Loo nor Dr. Lim had ever shown signs of growing callous; their hearts remained filled with as much compassion as ever. Repeatedly I heard that Surgeon General Loo had camped in a field at night in order to descend upon some military hospital for an early morning inspection. In Laohokuo, when I had been surprised to find a base hospital where the brightest rooms were given not to the staff but to the wounded, the Medical Director of the zone had said: "Yes, Dr. Loo told us to give the best rooms to the wounded. The staff was given what was left."

With these memories in the back of my mind, I followed a convoy of stretchers from the battlefield to a dressing sta-

Civilians aiding in transporting the wounded from the front.

(left) *A "walking-wounded" evacuating himself from the front to a hospital in the rear.* (right) *Inside the barracks of the 173rd Division (Kwangsi Army) I found soldiers studying, seated on their straw mattresses.*

tion. My secretary and I helped the soldier nurses lift the wounded to their feet or carry the severe cases to the long straw pallets on the earthen floor inside the building. Other wounded had lain on the straw on previous days and it was dirty with blood and mucus. We would shake it up or carry in new loads from the stacks outside.

I watched one soldier dresser tearing an old dressing off the hand of an unconscious man. The hand had been almost severed and the man was bleeding to death. I called the superintendent, a fairly well-qualified doctor, but he himself was suffering from hernia. After examining the hand, he took from his kit an ordinary sewing-needle and some silk thread, gathered up the few forceps, shears, and knives, and placed them in a wash-basin to boil. There were no sheets, towels, soap, hypodermic syringes or needles, and the "operating-table" was nothing but a straw pallet. The superintendent amputated the hand. I was his assistant.

Later I went about talking to the men. When I remarked how few were severely wounded, one soldier cried out: "The others couldn't get away! Some of us got out only because we could crawl. It took me eight hours to find the stretcher-bearers!"

Then one man's face attracted my attention. He sat in silence, his back propped against the wall, his head wrapped in a broad white bandage, his face exceedingly pale.

"Tell me how you were wounded," I said as gently as I could.

He seemed to be looking at me, but he did not answer. "He was a machine-gunner," someone said. Then the man himself tried to answer. He opened his mouth, but the words would not come. Finally with infinite difficulty he managed to say: "It is such a little thing — it is for my country."

As he spoke, his voice grew faint and his head sank onto his breast. Quickly a dresser and I stepped over to him and started to lift him so that he might lie flat on the straw. Even as we lifted him I knew that he was dead.

Of the 2,600 wounded men who left the north Hupeh battlefield during the first three weeks of the winter offensive, only 1,000 lived to reach the first field hospital at Fancheng, two weeks to the rear.

Sometimes I wrote my diary notes while jogging along on horseback. Then they looked like chicken scratches or as though I had been suffering from spasms:

December some time or other. Have lost track of time. Fighting deadlocked with heavy losses both sides. Ice on streams and hoarfrost turning dry grass white and brittle. Soldiers drill, practice old Chinese boxing — and sing national songs. They salute as I pass and their black, grave eyes make me think: "We who are about to die salute you, foreign woman, riding on a horse!" Thuds of bursting shells. Ghastly, droning enemy planes selecting targets before bombing. Planes like lazy sensuous animals of prey with victim which cannot protect itself. . . .

Am leaving Lishan market town on border battlefield. Today no sound of fighting shakes hillsides. Only bloody trails along paths.

Peasants plow dry, cheerless fields and grind corn. Some isolated mud farmhouses not destroyed; some big landlord mansions with watchtowers undamaged. Countryside strewn with military telephone wires stretched through trees on crooked improvised poles. Sentries challenge us from every hill. On one hillside a little boy cuts twigs with long curved knife; sometimes stops and sings shrill anti-Japanese song.

Szechuen Army very backward socially, but are filled with national, racial consciousness. Though no People's Work, still civilians transport wounded without conscription; trust Army and remain right near battlefield. They improvise stretchers by taking wooden doors off wooden hinges or turning bamboo cots upside down, string ropes beneath, and swing wounded along. Perspiration pours from them and they run in slow dog-trot with eyes on earth.

Have sent off report to Red Cross.

The Commander Who Sang

LIEUTENANT GENERAL WANG CHIH-YUAN, Commander of the 122nd and 123rd Divisions of the Szechuen Army on the Lishan front, had established temporary headquarters in an old temple on a high hill furrowed with trenches and dugouts. From there he could overlook the Lishan Valley and watch enemy positions beyond. With their strong field glasses the Japanese could also watch the whole valley and see every Chinese move. Their planes droned over the battlefield, and if they saw horsemen, they swooped down and machine-gunned them, knowing them to be officers. Headquarters had to be moved every few days to avoid discovery.

General Wang had formerly been a commander of the northern army of the Christian General Feng Yu-hsiang. He was a big, fat, hale and hearty man with a voice so tremendous that when he talked over the telephone, the man on the other end could never understand. His chief of staff usually took the phone and repeated the orders in a normal voice.

General Wang seemed a total stranger to cunning or dissimulation. He said what he thought — and no man could ever answer: "I'm sorry, I did not hear"! He belonged to the battlefield and I could imagine him speaking to a whole division literally without a man missing a word.

The fighting was not yet serious, he boomed at me, but the losses had been heavy enough for both sides to pause to reinforce. The Japanese were rushing troops from Hankow, but the General had sent men to destroy their communications. He himself had been waiting for two new artillery pieces; they had just arrived and on the following day would be in position. They had a longer range than the Japanese and he was going to blast the daylights out of the enemy's three nearest mountain positions. If I wanted, I could ride up with him next day and watch the first bombardment.

As he led me up and around the network of trenches protecting his mountain eyrie, he roared the glad news that he was a Christian and had been baptized in Peking years ago by an American missionary whose picture he still carried in a hymn-book.

I asked him why he became a Christian. "Well, it's something I can't explain — just a feeling," he said. "And I like to sing. I used to be in a choir. It's wonderful, singing — nothing like it."

General Wang and his chief of staff decided to celebrate my arrival with a dinner in the peasant home where I was to stay. They bought a chicken and some turnips and told the peasants they would pay to have it prepared. The peasants refused to accept any money. They adored General Wang and stood around talking with him as to a friend. That night four of us sat around a rough, square table with a peanut-oil lamp between us and talked about the war and the world.

The General always carried his big black Chinese hymn-book with him, and when he felt in need of a little spiritual comfort he sang. Once the dinner was finished, the General laid the book on the rough table, smoothed the soft rice paper lovingly with his big hand, and heaved a deep sigh.

"Ah! I remember singing this hymn with Feng Yu-hsiang!" he said. "Those were beautiful days. We used to sing and sing!"

He was a humble, unpretentious soul and the moment I asked him to sing he opened his mouth and let his deep but tender voice fill the peasant hut like a mighty pipe-organ. I recalled the Tuskegee Negro singers and the voice of Paul Robeson. When the General ended the hymn with "Allelujah! Allelujah! Allelujah!" the very rafters trembled!

Caressingly he thumbed the worn pages, found another song, and without any urging sang once more. He sang and sang, and when at last I heard the mighty line: "Holy! Holy! Holy! Lord God Almighty!" I could remain seated no longer. I walked to the door and stared into the night. The very earth seemed to be singing. Outside the two armed sentries set to guard my house had been walking back and forth across the hard-packed threshing-floor, but now they stood perfectly still. The wintry wind lifted the edges of their long coats and the light of the half-moon glinted on their fixed bayonets and on the still pond beyond. The wind rustled a few dried leaves and pods clinging to the long branch of a tree, and the moonlight through the branches turned the threshing-floor into a delicate wavering network. In the somber shadows at the foot of the tree I could see a small shrine to the Earth God.

The voice stopped suddenly. We listened intently. From the south came the roar of artillery.

General Wang spoke abruptly. "It's from Maping," he said to his chief of staff. "I'd better go. You stay."

He closed the hymn-book and went without another word. For a long time we sat listening to that distant roar coming from the south.

In the afternoon of the next day we rode up over a high level plateau criss-crossed by carefully camouflaged trenches. On every hillock was perched a wigwam-like look-out post.

From the plateau we could look across at the enemy positions. Directly at the foot of the eastern cliffs of the plateau ran the Yung River, along which our troops were stationed. Seven miles to the east towered the peak of Kuenshan, and on its summit was a Buddhist monastery which had been heavily garrisoned by the Japanese. Through field glasses we could see a long encompassing wall half-way down the mountainside, and another nearer the buildings themselves. To the southeast lay Juikuotan and in between that and the mountain lay Changchiakan.

That day I would have given my right arm for the privilege of handling a big gun. But there were so many Chinese who shared the same desire that I didn't have a ghost of a chance.

We dismounted at the sprawling farmhouse which had been selected as temporary field-artillery headquarters. The farmhouse was sheltered by trees, and near by was a scraggly pine grove; as usual, in a small shrine at the base of a spreading oak the Earth God and his wife sat in stoic dignity.

A wedding was being celebrated in the house and, to my disgust, the bridegroom and the bride turned out to be fourteen and sixteen respectively. The women ate in one room and the men, including the boy groom, in another. Some of the men had stuffed themselves unconscious and lay in a haystack sound asleep. Before we left that night, they had come to life long enough to go in and eat again.

General Wang and I went in to admire the alleged beauty of the bride. Gaudily dressed and painted, she knelt in front of us and offered us cakes and tea; we ate and placed a wedding present — a small sum of money — on the tray. I asked the women how the Japanese had acted when they had held these heights three months before. They told me that the enemy had found porcelain teapots and rice-bowls in the Chinese trenches and had realized that the peasants had fed their own soldiers. So they had slit the throats of the two old women and the one old man who had remained behind to guard the farmhouse.

One room of the house had been turned over to General Wang and he began roaring into a telephone connected with the artillery positions. The chief of staff waited patiently for the General to finish, took the telephone, and repeated the orders in a normal voice.

"Well, we may as well eat!" exclaimed the General, and the cook brought out some food and spread it on a board in the courtyard. General Wang lowered his huge bulk onto a low three-legged chair used by children and began muttering over a map. We had just started eating when the first shell shook the courtyard from end to end. I stood up, my rice-bowl poised in mid-air, and listened to the shells tearing through the heavens. "This is the first Chinese offensive since the war began," I thought, "and here we sit eating rice!"

We went along a gully so that enemy field glasses could not spot us, and moved slowly into a pine grove. General Wang possessed the only pair of field glasses among the lot of us and after each shot he would train them on Kuenshan to the east and then pass them around. We would watch the enemy position and after what seemed like a long time a fountain of smoke and debris would spout from the landscape. A moment later the sound of the bursting shell would come back to us.

A field telephone hung from a tree in the grove, and from time to time General Wang would pick it up, start to bawl orders to the gun captain, and then, with a tremendous effort, lower his voice. When he hung up he would mutter contemptuously about telephones that had to be handled like babies. Once he thrust his field glasses into my hands just as a shell crackled across the sky. I watched and watched and finally saw a column of smoke and debris arise right out of the heart of a Japanese defense position on Kuenshan. I shouted, and everyone else joined in, and someone ripped the glasses from me. General Wang picked up the telephone and bellowed as quietly as he could: "You've got it! Now get to work!"

At exactly half past four the valley and the hills beyond were split open by sound. We heard the hollow booming of trench mortars, punctuated by machine-gun bursts and accompanied in a kind of counterpoint by the crackling of rifles. Night fell swiftly here, and the small flame that spurted up as each shell was fired betrayed the gun positions and the artillery captain asked permission to stop firing. General Wang agreed and added that the guns must be moved to new stations, for in the morning the enemy's planes would certainly come over to bomb them.

Later we rode down the Lishan Valley. When the clouds parted we saw a small Catholic church on our right. It was totally gutted and without windows or doors. Only the walls and roof remained standing. General Wang asked us to wait while he went in to pray. Someone remarked: "That is a Catholic church; you are a Protestant," but he answered: "It's all the same in the eyes of God!" We remained seated on our horses outside, and from the hollow shell of the church we heard his voice roaring to God, pleading for guidance, for the protection of his men, for victory over the enemy.

With the dawn the wounded began to come in, and at the same time the fighting rose in crescendo. The walls of our building trembled, but we listened proudly to our two guns holding their own against the thirty-eight enemy pieces. Airplanes began to drone above, reconnoitering, seeking targets.

I took my medical kit and hurried to the nearest dressing station. As I approached, I saw two teams of slow-moving oxen dragging a captured Japanese field gun along the highway. Green branches camouflaged the gun, and out of their foliage stuck the laughing face of a soldier who was sitting astride the barrel. The civilians and soldiers who had dragged the field piece down the mountainside milled proudly around it, and many of them strutted about with shells on their shoulders. Just as I was photographing this apparition, I heard a roar and up came General Wang. He examined the gun and declared it a fine piece of workmanship, a 9.3 cm. gun with a Tokyo number plate, made in 1940.

Kuenshan had been surrounded and ten Manchurian Chinese puppet soldiers had been captured on its slopes. A number of enemy points had changed hands. Some had been captured, their garrisons exterminated, and their defenses demolished. One battalion, however, led by a young officer, Loh Huh-ping, seemed to have disappeared. When last seen they had been attacking an enemy position in Miaoerpu in the rear. In the late afternoon a unit found Battalion Commander Loh and his one hundred remaining men holding the fort. They had captured another field gun and were using it against the enemy.

Juikuotan had been taken. Forty members of the secret peasant "Big Sword" society, the *Hwang Shih Hwei*, had led the Chinese troops along the narrow paths leading to the town. They carried long spears and huge native-made iron shears with which they cut the enemy's barbed wire. Once while they were cutting the wires a Japanese officer came to the door of a near-by house; one of the peasants rushed the building and other soldiers hurled hand-grenades into it. The Japanese soldiers fled into an underground tunnel and pulled close a steel door which could only be opened from below. The tunnel had an outlet farther along the hill, and the Chinese caught the Japanese pouring out of it, throwing off their overcoats as they fled.

In Juikuotan the Chinese had found two American trucks, one of them loaded with shells. They unloaded the shells, destroyed the trucks, and sent soldiers and peasants down the mountainside with the shells and a field gun. Sometimes the men had literally carried the field gun over destroyed roads. Japanese banners, work tools, automobile spare parts, rifles, pistols, and ammunition began to pour into headquarters, and hundreds of men got blankets and overcoats.

Wounded members of the peasant secret society lay on stretchers with their long spears at their sides and the magic yellow sash of their society soaked with blood.

"Someone said that if you wore this sash you could not be wounded and would have no fear," I said to them. "Do you believe that?"

"If we had fear, we would not be fighting!" one answered; and I was silenced.

I rode swiftly along the outer Chinese defenses on the battlefield that stretched from Lishan eastward. We had been warned by General Wang to reach the headquarters of the 124th Division before nightfall, because news had come that the Japanese were concentrating heavy forces around the mountain fortification of Kuenshan.

After passing through the foul streets of half-destroyed Lishan, we came upon hundreds of civilians with picks and shovels; they were returning from the battlefield, where they had been digging defenses. Ragged beggars suffering from trachoma stood along the roads and wailed, but we gave them nothing. They were lost souls. Near a small town two hours out of Lishan we passed a company of exhausted, sleeping soldiers who lay strewn about like leaves.

We rode rapidly, our horses' hoofs kicking up billows of dust. From Kuenshan ahead came the ceaseless roar of guns.

At the western base of the mountain the forests had caught fire and a pall of smoke shrouded the slopes. Reconnoitering enemy planes circled like birds of prey over the hills and plains, and now and then a squadron of bombers came up out of the south, split into groups of three, selected targets, and opened their bomb racks.

Later while moving through a narrow valley we came upon a mud hut which a regiment of the 124th Division was using as a first dressing station off the battlefield. There was but one entrance, and the door was missing. Inside, in murky darkness, lay a row of wounded men on a straw pallet along the earthen floor. On a crude table near the door stood half a dozen half-filled bottles, a pair of black native scissors, a few compressed bandages, and some small squares of gauze. From the dusty rafters dangled a big open wad of native cotton. These were the medical supplies in this station.

I looked down at the dim faces of the wounded and their sad eyes gazed up at me. One man asked for water. A dresser brought some in a rice-bowl and placed it near the man's head, but did not offer to help him drink. I choked off an angry exclamation, knelt by the man, and helped him drink.

All the men watched me in silence, and when I rose I saw that the five dressers in the room — not one of them was more than seventeen or eighteen — were standing with lowered heads as if they had been reprimanded. Pity smothered my anger. They were peasant boys from the Army, and in China the poor take care of themselves. Perhaps not one could read or write. All the graces of human culture that spring from comfort and sufficiency were strangers to them.

The tramp of marching feet from beyond the hut caught my attention. Past the doorway marched a line of gray figures with rifles and packs. I went out and watched them come to a halt, remove their packs, and sit down with their rifles propped between their knees. Two of them went away and after a time returned with a big wooden bucket filled with boiled water, and soon all the men had drunk their fill.

This was a company moving up to the battlefield and

here was their last stop for rest. There was a moon and they would fight all night. Their commander came toward me and saluted, and after we had talked he said: "Will you say something to my men? We have half an hour here."

Because I was depressed I answered that this would be difficult at such a moment. He answered that it would encourage them; so I went with him, and at a command the soldiers rose and stood at attention. The commander shouted: "Salute!" and the men saluted. I returned the salute — with better reason than they had given it.

What does one say to men going out to die? I looked at those gray and solemn faces and I tried to think of those of my own people and of the common people of Europe who sympathized — in their spare moments — with China. So I began to tell the soldiers about those people who gave, I said, a part of their wages to help China. I hesitated, for I had not seen one ounce of foreign medicine at the Chinese fronts, but all of us there had seen many bombs, trucks, and other supplies from America.

"We have not done enough, but we have tried to do something," I finished. "I give you my pledge to tell the people of other countries what I have seen. I shall try to describe how you fight, and the spirit that moves you to continue until China is free."

The men saluted, sat down, and remained silent for a time. Then a murmur came from them. I spoke to the commander and he said to them: "She wants to know what you are saying."

One soldier summoned up the courage to rise. Standing stiffly at attention, as if reporting to an officer, he said: "We should like to know why your country sells arms and ammunition to the enemy to kill us with. We have done you no harm!"

There it was again, that specter of my country's betrayal of China. These soldiers were not content with "morale" lectures. They were as realistic as the earth they trod. I answered as I had answered so often before — that in all capitalist countries there were traitors to humanity who coined money out of death. But I added that there were also millions of common men like themselves who hated this policy, and these millions were bound in solidarity with the soldiers of China. I said this mechanically — a lesson learned by rote.

The soldiers were not satisfied. The same man asked: "What are these friends of ours doing against the rich traitors?"

I told them, describing organizations and individuals and the work they were doing. I mentioned President Roosevelt's call for medical supplies to aid China, and the same call by the Lord Mayor of London — but I did not add how inadequate the response had been.

One of the soldiers jumped to his feet and shouted: "Long live Roosevelt! Long live the Mayor of London!"

The whole company repeated these vivas after him and then echoed slogans in praise of the people's organizations I had mentioned. The commander smiled proudly and saluted me; he then shouted to the men and they also saluted. At last they shouldered their packs and rifles and began to move up the mountain.

General with a Conscience

As I thumb through the soft, cheap pages of my diary notes, the personalities of two or three of the men whom I met at this time keep thrusting themselves into the foreground. First there is the strange figure of General Chang Tze-chung, whose conscience hounded him across every battlefield of China. Another is the clear, chaste outline of his chief of staff, Chang Keh-hsia, younger than General Chang, brilliant, without illusions, his eyes fixed on the future. A third is General Wang Tsan-hsü, a fantastic fellow characterized by an unpleasant boastfulness that reminded me of certain Americans.

I reached the field headquarters of General Chang Tze-chung in Changjiaji, a town in the Ta Hung mountain range of central China, on January 9. General Chang commanded the right-wing Chinese forces in the winter offensive; he also commanded his own northern 33rd Group Army, containing the brigade — led by the heroic Fang Chih-an — that had first challenged the Japanese at Marco Polo Bridge and begun the Sino-Japanese War. The remnants of that brigade still constituted the core of the Seventy-seventh Army of the 33rd Group Army.

As my small party rounded the village houses, I saw a bareheaded, strongly built man at least six feet tall and wearing the blue cotton uniform of a common soldier. He held a paper-bound book in his hand, the pages folded back as if he had been reading.

General Chang led me into his headquarters and sat across the table from me, talking about the central front which he commanded. Through the open doors to the south we could see the great heights of a mountain range from which came the incessant roar of artillery and the drone of planes. As I sat there, I thought of the officer who had kept assuring me that this General Chang was a patriot, a brave man, a student — almost as if he were defending him. It was then that I had recalled that General Chang had once been called a traitor. Before the war he had held high positions in north China and had associated with the Japanese. On one occasion he had been a member of a delegation to Japan. When the war had begun at Marco Polo Bridge, he had been Mayor of Peiping, and while the 29th Route Army of General Sun Cheh-yuan was fighting for the city he had surrendered it to the Japanese, transferring authority, he said, to save it from destruction. *Han chien*, traitor, the people called him.

But could an individual be responsible for the policy of a government? For six long years the Chinese Government had settled each act of Japanese aggression as a "local incident," submitting or compromising at every step. All of Hopei Province had already been almost entirely demilitarized in the face of Japanese threats, and General Chang, like everyone in the north, including the 29th Route Army, of which he was a part, had become accustomed to being treated as a buffer between China and Japan.

For three whole weeks, while the 29th Route Army fought, General Chang was reported to be in Peiping and he was reviled by all Chinese. Actually, during the last few days of that period he lay in the German hospital inside the Legation quarter. But one day a foreign motor car drove out of Peiping, and two Chinese chauffeurs, instead of one, sat in the front seats. One of them was General Chang. In the German hospital, the man who was supposed to be the General, threw back the covers, stepped out of bed and walked out of the building!

When the Japanese next heard of General Chang Tze-chung he was Commander of the Fifty-ninth Army of the 29th Route Army and was fighting with them in every section of northern China. He led them through fierce fighting in northern Shantung, withdrawing only to fight again and again — to become, in fact, one of the main factors in the great victory of Taierchwang. His army retired to the west after the fall of Hsuchow, still fighting every step of the way. Generalissimo Chiang had appointed him right-wing commander of the central China front for the offensive of 1939–40.

General Chang had thus proved himself on a hundred battlefields, but the condemnation that had once been heaped upon him still haunted him fiercely. Two Chinese newspaper men were with me when I first talked with him. He talked so cautiously and watched them so suspiciously that I later remarked to his chief of staff, Chang Keh-hsia, that I could neither understand nor trust such a man. The chief of staff said: "You are wrong. The past still haunts him. In our literature we have an elegy about a general who once said that until he had achieved his aim, his life was no more than dust and sand. . . ."

It was not easy to be Chang Tze-chung. He had lived through forty-six years of confusion and turmoil, and the shadows of his past, stories of "opium" and "concubines," still trailed him. But in his headquarters I saw no signs of that past. Everywhere there were piles of books on military and political subjects, and in his few leisure moments in headquarters he discussed his reading or his reflections with his young officers and in particular with his chief of staff. For the two days and nights before I arrived, he had been up on the battlefield, inspecting defenses. Men said he courted death, trying to still his conscience.

Sometimes his humanity broke through his wooden reserve, but generally it hid in fear. With me he talked only of the war. The heavy bombardment, he told us, came from six Japanese field pieces on two mountains twenty miles to the south. The enemy had discovered a cavalry regiment which had been dispatched to destroy their rear communications. But the regiment had returned to its base and reported its mission completed. The General pointed out that the enemy had spent hundreds of shells on that one regiment, but had killed only sixty men; Japanese marksmanship seemed to be becoming poorer and poorer.

These troops, however, had difficulty in getting shells, mules and men being their only means of transport. And the 33rd Group Army alone had suffered four thousand casualties within three weeks. The wounded trickled to the rear over many routes, generally slipping through the Japanese lines at night. Despite all this the General declared that the spirit of his troops was very high. "They are proud to be on the offensive," he said. "We hope to smash the enemy's outer defenses around Hankow and take back their chief fortified city, Chunghsiang."

But no one could say whether the whole offensive would succeed. The enemy had been in their positions for months and had constructed strong defenses; they had the support of planes; and they could bring up reinforcements and supplies on trucks from Hankow and swiftly shift men from one interior position to another.

I learned, too, that one tenth of the enemy forces were Manchurian Chinese puppets. Since the Japanese usually were afraid to use puppets at the front and reserved them for garrison duty only, I became curious about this. Unthinkingly I asked General Chang what he considered to be the chief reason for so many puppets in China. "Ignorance," he answered, but no sooner was the reply out of his mouth than his body stiffened, his face froze, and his stare fixed itself on me. With difficulty I suppressed an impulse to cry out that I hadn't meant that at all!

The man whom I came to know the best of all those whom I met on the central China front was General Chang's chief of staff, Chang Keh-hsia. He was the brother-in-law of the Christian General Feng Yu-hsiang, and had once studied military science in Moscow. Before the winter offensive he had been the head of the training camp of the 33rd Group Army during one of its periods of reorganization.

Chang Keh-hsia's face was thin and keen, and his blue, shabby soldier's uniform hung loosely from his shoulders. Sometimes I met him at headquarters, sometimes in the house where I was billeted, and once we sat under a tree and talked while an air-raid took place a short distance away. With him, too, I spoke only of the war and the problems of the front.

When we talked about the Japanese as soldiers he said:

"Don't let anyone tell you that the Japanese still fight merely by book-rules. They have practiced on us for nearly three years and have learned much. They can make every kind of assault — frontal, flank, or even guerrilla. What is far worse, they have studied our military, political, and social weaknesses and use them against us."

He went on to point out that most Japanese soldiers were literate and had some education and that their conscription system was better than that of the Chinese and their physical and cultural standards higher. The Chinese, he admitted, really had no conscription standards at all; even young boys were taken, and new conscripts were sometimes led away tied with ropes. The political training which such soldiers needed was non-existent. This weakness, he said, was true of all the Chinese armies except the Eighth Route and the

New Fourth. When he implied, however, that the Political Directors of the latter armies did not, unfortunately, permit their soldiers to come in contact with other Chinese armies, I said that I had found that it was the other way round. He replied that it perhaps worked both ways, and that it was, in any event, not a good thing for the country. "However, we Chinese have improved in many ways since the war began," he continued. "One army no longer tries to save itself at the expense of another. What we must realize is that we can win only by a combination of all our military strength with continual political and economic progress."

Also under the command of General Chang Tze-chung, but interesting in a very different way, was General Wang Tsan-hsü, leader of the 29th Group Army, a Szechuen force. General Wang was one commander in whose presence I felt no sense of fellow-suffering and for whom I was unable to develop any respect.

Along with the two Chinese newspaper men I walked out to the village where General Wang had his headquarters and listened to him boast. He was a thin, hard-faced man who loved to be interviewed and have his picture taken in many poses. As soon as we were seated, he threw himself back in his chair and nonchalantly announced that the situation at the front would not have become so serious had he not been detained in Szechuen. He now had the job of taking back all that the Japanese had won. Generalissimo Chiang Kai-shek, he modestly informed us, had agreed to fill his place as Governor of Szechuen while he cleaned up the front! He implied that he had thereby greatly honored the Generalissimo, but I wondered if he himself had not been merely maneuvered out of the way. Such men were notorious in China.

General Wang discussed military problems intelligently, but his best explanation of the puppet traitors was: "There are so many of them because they have not studied the Confucian classics. Each military man must become a scholar."

A strange expression appeared on the face of the reporter

by my side. He kept silent, but I just waded right into General Wang's theory, remarking that most of the leading Chinese traitors *were* Confucian scholars. He looked at me with pity and remarked that such traitors had only "studied superficially." I decided not to remind him that General Chang Tze-chung had once studied the classics, but now read only modern military and political books, whereas General Wang did not have one book in his headquarters — not even the classics.

Apparently to demonstrate his theory of superiority, he told us that his army had just captured six Japanese. Unfortunately for him, we had seen these captives and knew that his army had nothing to do with their capture. They had been brought in by a "Storm Guerrilla Detachment" which operated in enemy-occupied territory beyond the Ta Hung mountain range to the north and northwest of Hankow. If their capture had any literary significance, it was not classical, for the "Storm Guerrillas" were led by the Chinese Communist Party. I took the cue from my newspaper colleagues and sat listening to General Wang with what I hoped was a perfectly impassive and respectful countenance.

As we left, one of the newspaper men with me remarked: "A typical Szechuen boaster — whew!" and spat.

Late one afternoon my secretary and I were returning from the market town of Changjiaji when we fell in with a company commander and his squad of soldiers returning from the front lines. The commander told us that on the previous night, as his company was crawling up a hillside to storm an enemy position, his men heard a Chinese voice somewhere above them say:

"*Lao hsiang* [countrymen], come no farther! We have orders to use poison gas!"

"Traitors!" the company commander exclaimed.

"There is no other way," said the voice.

The company crawled down and around the hill, intending to attack the position from the rear, but found itself completely surrounded by a whole battalion of Manchurian Chinese puppet troops. The puppet commander told the company that he would give them back their guns if they would retire at once. He said that his men would fire high in the air. "You are traitors!" the company commander again exclaimed, but the puppet leader answered that when the puppets were conscripted by the Japanese in Manchuria, their families had also been registered; if they deserted or refused to fight, their families would be killed.

The commander argued with the puppets, telling them that the families of loyal Chinese were also in Japanese-occupied territory — that all Chinese were men without homes. He pleaded with the Manchurians to come with him. The puppet soldiers stirred uneasily, and the company commander said that if it had not been for the officer they might have deserted. Even the puppet commander had hesitated and his voice had sounded deeply troubled as he told the soldiers to take back their guns. Before leaving he had said: "Don't go in that direction; there are machine-gun nests there and the gunners are Japanese."

Upon returning to my living-quarters I found a guerrilla leader and a Korean (who had just brought in some captives) waiting for me. My two visitors began to report on conditions in the enemy-occupied territory north of Hankow. When I asked why I should not go there and investigate for myself, they said there was no reason except the danger. The guerrillas were leaving at dawn the next morning, and their route lay to the east through the Japanese lines in the Ta Hung mountain range. The guerrillas marched and fought constantly and often camped within a mile of the enemy.

I sent my secretary to General Chang Tze-chung with a note asking for permission to go. I later learned that General Chang was in conference with a high military officer from Chungking when my note arrived. The officer remarked that the "Storm Guerrilla Detachment" of the New Fourth Army was illegal and had no right to be in this region!

"Illegal?" asked General Chang. "What is legal or illegal?

They have cleaned out many puppet armies in our rear; they've organized the people into anti-Japanese associations; they've sent us Japanese captives. Is that illegal? If it is, what is legal?"

He then took up his pen and began writing a permit for me to visit the guerrillas, and as he did so he declared: "It's just another political matter. These guerrillas are illegal only because their commanders are Communists. I care nothing for a man's political opinions if he fights the enemy!"

Not everyone was so objective. When he heard of my intention, one of General Chang's adjutants, a Christian who had once been a deacon in the First Methodist Church in Peiping, brimmed over with prejudices. He declared that I would be killed if I went into the guerrilla region — and tears filled his eyes.

"Save your tears for my funeral," I remarked impatiently. He burst out that the guerrillas were Communists and I replied that I didn't care if they were all deacons of the Methodist Church!

I left with the guerrillas the next morning.

It was March, nearly three months later, before I saw General Chang Tze-chung again. I had made my way back through the Ta Hung mountain range and I reported on the dangerous situation which was developing in central China. I told him that General Wang Tsan-hsü, that great braggart, had informed me that he had received orders from the Ministry of War to wipe out the storm guerrillas with whom I had been traveling.

General Chang cautiously asked: "Are you certain of his words?"

"Definitely! He told me so repeatedly. Of course, I argued with him that such civil war would help no one but the Japanese."

General Chang sat in dead silence and I kept my thoughts to myself. I had been told that he, too, had been ordered to turn his guns on the guerrillas, but had found excuses to evade the order. Only the backward Szechuen Army would agree to carry out such a fratricidal policy.

That was the last time I saw General Chang. I was already ill and he sent me by military truck to a foreign hospital in Ichang on the Yangtze. In early June 1940, when I was in a hospital in Chungking, one of his wounded staff officers called on me and told me this story:

On May 15, at the height of the Japanese spring counter-offensive, General Chang was again ordered to take command of the central-front armies engaged in driving the enemy out of Tsaoyang and a number of other towns. General Chang had kept only two guard regiments with him west of the Han River, and he doubted his ability to make contact with the rest of his 33rd Group Army, let alone with other armies. Before obeying the command, he wrote a final letter telling his vice-commander, General Fang Chih-an, to assume command of the Army in case any misfortune befell him.

On May 18 he and his two regiments were surrounded near Fengjiaji by 6,000 enemy infantry and cavalry. They fought for eight hours, suffering fearful losses, and General Chang was wounded in the left arm. The staff officers urged him to retreat while there was still time, but he refused, saying he had not yet done his duty to his country. Even as they debated, the enemy closed in and a burst of machine-gun fire hit General Chang full in the chest and wounded one of the officers. He ordered the two men to get out, but refused to allow them to burden themselves with him. "I've done my duty," he kept saying.

A few hours later General Fang Chih-an met the same Japanese force and all but decimated them. Among the dead they found the body of their own Commander-in-Chief. The Japanese radio had been crowing that the body of General Chang would be taken to his native Shantung for burial. They had talked of the "traditions of chivalry" and "the spirit of bushido."

The Chinese brought the General's body to Chungking (at the same time as that of Major General Chung Yi) and a state funeral was held at Peipei, thirty miles outside the capital. The Japanese learned of the funeral, and planes came and bombed it. After they were gone, the funeral continued, and Generalissimo Chiang conferred posthumous honors on the dead leaders. I was told that thereafter there stood on the Generalissimo's desk a photograph of General Chang Tze-chung, whose conscience was finally at rest.

Mutiny

A FEW days after I had left the headquarters of General Chang Tze-chung, I was sharply and unpleasantly reminded of the boastful Szechuen General Wang when I came to one of his regimental hospitals in the Ta Hung Mountains. The medical officer in charge of the hospital surprised me, although I had thought myself long past surprise in such matters. He was in no sense a physician and how he had secured such a position I could not imagine. The regimental commander in the village was intelligent and capable, but this man looked like a butcher. Perhaps he had been a butcher.

He kept making all kinds of excuses for not showing me his hospital, but when these had failed to quench my interest he reluctantly accompanied me on a tour. We approached a small group of buildings with rotten thatch hanging in clumps from the roof, and entered a courtyard surrounded by four rooms. As soon as we entered the courtyard I looked about in consternation, for a ceaseless moaning seemed to come out of the earth. Turning, I pushed open a door near me. The moaning rose to meet me in a wave.

The room was long and dark, the only light coming from the open door and from a narrow window at one end. Down the entire length of the room was the usual straw pallet on the earthen floor, and along it, like bodies on slabs in a morgue, lay two or three dozen sick and wounded soldiers. Between the foot of the pallet and the wall was a narrow aisle in which stood four or five big wooden buckets filled with urine and excrement, sending up an odor so foul that it was staggering. Some of the men lay huddled together to keep warm, sometimes three or four under one blanket. And from all of them came that ceaseless moaning.

One sick soldier staggered to his feet and started toward one of the big buckets. I reached out, grasped his hot, feverish hand, and helped him reach the bucket.

All politeness forgotten, I strode down the aisle and talked with the men. Then I walked out and turned into another similar room. Here I saw a number of dead men lying side by side with the living. I pushed open a door in a corner of this second room and found myself in a chamber so small and dark that I had to stand for a moment until my eyes could adjust themselves to the gloom. Slowly I made out the faint outlines of men lying on the floor. I turned one man over. He was stiff in death, and his clothing and the straw beneath him were covered with excrement. A hand reached out from somewhere and tugged at my trouser leg. Looking down, I found myself staring into glittering black eyes. "Help me!" a hoarse voice whispered.

This was a room for those abandoned to death. I staggered out into the courtyard and then into still another long room where still other men moaned their misery. The doctor kept following me and protesting that the staff had finished work for the day — that there was no medicine — that there was not enough help. . . . But from the pallet in this last room a derelict of a soldier stood up and cried out desperately:

"This isn't a hospital! This is a death-house. The doctor says we must sacrifice. *He* doesn't sacrifice! He saves money on our food! He doesn't care. No one cares!"

The "doctor" stepped forward and struck the man in the face. When I cried out, he turned and peremptorily ordered me to leave the hospital. I went in silence, but once outside I confronted him, swearing that I would tell this story to General Chang Tze-chung — to everyone in Chungking — to the whole world!

In a blind rage I started out to find the regimental commander, but before I had begun to talk to him, the matter was settled with terrible finality. The soldier whom the doctor had struck had stumbled to the house where his company commander lived. He had told what had happened, but the company commander had cursed him and threatened him with court martial. The soldier staggered away and came back with a rifle. A number of soldiers saw him approach, but watched him in silence and without stirring.

The soldier called the company commander, and when the officer came out, shot him in the guts. He then turned and started toward the house where the doctor lived; the soldiers followed him, watching from a distance. At the doctor's door the soldier told an orderly to tell the doctor that someone wanted to see him. The doctor was having dinner with two friends and came out angrily. The soldier emptied his gun into him. Then he staggered forward into the house itself, but the two friends of the doctor had fled. The soldier brought his gun down on the dinner table, smashing and scattering everything. This done, he staggered out, through the group of watching soldiers, down the short street, and along the path leading into the mountains.

In a short time the whole village was in an uproar. Before any officer could learn what had really happened, darkness had fallen and the mutineer was somewhere in the mountains. An officer found some of the soldiers who had watched the whole affair and began screaming at them. One soldier answered that none of them had had a gun or cartridges, while the mutineer had a good rifle.

Beyond this the officer could learn nothing. Special guards were on duty that night, but it was useless, and after talking with his staff, the regimental commander called all the soldiers and delivered a speech. He said the mutineer had murdered two men and, if found, would be shot. But he also said he would reform the hospital and he hoped that soldiers with complaints would thereafter come directly to him instead of shooting their officers.

Afterwards a small group of young soldiers went to the regimental commander to talk things over. They had heard that some armies put committees of convalescing soldiers in charge of food money and purchasing; if their hospital could have such a committee, they said, no one could complain about the food or accuse the doctors of stealing the money. They wanted to fight the Japanese and didn't care if they were killed, they said; but they didn't want to go to the hospital to die. They thought that the doctors should attend to their duties and that the attendants ought to keep the place clean and occasionally bring in fresh straw for the pallets. The dead ought to be removed, they said, and sick men should not have to watch their comrades dying by their sides. In the middle of the winter wounded men ought to have covers. . . .

The regimental commander said that the officers had always been too busy to look into such matters, but henceforth would do so. He was quite formal, but friendly, and the men did not take advantage of the situation. Finally they saluted with military precision, but as they went out I saw one or two who could not hide the gleam of satisfaction in their eyes.

During the remainder of that evening the whole place seemed to be whispering, and now and then I heard low laughter. Next morning we heard from the guards around headquarters that the soldiers had lain in their barracks and talked at length about the day's events. Too bad, too bad, some of them said; but more than one had laughed harshly as if thinking of a joke that was none too pleasant.

BOOK IX

With the Guerrillas Again

1940

BOOK IX

With the Guerrillas Again.

1910

1940

With the Guerrillas Again

ONCE while resting I wrote:

> We move on. . . . A motor highway stretches before us and we hover in the forests while our soldiers fan out up and down the highway. Then we make a dash and within fifteen minutes have crossed the highway and entered a forest beyond. . . . On and on and at last we see the shadows of guerrilla sentries standing under trees. We reach the first guerrilla village on the eastern slopes of the Ta Hung Mountains. Our route is now a march of triumph — patriotic songs, laughing faces, curious eyes. . . . Night comes under candles in a large temple packed with men, women, and children, and with the staff of the Storm Guerrilla Detachment of the New Fourth Army. A long board table lit by candlelight is loaded with peanuts and small red winter turnips. Turnips are the only vegetable these people now have, and once during the long evening of speech-making, singing, and laughter I hear someone say: "Our headquarters must move to a new place; over there the turnips are bigger and redder than here."
>
> A guerrilla staff officer tells me the story of a battle at Machiachung Valley three weeks earlier. Many men were killed, including wounded soldiers, and the editor of *Chichi Pao*, the guerrilla newspaper, was captured and slain. He was Li Chang-hiang, a former member of the Agrarian Research Society of Shanghai. Now the editor is Hsia Wen-yao, a graduate of Wuhan University. The staff officer then adds:
>
> "It's remarkable what a Japanese attack can do to one! I had been sick for two weeks when it began. I got up

and before the night was finished had walked ninety *li* [thirty miles]! I've never been sick since. It cured me completely."

"It's adrenalin," I reply. "I myself could do with a little machine-gunning, for I've been ill."

"You'll be cured here!" he laughs.

Well, I soon found that I was once more with a group of men to whom knowledge was as important as guns. The *Chi-chi Pao* called a conference to which almost everyone came. They sent me the list of subjects I was expected to discuss and my heart sank into my cotton cloth shoes. They included (1) the present European war, (2) Soviet-Finnish hostilities, (3) Chinese-American relations, (4) the present military situation in China, (5) relations between the Chinese political parties, and (6) suggestions for improvement.

The women leaders of the guerrillas — one of them a military commander known as "Big Sister Chen" — also informed me that they were calling a conference of women from eleven districts in the enemy rear and that I would be expected to speak on the international woman's movement and the achievements of Chinese women in the war. And I would be asked, of course, to "guide them"!

The letters began to trickle in from that vast guerrilla belt north of Hankow, urging me to visit the regiments in the field and participate in the mass educational campaign preceding the "first democratic elections of lower officials in the enemy rear." I would be expected, as a citizen of a democratic country, to lecture before civilian mass meetings on democracy and attend delegate conferences before the final elections. Two magistrates also invited me to visit their districts and lecture to their Self-Defense Corps. One signed himself "Shong Yi, your 70-year-old friend."

On the heels of these came a letter from a sailor, chief of the secret anti-Japanese civilian organization known as the "Ten-Man Group," informing me that some 100,000 civilians had been organized in the enemy rear and would soon hold a delegate conference in the lake regions northwest of Hankow at which I would be expected to speak about everything on earth. With the letter came five cartons of captured Japanese cigarettes, a Japanese flag, five beautiful new Japanese notebooks, a bottle of ink, and a Japanese woman's silk kimono!

For nearly three months I marched and talked and marched and talked. The snow fell and piled in drifts; the Japanese came and fought us; we moved at night and slept during the day while armed civilians guarded every path for miles around. One black night in a freezing, penetrating rain I skirted a Japanese-occupied town, crossed a Japanese-patrolled highway, and made my way to a guerrilla hospital in which two hundred men lay wounded. To prevent the Japanese from discovering it, the hospital moved once or twice a week. The only "doctor" was a Miss Li, a qualified nurse graduated from an American Baptist mission hospital in north China. She had trained a dozen men and women and with their help performed major operations, disinfecting everything perfectly and enforcing the most rigid rules of sanitation. She dressed in a shabby soldier's uniform, rode from village to village, and hid her small supply of medicine in a mountain cave. I rode with her and began to believe that there were indeed miracles on this earth.

While I was in this hospital, the guerrillas told me of a young Irish Catholic priest in Shuihsien, the most strongly fortified Japanese city in the region. He had often helped the guerrillas, had protected Chinese civilians, and had just distributed free rice to thousands of villagers outside the occupied city. I wanted to meet him. One night while I lay ill with bronchitis in the home of a landlord who helped the guerrillas, I wrote an invitation to the priest to visit me if he dared leave the Japanese-occupied town. A civilian took my note, and on a stormy night, while guerrillas fought a column of Japanese along the highway just three miles from where I lay, the priest walked fifteen miles and arrived at dawn bearing presents of medicine, three cans of Australian butter, and some sugar.

I got up and together we rode to the village where the

guerrilla wounded lay. I had already given all my money to the hospital; the priest gave all he had — fifty Chinese dollars. Many of the wounded still lacked coverings. The priest was so affected that he left at once to get help in Shuihsien, where his Church had a small hospital.

At the Shuihsien city gate the Japanese guard ordered him, as was the custom, to remove his hat and stand with head bowed for half an hour. The guard then slapped him in the face and allowed him to enter. After the young priest had slept a few hours, he presented my appeal to a large Protestant hospital in the city, asking for medical supplies and pleading with the hospital's Chinese doctor to come and help. The missionaries sent me only one pound of boric acid, and a bottle of medicine for myself. The Chinese doctor refused to come. He had only recently gone to Tientsin and brought back a wife — all with Japanese permission.

The priest returned to his own mission and practically looted it of its medical supplies. He put such substances as anti-tetanus toxin in the bottom of cocoa tins and covered them with cocoa. Underneath his clothing he had wrapped his body with surgical gauze. When everything was ready, he packed his supplies in four big bamboo baskets and covered them with cabbage leaves and turnips. Two Chinese servants from his hospital lifted them on carrying-poles and they all waited in a shop near the gate of the city until the Japanese changed guards. During an interval of four or five minutes the gates remained unguarded. Within this period the priest, carrying his hat respectfully in his hand, walked through, the two carriers following.

After he had delivered his precious gifts, we rode to guerrilla headquarters, where he remained as a guest for three days. To protect him the guerrillas spread rumors everywhere that an American doctor from Chungking had arrived.

One night the guerrillas selected some fifty of their leaders, pledged to secrecy, and we all gathered around two long boards on which a feast of rice, turnips, and peanuts was spread. It seemed like a glorious dinner, and after we had eaten and made speeches in praise of freedom, we sang the songs of our countries. In a strange, strong, metallic voice the priest sang first a Chinese song and then the Irish Soldier's Song. The Koreans gave us the beautiful *Song of Ariran*, which Nym Wales later immortalized. An Annamese who had been with the guerrillas for years raised his voice in a revolutionary song of Indo-China, and four Chinese-Malay boys, one of them from Java and three from Singapore, sang songs in Malayan. Then we all rose for the *Vanguard Marching Song*.

At the end of three days the priest crept back to his mission station, removing his hat and standing respectfully before the Japanese as he entered.

My Chinese Son

WHEN I first reached the Storm Guerrilla Detachment of the New Fourth Army, a *hsiao kwei*, or "little devil," was assigned to serve me as orderly. The woman reporter who accompanied me was similarly provided. Although this was the custom of the guerrilla armies, I still had to face an old problem — not only of having a child serve me, but of exposing children to battle.

Children have taken part in people's revolutions in all lands and in all periods. They had taken part in China's 1911 revolution and in the "great revolution" of 1925–7. When the civil wars began in China in 1927, the rising Red Army had faced this problem on a mass scale, for thousands of young boys entered their ranks and sometimes whole families of men, women, and children fought with the soldiers.

As in the main New Fourth Army, these children were given such light work as bringing hot water each morning, keeping clean the room of an officer or political leader, and carrying messages. For a number of hours each day they had to study reading and writing or attend classes. From orderly they "graduated" to guard or soldier, and many of them later became commanders in the field. With them an entirely new force entered Chinese society — a force that had grown up in a world of war and was literally rooted in revolutionary consciousness.

In many ways this was a sad phenomenon, yet I could see no other path for these children to follow. If Army life was too rigorous for children, it was still not half so bad as their fate in factories and small workshops. With the exception of those in well-to-do families, China's children bore the brunt of all the storms of misfortune that swept the country.

Time and again I heard foreigners in China declare that the *hsiao kwei* in the guerrilla armies were kept by the officers for homosexual purposes. These were stories invented by diseased minds. It may be said that I am naïve or that I was lied to; but few things can be hidden in an army: its life is communal; it is, in truth, the greatest goldfish-bowl of them all. There is absolutely nothing that Chinese soldiers do not gossip about; war conditions them to utter frankness, and even if one man lies to you, the next will tell you the truth.

The *hsiao kwei* assigned to me was typical of most of the "little devils" who joined the guerrillas. His name was Shen Kuo-hwa, and though he said he was ten or eleven years old — he did not know which — he looked much younger. With that curious wisdom of China's children, he told me that he was small because he had never had enough to eat and had been sick so much when he was a "beggar boy." That was long ago, he explained, when he was "very little." Bandits had fallen upon his poor home in Honan, burning it to the ground, killing his father, and injuring his mother. His two elder brothers had both joined the Army to make a living, and after this disaster he had become a beggar boy to earn money to support himself and his mother.

He could not remember how old he had been at that time. His mother had told him to take a bowl and stand in front of a rich man's house. So he had toddled out and stood before a big house all day long. Since he did not know how to whine and cry out or beat his head in the dust, no one paid the least attention to him. Only at the end of the day did a man who was coming out of the house ask him why he didn't go home. Kuo-hwa told the man that his house had been burned, his father killed, and his mother hurt. He himself was a beggar, he explained. The man gave him some coppers and sent him away.

When the snow fell and the wind howled, the woman reporter and our two little orderlies often remained in my room all day long because I was one of the few persons in the Detachment for whom a charcoal fire was provided. Like every soldier in the detachment, the two children had lice. One day I decided to delouse them. While they bathed in a small wooden tub in the corner of the room, I heated the fire tongs red-hot in the coals, then drew them down the wet inner seams of their uniforms. When Kuo-hwa had bathed, he came up in all his naked innocence and stood by the table watching me, talking all the while about the years before he joined the guerrillas.

"All the *lao pei hsing* (common people) have lice in winter time," he said. "I had them when I was a beggar boy and when I worked for the big landlord. If you have just a few lice, you have to scratch all the time. But if you have very many you no longer itch, but get a headache which does not go away. Yesterday another soldier died of this louse sickness. While he was dying many, many lice crawled off his body into the straw."

Kuo-hwa took the lack of medical care entirely for granted. When he had been a beggar boy, he said, he himself had often been ill. He would simply lie down somewhere until he felt better. Sometimes people had set their dogs on him, and one dog had bitten him on his leg, leaving a long scar.

"I'm afraid of dogs," he added. "I'm afraid they'll catch me." He had a scar on his left cheek, but that was a result of the time when the bandits had burned down his home.

Having no conception of time, Kuo-hwa did not know how long he had been a beggar. He had watched the "rich little boys" go to school, because they had thrown stones at him. He wanted to study, but found he could not because he was not "rich." By tracing in the dust the inscriptions he saw on scraps of paper he had learned to write such simple things as "one, two, three," but after that the numerals were too difficult. When he had asked people to teach him to write his name, they had laughed and asked why a beggar boy should want to learn to write. He had learned to write his name only after he had joined the guerrillas.

He must have been about six years old when his mother got a small landlord to guarantee him to a big landlord as a reliable cow herd. The landlord paid him eighty Chinese cents a year and gave him food, shelter, and the coats and trousers occasionally thrown away by his own sons. When he was paid each New Year's, the child gave his mother the eighty cents, and she bought cloth and made him the shoes he used during the winter.

When I was finished delousing Kuo-hwa's uniform, he put it on. Then he said to me: "You are both my father and my mother."

I drew him to me, held him between my knees, combed his hair, and helped him button his jacket. This embarrassed him a little, for no one had ever done it before. He was supposed to take care of me, not I of him.

The Army was everything to Kuo-hwa, it was his Rock of Ages, and he gave it credit for everything he had learned. But, he explained, he had not been with it very long — only a year now — and thus he had a great deal still to learn. Listening to him talk, with his small melancholy face turned up to me, the woman reporter exclaimed in a low voice: "What an existence!"

As Kuo-hwa talked, the wind wailed outside. He went to the window and peeked through the hole in the paper stretched across the frame. The storm would not last long now, he assured us, for when the wind sounded like that and the snow lay on the earth as it did, the storm would soon stop. That he had learned by watching many storms while he worked for the rich landlord.

We asked him how he had come to join the guerrillas. He had once been sent into Kioshan, on the Peking-Hankow railway, he said, and had stopped to watch an army of soldiers march through. Then suddenly he had seen one of his brothers among them! But this had been his "bad brother," he explained, his "good brother" having been killed in the battle at Marco Polo Bridge at the beginning of the war. His "bad brother" talked with him, but would not give him or his mother any money. Instead, he called Kuo-hwa a fool for working for eighty cents a year and advised him to get a job that paid good money.

From the soldiers Kuo-hwa had heard talk about the Eighth Route Army. It was a good Army, a poor man's Army, the soldiers said. Officers could not beat or curse the soldiers, and everyone learned to read and write and there were clubs and singing groups. Kuo-hwa asked where he could find this "poor man's Army" because, he explained to the soldiers, he himself was a poor man and would like to join it. They laughed at him and told him the Army was far, far away. So he went out and asked a policeman, but the man only shook him and said that the Eighth Route Army was made up of bandits.

Shortly after, he came across a bearded old soldier dressed in a shabby military uniform, and asked him the same question. The old soldier, named Wang Lao-han, also said that Kuo-hwa was too little to join an army, but that the Eighth Route was months away if you walked straight north. Then old Wang added that he himself came from a poor man's army and that it was not far away. It was the Storm Guerrilla Detachment. The old man laughed at Kuo-hwa's announcement that he was going to join the guerrillas. "Do you know," replied the old man, "that the guerrillas live a bitter life, with little food and poor clothing, that they march and fight all the time, and that sometimes they get no money at all?"

For one whole day Kuo-hwa dogged the footsteps of Wang, and all day long the little fellow pleaded his case: because of too little food and too much sickness he was smaller than he should be, but he didn't want to get rich and he could walk long distances and carry heavy burdens . . . here the landlord's servants beat him and made him do much of their work . . . and no one would help him write even his own name. . . . Finally, at the end of the day, Wang Lao-han grew so weary that he said Kuo-hwa might go with him and try out the guerrilla life. Kuo-hwa followed him into the mountains, and since then he had been an orderly.

The woman reporter often sat with the two children, helping them with their lessons. Each of the boys had a small primer written and published by the detachment itself. It began with the words "man" or "human being," and went on to "worker," "peasant," and "soldier," then to the name of the Army, the name of the Japanese Army, and so on to sentences. Across the bottom of each page was a question for discussion. Some of these read:

"A peasant produces rice, a worker weaves cloth. Why can't the peasant eat the rice he produces and the weaver wear the clothes he weaves?" . . . "Why is there a distinction between the rich and the poor?" . . . "Why are both the rich and the poor anti-Japanese today?" . . . "What prevents human beings from relying on each other?" . . . "Why is the Japanese Army the most cruel on earth?"

It was such questions, I feel, that were accountable for much of the opposition to the Eighth Route and New Fourth Armies.

"When I grow up I want to join the cavalry and fight the Japanese," Kuo-hwa said to me more than once. And each time I thought of lice and typhus and wondered if he would live to become a man, to lead poor men into battle.

Soon I had an opportunity to join a platoon of troops going to join a field regiment in the lake regions to the northwest of Hankow. The woman reporter decided to go with me, but we both felt it would be dangerous to take our *hsiao kwei* with us. Yet when I thought of leaving them behind, I could not shake off the memories of the lice and the relapsing fever that menaced them constantly. When I told

Kuo-hwa that I was leaving, he seemed to be struggling to keep from crying. I could not endure it and wrote a request to the detachment commander asking for permission to take the child with me. Kuo-hwa took the message and shot away like a streak of light, but I later heard from the commander that he did not really deliver it. Instead, he popped into the room of the commander, saluted, and announced that I wanted him to go with me! The commander was somewhat surprised, but the boy stood his ground. He argued that he had often marched with the Army all night long, carrying heavy loads. Furthermore, he pleaded, I needed him because he knew all my habits and needs.

The commander replied that since I really wished it, Kuo-hwa could of course go with me. The child asked him to write this down, and soon came running back with the written permission. I was surprised, but thought that the Army knew what it was doing.

So I took Kuo-hwa with me into the lake regions. On the third night out we stopped at a village about five miles from the motor highway which we planned to cross at midnight. A group of new volunteers, as yet without arms, had gathered to join us in the village, and a number of travelers carrying bundles were also waiting for us; for the highway was used by the Japanese to send reinforcements up to the Ta Hung mountain front, and they had established garrisons in all the larger villages near by.

When the darkness was deep enough, we lined up to march. A number of peasants had gathered to see off their sons who had volunteered. I remember one old woman standing on a little knoll, wiping the tears from her eyes, and a young woman with a baby in her arms who kept running by the side of one of the men and crying: "Come back as soon as you can!" And then out of a house on the outskirts of the village we heard an Amazonian voice bawling the name of a youth. Before the woman reached us we were already marching rapidly, but she caught up with us and ran up and down the column, peering into the face of each man. We learned that her son had run away to join the guerrillas and she was trying to find him. But not a sound came from our marching column, and long after we had left her behind we heard her voice wailing in the night.

A few hours later we skirted the walls of a village, intending to cross the highway beyond, but just as we came within sight of the road, we stopped dead in our tracks. There, about a hundred yards ahead of us, were a dozen or more Japanese soldiers, rifles slung across their backs, standing around a huge bonfire in front of a building. As we watched, several Japanese came out of the building with tables and chairs and threw them on the fire. Then they all stood about, warming themselves contentedly.

We drew back behind the village walls and the guerrillas put their heads together and began whispering. The woman reporter and I joined them. They were planning to wipe out the Japanese! We both protested. We had just passed a Japanese garrison a mile away, we argued, and they would come out and attack us from the rear. We also pointed out that we did not know how many more Japanese were inside the house or what their equipment was. We had no more than twenty-five rifles and one machine-gun, and the machine-gun had only two dozen cartridges.

Finally we persuaded them to make a short detour and cut in toward the highway a few hundred yards away. The woman reporter and I were both riding our horses. Just as we approached the highway we heard the roar of approaching motor trucks. Immediately a wild whisper fled down the column ordering everyone to run and all non-fighters to get into the shelter of the hills. I saw the small figure of Kuohwa speeding across the highway ahead of me. In the darkness and confusion my horse dashed out to the end of a low, half-destroyed bridge, crouched and sprang. We landed on a road in the midst of figures scurrying in every direction. My muleteer grabbed the bit of my horse and ran toward the rice-fields. Ahead of me were three of the new volunteers in long gowns, running as I had seldom seen men run, and my muleteer kept whispering fiercely: "Beat the horse! Beat the horse! The enemy is coming!"

We went over an embankment in one leap and out over the dark fields, while from behind us bullets began singing to the stars, hand-grenades burst, and a machine-gun rattled. We heard the engines of enemy motor trucks grind to a stop, then one of them roar on down the highway.

"Stop!" I cried to the men. "The enemy isn't coming! We will get lost!"

"Beat the horse!" gasped the muleteer from behind me, and ran farther. I began to feel like a coward. We were abandoning our men, and I was the only one of our group with even a small pistol! I flung myself from the saddle and struggled with the terrified muleteer.

"We must go back! We must find our men!" I cried.

Through his hard breathing I heard the strange singing of the bullets.

"The devils! The devils!" he gasped, but ceased struggling. I grasped his hand and we led the horse behind the towering grave-mound of some rich man of old. Two of the volunteers had already disappeared.

The fighting had died down and all was as silent as the dead. There was no moon and only the stars gave a faint light. My horse began to champ the grass at our feet and the volunteer whispered: "Your horse is white and the enemy can see! He is eating grass and the enemy can hear!" With these words he turned and disappeared into the darkness.

My muleteer, now perfectly calm, whispered: "Now what?"

"Wait," I answered, and leaving him behind the grave-mound I crawled to the summit, lay down on my stomach, and in the darkness watched for any sign of movement. Nothing moved. Beyond was the dark outline of the hills along the highway. I strained my ears for any human sound; when none came I went down the hill and said: "I'll give the guerrilla signal."

"No! No!" cried the muleteer. "The devils may know it!"

"I *must!*" I said in desperation, and crawled up the hillock again, lay down, raised my hands, and clapped softly. No answer came back. I tried again, this time a little louder, and heard whispered protests behind me. No reply! I clapped again sharply, and from far away a cautious signal answered. I tried again and it was repeated. I grabbed my muleteer by the hand and my horse by the bridle and began to drag them in the direction of the signal. The muleteer kept saying: "It may be the enemy!" We moved forward, cautiously giving the signal at intervals and hearing the answer drawing ever nearer. Soon we were very near. We stopped short and stepped behind our horse. I drew out my pistol, released the safety catch, and waited.

Out of the darkness in front of us came three dark shadows. "Password!" they demanded harshly and we saw their rifles trained upon us.

"Asses!" cried the muleteer in wild joy, and ran toward them and fell upon their necks.

The three guerrillas slung their rifles back over their shoulders and, laughing, gave me pats of joy that almost knocked me down.

"We got 'em! We got 'em!" they cried, and holding hands, we walked across the rice-fields. One of them whistled softly in pure joy, broke off, and laughed: "Ai-yoh! When my hand-grenade landed right in the body of that truck, did the devils scatter! Did they scatter!" He turned to another and said: "Now listen here, remember that when a truck is running, you must not throw your hand-grenade right *at* it, but *ahead* of it! That's the reason we failed to get that first goddam truck!"

"Ta Ma Di!" the other cursed. "Of course our machine-gun had to jam! It couldn't wait until later. And of course we had to have only one."

Cursing the machine-gun and making uncomplimentary remarks about the mothers of Japanese soldiers, we finally reached a market town three miles from the highway. Here the Japanese had established a puppet government, but without troops, and every puppet was one of our men. The whole government came out to welcome us, and its chief stood in the midst of our troops talking excitedly.

As we came into the village I was surprised to see Kuo-hwa standing by like a lost soul. As soon as he saw me he ran to me, placed his two small hands on my arm, and stood in perfect silence looking up into my face. When the order had been given for us to scatter, he had fled with the woman reporter and a young poet, Loh Fan, who had become my assistant. But when he had learned that I had disappeared, he had begun running about in the darkness crying out, asking if the devils had caught me. The woman reporter had taken him by the hand and told him to be silent, but he had said that he *must* go and search for me, that I would answer to his voice, but no other. When they told him he was a child and would get lost, he ceased crying, looked around at the hills and trees, and answered: "I will find her and come back! When she came to our Army, they told me to serve her and said I must take care of her. It is my duty."

A heavy fog from the lakes that stretch for miles to the west and northwest of Hankow blanketed the earth, and at dawn we began marching onward through it. We passed villages from which all people had fled, thinking we might be Japanese clad in Chinese uniforms. As the light increased and the fog lifted we entered a market town on the shores of a great lake. Only three or four old men and women and a few children remained behind; all the rest of the population had rowed far out on the bosom of the lake. One of the old women took a huge brass gong, beat it, and bawled like a foghorn to the people on the lake: "Come back! Come back!"

They came back and gathered about us in joy, but their excitement was greatest when they saw me. They gathered about me in crowds and I heard men trying to decide whether I was a man or a woman, American, German, or English. One woman pulled back her little child in fear and declared: "She has eyes like a cat!"

My little Kuo-hwa could not endure this. He stood up before them and cried: "She does *not* have eyes like a cat! She is a woman and our American friend! She helps our wounded! In Tingjiachun she found a wounded man and fed him and gave him a bath. She even helped him do all his business."

The people turned their eyes on me in amazement. My "son" would not stop. "Look at her bandaged hand!" he demanded, taking my hand in his. "She got this when she picked up a pan of hot water while she was bathing a wounded soldier. She is both my father and my mother! If any of you are sick, she will cure you."

When at last I decided to leave the Storm Guerrillas, the thought of typhus or relapsing fever haunted me, and I decided to adopt Kuo-hwa as my son — if the detachment and he himself were willing. True, I argued with myself, he was not the only one. But in west China, I had learned, an American-trained professor of child education had established a school that laid great emphasis on science. The life was austere and the children did all their own work, and for relatively little money the children were well fed and clothed. I questioned very much the desirability of having a foreigner bringing up a Chinese child and perhaps thereby isolating him from his own people. Yet I allowed my mind to stray to some far-off time when I might even be able to send Kuo-hwa to a foreign country for advanced scientific studies. But my own life was so dreadfully insecure and uncertain, dare I undertake such a project? I would try.

So I went to Li Hsien-nien, the commander of the Storm Guerrillas and, while many men stood about, talked with him about adopting Kuo-hwa. Li had once been a Red Army commander and before that a carpenter; life had been bitter for him and for his people, and individuals must have seemed of little importance to him. When he asked me why I wished to adopt Kuo-hwa, I tried to give my reasons a scientific basis. The child had a scientific turn of mind, I argued, and I mentioned his observations of lice, of wind and snow, the way he learned to read and write so quickly, and how he could tell the directions from the stars at night. Good, Li Hsien-nien said, I could adopt the boy if I wished and if the boy himself consented.

A burly fellow leaning against the door-frame remarked that he could do all the things I said Kuo-hwa could do. And he felt certain that he knew much more about lice. Would I like to adopt him too? Li Hsien-nien smiled dryly and added that it wouldn't be a bad idea for me to adopt the whole lot of them! The conversation became a little rowdy.

But it was a very serious matter with Kuo-hwa. He asked me about the school in west China and said he was afraid of rich little boys. He belonged to the Army, he explained. I argued that he might try the school for a time, and then return to the Army and teach others what he had learned. The Army needed teachers, I urged. He thought in silence, then asked to be allowed to talk it over with the other little orderlies. The following day he came in with another orderly and gave me his decision.

"We think all men must remain at the front," he said. "You can adopt me after the final victory."

We could not sway him.

But before leaving the lake region I arranged for my "son" to join the Children's Dramatic Corps of the Storm Guerrillas. A young woman teacher was in charge of the corps, which spent half the day in study and the other half writing and rehearsing patriotic dramas, songs, and folk-dances which were to be presented to soldiers and civilians.

As the small boat which was to take me out of the lake regions pulled away from the shore, I saw Kuo-hwa for the last time. He and two other boys stood on the bank, washing their clothes in the waters of the lake. He cried to me and waved, then stood perfectly still, watching as my boat disappeared into the mist.

Storm Guerrillas and Salt-Miners

DOWN in the dreary lake regions which stretch for miles and miles to the northwest and west of Hankow, regions in which the annual floods of the Han River force hundreds of thousands to live on small boats for months at a time, we were both hunters and hunted. There I spent weeks with the 4th Regiment of the Storm Guerrilla Detachment, living in a nightmarish world. In addition to their own activities, the guerrillas had called to life that vast underground civilian organization the "Ten-Man Group," and together they hunted their enemies like bloodhounds.

The 4th Regiment was one of the six guerrilla units of a detachment which was separated by thousands of miles from the New Fourth Army, but bore its name — perhaps because the New Fourth had been legally constituted by the Government while the Storm Guerrillas had not. Three or four guerrilla detachments in the Fifth War Zone had official status, but the "Storm Guerrillas" continued to function only because no Chinese force had so far been willing or able to wipe them out. I had taken this fact lightly while in General Chang Tze-chung's headquarters; but once in a contested zone, it sometimes seemed that beside this internal problem the Japanese threat was only a sideshow.

Each regiment of the Storm Guerrillas had its own peculiarities: the 4th was composed primarily of peasants and artisans from the one-time Chinese Soviets. This whole territory had been the "storming ground" of Ho Lung, commander of the old Second Red Army Corps and now commander in the Eighth Route. Here the Communists laid a foundation of Marxian thought and a machinery for resistance which years of ruthless Kuomintang control had suppressed but not destroyed. The Communists always looked upon the region as theirs — and the Kuomintang did too. Each side knew all the moves made by the other.

Even when the Japanese hammered at the doors of Hankow in 1938, the Kuomintang refused to permit this old Soviet region to be mobilized or the people armed for guerrilla warfare. The Communists argued that an armed people would make it impossible for the Japanese to consolidate their base around Hankow, but the Kuomintang knew that an armed people would also be a permanent danger to itself. The Communists were called "insincere."

When the Government armies retreated before the Japanese around Hankow, many sick, wounded, and exhausted Chinese soldiers dropped or threw away their guns as they moved westward. The civilians who had once fought for the Soviets, gathered up and hid these guns — although bandits gathered others and became a menace almost as fearful as the Japanese.

As official Chinese authority disappeared under the Japanese tide of conquest, Chinese Communist organizers began to filter into the region, knocking on doors at night. And well did they know every door! The chief of these organizers was a thin, restless man named Tao Chu. With his tousled hair and his mustache he did not look Chinese at all. He worked secretly with a young man named Tsai, heir to some salt mines near occupied Yingchen. Tsai was a capitalist, but he had been educated in Peiping and had become imbued with modern thought. While the old merchants in the Chamber of Commerce in Yingchen formed the puppet government for the Japanese, Tsai called upon the miners from his own and other mines to fight the enemy. A few hundred of his workers followed him. They were given guns salvaged by the people, and Tsai used his fortune to finance them. Eventually the young capitalist became the Communist commander of the 5th Guerrilla Regiment, and I frequently saw him striding about in a captured Japanese coat, sharing the same fate as everyone else.

The 5th Guerrilla Regiment often joined the 4th to make assault on some puppet army or Japanese garrison, and at such times I had an opportunity to talk with the salt-miners. They were like no other men on earth. Once I put my arm across the shoulders of a lad whom I took for a child, a "little devil"; but when the "child" looked up I saw the sad, lined face of a mature man.

The salt-mine tunnels around Yingchen were so low that only children could work in them, and even they could hardly stand upright while working. Many began to work at the age of seven or eight, and spent their lives digging salt. Naked in the hot tunnels, they often remained in the mines for weeks at a time, sleeping and eating underground.

The owners fed them and paid them a wage of about twenty coppers a day — although the children never knew when a day began and when it ended. They worked until exhausted, and they told me that foremen with little whips crawled along the tunnels to beat those who fell asleep.

Because of this slave existence, the bodies and minds of the salt-miners were undeveloped. They followed Tsai against the Japanese because he was the owner who clothed and fed them — to them it was only another kind of work. Once, in the early months after Hankow fell, they demanded higher wages, refusing to fight if he did not pay. He explained that all his wealth was being used to support them and other guerrilla units; but they did not understand. If they could get more money elsewhere, why not, they thought. So the first months had been filled with confusion and despair, whole companies of salt-mine guerrillas going over to the Japanese or their puppets, then later coming back to bargain with Tsai.

But most of them eventually remained with the guerrillas. By the time I arrived in the region, they had become a pillar of resistance, and wherever any new guerrilla unit needed a backbone, units of salt-miners were sent to stiffen it. I watched them curiously. The casual, uncomplicated spirit which distinguishes men who have enjoyed a normal childhood and youth was a stranger to them. They were gray and grim. They did not know how to play. They had learned to sing — but only fierce songs of revolution.

Shortly after my arrival in the guerrilla region I witnessed the founding of the 6th Regiment of the Storm Guerrillas, and it was almost as strange in origin as the salt-miners' regiment. Fifteen hundred men who before the war had been the Peace Preservation Corps of Yingchen and had transferred their allegiance to the Japanese-controlled puppet government after the fall of Hankow, came over to the Storm Guerrillas. They had never been real puppets, for their officers, the chief of whom had been a foreman in the salt mines, had kept the guerrillas informed of all orders issued to him by the Japanese. For a year and a half they had walked a tight-rope until, fully armed, they had at last mutinied.

The guerrillas received the new regiment in a night mass meeting at which all the leaders spoke, and at which I told the amazed mutineers why foreign people supported China instead of Japan. Some of the new officers had exceptionally alert and handsome faces, but I had the impression that they had not quite made up their minds. The Storm Guerrilla commanders assured and reassured them — too much I thought — that they did not have to be Communists to belong to the detachment.

During this very meeting a peasant messenger arrived with a letter to the Storm Guerrilla Detachment. When the commander opened it he found it to be from a Japanese officer who was urging the whole detachment to mutiny and join the Japanese. The letter read in part:

> I am a Japanese Colonel and I feel very sorry about the war between China and Japan. I am a man of East Asia; you are men of East Asia. Why, now, do we men of the same race wage war? My Empire is now building a happy world in which Japan, Manchuria, and China will go forward together. . . .
>
> Open your eyes and look at the condition of the world. Russia, France, England, and America are all occupied with their own affairs and are at odds. They have no time to think of China. Why does your Army not realize this? Look at the condition of the Chinese armies that come over to us. They are very happy. Hand in hand with the Japanese Army they are rebuilding East Asia. . . .
>
> I will wait for you in Pinglingshih. If your representative comes to me there, I will not kill him. . . .

It was dated January 23, 1940, bore a seal, and was signed by Ta Nieh Pan Tze, a Colonel of the Empire.

The guerrilla commanders laughed contemptuously and announced that they would meet the Colonel's troops in their own way and at a time and place of their own choosing. It might be by night or by day — he would certainly not know in advance. And they would return from the rendezvous with guns and ammunition.

Shortly after this incident I sent two plain-clothes guerrillas through the Japanese lines to Hankow with letters to friends and to the International Red Cross Committee, reporting on the desperate need for medical supplies in the guerrilla region and asking for Chinese doctors and nurses. My messengers delivered the letters safely. Two foreign friends, one of them a young missionary, pounded the streets of Hankow trying in vain to induce the International Red Cross Committee to grant my requests. They refused, fearing, like timid rabbits, that the Japanese would learn about it. So my friends took up a collection and bought quinine, disinfectants, and gauze. But there was no cholera vaccine.

My friends also sent personal gifts to me, including a box of such American magazines as *Time, Life,* and the *New Yorker.* Scattered among them were small match-books. Chinese matches were really poor things, and the American matches with blue heads and a tiny white dot on the end sent the guerrillas ah-ing and oh-ing.

All of these precious gifts had been protected by my friends in a covering letter, in case the Japanese should capture my messengers. This letter consigned the stuff to

> Miss Betsy Ross
> Mission of the Latter-Day Saints
> Tanyang, Hupeh

I sat in my small boat on the Chao Lakes and laughed at the letter. Only I could understand the humorous implications in the address; and the enclosed letter was a marvel of disguised information. Respectable Americans in Hankow were learning a great deal about secret conspiracy.

This was the first personal letter I had received for nearly a year, and it lit a small flame within my heart. The shipment was so unusual that many small guerrilla sampans — some with machine-guns — drew up and tied themselves to our cluster of boats. Copies of *Life* began to circulate, the guerrillas staring over one another's shoulders at the pictures.

I ran through the magazines to see what new books were out, what plays were being given in New York City, and what was new in the medical world. Then with pleasant anticipation I took up the *New Yorker* and scanned the "Talk of the Town" and "Ho Hum" sections. But my sense of humor seemed to have changed, for all the notes meant to be so wise and witty seemed to me incredibly thin and trivial.

The guerrillas asked me to explain the advertisements and photographs and I began to scan the "Christmas shopping" pages. Here was a fur coat that could be bought for the trifling sum of $1,500 — or up! . . . Here were motor cars, houses, necklaces, sets of silver, bed linen — all at fabulous prices. Here was "Vampire Perfume" at $100 a bottle. *Life* seemed to be filled exclusively with photographs of women in bathing suits. These photographs staggered the guerrillas and I did not know how to explain them.

My friends in Hankow had been able to collect only six hundred Chinese dollars to buy medical supplies for a region in which millions of people suffered from malaria, dysentery, typhoid, and in which cholera epidemics killed thousands each year. Sitting in that little boat under a lowering sky and staring at these American magazines, it suddenly seemed that I could not endure the contrast between America and China.

Traitors and Patriots

OCCASIONALLY members of the Ten-Man Group and the guerrillas brought in supplies taken from enemy boats along the Han River. The guerrillas would set up machine-guns along the bank, fire a few shots, and order the boats to shore. If the enemy refused, his boats were often riddled and sunk.

I once saw men bring in the cargo of eight enemy junks.

It consisted of hundreds of pounds of brown sugar, five-gallon tins of American gasoline and kerosene, bolts of cotton cloth, and a vast variety of such miscellaneous stuff as paper, notebooks, cheap fountain pens, and ink. There were also a few hundred pairs of flannel underdrawers and the usual Japanese flags. These flags were a drug on the market in the enemy rear; some of the better ones saw service as curtains or table covers, but many were used just to wrap up bundles. The choicest part of this haul was crates of fine Japanese cigarettes in delicate cream and gold cases engraved with the word "Reward." These had been intended as gifts from the Japanese Emperor to his troops in China. They had short pipe-stems, somewhat like the tips of Russian cigarettes. We smoked them for weeks, making facetious remarks every time we offered one to a friend.

The guerrillas got all their uniform-cloth from the enemy, which explained why some of the units looked like beds of peonies. They were dressed in black, green, blue, and various shades of gray, and once I saw about a dozen of them sporting the white flannel drawers.

Chinese traitors were brought in every week, and in the middle of February I talked with twenty puppet soldiers who had been captured in a battle between the guerrillas and a puppet army commanded by Wang Bu-ching. The captured puppet soldiers were sad-eyed, dreary-looking men who said they had been forced into the puppet army. After the capture of Hankow, one said, the Japanese had come to his village in Hwangpei and burned it to the ground. Hearing that coolies were wanted to build a Chinese railway, he and five friends had gone to a Chinese recruiting agent; they were led up the Han River to Chujhushan and then told they were in Wang Bu-ching's army. They knew nothing at all about political matters, but Commander Wang had delivered a speech in which he said that his chief, Wang Ching-wei, had really been sent by Generalissimo Chiang Kai-shek to make peace with the Japanese, and that that was why Wang Ching-wei was in Nanking. He also told them that a representative of the Central Government served in his headquarters as adviser. The soldiers said they had had no means of knowing if such things were true or not.

The guerrillas never punished such puppet captives. Instead, they gave them a little training and then asked them to join the guerrillas. The puppet commanders, who were often educated men, were treated more harshly, and some were even executed.

I often attended the military courts before which traitors were brought for examination. The chief judge in this martial court was a young officer with a long, deep scar down his left cheek — a wound from a Japanese sword. He had had some five years of regular schooling before the war had begun, but his chief education had been in the Army. Fighting in the enemy rear he had in a short time picked up what would otherwise have taken him decades to learn. Of ordinary law he knew nothing, but he knew patriots, he knew traitors, and he knew politicians who would be traitors if they could.

One day I saw two prisoners brought into the courtroom. One was a short, degenerate-looking creature about thirty years of age, sallow from opium-smoking. In his first hearing he admitted that he had owned an opium shop in Fengshuiji, a Japanese-occupied town, and that while his brother tended the shop he went into the countryside to gather military information about the guerrillas for the Japanese. He had been paid by the piece — five dollars for each item of information. Because of this low pay, he argued that he was one of the oppressed, only a "small traitor"!

The other prisoner, a puppet chief, was in his middle forties. He was short and filthy, had a scraggly black beard, and looked as if he had not taken a bath since the outbreak of war. He wore a greasy blue gown and a small black silk cap. He bowed and smirked like a slave, a habit he had picked up in Fengshuiji while serving his Japanese masters. Before acquiring his high position he had been a poor man, a dealer in quack medicines. He boasted of his skill, describing himself as an "injection expert" who could cure almost any disease by aphrodisiacs or concoctions of herbs, tiger's bones, coffin nails, and snakeskins. He even argued that the guerrillas ought to take him into their medical service.

The guerrillas knew little of medicine, but they knew a great deal about traitors. They told him that if he would send a messenger to his wife and brother telling them to disgorge all the loot he had acquired since he had become a puppet chief, they might think twice before shooting him. He offered them a bribe of $1,000 and then gradually raised it to $10,000. The guerrillas said they would think about it if the money were placed in their hands. Although he had acquired his wealth by usury or by keeping the proceeds from the "Good Man" badges which those in the occupied zones were compelled to wear, he argued that his wealth was innocently won because he had received not one cent from the "Consolation Houses of the Imperial Japanese Army."

After a while a great depression seemed to settle on the man and he decided to send a messenger to order his family to give up all the loot. I argued that his family might betray the guerrillas, but the judge thought that unlikely, since it would most certainly mean the man's death. I looked at the greasy old customer and suggested that perhaps his wife would like him shot. The judge smiled a little and remarked laconically: "We will attend to that too."

Finally the witnesses were called. It was then that I learned that the chief witness, a man with a bandaged hand, was the redoubtable leader of the Ten-Man Group, he whom the Japanese called "Kan the Bandit."

The four witnesses looked much like ordinary civilians. They wore no hats and their faces were hard and brown. Yet the minute I saw "Kan" (this was not his real name), I knew he was no ordinary fellow. He wore civilian clothes, perhaps, but he walked with the quick decisive step of a military man; and there was nothing unconscious about that lean, alert face. He had all the earmarks of a patriot who would not spare his enemies. Were I a Japanese, I thought, I would arrest him on general suspicion.

I had already heard a great deal about this man. He had

been the son of a peasant of moderate means, which meant he had studied in a public school for a number of years. In his youth, like many other peasants, he had joined the Han Liu Ban, branch of an ancient peasant secret society said to have been organized to fight the Manchus who overthrew the Ming Dynasty. This organization had gradually degenerated into a cult that practiced superstitious rites not unlike those popular in American "lodges." They pledged blood brotherhood, exchanged the "eight characters of destiny," and kowtowed before burning incense. Their leaders had been given high-sounding names. When he had ruled in this region, Ho Lung, the Red Army commander, had borne the title "Double-headed Dragon."

Like many other members of the Han Liu Ban, Kan had become a Communist during the civil war. When the Red Army was defeated, he had been arrested and sentenced to seven years' imprisonment. But even fearful prison conditions had not broken his body and spirit, and when the Japanese invasion stimulated a national united front, he had been released. He had gone directly to Hankow and served as a guard in the Government military airdrome. After the Japanese had occupied Hankow, he had returned to his native haunts along the Han River and begun tapping on the doors of his Han Liu brothers, organizing them for resistance against the enemy.

When the Japanese had first occupied this vast region around Hankow, traitors had been shameless and bold, for Japanese power was great. When, however, certain puppets disappeared mysteriously or were found in their beds with knives through their hearts, the others became shaky. The name of "Kan the Bandit" got around, and the Ten-Man Group, operating right inside Japanese garrison towns, became a force to be feared.

Seeing Kan's bandaged hand, I asked about it. A few weeks before, I was told, he had, while prowling along the Han River, come upon a Japanese motor launch anchored under cover of some trees. He crept up and saw a Japanese officer and two women on the deck. He aimed a pistol and pulled the trigger, but it jammed and could not be fired. He crept close, leaped onto the launch, and grappled with the officer. In the struggle the two men tumbled into the river. They fought with their feet miring in the muddy bottom. Kan forced the Japanese under the water, and although the latter managed to sink his dagger into Kan's hand, Kan held him down and then trampled on him.

Kan then leaped onto the launch again, bound the women, and searched the boat. Within a few hours he had delivered the women and the boat's supplies to a guerrilla battalion and calmly proceeded with the work in which he had been originally engaged.

Now I listened to this same Kan and three other men testifying before the guerrilla court martial.

"This man Wang," Kan began without any formality, "is a spy connected with the enemy Special Service. He used to come into the villages and sit around gossiping, picking up what he could about the guerrillas and the Ten-Man Group. Our men began to watch him and I smoked and gossiped with him once and then followed him to his home in Fengshuiji. He lives in a house near the devils' barracks, and keeps an opium and drug shop on the ground floor. I got these three of our men to help. We had knives, because my pistol always jams. We thought —"

"Why does your pistol always jam?" the judge interrupted.

"It was buried for a year. Sometimes it shoots; sometimes it doesn't."

The court waited while the judge turned the pistol over and over, then drew out his own gun, a neat little Japanese piece, and presented it to Kan with his compliments. He would try to have the other weapon put in shape, he said. Kan examined the Japanese pistol admiringly, then returned to his testimony:

"Well, these three comrades went with me one night. We wore 'Good Man' badges and I showed Wang the Special Service papers which I had taken from that Japanese launch. I told Wang that we had proof that he was going out in the villages and selling the guerrillas information *against* the Japanese. He denied it and said he could even get the head of the puppet government to guarantee his loyalty to the Imperial Army. That gave us an idea and we went with him to the house of this other maggot here. This worm said he would guarantee Wang's good character to the Special Service. So we stuck our knives against their ribs and told them that if they so much as peeped, we'd cut them to pieces on the spot. In this way we got them outside the town and delivered them to your battalion. *Wan-la* [Finished]!"

Turning to the two prisoners, the judge asked them what they had to say. The head of the puppet government bowed from the waist, as if he were Japanese, and pleaded that he had been forced to act as head of the puppet government. Kan interrupted laconically:

"The only thing a man can be forced to do is die!"

Wang the spy again pleaded that he was but a "little traitor" with a large family to support. One of the witnesses snorted and the judge turned and asked me if I wanted to ask the prisoners any questions. "I'm new at this court business," he explained; "maybe you can help." I asked Wang where he got his opium and drugs, and the judge exclaimed in surprise: "From the Japanese, of course!" and then remembered to ask the spy to reply. The spy repeated the judge's words, but added that the Japanese charged too much — which again, he said, made him one of the oppressed!

The judge stared at him for a long time, then told him it was a crime punishable by death for any man to be a spy or to deal in opium or drugs. The spy sighed heavily and explained that he was poor and had a large family. Kan turned on the fellow, and for a moment I thought he was going to brain him with his new Japanese pistol. But he only exclaimed: "We're all poor and we all have large families; but we don't sell out our country!"

A few days later I stood outside the village and saw the two traitors shot. Villagers were not allowed to watch executions, but a small group of guerrillas gathered near me and shouted: "Death to all traitors!"

Kan had already gone on another mission. I had examined his hand before he left; the Japanese dagger had cut the nerves and the hand was paralyzed.

"It's good it was my left hand," Kan remarked. He still had a good right hand and he had a new Japanese pistol.

Some men were lucky.

Farewell!

As spring approached, the atmosphere in the enemy rear was like a threatening sword. Word came from General Chang Tze-chung that he was taking his 33rd Group Army west of the Han River for rest and replenishment and that I could reach him there. But the Chinese winter offensive was petering out. And as the offensive slackened, the Japanese began preparations for a spring counter-offensive. The roar of artillery from the mountains to our west had never ceased and the highways were an endless stream of enemy trucks carrying supplies and troops up into the mountains encircling Hankow. We knew what that would mean. Once again the mountains and the plains would run with blood. It was clear that we were all in for it.

The first elections of lower officials of towns and villages in the enemy rear had served to replace old officials with militant members of the Ten-Man Group — local schoolteachers, blacksmiths, peasants, and even a woman. "True men" the new officials were called because they had never wavered in the war, were honest, and did not smoke opium or gamble. The Ten-Man Group had finished a winter congress in which it had decided to mobilize every person in the enemy rear for the coming struggle. While the guerrillas fought, the Ten-Man Group was to train new fighters and destroy traitors.

After that, everyone went gunning for puppets. One day I saw the leader of a puppet government hustled before the guerrilla court martial, condemned to death within ten minutes, and executed within another ten. There's something dreadfully decisive about a beheading.

Within a week the guerrilla regiment with which I moved had fought three battles. We slept in our clothing and almost every midnight a warning knock at our door would send us scrambling to our feet. We would roll up our blankets and within five minutes be in small sampans out on the lakes. I sent off another messenger to Hankow with an appeal to the International Red Cross Committee for medical supplies, but knew that we would get nothing. A feeling of despair took hold of me. Malaria returned to sap my strength, and together with malnutrition it was causing my toe-nails to fall off, my teeth to loosen, my eyes to become inflamed; and a skin rash and hives sometimes made my life a torment. Yet I tried to keep my shame to myself, for all this seemed to prove that I was unable to stand what all Chinese must endure or perish.

In the middle of March I made my last trip within the enemy rear, moving across the lakes, then marching through a pouring rain to visit that very old Magistrate Shong Yi. The old man had built up a fairly strong local militia and kept on the move, trying to serve his country in his own way. I found him in Tienerhoh, a dark and dreary town which had been repeatedly attacked by Japanese raiding columns.

The old Magistrate and his *hsien* government led an exhausting life, trying to keep the wheels of Chinese administration going. They showed me a clever letter from a Japanese named Maruyama which flattered the old man's classical learning and urged him to "mount a horse and get on a platform" — that is, leave Tienerhoh and come to Hanchuan to head the puppet government. Old Shong Yi, a devout Buddhist, penned a contemptuous reply in the old classical *wen-li* poetry.

The old Magistrate had spent hours composing a report to Generalissimo Chiang Kai-shek. This he entrusted to me to take to Chungking. For I was leaving for western China, hoping to get through the Ta Hung Mountains before the enemy counter-offensive began.

That trip to the west was one of the hardest I had ever made. It took us ten days to get through the lake regions and the mountains. We traveled day and night, changing boatmen when necessary and scattering when enemy airplanes hummed overhead. At night we slept packed like fish in the bottom of our boats — five guerrillas, Loh Fan, and I, head to foot in one small boat.

Late one afternoon we reached a small island near the northern shore of the lakes and waited for darkness, intending to row to a market town about a mile away and strike across country into the foothills. But the boatmen scouts who went out returned after a few hours to say that the market town had just been occupied by the Japanese and that only one town on the whole north shore was still accessible. We could land there, but must pass two enemy garrisons before we reached the highway.

Our platoon mounted their machine-guns and we slid into the darkness. To protect ourselves from spies, we started toward the market town, but then turned sharply and rowed swiftly and silently toward the unoccupied town on the north shore. Hardly had we done this when I heard gasps from the men around me. I turned quickly and saw the island we had left illuminated by a signal flare that lit up the buildings and the sky. Traitors used such signals to warn the Japanese of danger.

Our boatmen bent feverishly over their oars, and the rest of us sat like statues, every nerve taut. But the only sound was an eerie one that came from a distant lake where some watchman was beating on hollow bamboo, telling the time.

Finally our dark boats slid up into a cove on the northern shore of the lake. We sprang out swiftly and stood motionless under a clump of trees while men went forward to scout the land. When they returned, we began walking swiftly along the winding narrow paths between the rice-fields, making our way toward the first highway.

Just before we crossed the enemy-patrolled highway we sat down to rest, leaning against the high encircling walls of a village. A fog hugged the earth around us. Glancing up at the walls above, I whispered to Loh Fan that if I were a Japanese I would occupy and use just such a village as this. Loh Fan whispered back something that men always say to women: "Now, don't get excited! Don't get panicky!"

Before I had time to retort, a sharp order to march came and Loh Fan and I began to run, grasping each other's hands to keep from falling. We fled through a dark tunnel that cut right under the highway, and continued to run until our whole column was brought to a dead stop by a guerrilla who cried out: "Look — the enemy!"

Looking back toward the highway under which we had rushed, we could see the flare of lights moving about, first on the road itself and then down in the tunnel. Clearly outlined by the lights were the moving figures of Japanese swinging flashlights and rifles. The Japanese, we realized with a shock, had been inside the walled village against which we had rested! Perhaps they had not come out to fight because they had not known how many of us there were.

The guerrillas wanted to go back and fight, but we knew the Japanese would retire behind the village walls and get reinforcements from every direction. Complaining bitterly, we continued on our way.

A few days later we left the headquarters of the Storm Guerrilla Detachment and began passing through the Ta Hung Mountains once again. An official guerrilla detachment under a commander named Tsao Sho had just occupied a long valley through which we had to pass. I became nervous as we approached this valley, for many of these "official guerrillas" had really been bandits. Tsao Sho himself was known to be Fascist in outlook and connected with the notorious Blue Shirts. He had only recently informed many people that the Minister of War of the Chinese Government had ordered both his guerrillas and the 29th Group Army to attack and annihilate the Storm Guerrilla Detachment. There seemed to be no end to the complexities of Chinese politics.

My fears seemed to be confirmed the moment we entered

the forbidden valley. Voices challenged us from the hillside and then in a trench directly in front of us we saw a row of bare heads and a line of leveled rifles. A voice demanded our name and mission. I removed my cap to show my blond hair and started forward. I was ordered to halt in my tracks. An officer with the face of a bandit took my passport and military pass and disappeared. After what seemed hours he returned and took Loh Fan and me to a village where I argued with a commander for the right to pass through the valley. The permission was granted, the officer cynically adding: "Remember — to Tsao Sho's headquarters only."

At last we reached the large village in which Commander Tsao Sho's headquarters were located. I had visited him once before in the foothills of the Ta Hung Mountains, and he had been very pleasant. But now he seemed to be mentally preparing himself for conflict with his own countrymen. In a loud voice he accused the Storm Guerrilla Detachment of inspiring democratic elections in the enemy rear and of organizing the people into Ten-Man Groups — all of which he branded as Communism. When I asked him what was wrong with democratic elections, he charged that they had been held by violence. When I declared that I had seen no violence of this kind, he would not listen.

He continued to work himself up until I began to fear that he might act against us that very night. Finally I told him that I knew that many of his guerrillas and officers had been bandits and that our party therefore had to have protection to get through the valley. To my astonishment, he admitted the charge, but added that he was trying to retrain them. At last he agreed to send a guide to take us through the mountains to the point where "his territory" ended. His last words, however, were: "It's the last time I'll grant such a request."

Even then we doubted at times that we would ever get through the valley. For hours on end we stumbled through the dark forests, tripping, falling, getting lost, clapping, and calling to each other in the night. At last we approached the small village where Tsao Sho's domain ended. Completely exhausted, we dropped onto a threshing-floor outside the village while the guide went up to the dark houses, banged on the doors, and shouted the name of his guerrilla detachment. Not a sound answered, not a light glimmered.

Finally our own commander gave the guide some cigarettes and dismissed him, telling him we would make our own way through the mountains. We all sat perfectly still and listened to the stones rolling from his path as he went farther and farther down the mountainside. Then our commander went up to one of the village doors, tapped, and called: "Comrades — open! We are Storm Guerrillas passing through the mountains. We need a guide."

A faint light showed and a moment later the heavy, weather-beaten door swung back revealing a peasant woman holding a candle and, behind her, the haggard face of a man. In another moment all the doors within sight had swung open, and men, women, and children came flocking out! Chattering freely, some began carrying rice straw into the houses to make pallets for us, while others fanned the fires under the large rice-pots. Our guerrillas hustled about, talking with the people like brothers.

BOOK X

Chungking and After

1940 — 1941

BOOK X: CHUNGKING AND AFTER

1940 ~ 1941

Chungking

THE NEWS trickled into Ichang on the Yangtze that the Japanese had blasted their way across the Han River to the plains beyond, scattering the Chinese armies like sparks from an anvil. First we heard that Shasi on the Yangtze had fallen, then that it hadn't. The Chinese had little to live on except hope, and it was not easy to admit the loss of new territory. Each spring and autumn the Japanese had moved out of their strongly prepared defenses and tried to annihilate the main Chinese armies, but never before had they crossed the Han. Then we thought the high mountain ranges guarding Ichang on the east could hold them, but soon their planes began blasting a way for troops and tanks. And Ichang was bombed.

Despite official statements that the Japanese were being beaten back, every steamer and junk going up river from Ichang was jammed with evacuees and wounded; and every mountain road was lined with refugees.

I left Ichang on a river steamer shortly before the city fell on June 11. Soon afterwards I met a Red Cross doctor who had escaped from Shasi with his staff and supplies. Of the one hundred and fifty military hospitals on the central front, he said, only five had turned up. "What about the wounded?" I asked. He said nothing and I knew the answer.

The Japanese had cut right through the 29th Group Army, commanded by General Wang Tzan-hsü, he said. That Army was still running back toward Szechuen, and General Wang had been shot by his superior officer. I recalled that, in January, dapper General Wang Tzan-hsü had boasted that he would send the Japanese scurrying back to Hankow. And in May, before the Japanese offensive had begun, he had added that he was also going to exterminate the Storm Guerrilla Detachment in the enemy rear.

My trip from Ichang through the swirling Yangtze gorges and on to the upper river was made under a perpetual air-raid alarm. The winter fogs that hover over the upper river in winter and early spring had lifted and the Japanese had begun their annual blitz raids. Every town and village along the way had already been bombed, and the British flag painted on the decks of our steamer certainly would not protect us. The lower decks were packed with wounded and everyone's nerves were ragged from the tension.

As our boat approached the Chungking pier, a Chinese official and I became engaged in a violent argument with a young Englishman who insisted on defending the Munich Pact and Chamberlain, declaring with all the ignorance of a Far Eastern Britisher: "Our old graybeards know what they are doing."

We stopped suddenly, alarmed by a dull roaring noise. It turned out to be a series of dynamite blasts set off by men preparing new tunnels under the high cliffs of Chungking. Chungking was pitted with these deep dugouts, some of them equipped with ventilating and lighting systems and capable of accommodating thousands of people. When an air-raid began, the city lay as silent as the dead, not a soul stirring except for a few soldiers ready to shoot down anyone who might give the enemy a signal. When the planes came at night we always heard the soldier guards as they fired at any flicker of light. Even after the planes were gone, Chinese planes roared low over the city, machine-gunning any light that showed before the all-clear signal sounded. And each day we saw the bloated corpses of human beings slowly floating down the river, drifting against junks, and being shoved away by boatmen with long spiked poles.

The Japanese planes would come over in three or four formations of thirty to fifty bombers each. Sometimes we would stand on the south shore enjoying an illusory sense of safety and watching the bombing of the northern city. When

I first arrived, as many as twenty-four Chinese fighter planes were going up to challenge the bombers, but as the days passed there were fewer and fewer of these. Once I saw one solitary Chinese fighter turn and go after a formation of bombers coming up river. At such a moment I longed for the ability to write just one deathless poem to that little plane.

Sometimes the incendiaries landed in the Yangtze and sent up white clouds of fumes and obscured our view of the northern city. We would hear the crackling of the fires beyond, and as soon as the "all-clear" had sounded, the people would pour from their underground havens to try to save the city. When the fires had died down, the whole city would resound with hammering and sawing as the people rebuilt their homes and shops.

But life in Chungking went on. The Industrial Co-operatives held a national exhibition of home industries from every part of the country. I lectured before clubs in the northern city and raffled off war trophies to buy medical supplies. The wife of the British Ambassador took a theater and gave a performance of Snow White to raise money for Madame Chiang Kai-shek's war orphans. Foreigners gave air-raid parties, and every foreign home on the south shore was filled with bombed-out people. The British Ambassador ignored the Japanese warning to all foreign embassies to move to the south-shore "neutral zone," and a number of us sometimes gathered in his home for afternoon tea. The blasting of tunnels sounded continually; soldiers drilled and sang; Government institutions set up new communities out in the country; gangs of coolies hovered near the airdromes, repairing them after each raid; and factories and arsenals hummed on. And right at the height of the air blitz the people celebrated the annual Dragon Boat Festival, gaily clad crews of boatmen covering the Yangtze and its tributaries.

Of course the time came when the Japanese began dropping bombs in the "neutral zone." No one in the zone had trusted them anyway. When Colonel Dave Barrett, American military attaché, and I were once caught in such a raid,

Barrett, who knew the dangers of America's Japanese policy, drawled: "Wa-a-a-l, our chickens have done come home to roost!"

One June night I attended a play given by Japanese captives organized in the "Japanese Anti-Imperialist League." About twenty young Japanese soldier captives under the leadership of the Japanese revolutionary writer Kadji wrote their own plays, published their own magazine, and put on plays for the Chinese population and for war prisoners. The day after the play was given, the theater was suppressed by Mr. Chen Li-fu, Minister of Education. The plays were considered revolutionary because they showed the effects of war upon the poor people of Japan!

Great changes had taken place in China since I had left Hankow in 1938. Many reforms had been introduced in the Army Medical Administration, headed by Surgeon General Loo Chih-teh, and the National Health Administration under Dr. P. Z. King had built up a network of free medical clinics throughout "free China." The foundations of socialized medicine had been laid. The War-Time Emergency Medical Schools, headed by Dr. Robert K. S. Lim, now had two additional branches, one on the eastern and one on the northwestern front. Nearly five thousand medical officers and nurses had already been retrained. Mobile anti-epidemic units trained in these schools now operated in the war zones, inoculating the armies and the people against epidemics, constructing wells, and purifying the water supply.

But while the Chinese Government had transformed western China into a powerful base of resistance, and institutions of historic importance had grown up, these very changes had unleashed numerous reactionary forces. Many officials, industrialists, and landlords now looked with fear upon the swift growth of the Industrial Co-operatives and other institutions in which millions of men and women were learning the meaning of social progress and economic democracy.

Upon arriving in Chungking one of the first things I heard was of the power of General Tai Li. He was said to have 150,000 uniformed men and 150,000 plain-clothes agents under his direction. No one knew whether Generalissimo Chiang controlled him or he exerted control over the Generalissimo. Of the many reports which he had placed before the Kuomintang, one was a charge that leaders of the Industrial Co-operatives were "agents of the Communist International" — a charge which covered anything from mild liberalism to actual membership in the Communist Party. As a result many Chinese leaders of the Industrial Co-operatives had been driven out and others arrested.

At a small dinner party I heard a foreigner and a Chinese discussing a secret report said to have been given to General Tai Li by Dr. Pan Chi, secretary of the Chinese Red Cross board of directors, charging that Dr. Robert K. S. Lim was corrupt and was using Red Cross trucks to transport Communist literature into China. I interrupted their conversation to remark: "If you lived in a country with decent courts, both of you, and Tai Li, could be brought up for criminal libel."

Educational institutions had become centers of witch-hunting and two centers modelled after Nazi concentration camps had been established, one near Sian, and a smaller one near Chengtu. In the northwest the major part of the most powerful group army of China, that commanded by General Hu Chung-nan, still spent its time keeping the Eighth Route Army encircled. A convoy of British relief trucks led by Edward Barger was allowed to distribute supplies to every army except the Eighth Route. General Kuo Shuen-chi, commander of the 50th Army along the lower Yangtze, had been removed because he had refused to allow his army to be used against the New Fourth Army. Sporadic attacks had been made against the Eighth Route and New Fourth Armies in many places, and the nation seemed to be on the brink of civil war.

The whole atmosphere of Chungking reminded me of the terror and discord before the Japanese invasion. Many Chinese writers, editors, organizers and other intellectuals had fled to Hong Kong or were trying to flee. The full seriousness of the situation became clear to me when I went to call on Sheng Chung-ju, a mild little old lawyer who was leader of the democratic National Salvation Association. He was not at home and his family told me that he and Chow Tao-fen, the editor and publisher, had gone to protest to the Minister of War because the Minister had just charged that the lawyer and Mr. Chow were plotting an armed uprising in the city!

The "peace elements" in the Government, I was soon informed, were themselves plotting an uprising in which the Generalissimo was to be killed because he wished to continue the war. The blame was to be placed on the Communists. Another "Reichstag fire" was being planned, men said. Just how much of this was wild speculation, how much true, I could not determine, but it was a serious situation if charges such as these could be brought against such an organization as the National Salvation Association.

Next I heard rumors that the Christian General Feng Yu-hsiang, and a number of high Kuomintang officials who shared his liberal outlook were being called the "outer defense line of the Communists." Then I heard from two foreign women that they had been approached by representatives of General Tai Li to act as spies and ferret out the political opinions of foreign correspondents. One had accepted. The other had refused and had thereafter been accused of being a "spy who slept with military men." The accused woman shook off the charges contemptuously; she had extraterritorial rights. But no Chinese could have afforded to ignore such a charge.

Close on the heels of these reports I heard that the Kuomintang in Kweiyang, capital of Kweichow Province, had accused the Y.W.C.A. and the local Women's New Life Movement of being Communist. One day as the Y.W.C.A. gathered to discuss "What is Democracy?" two Kuomintang officials stalked in and ordered them to go home. The officials announced that no meeting of any nature could be held without Kuomintang permission and without a Kuomintang member in the chair. Immediately afterwards Kuomintang officials went through the streets of this city during an election of women delegates to a Kuomintang conference and paid illiterate women ten cents each to vote for women whom they nominated. This incident was carried to the high authorities in Chungking and they condemned it as political racketeering.

Waves of political reaction got under way whenever new Japanese peace proposals were made to the Chinese Government. As a rule the Germans were the channel through which such offers were made, though Chinese of Hong Kong and a few followers of Wang Ching-wei — one of them a high official in the Ministry of Communications in Chungking — always took a hand. No one believed that Generalissimo Chiang would consider peace until China was victorious, but the Germans entertained other hopes. After a German war film was shown to a selected group of officials, I heard open expressions of admiration for the war machine which was flattening all Europe. When Paris fell in the middle of June, admiration for the Nazis mounted. Chinese remembered the corruption and the maltreatment of the people of Indo-China by the French rulers: a Red Cross official told me that even before Indo-China had been occupied by the Japanese, French officials in Indo-China had accepted huge bribes from the Chinese who wanted to get their supplies through.

When the British closed the Burma Road in June, these international developments, combined with the British and American policy toward Japan, gave impetus to a powerful tide of anti-foreign feeling throughout China. The hatred for the British was the strongest of all, and never before had China been so near surrender. The Generalissimo still did not waver, but the "surrender elements" in the Government were provided with new fuel.

I could well understand the anti-foreign feeling. For three long years the Chinese armies had been regarded with contempt by many foreigners. China, they said, couldn't fight; its generals were rotten; its soldiers illiterate coolies or mere boys; its people ignorant; the care of the wounded an abomination. Some charges were true, some untrue, but almost all were based on a lack of appreciation of the fearful burdens under which China staggered.

I was particularly affected when my own countrymen thought of themselves as true friends of China or declared that they were furnishing China with its medical supplies. It was the overseas Chinese upon whom China depended for its chief medical supplies and ambulances, and in comparison with such aid the help of my own country was infinitesimal. The only help that ever reached the Chinese wounded from America came through the American Bureau for Medical Aid to China, whose leader was a Chinese. One high Chinese official in the Army Medical Service told me that America had indeed recently given China a million dollars to buy quinine, but that American business men had demanded that the purchase be made through them. Accordingly they bought the quinine in Java, shipped it to America, repacked it, and then shipped it back to China; in the end the Chinese received about $300,000 worth of quinine!

My attitude was therefore much the same as that of the Chinese. China was a pariah, treated with contempt or condescension, while, with all its internal conflicts, it was really fighting the battle for world democracy. Many foreigners whom I knew shared aspects of my point of view; some shared it in its entirety. Not all the color lines or race prejudices in the world could blind such people to the bitter facts.

The American public seemed so uninformed or misinformed, or so very soft, that it seemed incapable of facing a situation so serious. Because of this the foreign correspondents feared to send out the true facts. "The truth?" one foreign correspondent said. "I simply don't know what the truth is!" So we all suffered from a kind of mental paralysis.

Gathered in the ward room of the *Tutuila*, an American gunboat anchored in the river in front of the American Embassy, many of us argued about these issues repeatedly. Sometimes there were a dozen people shouting at each other. China would make peace! China would not make peace! America should enter the war! America should not! And once the Belgian chargé d'affaires, a Fascist, challenged another Belgian to a duel for calling the Belgian King a traitor. I was called an idealist, an illusionist, and so forth. Only when the Japanese bombers came over did we all realize our common danger.

One evening while Captain Bartlett was still commander of the *Tutuila*, I was his dinner guest. During the visit an air-raid alarm sounded. The men took up their battle stations and the Captain gave me a steel helmet and a life-vest and led me above, where he had only the sky for cover. When bombers had come I had been accustomed to falling on my face in a ditch, but now I had to stand out in the open. I asked the Captain if bomb fragments ever fell around the gunboat, and he answered that they did indeed, that one fragment had cut a hole in the deck and another had hit the helmet of a gunner. The chief thing, he said, was to note where the first bomb fell and then in what direction the bombers were going.

"And if we are hit?" I asked. The Captain replied that in such a case we would know exactly where the bomb had landed! The bombers went to Chengtu that night, but never have I felt more like a rat in a trap.

I recalled a conversation with Jack Belden, the foreign correspondent, who had made a short trip to the headquarters of the New Fourth Army while I was there. He had asked me if I was afraid of air-raids. I admitted that I was, and to my surprise he admitted that he was too, and that the fear grew greater instead of less. We both thought this fear might be overcome if we were permitted to fight in a few battles. A gun seems to absorb fear. Many Chinese soldiers had told me that when they first went into battle, they were afraid; but as the fighting had progressed, fear had vanished.

Jack Belden carried a copy of Tolstoy's *War and Peace* with him and said that if the names and places were changed into Chinese, it might easily seem like a version of the present war. He asked me who could write such a book on

China and I said that I thought it could be done only by a Chinese who had actually fought throughout the whole of it. But I also thought that Jack might one day write a very fine book. He had been with many Chinese armies and in order to reach them had had to use all kinds of maneuvers to get past officials. He was more objective than I; he represented no cause and could stand aside and observe, whereas I always forgot that I was not a Chinese myself. To me the problems, strength and weaknesses of China seemed to be those of the whole world.

The Medical Corps Fights On

As June drew to a close, and while the air blitz was still trying to reduce Chungking to ashes, Dr. Lim came and took me back to Kweiyang, headquarters of the Red Cross Medical Corps. To get through the masses of trucks and people waiting to leave Chungking was a problem, and once on the road our trip was made under continual air-raid alarms. Because we were in a Red Cross car, the armed guards in the silent, deserted villages allowed us to whirl through and take our chances. We intended to take cover only when we saw planes coming directly at us. If we stopped for air-raids, Dr. Lim kept saying, China would get nowhere. An urbane gentleman before the war, this little doctor had become as hard as steel. If fear ever gripped him, a greater fear of subjection and slavery overcame it. He had tasted too much of his country's bitterness.

Dr. Lim gave me a room in his small cottage and undertook to treat me. It was on his advice that I had refused to have my gall-bladder taken out in Chungking. While lying in bed, I read books from his small but excellent library, and when he could steal an hour from his numberless tribulations, I would outline for him what I had read. He had little time for reading anything but reports and medical books, and to his organizational and administrative duties he had added another which would occupy many months: he was writing a series of medical manuals with which he hoped one day to equip every Army medical worker in the field. His light always burned until the small hours. The Medical Corps had grown tremendously under his leadership, and ambitious men had already decided that it was too powerful and lucrative to function under a man of non-partisan democratic outlook. Political intrigue was hampering his work and he was already spending too much of his time in protecting himself and the Medical Corps from snipers who were trying to use the Chinese Gestapo against him.

My affection for Dr. Lim was very deep and my admiration even deeper. His education and culture were, as I have said, the best that British liberalism had to offer, but he was lonely in his own country and a stranger in England or America. One evening he told me how he had once set out for America to attend a scientific congress. Missing him, his colleagues had sought him on Ellis Island. They had found him in the immigration pen with a "Deloused" button pinned on his coat.

He was a man whose mind worked in the broadest terms — terms perhaps too broad for his age. Upon him depended in large measure the fate of all the wounded of China. Only his plan to re-educate the medical personnel of the entire Army could bring permanent relief to the sick and injured. But political intrigue can wreak havoc with such work and such a man. I was never without deep concern for his future, for he was tough and stubborn, determined to fight to the end.

Japanese naval planes came up from the south each week to bomb Kweiyang, and before they had left, Red Cross ambulances were clanging and roaring down from our headquarters in the hills to bring back the injured. International publicity had long since revealed our location to the enemy, and in addition our headquarters was now connected with the great medical training school, hospital, and orthopedic center. This center had been equipped and financed with British aid, but the entire Medical Corps still depended for most of its support upon the Chinese of Java.

On July 28, enemy naval planes made a special detour to bomb the Red Cross headquarters and the medical center. After that raid — when doctors had to operate on wounded men injured a second time and convalescent soldiers had to help prepare temporary shelters for the night — Dr. Lim began plans to decentralize and scatter the wards — a lay-out which would make medical work still more difficult. That evening Dr. Lim brought in a huge bomb fragment and, looking at it speculatively, said: "I've half a mind to make special medals of it and confer them on American firms that sell war materials to Japan."

While under treatment, I began work on a chapter on Red Cross work for Madame Chiang's new book, *China Shall Rise Again*, and I also began lecturing in Kweiyang educational institutions. On July 7, the anniversary of the war, Dr. Lim had introduced me as the main speaker before a conference of Red Cross and Army medical workers in the region. I reported on conditions in the war zones. That large hall filled with blue-clad men and women war-workers was an inspiring sight, and I considered that opportunity the greatest honor that had ever been accorded me.

There were now sixteen European doctors in the Medical Corps and they had already been in service for almost nine months. Although they represented many nationalities, we called them the "Spanish doctors" because they used Spanish as their *lingua franca* and because they had all served in the Spanish Republican armies. The Norwegian Red Cross had secured their release from French concentration camps, paid their passage to China, and maintained them while they worked as volunteers.

These men were entirely different from any other foreigners I had met in China. Despite definite political differences, they were united as anti-Fascists. Unlike several other foreign doctors whom I had known, moreover, they dressed, ate, and lived like the Chinese. They saw all the sanitary and scientific backwardness of China, but they saw these conditions in their proper perspective and responded by shouldering whatever burdens they could. Sometimes they told amusing stories of lesser Chinese commanders who had become passionately imbued with scientific medical attitudes. When a D.B.S. station was erected on one front a commander had announced to his troops: "Now you've got no right to have scabies!"

These "Spanish" doctors had gathered in Kweiyang for another reorganization: the Medical Corps was changing from an old boat to a new one in midstream. Henceforth they were to retrain every Army medical worker, lecture to the troops on hygiene and first aid, build D.B.S. stations out of whatever material was at hand, purify wells, and do other anti-epidemic work. Education and more education was the cry.

The loss of Indo-China and the Burma Road had cut off China from the outside world. The Red Cross was beginning to manufacture some of its own disinfectants, and the National Health Administration had established small factories to manufacture what drugs and equipment it could, but the armies would have to depend more and more upon *prevention*.

By early September, it had become clear that I could not recover from my chronic illness if I remained in China, so Dr. Lim put me on a Red Cross truck headed for Kweilin, capital of Kwangsi Province. The medical unit would go on down to the Indo-China front, where heavy fighting had now started, and I would fly over the Japanese lines to Hong Kong.

Our truck made its tortuous way up the new roads through the mountains of the southwest. There were no guard walls at the edge of the road and we often looked down into deep gorges into which other trucks had tumbled. Again we traveled in a perpetual air-raid. Exhausted, emaciated troops, most of them suffering from night blindness and malaria, were moving to the rear, and fresh troops were marching in endless lines toward the front. Thousands of good trucks, all intact but unable to get gasoline, were stranded along the highway. Frequently we passed through towns and villages that had been destroyed by raids. One afternoon we halted to aid the injured in a town which had just been attacked and was still smoking; but by dawn the next day we were on the road again.

I stopped at Kweilin to lecture and broadcast, much as I had done in Kweiyang. But Kwangsi Province was very different from other sections of China. It was still a democratic stronghold, permitting free speech, press, and assembly. Writers and editors driven out of other parts of the country had gathered here to continue their work. I hoped that after treatment in Hong Kong I might return to Kwangsi and go to the Indo-China front.

One evening as I finished a broadcast over the Kweilin radio, I found a Japanese, who had broadcast before me, waiting to speak to me. He was not being guarded and was living and working as a Chinese. We spent an evening at an outdoor tea garden and I found him a remarkable personality. His name was Seisaku Shiomi and he spoke three foreign languages — Chinese, English, and French. Up to December 1938 he had been secretary in the Japanese Consulate in Hanoi, Indo-China, and at the same time in the pay of the Japanese Secret Service. He had been captured by Chinese troops while on a spying tour of the frontier. For one year he had refused to help the Chinese in any way. During this time, however, the Japanese revolutionary writer Kadji, who worked in all the camps for Japanese war prisoners, had given him books and talked to him, and he had finally decided to participate in the anti-Fascist movement.

"My entire life's training," he said, "was as a diplomatic official. I used to believe that I was blessed to have been born Japanese, and I thought my Government was doing the right thing in invading China. I could not help seeing that we Japanese were the only men of color who had not been conquered by the white race. The militarists of my country were able to use this fact to inspire us with the belief that we were fighting for the liberation of all colored people. But since I have studied and thought, it has become clear to me that our own militarists merely wish to take the place of the white imperialists. It took a long time for me to change my whole life's training and take a step which the Japanese brand as treason. However, I see that the rulers of Japan, like those of most other countries, merely use the common people as sources of wealth in time of peace and as cannon fodder in time of war. Now I broadcast in Japanese to the Japanese troops and people, trying to explain what I believe. I work for real peace and justice, and my mind is at rest."

He spoke quickly, nervously, as if torn by internal conflict. He kept assuring me that he was "happy," but I could hardly believe that a man of his training could slough off the outlook and attitudes of a lifetime. Before we parted, however, he asked me to tell his story wherever I went, because the Japanese had denied that it was the voice of their consular official that was coming over the air. "Tell everyone that you have seen and talked with me," he urged. And then I almost believed him. I wondered what I would have done under similar circumstances.

That same night official friends took me by car to the airdrome and we stood in the pitch dark and watched a small red gleam come out of the east high over the dark rim of the mountains. It was a special plane which brought bank-notes from Hong Kong. I was the only passenger going out. A truck rolled up to load the plane with a ballast of stones, and a little later we soared into the night and began nosing our way through total darkness over the Japanese lines toward Hong Kong.

Hong Kong

AT three in the morning I looked down from the plane on Hong Kong, its soft lights reflected in a dark, slumbering sea. Surely no scene on earth is so lovely. On such dark nights, I knew, Chinese junks slid silently across the water to hidden coves along the Kwangtung coast where scores of undernourished coolies picked up cargoes and began trotting toward the far-off interior. So it had gone since Canton had fallen in late 1938, and so it would continue until Hong Kong fell to the enemy.

We landed in a flood of lights. The polite British official who received me refused to search my suitcase; he paid my taxi fare and sent me to the luxurious Peninsula Hotel, where a room had been reserved for me. Once in the room, I moved about gingerly. It was clean and spacious, and provided with thick carpets, easy chairs, and sparkling mirrors. It seemed a shame to dirty the spotless linens and the white bathroom; and the soft bed kept me awake most of the night.

But the morning brought my friend Mrs. Hilda Selwyn-Clarke, wife of the Medical Director of the Hong Kong Government. We crossed the bay, but before going to the palatial Queen Mary Hospital, where I was to be treated, she asked me if there was anything I wished or needed. I said I wanted some ice cream; so at eight thirty in the morning we went into a deserted hotel lounge and confounded the waiter by ordering ice cream. Hilda then suggested that I get some nightgowns; we bought two — another useless luxury when all is said and done. Later we had occasion to stop at a pharmacy, and that to me was almost unbearable, for it was stocked with far more medical supplies than I had seen in any Chinese army on the whole front. Its glittering cases overflowed with beauty accessories for women. All that I needed was a toothbrush, paste, and some soap.

The superintendent of the Queen Mary Hospital stared at me, but kept his composure until he had settled me in a beautiful room overlooking an azure sea; then he fled to Professor Paul B. Wilkinson, chief medical consultant to the Hong Kong Government, who had been retained to direct my treatment. Waving his arms in the air, the superintendent declared that an impossible-looking woman dressed in a "boiler suit" had just blown in. Dr. Wilkinson tried to comfort him by assuring him that, despite these disadvantages, I possessed a "fascinating gall-bladder."

In the months that followed, I argued with Dr. Wilkinson

up and down Hong Kong, but we still remained friends. He was one of those Englishmen who become very patriotic when they find themselves in a far-away place. He was a recluse, or liked to think he was, living in a world of classical literature and medical research, quoting Latin and Greek at the drop of the hat, and winning the fear of his medical students. Before coming to Hong Kong a few years before, he had been stationed in isolated regions of Africa, where he had seen and treated only Negroes. He seemed to like them much better than officials or Americans, whom he regarded as semi-savages. The Negroes, he always said, possessed great pride, dignity, and sensitiveness. Before coming to him for treatment, the women would always bathe and make fresh little aprons of green leaves.

To the rich Chinese the professor was indifferent, but for the Chinese poor his heart was filled with tenderness and respect. Though the Hong Kong police had forbidden me to speak, write, or otherwise take part in public life, Dr. Wilkinson one day surrendered the rostrum of his lecture theater to me and I spoke to the medical students of Hong Kong University about the conditions and needs of their wounded countrymen at the front. The doctor followed this up by urging graduates to join the medical services of their armies. After I concluded, he quoted from Shakespeare in the suavest of British accents, and then added that he thought my speech had made no more impression on the students than water on a duck's back! We got three volunteers out of the lot.

After treatment in the hospital, I took up residence in the country home of Dr. Ronald O. Hall, Bishop of Hong Kong. The Bishop and I soon became fast friends. Like my friend Hilda, he was engaged in every kind of relief work for Chinese soldiers and civilians. He was a devout Christian who tried to live a Christ-like life — no easy task in a British colony founded on race and class discrimination. From my viewpoint, it was an utter impossibility. Along with Hilda and her husband, Dr. Percy Selwyn-Clarke, he campaigned against discrimination and tried in vain to force through such social reforms as an eight-hour day and a minimum wage. But the trade unions which might have supported him had long since been suppressed by the British rulers.

Bishop Hall once told me of a typical incident which he had witnessed while on a trip which the Japanese had permitted him to make to Canton. A poor Chinese woman with a baby on her back had stepped off the boat before him. She carried one precious can of powdered milk for her baby. Noticing it, a Japanese sentry had ripped it from her hand, opened it with his bayonet, and scattered the powder in the mud at her feet. Then he let her pass.

I was soon a member of a small but very active group of British men and women engaged in relief work for China. Hilda, the leader, was secretary of the Foreign Auxiliary of the Chinese Red Cross and thus the agent through whose hands went the supplies sent by British relief groups and by the American Bureau for Medical Aid to China. She was also secretary of the China Defense League (Madame Sun Yat-sen was the Chairman) and without her help the League could never have functioned. As the wife of a high official, she might easily have been content to give her patronage to organizations. But she came from the British labor movement and thus did not scorn to do her own typing, telephoning, and similar work. In her office I met every kind of relief worker from Hong Kong and China — among them a representative of the American Red Cross who drew a salary so fabulous that it was almost sickening. Officials called Hilda utterly unscrupulous — words which, in the mouths of such individuals, always amused me. Some men held that she twisted the Governor, Sir Geoffrey Northcote, around her finger. When it came to her aims, Hilda was certainly as tough as nails.

Though Hong Kong considered itself a British colony and, as such, was neutral in the war, it was in reality a part of China and was rent by the same problems as the mainland. All the distortions of the Chinese Revolution were reflected in the whirlpool of its life. It teemed with enormously wealthy bankers, both Chinese and foreign, and among other circles in its midst was that of the four hundred Chinese millionaire families who had fled to it for shelter. Some were on their way to America, where, I later heard, they posed in high society as representatives of China. Had they been its representatives, there would have been no China. When hundreds of thousands of poor Chinese refugees tried to find shelter in the colony, thousands of them had to sleep in the streets or on the roof. Poor refugee girls — some no more than fourteen — learned to wait in the shadows of doorways and then offer themselves to men leaving restaurants, hotels, or theaters. Policemen and porters alike collected a percentage of the earnings of these girls.

In the great hotel lounges every afternoon well-to-do Chinese and foreigners gathered for cocktails, intrigue, business, or just to while away the years until Chinese soldiers made it possible for them to return to their old hunting grounds. Chinese agents of Wang Ching-wei moved quite openly among them, never lacking money. Hong Kong was thick with such men.

Once, for example, a friend of mine rose hastily from a tea table and disappeared through a door behind me. A certain Mr. Tu Yueh-seng, one-time opium Czar and leader of the Green Gang of Shanghai, had entered the room! Mr. Tu was now vice-president of the Board of Directors of the Chinese Red Cross. He and several members of his gang had become anti-Japanese, although other members still worked for the enemy. Yet even he was less obnoxious than those two or three other members of the same Red Cross Board who were trying to drive Dr. Robert Lim from his position and make room for one of their own henchmen. I knew that such men were interested only in their own power and prestige and not at all in the wounded. I never hid my opinion of them, even when they stood before me — thereby virtually ending my chances of returning to China.

My friends, both foreign and Chinese, were sometimes called the "political-literary set." We were united in work for China, but, like other Chinese political groups, were torn by bitter ideological conflicts. Take the case of the two British Communists in my "set." At the beginning of the war in Europe, one of these young men had gone to England to join the R.A.F., but learned upon arriving there that the British Communist Party considered the war imperialist. So he came wandering back to Hong Kong, his passage paid by a relief organization. I personally could not see how on earth any Englishman, Right or Left, could want to do anything but fight when threatened by a Nazi invasion.

One day one of these Englishmen, finding me reading Tom Wintringham's book on tactics, announced that Wintringham was a traitor. Wintringham had commanded the British Battalion of the International Brigade in Spain, but when the Battle of Britain had begun and British cities were being destroyed from the air, Wintringham had volunteered to teach the Home Guard the military tactics he had learned on the Spanish battlefields. He rejected the Communist Party line and for his trouble was called a "traitor." For similar reasons John Strachey, the political economist, was called a contemptible idealist.

We got echoes of the American Communist Party line (it was the same as the British) from American travelers. True, the Communists had fought the Fascists in Spain, and they had added their voices to those of trade unions, liberals, and other Americans opposing the sale of war materials to Japan. But when I heard these men talk about the war, I could see little objective difference between their policy and that of the America Firsters and the various religious pacifist groups. I agreed that the Soviet Union should be defended against attack by any capitalist power — which included the Nazis — but why advocate a "peace" with Germany? I regarded all these peace movements in America as poisons drugging the American people and keeping them totally unprepared to meet the coming attack. But what was wrong with the American people that they permitted this?

Even the most obtuse person in China and Hong Kong

knew that the Japanese intended to attack the colony, and that this would be merely a small episode in some greater strategy. The Japanese had boasted that they were going to do it, and their *Tanaka Memorial* had even outlined the plan of attack. They had been steadily moving troops southward through Indo-China. They had prepared Siam for occupation. Their activities in Burma had for years been so effective that all but two Burmese nationalist papers were pro-Japanese. When the Burma Road into China was first opened, Japanese influence had been so great that the workers of Rangoon had declared a general strike against the shipment of arms to China. Japanese agents had been working for years in Afghanistan, India, the Dutch East Indies, and the Philippines. Though the Indian National Congress supported China and was anti-Japanese, many Indian terrorists were connected with Rash Behari Bose, an Indian who had for years lived in Japan.

So we knew the Japanese attack was coming. One Japanese naval officer in Hong Kong had in fact gone so far as to remark that it would not be necessary to fight for Hong Kong because it would merely fall into Japan's lap "like a rotten fruit." Another Japanese official informed the American Consul General that his Army could capture Hong Kong simply by destroying the water system. Nor did the Japanese confine themselves to mere talk. They began occupying the entire Kwangtung coast about Hong Kong, cutting it off from the mainland. They took thousands of Chinese by force and used them in building new motor roads along the coast, and in constructing a new airdrome about five minutes' flying distance from the island.

The British Government had spent tens of millions of pounds on Hong Kong defenses and were still constructing new military highways through the mountains in the New Territories. Buildings were sandbagged and special guards stopped all motor cars passing through Kowloon and searched them. But the Japanese knew every gun emplacement, every ammunition dump in all the gulleys, every twist in the military highways, and far too much about the new underground shelters on which the British were spending a fortune.

Just when a conjunction of international developments would enable the Japanese to attack, we did not know, but we felt they were not quite ready because many Japanese still remained in the colony. Some American business firms had already received orders to close down and leave, and a printing house began printing thousands of death certificates for the Government. One day a Chinese friend anxiously informed me that he had seen a number of Japanese carrying all their possessions to a steamer. I went with him from one Japanese shop to another to see whether all the rats were really leaving the sinking ship. They were not. Apparently the time was not yet ripe.

Another Chinese friend said: "Watch the National City Bank, and when it moves out its reserves, take the next plane to China."

Hong Kong's air force consisted of just three old planes. At night they droned over the islands at a hundred miles an hour in order that the searchlight squads might practice on them. Sitting on the terrace of Norman France's home (he was Professor of History in Hong Kong University), we used to watch the planes and say: "The air force is out tonight — all three of them." Professor France, a member of the artillery section of the Hong Kong Volunteers, was later killed in the fight for Hong Kong — as was one of the British Communists who had opposed the war, but who had fought when the Japanese attacked.

British authorities estimated that their forces would be able to fight for about three months; the more optimistic expected that British naval support would have come up from Singapore by then. And perhaps America would have entered the war by that time and naval help would have come from Hawaii, the key to the Pacific. The American Pacific Fleet, based on Hawaii, could hold Asia, and then, of course, there were our bases in Alaska and the Aleutians. . . .

Some Englishmen argued that Hong Kong was of too little importance to warrant either British or American naval help. The colony seemed to be nothing but a sacrificial outpost intended to detain and absorb Japanese troops that would otherwise be thrown against more important objectives. I heard one English doctor argue that thousands of people would be killed for the sake of British Imperial prestige. But what should Hong Kong do? Should it lie down and do nothing, or should it be returned to its rightful owner, China — which also could not defend it? A great many Englishmen and Englishwomen — including Professor France and the Communist and many other men who died for it — cared little or nothing for the whole British Empire; they were passionately interested, however, in the preservation of the British Isles. They remained in Hong Kong out of a sense of duty and because it would have looked cowardly for them to leave. While most British women and children were evacuated to Australia and a few to the Philippines, some remained in Hong Kong getting medical training in anticipation of a Japanese attack. Among the latter was my friend Hilda. She and her husband, together with a number of my other friends, were later taken prisoner by the Japanese.

While some of the British were alert to the danger, they themselves had an Achilles' heel in their own racial and class prejudices. For instance, British women and children were evacuated from the Colony, while Chinese, Indian, and Eurasian women and children were not, despite the fact that they were British subjects. To help support the evacuated English women and children, the Hong Kong Government imposed a sales tax on certain goods which everyone, rich and poor, had to buy. There was no income tax on the wealthy of the colony. Of course many of the English themselves — among them my friends — challenged such shameless actions.

Often, moreover, I heard British officers make contemptuous references to the Chinese as a "third-rate power"; when the Japanese fought the British "they would learn what real fighting meant"! There were a few hundred Chinese in the Hong Kong Volunteer Corps, fine men, but British soldiers refused to bathe in the same pool with them. Not only this, but the British had not considered it worth while to negotiate with the Chinese Government for the joint defense of Hong Kong. Over an official dinner table I once argued with a British officer who declared that had the Chinese been worth anything, they would have held or recaptured Canton. Had the British been worth anything, I thought, they would not continue selling scrap iron to Japan as they were doing right down to that moment. One British General struck new depths when he remarked that Sir Robert Craigie, known as pro-Japanese and an appeaser, should have been stationed in China instead of Sir Archibald Clark Kerr.

I moved about in many circles, often like a fish in alien waters. The Hong Kong police still forbade me to speak or write, and when I argued with them, they declared that Hong Kong was neutral and a fortress, and to permit me to speak would be a violation of neutrality. To the Japanese I was *persona non grata* and was one of many foreign journalists and broadcasters on the Japanese blacklist. We were to be treated as Chinese belligerents in case of capture.[1]

The ban against me was eventually lifted, but only after the Chinese representative in the Hong Kong Government threatened to take the matter up to the House of Commons. Even before this, however, I had been lecturing in what my friends conveniently called "private gatherings." These gatherings took place before students of Hong Kong University, relief organizations, the Sino-British Cultural Association and, on one occasion, in the home of Captain Royal

[1] Mr. J. B. Powell, editor of the *China Weekly Review*, informed me of two or three Japanese blacklists. Over sixty Chinese newspaper men were booked for death and many were assassinated in Shanghai. One list of American names — Powell, Gould, Allcott, Allman, Mills, and Starr — was compiled for the Japs by the Chinese traitor Tang Leang-li, who had the help of an American. Edgar Snow, the author, and H. G. W. Woodhead, the Englishman, were also on a blacklist, as was my own name. Arrested in Shanghai after the fall of Hong Kong, Powell was imprisoned under such barbarous conditions that his feet had to be amputated.

Leonard, pilot for the American Aviation Corporation.

Hong Kong was, however, a small place for one engaged in "criminal" activities. During one of my "private gatherings," just as I was ardently urging Chinese university students to demand daily military training, I found myself looking right into the pudgy face of the British Colonel who had been put in charge of Hong Kong's internal defense! The only comfort I got from the gentleman's presence was a story then going the rounds. The Colonel had previously tried to expel or intern all anti-Nazi German refugees in the colony, and the liberal Governor, Sir Geoffrey Northcote, had asked him to explain why.

Said the pudgy Colonel: "Well, to tell you the truth, I don't like their faces."

Said the Governor: "Well, to tell you the truth, I don't like *yours!*"

Despite its turmoil and conflicts, or perhaps because of them, Hong Kong was a fascinating place. It was the gateway to China. To its crowds of Chinese was added a constant stream of foreign newspaper correspondents, writers, military observers, and just plain tourists. Many of the foreigners lingered longer than was necessary over its bars and in its pleasant hotel lounges. It was a "wet spot," and frustrated young Englishmen, aware of social thought but harnessed to an antiquated imperialist machine, saw to it that it remained wet. The danger of imminent attack was a constant strain on all of us and we tended to say to one another: "Drink, for tomorrow you may die."

I came to like many things about some Englishmen and in particular about the Scotch. Though hard and dry, the Scotch had in them a curious streak of imagination and fantasy. But certain Englishmen had the ability to turn me not only into a nationalist Chinese but also into a chauvinistic American. There was, for instance, the Englishman who informed me that Americans disliked the British because they were jealous. "In God's name, jealous of what?" I asked. Another informed me that Britain was fighting for America and that Americans would fight "to the last Englishman." When I retorted that Britain would fight "to the last Greek," the sparks flew. Some Englishmen talked in a most unreticent manner of how very reticent and cultured the British were and how vulgar and flamboyant the Americans. But some of my friends, although they were English to the bone, were neither reticent nor stodgy, and some of them were as flamboyant as the Star-Spangled Banner.

One of my Scotch friends was young David MacDougall, who had been sent out as a civil servant and given the job of distributing the dull pamphlets published in Singapore by the Ministry of Information. MacDougall was head of the Hong Kong office, but I never caught him reading one of his own pamphlets. He read "undesirable" Leftist literature instead. He served in the Volunteer Defense Corps and was wounded in the defense of the colony. Later he escaped to the mainland with a number of other Chinese and British officers and officials and was transported into the interior by guerrillas.

Another was Colin MacDonald, correspondent for the London *Times*. He had been so thoroughly influenced by China's timelessness that the *Times* was eternally finding it necessary to cable or write him, delicately suggesting that he ought now and then to send in an article. Colin said he took these suggestions so seriously that he thought about them for weeks and weeks, wondering if he really ought not to write something. . . .

One of the Englishmen, a military attaché, had also been deeply affected by China. He had been, he said, consistently abused and insulted by ninety per cent of the Chinese people; but the other ten per cent had been so "damned decent" that they made up for the rest!

The Americans who blew through Hong Kong were distinctive. Breezy, self-confident, virile, some were quite capable of making a three or four weeks' trip to China, then writing a couple of books. There were some serious men, but the loud-mouthed ones held the center of the stage, making a fearful din that gave all Americans an unenviable reputation. Once quiet, soft-spoken Evans F. Carlson passed through, and won the hearts of all who met him. He was making another tour of China, this time for the Industrial Co-operatives.

Whole droves of American military and naval intelligence officers soon began to heave in sight, but all of them seemed to be on their way to Egypt. Their route lay through Chungking, by air over the Burma Road to Rangoon, and thence through Singapore, India, and the Middle East. I wondered if something were not in the air and if they were not perhaps the first swallows of spring. They were frank, hearty, technical men, but I wondered if they had any idea of the significance of the political factors involved in resistance.

There were writers, too. Erskine Caldwell and Margaret Bourke-White passed through en route to the Soviet Union. Ernest Hemingway blew in, offering to stand everybody to drinks with the lucre won in his last literary victory, and entertaining us with tales of far-off places. He described how he had beaten up a relative of Quisling in a bar-room brawl in Idaho; and one evening he and a Marine officer demonstrated dagger and sword tricks by which, it seemed, a man's head could be cut off as easily as you could spit.

Madame Chiang Kai-shek came to town for treatment of an old back injury and I met her for the first time in the home of one of her sisters, Madame H. H. Kung. A few foreigners had once tried to arrange a meeting between Madame Chiang and myself, but I had been unwilling to run the gantlet which her followers had arranged for my benefit. Once her devotees were out of the way, I met her and found her cultivated, tremendously clever, and possessed of charm and exquisite taste. She was groomed as only wealthy Chinese women can be groomed, with an elegant simplicity which, I suspect, must require a pile of money to sustain. Next to her I felt a little like one of Thurber's melancholy hounds. She was articulate, integrated, confident. As the years had made her other sister, Madame Sun Yat-sen, older and sadder, so had they increased Madame Chiang's assurance and power.

Emily Hahn, living in Hong Kong, had just finished her

book on the three Soong sisters. They well deserved a book, but contrary to the belief of some foreigners, they were not the only capable women of China, and I always considered it unfortunate that publicity should be given to them alone. I often wondered what would have happened to the whole Soong family if they had been born in the obscurity and poverty that bound most of the Chinese doing duty in the war zones. I thought of those Chinese women who were doctors, nurses, political organizers and educators in the armies and among the people, and who, despite the indescribable hardships under which they worked kept growing in power and ability with the years. And I thought too of those others who lost the bloom of youth in the struggle, and died at obscure posts.

A new Chinese womanhood, in many ways far in advance of American womanhood, was being forged on the fierce anvil of war. One such woman lived with me for a time in Bishop Hall's country home. Her name was Hsiao Hung and her fate was typical. When the first Japanese attack on Manchuria had begun in 1931, she had fled. She had fled not only from the Japanese, but also from rich parents who wished to marry her off to a husband of their choosing. She had kept just ahead of the Japanese advance, living first in Peiping, and then successively in Shanghai, Hankow, and Chungking. Her first book, *Fields of Life and Death*, had been introduced to the Chinese public by no other than Lu Hsün, and he had spoken of it as one of the most powerful modern novels written by a Chinese woman. After this the girl published three other books, including a war novel which she completed while living in my home. Like most modern Chinese writers, she lived in perpetual penury. The money such writers earned placed them on the economic level of the coolie class. So Hsiao Hung, like many of her colleagues, contracted tuberculosis. I had her admitted to the Queen Mary Hospital and kept her supplied with money until Hong Kong fell. She died a few days after the Japanese occupied the island. She was twenty-eight years old.

The Japanese had learned enough in China to develop

some political cunning, and they began applying it soon after their first days of orgy in Hong Kong. They began posing as men who were liberating the Chinese from white imperialism. Thus when Hsiao Hung's husband [1] asked for permission to cremate her body and take the ashes to Shanghai to be buried beside her "master," Lu Hsün, the Japanese granted the request. So clever were Japanese tactics in some respects and so emasculating had been the influence of British policy on the Hong Kong Chinese that many Chinese chose to live under Japanese rule in Hong Kong rather than go into China.

I entertained no illusions about my fate should I become a prisoner of the Japanese; the American Consul General had already placed my name on a list of those who were to be taken to China by emergency planes when the attack came. I had not recovered from my chronic illness and, under the perpetual zero hour in which we lived, could do little writing besides publicity stories to raise money for the orthopedic hospital under Dr. Robert Lim's direction. If I returned to China I knew I should be unable to write at all. In addition, reactionary forces were mounting in China and had affected not only Leftists, but even such non-partisan organizations as the Industrial Co-operatives and the Red Cross Medical Corps.

I therefore considered returning to America. But I lingered on, hoping that some magical combination of circumstances would enable me to return to China. One day an American pilot amused me by the way in which he urged me not to return to America. In his soft drawl he said: "Why, honey, don't you know you'll be unhappy back there with all those foreigners?"

He was quite right, yet I decided to return, hoping to be able to tell Americans about the way Chinese lived and how they fought for freedom. I had become a part of the vast struggle of China — how much a part I first began to realize when I met Americans and Englishmen in Hong Kong —

[1] Her husband, Tien Chun, was author of the well-known book *Village in August*.

yet I had remained American in many ways. I had, in truth, become one of those creatures who have no home anywhere.

In the summer before Hong Kong was attacked, I took passage to America. I dared not travel via Japan, for the Japanese were taking "wanted" Americans off American ships in Japanese harbors and putting them through an inquisition. So I decided to take my chances with a Norwegian shipping firm, fully aware that some of their ships had already been sunk and captured by German raiders. We crept across the Pacific in an unbroken blackout.

Among the twelve passengers on board were three Pentecostal missionary ladies, one of whom was my cabin-mate. She did not even know who Hitler was. These ladies had originally come from the American South, where they had had Negro servants; and in China they had had Chinese servants. Thus when they once discoursed on heaven, they described it as a place where truly pious Christians would sit on the right hand of God through all eternity while the less pious would be their servants.

Another passenger was a young Belgian priest who had become a Chinese citizen. He and I agreed about most things in China, so we spent four weeks on the Pacific arguing about religion and the future of society. Upon entering San Pedro harbor, the two of us leaned over the rail and stared dejectedly at three big Japanese tankers, riding low in the water, and steaming slowly out toward the Far East.

"Look," remarked the young priest as we stared at the Japanese sun painted on the tankers. "That sort of thing has been going on since September 18, 1931! Everything that is happening in the world today can be traced back to that date!"

A new generation had been born and come to maturity since I had first left America twenty-two years before. There had developed an attitude and a way of life that were entirely foreign to me. Among other things, commercialism seemed to have eaten into the very heart of American life and culture. Shortly after I landed, a newspaper woman in Los Angeles took me to a broadcasting station, hoping to have me broadcast on China. The first question the young station official asked me was:

"What's your radio sales record?"

I didn't even know what he meant; later I learned that in order to tell the American people a few facts you must first sell them soap, dandruff cures, or Crazy Crystals for Constipation.

Nevertheless, I did lecture occasionally. Once when I told a group of business men what I thought of the sale of war materials to Japan, one of the men declared that I "wished to destroy everything." I asked another young business man what he read. He used almost the same words that I had heard from a Chinese official: "Since leaving college I have not read. I go home from work at night, have dinner, and sometimes take in a movie." I compared him with the Chinese soldiers I had met and I was glad he couldn't read my mind.

What appalled me most of all were American women. Working-class women had their homes and children, but besides these there seemed to be a sea of middle- and upper-class women, few of whom had anything to do. They had less connection with most of the main activities of their society than even Chinese women. Men members of the Town Hall of Los Angeles told me that if women were admitted, they themselves would resign. And women's "clubs" seemed to be places where women made weak attempts to fill up their empty lives. Speaking before one of them, I kept seeing in front of me a great room gleaming with white linen, cutlery, elegant clothes and costume jewelry as useless and artificial as the creatures who wore them.

In San Diego I met Evans F. Carlson once again and we discussed with foreboding the state of the nation around us.[1]

[1] Following the attack at Pearl Harbor, Carlson, then back in the Marines, was transferred to Hawaii. On August 17 he led a specially picked battalion of Marines (whom he had trained in guerrilla warfare and had "ethically indoctrinated") in the raid on Makin Island in the Pacific, annihilating the Japanese garrison and destroying stores of American gasoline which the

There was waste and softness on every hand. No person in California could think of life without a car. Mystic cults of every kind grew as scum forms on the surface of a stagnant pond. Even radio broadcasters lectured on astrology, telling people how to plant their gardens and regulate their entire lives by the stars. Lindbergh drew a crowd of twenty-five thousand in the Hollywood Bowl, Senator Wheeler howled over the radio, and up to June 22 the Communists attacked President Roosevelt and called the British imperialists. That the British Government was imperialist, no objective mind can deny, and India provides the bloody proof. But our own unclear tendencies leave room for speculation. These did not change after either June 22 or December 7.

My decision to leave China had brought to a close the most important chapter of my life. Looking back I was far from satisfied. I knew I had made countless mistakes; I hoped I had done a little good. For the future I still had one great job to do — to tell America the truth about China, how the Chinese had fought and were still fighting. I had vowed by everything that I believed not to forget Chung Yi's words: "Tell your countrymen. . . . Tell your countrymen. . . ."

Japanese had collected there. On December 7, 1942, Major General A. A. Vandergrift, Commander of the U. S. Marine Corps in the South Pacific, cited the whole Second Raider Battalion, commanded by Lieutenant Colonel Carlson, for outstanding service to the nation. The only other unit that had been so honored was the Marines and workers on Wake Island. The battalion, including all officers and men, was cited for "training, stamina and fortitude . . . and for its commendably aggressive spirit and high morale."

Thus was Evans Carlson vindicated, temporarily at least.

Index

Abyssinia, 109, 134
Academia Sinica, 111, 113
Afghanistan, 517
Agrarian Research Society, 459
Agrarian survey, 64–9
Air attacks, Japanese, 184, 188 f., 193, 195 f., 214, 227–8, 232, 236, 241, 319, 336, 339, 343, 347, 355, 379 f., 382, 385, 391, 393 f., 397, 408, 410, 412, 427, 430, 438, 440, 451–2, 498 ff., 505 ff.
Air Force, Chinese, 429 f., 499
Air power, Chinese lack of, 427
Allcott, Carroll, 520
Alley, Rewi, 211 f., 227
Alliance of Anti-Japanese Armies, see Anti-Japanese Alliance
Allman, N. F., 520
Alps, Bavarian, 17, 19
America First movement, 516
American Aviation Corporation, 520
American Bureau for Medical Aid to China, 504, 514
American Expeditionary Army in Siberia, 125
American Pacific Fleet, 518
American Red Cross, Special Advisory Committee of, 277
American War of Independence, 217
America's Siberian Adventure, 125
Anhwei Military Education Corps, 343
Anhwei Political-Military Training Camp, 348
Anhwei Province, 255 f., 299, 317 f., 320, 322, 336 f., 338, 343 ff., 349, 368, 372 ff.; intrigue in, 344, 349–51, 356–64; Japanese occupation of, 348
Anhwei Provincial Government, 339, 351
Anhwei Student Army, 343 ff., 359
Anking, 355
Anti-Epidemic Commission, 214
Anti-Fascists, 508–9, 510
Anti-Japanese Alliance, 136, 148 f.

Anti-Japanese organizations, 103, 154 f., 189 f., 251, 260–1, 338, 353, 450, 460
Anti-Japanese Resistance Theater, 179
Anti-Japanese Seasonal Song, 249
Anti-Japanese student movement, 139–40
Anti-Red Military Conference, 138 f.
Appeasement, bitter fruits of, 109 f., 185
Apprentice system, 242 ff.
Ariran, Song of, 463
Arizona, 7 f.
Army Medical Administration, see Medical Administration, Army
Army Medical Service, see Medical Service, Army
Ashland, Dr., 241
Atal, Dr., 230
Australia, 519
Austria, 18
Axis, 108

Banditry, 320, 374
Barger, Edward, 501
Barrett, Dave, 499–500, 505
Bartlett, Vernon, 232
Battle Hymn of the Republic, 199, 209
Bavaria, 17 f.
Beggars, 37 f.
Bei-gar, 55
Belden, Jack, 505 f.
Berlin, 11, 20, 22 ff., 95, 147, 167
Berlin, University of, 18
Bernhard, 97
Bertram, James, 149, 197
Bethune, Dr. Norman, 229
Bezprizorni, 24 ff.
"Big Brother" secret societies, 157
"Big Sister Chen," 460
Blue Shirts, 72 f., 93, 98, 112 f., 116 ff., 120, 134, 137, 139 ff., 144, 148, 165, 178, 205, 256, 367, 491

i

Blut und Boden, 19
Borcic, B., 213 ff.
Borodin, Michael, 34, 59
Bose, Rash Behari, 517
Bourke-White, Margaret, 523
Boycott of Japanese goods, 103, 230
Britain, Battle of, 516
British Government, 14, 16
British Medical Journal, 251
British Relief Fund, 277, 282
Brown, Richard, 229
Brussels, 24
Buck, Pearl, 234
Buddhist priests of Omei Mountain, 359
Burma, 517
Burma Road, 517, 523; closing of, 33

"C. C. Clique," 344, 349 f., 356 ff., 361, 363
Calcutta, 16
Caldwell, Erskine, 523
Canosian Sisters, Convent of, 391
Canton, 35, 74, 86, 93, 167, 236, 255, 257, 413, 512, 514, 520; *see* Silk Guild, Canton
Canton Army, 239
Canton Commune, 257
Canton Government, 34 f.
Carlson, Evans F., 197 ff., 206, 208 ff., 222, 402, 522, 527 f.
Carmen, 78-9
Cattaneo, Erminietta, 392 ff.
Caucasus, 26, 120, 124, 126
Cell Mates, 9
Central Government, *see* Chinese Government
Central Military Academy, 59
Central Military Council, 173
Central University, Nanking, 63, 65
Chang Chung-chang, 36
Chang, Dr., 267 ff., 282, 284 ff., 289 f.
Chang Hsueh-liang, 33, 36 f., 43 f., 47 f., 101, 103, 134, 136, 137 ff., 145, 148 ff.; his Student Military Academy, 136
Chang Keh-hsia, 442, 444, 446 f.

Chang, Merchant, 272 ff.
Chang Nai-chih, 343 f., 351
Chang Pei-chuan, 351, 362, 364
Chang, Samuel, 175 f.
Chang Tso-lin, 33
Chang Tze-chung, 220, 426, 442 ff., 449 ff., 488
Chang Yen, 325-7
Chang Yun-ee, 317 ff., 327 ff.
Chang'an, 135
Changchiakan, 435
Changjiaji, 442
Changsha, 219 ff., 223, 225, 234 ff., 291
Changtaikwan, 384, 426
Chao Lakes, 480
Chapei section, Shanghai, 106; evacuation of Chinese civilians from, 107
Chattopadhyaya, Virendranath, 11, 14 ff., 22 ff.
Chekiang Province, 255
Chen, Eugene, 74
Chen Fang-chuen, 330 ff.
Chen Ken, 194
Chen Kuo-fu, 349
Chen Li-fu, 205, 349, 500
Chen Liang-chu, 357 f., 361
Chen Lin-hung, 304
Cheng Chien, 380
Chengtu, 501, 505
Chennault, Claire, 208
Chentai Railway, 187, 191 ff., 195
Chiang, Jean, 235
Chiang Kai-shek, 43, 59, 102, 104, 110, 116, 137 ff., 145, 147 ff., 156, 162, 172 f., 182, 197, 205, 212, 227, 229 f., 233, 236, 239, 254, 257, 318, 366, 368, 371, 387, 413, 425 f., 429, 444, 447, 452, 482, 490, 502 f.; his first *Putsch* against Canton Government, 34; commands army in Northern Expedition of 1926-7, 34; establishes Nanking Government, 35; joins Southern Methodist Church, 69; captured and held at Sian, by Chang Hsueh-liang, 141 ff.; the eight demands, 144; released, 148 f.; issues four-

point statement on war with Japan, 182
Chiang Kai-shek, Madame, 59, 148, 172, 212, 227, 230, 233, 387, 499, 508, 523
Chicago Daily News, 208
Chicago Tribune, 177
Chichi Pao, 459 f.
Children, in New Fourth Army, 463 ff.
Ch'in Dynasty, 135
Ch'in Shih Huang Ti, tomb of, 135 f.
China Defense League, 514
China Shall Rise Again, 508
China Tribune, 97
China Weekly Review, 75, 177
China's Red Army Marches, 124
"China's Sorrow," valley of, 53
Chinese Eastern Railway, 43
Chinese Government, 58 f., 62, 73 f., 101 ff., 109 f., 120, 134, 136, 147 ff., 154 f., 158, 162, 172, 175 f., 178, 182, 185, 213, 217 f., 238, 292, 294, 337, 341, 349, 363, 365 ff., 390, 429, 482, 491, 500, 502 f., 520; refuses supplies to Communist armies, 370 f.
Chinese Law, 98
Chinese millionaire families, 514
Chinese newspaper men, assassinated by Japanese, 75
Chinese officials, *see* Officials, Chinese
Chinese press, its venality, 175; corrupted by Kuomintang and Japanese, 176 f.
Chinese Republic, 33, 101
Chinese Revolution, *see* Revolution, Chinese
Chingkanshan Mountain, 160, 167
Chinkiang, 112, 255, 260, 365
Chinpu, 325
Chou Chien-ping, 123 f.
Chou Dynasty, 379
Chou En-lai, 147, 167, 170-1, 172 ff.
Chou Li-po, 183
Chou Ping, 252 f.
Chow Tao-fen, 502

Christianity, 47, 334
Christians, Chinese, 47 f., 69, 433 ff.
Christians, rice, 69
Chu Cha Li, 65
Chu Ching-hsia, Miss, 353 f.
Chu family, 65 ff.
"Chu-Mao" Army, 167; *see also* Red Army, Chinese
Chu, Mr., 64 ff.
Chu Tang, 85
Chu Teh, 35, 73, 159 f., 164 ff., 170 f., 183, 190 f., 193 f., 197, 229, 367, 371; revolutionary career of, 166 f.
Chujhushan, 482
Chung Yi, 403, 410 ff., 423 ff., 451, 528
Chungchuan, 331
Chunghsiang, 445
Chunghsiang front, 424
Chungking, 73, 230, 232, 259, 282, 286, 299, 344, 361, 366, 369, 405, 407 f., 414 f., 423, 425, 427, 451, 453, 598 ff., 523 f.
Chuyung, 366
Civil Rights, League of, 111 ff.
Civil rights, movement for, 110 ff.
Colorado, 4 f.
Colorado Fuel and Iron Company, 4
Communism, 52, 62, 367; in Germany, 18; Chinese and Korean nationalists falsely accused of, 41
Communist armies, Chinese, *see* Eighth Route Army, New Fourth Army, Red Army, Chinese
Communist Government, Chinese, 340
Communist International, 501
Communist movement, German, 42
Communist Party, American, 10, 516
Communist Party, Chinese, 72 f., 102, 114, 116, 122, 157, 172 f., 179, 256 f., 341, 365, 448, 501; Central Committee of, 121, 146, 369
Communist Party, Russian, 33
Communist publications, 69-70
Communist-sympathizers, 35
Communist Youth, 116

Communists, alleged Chinese, 88, 92, 112 f., 116, 216, 357, 502; executions of, 73 ff.; imprisonment and torture of, 85–6
Communists, American, 528
Communists, British, 516
Communists, Chinese, 23, 34 f., 47 f., 52, 54, 62, 70 ff., 79, 137 f., 148, 157 ff., 164 ff., 205 f., 243, 251, 257, 259, 301, 318, 324, 338, 349, 353–4, 358 f., 365 ff., 411, 450, 476 f., 485; executions of, 73 ff.; attitude of Chinese officials and foreigners toward, 102; in Kiangsi Province, 105; suppression of, 116; attitude toward democracy, 173 f., 175, 369; issue ultimatum to Central Government, 368; rumors spread by foreigners concerning, 369
Communists, German, 20 f.
Communists, Japanese, 41 f.
Concentration centers, 501
Confucian Street, 61
Congress, American, 105, 300
Conscription system, 339
Consolation for the Wounded song, 275
Consolation houses, Japanese Army, 293, 484
Contract labor system, 45 ff.
Co-operative farm, 278 ff.
Co-operative Headquarters, Industrial, in Chungking, 408
Co-operatives, 211 f., 227, 355, 378, 407–10, 499 ff., 523, 525
Craigie, Sir Robert, 520
Crescent Moon, 111
Crimean War, 217
Cultural Federation, Chinese, 79
Cultural Monthly, 352
Curie, Madame, 413
Czechoslovakia, 23; Nazi occupation of, 403

D. B. S. stations, 509
Dairen, 41, 48 f.
Danzig Harbor, 11
Dare to Die Corps, 189

Daughter of Earth, 23, 113
Democracy, 52, 349, 352, 510; and Communist policy, 173 f., 175, 369; economic, 212
Democratic system, demanded by Chinese communists, 368
Democrats, revolutionary, 74, 344
Denmark, 23
Dewey, John, 52
Disease, 379
Donald, 177
Dorn, Frank, 172, 208
Dragon Boat Festival, 499
Driscoll, Rex, 123 f.
Durieux, Tilla, 18
Dutch East Indies, 413, 416

Egypt, 13
Eight demands, *see* Sian Incident
Eighth Route Army, 182 ff., 186 ff., 206, 209, 216, 229 f., 234, 238, 251, 318, 354, 367, 369 ff., 378, 427, 446, 467 f., 476, 501; Political Department of, 190
Ellis Island, 507
Engels, Friedrich, 169
England, 12, 14, 25
Espionage, Japanese, 190, 239, 319 f., 486 f.
Eurasian Aviation Corporation, 75
Executions, mass, *see* 73 f., 83

Factories, 45, 53 f., 87 ff., 227
Fanchang Guerrilla Inspection Unit, 311
Fancheng, 403, 410, 412, 427
Fang Chi, 349, 358
Fang Chih-an, 443, 451
Fang Chih-ming, 123, 304; capture and execution, 123–4
Far Eastern Review, 176
Farmers, tenant, 64
Fascism, 134, 172, 205, 286
Fascists, Chinese, 491
Fascists, Italian, 205
Fascists, Spanish, 516
Fememord, 21
Feng Da, 73, 83, 94–5, 115, 118

Index

Feng Da-fee, 302, 304 ff., 312 f.
Feng Yu-hsiang, 181, 433 f., 446, 502
Fenghwa, 151
Fengjiaji, 451
Fenglingtohkow, 183
Fengshuiji, 483
Feudalism, 38 ff., 135, 242 ff., 428
Fields of Life and Death, 524
Fiftieth Army, 248, 277, 282 ff., 292, 501; study clubs in, 285; Medical Service of, 287–8, 290–1, 292; Training Camp, 288; Front Service Corps, 289; inadequacy of medical personnel, 290–1
Fight Back to Your Native Home, 150, 296 f.
Filatures, 87–8; girl filature workers, 87 ff.
Flood, 352
Folk-art, Chinese, 244
Foot-binding, 354
Fourth Army, 255, 318
Fourth Detachment of New Fourth Army, 317–29
France, 23 f., 25, 128
France, Norman, 518 f.
Frankfurt am Main, 24
Frankfurter Zeitung, 24, 38, 110
Free Love Club, 165
French, in Indo-China, 233
Fu Tso-yi, General, 136, 140, 148 f., 185
Fu-jia-tien, 37, 40
Fukien Province, 108, 254
Fushun mines, 45 ff.
Futan University, 78

Gandhi, Mohandas K., 24
General Motors, 21
Geneva, 102
Geneva Red Cross Convention, 213
Genghis Khan, 294
Geopolitik, Institut für, 19
German Government, 9, 15, 20, 110
German military advisers, 104, 227
German Republic, 10, 19 ff.
Germans, in China, 69, 232, 503
Germany, 10 ff., 23 f., 36, 108, 110,
147, 169; hunger in, 20–1; effects of inflation in, 21; signs Non-aggression Pact with Soviet Union, 300
Gestapo, 227, 232
Gorky, Maxim, 42, 78, 83
Gould, Randall, 520
Grand Canal, 64
Grant, U. S., 207
Great Britain, investments in China, 102
Great Wall, 37, 102, 135, 154, 182, 187, 249
Green Gang, Shanghai, 94 f., 517
Guam, 301
Guerrilla detachments, central Anhwei, training camp of, 322–7
Guerrilla Marching Song, 247–8, 312
Guerrilla warfare, 252–4, 260 ff., 318 ff., 328, 332, 347, 459, 489 ff.; conditions of, 327 ff.
Guerrilla wounded, 329–35
Guerrillas, 174, 230, 254 ff., 301 ff., 317 ff., 336, 340 f., 357 ff., 374, 376, 448 ff., 459–93; women leaders of, 460; see also New Fourth Army
Gung, N. C., 267 ff., 301, 305, 313, 317, 322, 327
Gunther, Frances, 232
Gunther, John, 232
Guo Ping, 420 f.

Hahn, Emily, 523–4
Hall, Kathleen, 367 f.
Hall, Ronald O., 513 f., 524
Han Liu Ban, 485
Han River, 403, 427, 451, 475, 481 f., 488, 497
Hangchow, 366
Hankow, 75, 157 f., 188, 205 ff., 214, 216, 219 f., 222 f., 225 ff., 247, 249, 254 f., 318, 335, 346, 348, 376, 384 f., 426 f., 433, 445, 449, 460 f., 475 f., 478, 480 ff., 485, 488 f., 497, 524; Canton Government removed to, 35; French Concession in, 228; Brit-

ish Concession in, 233; Japanese Concession in, 235; foreigners in, 232–4; missionaries in, 233–4; fall of, 231–36; evacuation of, 232, 234–5
Hanoi, 510
Hanshuan, 489
Hanyang, 205
Harbin, 37, 42, 45
Haushofer, Karl, 19
Hawaii, 518
Hearn, Lafcadio, 103
Heidelberg, 13
Hemingway, Ernest, 523
High school centers, 336 f.
Hinduism, 12
Hindus, 13 ff.
Hitler, Adolf, 19, 22 ff., 108, 110, 147 f., 150, 227, 403
Hitler movement, 18, 21
Ho Lung, 155 ff., 166 f., 169, 171, 476, 485; his family, 157–8
Ho Tung, Eva, 235
Ho Ying-ching, 148 f., 174, 365
Hogg, George, 378
Honan Province, 255, 318, 373 ff., 381, 394, 396, 464
Hong Kong, 176, 226 f., 235, 241, 343, 370, 429, 501 f., 510 ff.
Hong Kong Government, 225, 512, 519 f.
Hong Kong Rotary Club, 210
Hong Kong University, 513, 520
Hong Kong Volunteer Defense Corps, 518, 520, 522
Hoover, Herbert, 25
Hopei Province, 37, 181, 190
Hospitals, 213, 222, 240–2, 248 ff., 251, 274–5, 287–8, 330–5, 346, 383 ff., 412, 432, 438, 440, 461, 497
Hsia Wen-yao, 459
Hsiang River, 403
Hsiang Ying, 257 ff., 261, 300, 365
Hsiangyang, 412
Hsiao chirh, 55
Hsiao Hokuo, 250
Hsiao Hung, 524 f.
Hsiao Keh, 157 f.
Hsiao Kwei, 463 ff.

Hsiao Li-tze, 139, 145
Hsienyang, 151
Hsipei (Northwest) Army, 136
Hsu Chuen, 183 f.
Hsu, Mr., 114
Hsüan Tsung, Emperor, 134 f.
Hsuchow, 219, 221, 338, 420, 444
Hu Chia-chen, 323 f.
Hu Chung-nan, 136, 145, 367, 501
Hu Han-min, 34
Hu Shih, 98, 110, 254
Hu Wei-pei, 404 f.
Humanists, 52
Hunan bureaucrats, 349 f., 357, 361
Hunan Province, 255, 350
Hung Hwang Shan Mountains, 304
Hung Sheng, 78
Hungary, 25
Huntung, 196
Hupeh Province, 255, 299, 318, 346, 373 f., 401, 410, 426 ff.
Hwang, J. L., 59
Hwang Shih Hwei ("Big Sword" society), 438
Hwang Ti, 174
Hwangchuan, 375 f., 379; military clinics in, 381
Hwangchuan Youth Association, 374
Hwangpei, 482
Hwei River, 301
Hweiyuan, 331 f.
Hyderabad, 12, 16

I. G. Farbenindustrie, 110
Ibsen, Henrik, 78
Ichang, 451, 497 f.
"Incidents," provoked by Japanese, in Manchuria, 101; around Shanghai, 104; at Lukuochiao (Marco Polo Bridge), 168, 181
India, 8 f., 11, 13, 23 f., 127, 170, 299, 517, 523
Indian exiles, 9, 11
Indian government-in-exile, 9, 11
Indian Medical Mission, 229–30
Indian National Congress, 229 f., 517; boycotts Japanese goods, 230; China Medical Committee of, 230

Index

Indian revolutionary activity, 8 f., 11 f.
Indian students, 14
Indo-China, 127, 233, 463, 503, 509, 517
Indo-China front, 509 f.
Inner Mongolia, Japanese occupation of, 136
Intellectual renaissance, Chinese, 80 ff.
Intellectuals, Chinese, 110 f.; mass executions of, 83–4
Intellectuals, left, Chinese, 79; Japanese, 82
International Settlement, Shanghai; see Shanghai
Internationale, 92
Intrigue, political, 344, 349–51, 356–64
Investments in China, British and American, 102
Isaacs, Harold, 111
Isolationists, American, 300
Italians, in Hankow, 232
Italy, its occupation of Abyssinia, 108–9
Izvestia, 148

Japanese, assassinate Chinese newspaper men, 75; in Manchuria, 33, 37 f., 45 ff. *See also* Manchuria
Japanese agents, 354–5
Japanese air attacks, *see* Air Attacks
Japanese Anti-Imperialist League, 500
Japanese control of Manchuria, articles on, 61
Japanese factories, in Manchuria, 45
Japanese goods, boycott of, 103, 230
Japanese "incidents," *see* "Incidents"
Japanese labor organizers, 42
Japanese occupation of China, ineffectiveness of, 335–6
Japanese occupation of Inner Mongolia, 136
Japanese peace proposals, 366–7, 368, 503
Japanese peasant movement, 42
Japanese prisoners, 264–6, 276–7, 404 ff., 449 f., 500
Japanese schools for Chinese, 45
Japanese secret service, 239, 510
Java, 463, 507
Jehol Province, 108
Jen Pei-hsi, 163
Jena, 13
Jinnah, Mohammed Ali, 15 f.
Jinnah, Mrs., 15 f.
Johnson, Nelson T., 206
Jou Shih, 83
Juikuotan, 435, 438 f.
Junan, 396

Kadji, 500, 510
Kamala Devi, 12
"Kan the Bandit," 484–8
Kang Da (Resistance University), 155, 165, 169, 182 f.
Kang Di, 299
Kansu, plains of, 133
Kao Ching-ting, 318 f.
Keen, Victor, 75, 178 ff.
Kerr, Sir Archibald Clark, 172, 211, 520
Kiangsi Anti-Enemy War Service Association, 240
Kiangsi front, 222
Kiangsi Province, 35, 62, 105, 121, 152, 159 f., 167, 238, 255, 259
Kiangsu Province, 368
Kimen, 244
King, P. Z., 213 ff., 500
Kinghsien, 337
Kingtehchen, 242 ff.; potteries in, 242–4
Kioshan, 467; Lutheran hospital at, 383 ff.
Kirin, 40
Kislovodsk, 124 f., 127
Kit bag (*shubao*), contents of, 323–5
Kollontay, 163
Kollwitz, Kaethe, 81, 84
Koo Ting, 374
Korean nationalists, 48; imprisoned in Manchuria, 41
Korean Volunteers, 403 f., 449, 463

Kowloon, 517
Ku Chu-tung, 112, 365 f.
Kuenshan Mountain, 435, 438 f.
Kuling, 103, 181
Kung, H. H., 185
Kung, Madame H. H., 523
Kuo Shuen-chi, 501
Kuomintang, 23, 33 ff., 42 f., 54, 58 ff., 63, 65, 72, 75, 79, 83, 111 ff., 121, 137, 139, 145, 151 f., 161, 166, 170, 173 f., 176, 205, 251, 256 f., 338, 344, 349, 351, 354, 362, 365, 371, 375, 380, 411, 413, 476, 501 ff.; Third Plenary Session of, 173; Publicity Department of, 176; corrupts Chinese and foreign press, 176 f.
Kuomintang armies, 35, 122 f., 157, 160, 162, 167, 178, 251, 257, 318, 331, 353, 373, 376
Kuomintang Congress, 60
Kupeichung, 343
Kwanchang, Battle of, 121
Kwangsi Province, 122, 124, 136, 343 f., 348, 411 f., 426, 509; *pao-chia* (administrative) system in, 337–9
Kwangsi Provincial Army, 187, 336 ff., 346, 349, 357 ff., 374, 383, 403, 410, 425; *see also* Twenty-first Group Army
Kwangsi Student Army, 338, 343
Kwangsi troops, 355; character of, 341, 346
Kwangtung Province, 35, 343, 517
Kwangtung Provincial Government, 86
Kweichow Province, 122, 502
Kweilin, 426, 509, 510
Kweiyang, 502, 506 ff., 510
Kwo Shuen-chi, 282 ff.
Kwo Shuen-chi, Madame, 284, 286 f., 289 ff.

Labor: contract labor system, 45 ff.; labor conditions in Kingtechen potteries, 242–3
Labor unions, 60 f., 74, 375
Lady Windermere's Fan, 78

Lai Chuan-chu, 317
Lai Kang, 354, 359
Laiyuan, 190
Landlordism, 36, 64 ff., 79, 320 f., 354 f., 369, 428
Language School, Peking, 91
Laohokuo, 299, 401, 403 f., 407, 425, 430
Lattimore, Owen, 179
Laval, Charles, 177
Law, Chinese, 98
Leaf, Earl, 178 f.
League against Aggression, 402
League against Imperialism, 24
League of Civil Rights, 111 ff.
League of Left Artists, 79
League of Left Writers, 79
League of Nations, 101 ff., 213
Lenin, Nikolai, 163, 169
Leningrad, 23, 124, 127
Leonard, Royal, 520
Li Chang-hiang, 459
Li Chung-ren, 348, 363, 401 ff., 410
Li Hsien-nien, 474
Li, Miss, 461
Li, Mr., 115 ff.
Li Ping-hsien, 364
Li Teh, 122, 175, 179
Liberalism, English, 13
Liberals, 20
Liao Rei, 336, 343, 345 ff., 356 ff., 364; his War-Time Political-Military Program, 348 f.; his last will and testament, 360
Lihwang, 327, 337, 345, 347 ff., 354 ff., 372, 374; civic center, 355
Lihwang Preservation Corps, 363
Lihwang River, 342
Lihwang Valley, 343 ff.
Lim, Robert K. S., 212 ff., 219 f., 223, 226, 234 ff., 292, 430, 500 f., 506 ff., 515, 525
Lin Pei-chu, 174
Lin Piao, 169, 187, 194 f.
Lin Yu-tang, 85, 98, 111
Lincoln, Abraham, 207, 413
Ling Shih-fu, 264
Lingnan Christian University, 87
Lintung, 134 ff., 138 f., 141
Lishan, 439

Lishan front, 433 ff.; battle on, 436 ff.
Lishan Valley, 433, 437
Liu, Dr., 241 f.
Liu Liang-moh, 224
Liu Shih-li, 420
Liupiehtung, 339 f.
Loh Fan, 424, 473, 490 ff.
Loh Huh-ping, 438
London *Times*, 522
Long March, *see* Red Army
Loo Chih-teh, 214 ff., 218, 223 ff., 235, 430, 500
Los Angeles, 527
Lotus Lake, 62
Loyang, 391
Lu Hsün, 77–86, 107, 111, 133, 137, 152, 175, 524 f.; characterized, 77–8, 81–2; birthday celebration of, 77–81; illness, 83; protests executions of Chinese intellectuals, 83–6
Lu Hsün Art Academy, 138
Lu Hsün Library, first, 138, 166, 171
Lukuochiao, Japanese attack at, 168, 181
Luliang Mountains, 196
Lunacharsky, 85
Lunghai railway, 301
Lutheran Mission, American, 380; hospital, 381
Lytton Commission, 102

Ma Chan-shan, 101, 103
Ma Chang-yien, 304
Ma Chi-ying, 343 ff., 356 ff., 364
Ma, Dr., 241
Ma Hai-teh, 157, 164, 179
MacDonald, Colin, 522
MacDougall, David, 522
Macheng, 374
Madame Butterfly, 103
Mai Ta-fu, 380, 382
Makin Island, raid on, 527
Malinverni, Erminia, 392
Manchester Guardian, 220, 237, 298, 395
Manchouli, 31

Manchu Dynasty, 62, 80, 101, 166, 354
"Manchukuo," 103, 233
Manchukuo Government, 177
Manchuria, 33, 36 ff., 41 ff., 45, 61, 90, 115 f.; Japanese invasion of, 38, 101 ff., 158, 176, 257, 524; Japanese factories in, 45
Manchurian Army, 103 f., 136, 140, 146, 148, 150
Manchurian Daily News, 41
Manchurian Division, 108th, 294; training school of, 297
Manchurian Government, 37
Manchurian puppet troops, 438, 445 f., 448 f.
Manchurian Volunteers, 104, 115 f.
Mao Tun, 81, 84, 86
Mao Tze-tung, 35, 73, 122, 160, 167 ff., 174–5, 180 f., 183, 229, 318, 324; characterized, 168 ff.; his writings, 170
Maotangchang, *pao-chia* system in, 337 ff.; Mass Movement Council of, 338 f.
Maping, 435
Marco Polo Bridge, Japanese attack at, 168, 181, 442, 467
Marquardt, Admiral, 210
Marseillaise, 92, 416
Marx, Karl, 169
Marxism, 14, 52, 251 f., 324, 329, 476
Medical Administration, Army, 213 f., 219, 229, 251, 500
Medical Aid to China, American Bureau for, 504, 514
Medical center, 507 f.; bombed, 508
Medical Corps, Chinese Red Cross, 212 f., 216, 220 f., 222, 225 f., 229 f., 241, 251, 258, 292, 321, 363, 395, 429, 506 ff., 525
Medical Mission, Indian, 229–30
Medical Schools, War-Time Emergency, 214 f., 219, 222, 291, 500
Medical Service, Army, 218, 220, 249, 346, 430
Medicine, socialized, 214
Mei, General, 415

Mein Kampf, 19
Methodist Church, Southern, 69
Miaoerpu, 438
Mikado, The, 103
Military Council, National, 234, 365
Ming Dynasty, 58, 101, 148, 485
Ming Yao, 375
Missionaries, 207, 215, 233–4, 380 ff., 461 f.
Missouri, 4
Moh Hsu-chi, 425
Moh, Mr., 58, 61 ff.
Mohammedanism, 12
Mongolia, 171; Japanese occupation of, 102
Mongolia, Inner, 294
Mongols, 133
Moscow, 23 ff., 34, 42, 59, 124, 127, 446
Moscow University, 26
Moslems, 13 ff.
Moving pictures, educational, 341
Mowrer, Edgar A., 232
Mozart Festspiel, Salzburg, 18
Muenzenberg, Willi, 95
Mukden, 37, 43 ff., 47 f., 101, 109
Mukden Government, 37
Mukden Medical College, 301
Munich, 19
Munich Pact, 300

Naidu, Sarojini, 12
Nakamura, Corporal, 264–5
Nanchang, 35, 123 f., 167, 221, 237, 239
Nankai University, 49, 172
Nanking, 42, 58 ff., 63 ff., 108, 112 f., 147, 150, 152, 158, 163, 173 f., 190, 213, 255, 260, 262, 268, 292, 330, 366, 368, 420, 482; fall of, 205, 213–14; evacuation of, 214
Nanking broadcast, 163
Nanking divisions, of Chinese Army, 104
Nanking Government, 35 ff., 147, 167
Nanking International Club, 101

Nanking puppet government, Japanese-controlled, 321
Nanling front, 291
Nantao, 116
Nanyang, 389 ff.; Japanese occupation of, 397–8
National Health Administration, 214, 500, 509
National Military Council, *see* Military Council, National
National Resources Commission, *see* Resources Commission, National
National Salvation Congress, *see* Salvation Congress, National
National Salvation movement, *see* Salvation movement, National
National Salvation Union, *see* Salvation Union, National
National Salvationists, *see* Salvationists, National
Nationalism, 36, 47 f., 80
Nationalists, Chinese, 41, 47 f.; imprisoned in Manchuria, 41
Nationalists, Korean, 41, 48, 104
Navy Department, U. S., 209
Nazi movement, 18, 21
Nazis, 20 ff., 24, 35, 110, 205, 227, 300, 503, 516
Nazism, sources of, 22
"Negotiated peace" movement, 300
Nehru, Jawaharlal, 24, 173, 230, 299
Neutrality Law, U. S., 9
Neuwangmiao, 332
New China Daily, 205
New Fourth Army, 236 f., 239, 247 ff., 251, 254 ff., 259–66, 271, 277, 284, 286, 291 f., 299, 301 ff., 318 f., 322, 336, 339, 354, 359, 362 ff., 370 f., 378, 385, 447, 449, 463, 468, 476, 501, 505; Medical Service of, 249 ff., 257 ff., 266–70, 277 ff.; Political Department of, 251 f., 260–1, 271, 302; Air Training Camp, 262–3; Enemy Work Section of, 264; Medical Training School of, 266 ff., 302; Mass Movement Department of, 278, 281; Front Service Corps, 301; Fourth Detachment of, 317–29; physical ex-

amination system of, 321–2; training camp of central Anhwei, guerrilla detachments of, 322–7; Third Detachment of, annihilation of, 365; First and Second Detachments of, 368; Storm Guerrilla Detachment of, 463 ff.; its children, 463 ff.
New Life Movement, Women's, 502
New Mexico, 5
New York, 8 ff., 128
New York Herald Tribune, 178
New York Times, 147
New York University, 8
Ni Tao-liang, 320
Nichi-Nichi, 97
Nightingale, Florence, 217
Nineteenth Route Army, 104 f., 106, 108, 147
Non-Aggression Pact, Soviet-German, 300
Nonni River, Battle of, 103
North China Daily News, 178
Northcote, Sir Geoffrey, 514, 521
Northern Expedition of 1926–7, 34, 160, 255

Officers' Moral Endeavor Association, 59
Officials, Chinese, venality of, 105–6
Opium, traffic in, 40 f., 94, 112, 273 ff., 285, 515
Orphans, war, 227
Oxford, 16

Pacific Fleet, American, 518
Pacifists, 516
Pai Chung-hsi, 365
Pan Chi, 501
Pan Nien, 113, 120
Pao-chia (administrative) system, in Kwangsi Province, 337–9, 357 f., 375
Pasteur, Louis, 413
Patricians, Chinese, 49 ff., 74
Patterson, Miss, 381 f.
Peace proposals, Japanese, 366–7, 368, 503

Pearl Harbor, 527
Peasant leagues, 34
Peasants, "harvest uprisings" of, 79; "silk peasants," 86 ff.
Pei Wutienshan Mountain, 160
Pei Yen (White Bayonet), extracts from soldiers' diaries in, 421–3
Peipei, 451
Peiping, 53, 55, 57, 70, 80, 90, 101, 106, 109, 115 f., 136, 140, 172, 176, 181, 190, 213 f., 443 f., 450; its patricians, 50 ff.
Peiping-Hankow railway, 187, 384 f., 426, 467
Peking Government, 176
Peking National University, 110
Peking Union Medical College, 186, 359
Peng Teh-hwei, 159 ff., 169, 171
People's Mobilization committees, 189, 191, 349, 351, 361 f., 364; publications of, 352
People's movement, 205
Philippines, 83, 232
Pinghsinkwan, battle of, 187 f.
Pochow, serfdom in, 354–5
Poison gas, 413, 426, 448
Poland, 26; Nazi occupation of, 403
Poverty, 49 f., 54, 320, 373 f., 428
Powell, John B., 75, 177 f., 186, 520
Pragmatists, 52
Profiteers, 105
Proletarian literature, 79 ff.
Public Health Administration, 429
Public Health Service, German, 20
Purdah, 15 f.
Purple Mountain, 58
Pu Yi, Henry, 101

Quello, Miss, 381
Queue, wearing of, 354
Quo Tai-chi, Mrs., 106

Radio, 163, 235, 322
Rae, George Bronson, 177
Rai, Lala Laipat, 8
Rangoon, 517, 523
Rats, Lice and History, 171

Reaction, 205
"Reconciliation" policy, Japanese, 321
Red Aid, Chinese, 79
Red Aid, International, 95
Red Armies, Front (Chinese), 159 ff.
Red Army, Chinese, 36, 73, 79, 101 f., 105, 108, 121 f., 124, 133 f., 136, 138 ff., 145 ff., 151 f., 157 ff., 164 ff., 172 ff., 177 f., 180 f., 191, 197, 243 f., 259, 263, 302, 318, 321 ff., 337, 344, 375, 378, 463; Long March of, 36, 108, 121 ff., 133-4, 160, 166 f., 254, 259; declares war on Japan, 102; Political Department of, 161; founding of, 167; reorganized into Eighth Route Army, 182
Red Army, Russian, 24-5, 27, 125, 127; Academy, Moscow, 125
Red Army, Second, 157
Red Army, Workers' and Peasants', 160
Red Army Corps, First, 151, 154
Red Army Corps, Fourth, 373
Red Army Corps, Second, 155, 476
Red Army Corps, Tenth, 123, 304
Red Army Marching Song, 153
Red Army Training Academy, 124
Red Cross, American, 221 f., 226, 514
Red Cross, Chinese, 207, 214, 221 ff., 235, 237 f., 241, 258, 325, 429, 515; field units, 221 f., 225, 241, 301 f., 322; Japanese attack on, 325-6; Foreign Auxiliary of, 225, 514
Red Cross, International, 207, 381 f.
Red Cross, Scottish, 220
Red Cross Committees of China, International, 207, 215 f., 222, 229 f., 382, 385, 480, 489
Red Cross Convention, Geneva, 213
Red Cross Medical Corps, Chinese, 212 f., 216, 220 f., 222, 225 f., 229 f., 241, 251, 258, 292, 321, 363, 395, 429, 506 ff., 525
Red Cross, Norwegian, 508
Red Swastika Society, Buddhist, 338, 395

Refugees, 278 ff., 358, 408, 409, 515; students, 336
Reichstag, 22
Remarque, Erich Maria, 78
Resources Commission, National, 212
Reuter's, 176
Revolution, American, 7
Revolution, Chinese, 58, 109, 114, 322, 324, 514; of 1922-27, 23 f.; national, of 1925-7, 156-7, 167; history of, 167, 329
Revolution, intellectual, Chinese pioneers in, 78-9
Revolution, Russian, 10, 24, 125
Revolution, social, 54
Revolutionary Military Council, 159, 172
Ring, Wagner's, 19
Robeson, Paul, 434
Rockefeller, John D., 4
Rockefeller Foundation, 358
Rolland, Romain, 78
Roosevelt, Franklin D., 295, 442, 528
Roots, Frances, 206, 211
Roots, Logan, 206
Ruhr, 21
Russell, Bertrand, 52
Russians, White, *see* White Russians
Russo-Japanese War, 19

Salome, 78
Salt-miners, 477 ff.
Salvation Association, Women's National, 155, 271 ff., 298
Salvation Congress, National, 134
Salvation movement, National, 134, 144, 147, 151
Salvation Union, National, 145 f., 344, 502
Salvationists, National, 74
Salzburg, 18
San Diego, 527
San Min Chu I Youth Corps, 205
San Pedro, 526
Sanger, Margaret, 20, 94
Sano, 42

Sanyuan, 151, 155, 158, 163, 183
Secret Service, British, 12
Seeckt, Hans von, 122, 238
Self Defense Corps, 337 f.
Sellett, George, 96
Selwyn-Clarke, Mrs. Hilda, 225 f., 512 ff., 519
Selwyn-Clarke, Percy, 513
Serfdom, 46, 354
Seventeenth Route Army, 136
Shangchen, 374 ff., 378
Shanghai, 34 f., 46, 63 ff., 69 f., 75, 83, 85, 90, 92–8, 104, 110, 112, 116, 120, 123, 133, 137, 147, 165, 175 f., 178, 194, 212 ff., 227, 231, 243, 247, 254, 262, 268, 277, 282, 287 f., 325, 366, 411, 429, 459, 524; International Settlement, 46, 94, 98, 107, 118, 120; Japanese occupation of, 75; French Concession, 77, 94, 96 f., 116; Green Gang, 94; American Court, 96; Japanese attack on, 104 ff.; agreement terminating hostilities, 106; defense of, 104 ff.; demilitarization of, 106
Shanghai Evening Post and Mercury, 92–4, 107, 520
Shanghai Pao, 79
Shanghai Times, 176
Shanghai-Nanking fighting, problems of, 346 f.
Shanghai-Nanking-Hangchow triangle, 366
Shanghai-Nanking railway, 260
Shanpei (Northwestern Academy), 165, 169, 183
Shansi Province, 183, 185, 195
Shansi Provincial Army, 185 f.
Shantung Province, 36 f., 55, 136, 376, 444
Shasi, 497
Sheba, Kimpei, 177
Shen Kuo-hwa, 464 ff.
Sheng, C. C., 249
Sheng Chung-ju, 502
Shensi Province, 148
Shih River, 342
Shihchiachwan, 187, 192

Shiomi, Seisaku, 510 f.
Shong Yi, 460, 489
Shubao (kit bag), contents of, 323–5
Shuihsien, 461 f., 426
Shuikin, 121
Shun Pao, 520
Shuntek silk region, 87
Siam, 517
Sian, 134 ff., 138 f., 140, 146 ff., 152, 171, 178 ff., 183, 197, 417, 501
Sian Incident, 133–51; Anti-Japanese Alliance, 136, 148 f.; capture of Chiang Kai-shek, 141; his release, 148 f.; the eight demands, 144; civil war threatened, 147 f.; imprisonment of Marshal Chang Hsueh-liang, 150–1
Sikong, 159
Silk Guild, Canton, 87
Silk industry, 86 ff.; see also Shuntek silk region; Filatures
Sinclair, Upton, 78
Singapore, 463, 519, 522 f.
Singsong girls, 55
Sinkow, 187
Sino-British Cultural Association, 520
Sinyang, 426
Skinsness, Doctor, 383–8, 426
Slogans, 150, 294, 298, 321 f., 329, 339 f., 352, 374 f., 380
Snow, Edgar, 157, 171 f., 179, 232, 520
Snow, Mrs. Edgar, 179, 463
Socialism, 36
Socialists, 20 f.
Socialized medicine, 214
Sokolsky, George, 177
Soldiers, Chinese, characteristics of, 105
Song of Ariran, 463
Song of Unending Sorrow, 135
Soong, T. V., 60, 137, 148, 220
South Manchurian Railway, 48
Soviet advisers, Russian, in China, 34, 227, 370, 427
Soviet-Chinese frontier, 31
Soviet Government, Chinese, 340

Soviet Government, Russian, 25, 148, 369–70
Soviet region, Chinese, 353, 373, 375, 476
Soviet Union, 8, 11, 13, 23 ff., 52, 83, 102 f., 115, 120, 123 ff., 127, 136, 148, 169, 214, 256, 300 f., 329, 367, 370, 402, 413, 516, 523; signs Non-Aggression Pact with Germany, 300
"Spanish doctors," 508 f.
Spanish Republic, 172
Spanish Republican Armies, 251, 508
Spies, 190, 239, 319 f., 350, 358, 486 f.
Stalin, Joseph, 169
State Department, U. S., 206
Steele, Art, 208
Stennes, Captain, 233
Stilwell, Joseph, 172, 188, 207 f., 221–2
Stimson, Henry L., 295
Storm Guerrilla Detachment, 448 f., 463 ff., 491 ff., 498
Strachey, John, 516
Strauss, Karl, 95 f.
Studebaker Corporation, 216
Students, 52, 54, 336 f.
Students' Unions, 146
Su Tung-po, 63
Suencheng, 292 ff.; description of, 296–7
Suhasini, 16 f.
Suiyuan Province, 136, 148, 185, 413; Japanese invasion of, 134
Sun, Captain, 141
Sun Cheh-yuan, 443
Sun Chen, 427
Sun Lien-chung, 426
Sun Yat-sen, 33 f., 59, 174, 256, 413; "Three People's Principles" of, 36
Sun Yat-sen, Madame, 35, 59, 106, 111, 137, 514, 523
Sun Yat-sen mausoleum, 58
Sun Yat-sen Memorial Hall, 86
Sunchochuang, 331
Sung Cheh-yuan, 181

Sunyingtze, 331
Sweden, 13
Szechuen armies, 285, 426 ff., 433 ff., 450
Szechuen Province, 166, 238, 285, 287, 359, 428, 447 f.

Ta Hung Mountain Front, 469
Ta Hung Mountains, 423, 442, 448, 452, 459, 491 f.
Ta Nieh Pan Tze, 479
Ta Pieh Mountains, 317, 336, 339, 342, 353, 372, 374, 376, 379
Ta Pieh Shan Er Pao, 349, 351, 357
Ta Tao (The Great Way), 77
Tai Li, 148, 500 ff.
Taierchwang, Battle of, 219, 367, 402, 444
Taiping, 248
Taiyuan, 183 ff., 188, 195
Tanaka Memorial, 102, 221, 517
Tang En-po, 395
Tang River, 424
Tangho, 389 f.
Tanyang, 366
Tao Chu, 477
Tehan, 239
Tempe, Arizona, Normal School at, 7 f.
Ten-Man Group, 460, 476, 481, 484, 486, 488, 492
Teng Ying-chou, 173
Tercio, 5
Terror, Japanese, 320–1, 336 f.
Terror, Kuomintang, 35, 69–77, 113 ff., 206, 213, 257, 353
Theatrical Group, 355 f., 364
Third Detachment of New Fourth Army, annihilation of, 365, 368
Thirty-third Group Army, 443, 445, 451, 488
Three Generations, 163
Three Kingdoms period, 317
"Three People's Principles," 36, 340, 404
Tien Chun, 525
Tienerhoh, 489
Tientang Mountain pass, 342

Tientsin, 48 f., 97, 101, 109, 136, 178, 462
Tientsin-Nanking railway, 301, 318, 321
Tikang, 304 ff.
Ting Ling, 115, 118 f., 152 ff., 159 f., 163 f.; abduction of, 113, 120
Tolstoy, Leo, 80, 126, 217, 505
Torture, 112, 116 f.
Trade-union organizers, executions of, 74
Trade unions, 34, 48, 60 f., 74, 375
Training camps, political-military, 262–3, 288, 337, 348 f.
Traitors, 483–8, 490
Trotskyites, Chinese, 165, 357
Tsai, 477 f.
Tsai Ban-tang, 305
Tsai Loh, 302, 305 ff.
Tsai, Mother, 270 ff.
Tsai Ting-kai, 104
Tsai Yuan-pei, 111
Tsao Sho, 491 f.
Tsao Tsao, 317
Tsaoyang, 427 f., 451
Tsingtao, 136
Tso Chuan, 151, 153 f.
Ts'uan Tai Chen, 424
Tu Ti Kung-Kung, wayside shrines to, 396
Tu Yueh-seng, 94, 116, 515
Tungkwan, 148 f., 183
Tungli, 151
Tungpeh Mountains, 426, 428
Tungpei (Northeast) Army, 136
Tunling, 320
Tutuila, 504 f.
Twenty-first Group Army, 336 ff., 357 ff.; base of, 336; Political-Military Training Camp of, 337; Artillery Training Camp of, 339; *see also* Kwangsi Provincial Army
Twenty-ninth Group Army, 491, 497
Twenty-ninth Route Army, 181 f., 443 f.
Twenty-second Group Army, 426 ff.

United Front, 172 ff., 256; conditions for, submitted by Red Army, 173
United Press, 178 f.
United States, investments in China, 102; terminates commercial treaty with Japan, 402
Utley, Freda, 209–210

Vandergrift, A. A., 528
Vanguard Marching Song, 317, 463
Versailles Treaty, 21
Village in August, 525
Villages, sanitary conditions of, 64
Vladivostok, 125
Voltaire, 14
Volunteer Marching Song, 150, 249, 275

Wales, Nym, 179, 463
Wang Bu-ching, 482, 486 f.
Wang Chan-ping, 383
Wang Chih-yuan, 433 ff., 439
Wang Ching-wei, 34 f., 97, 104, 108, 147 ff., 174, 205, 231, 234, 339, 366, 368, 403, 482, 503, 515
Wang Lao-han, 467 f.
Wang Tsan-hsü, 442, 447 ff., 452, 497
Wanping, 181
War and Peace, 126, 217, 505
War materials, American, sold to Japan, 206, 220–1, 232, 236, 295 f., 340, 401, 403, 410, 413, 416, 439, 441 f., 500
War-time Emergency Medical Schools, 214 f., 219, 222, 291, 500
War-Time Service Corps, 240
Washington, George, 413
Wei Li-hwang, 187
Western Hills, 109
White Russians, in China, 38 f., 95 ff., 125, 227
Wilde, Oscar, 78
Wilkinson, Paul B., 512 f.
Wintringham, Tom, 516

Woman's National Salvation Association, 155, 271 ff., 298
Women, Chinese, handicaps of, 353 f.
Women's New Life Movement, 502
Wong Wen-hao, 212
Woodhead, H. G. W., 520
Woosung forts, defense of, 105
Workers, factory, evacuation of, 227
Workers' and Peasants' Red Army (Chinese), 160
Workers' tenements, 70
Wounded, care of, 212 ff., 239 ff., 285–6, 330–5, 380, 412 f., 429, 430 f., 438, 440, 452–5, 461 f.
Wounded Soldier Committees, 105
"Written in Deep Night," quotations from, 84–5
Wu San-kwei, 148
Wuchang, 205
Wuhan, 205
Wuhan University, 459
Wuhu, 255, 260, 292, 312
Wusih, 64 f., 269
Wutai, 188 f.
Wutai Mountains, 187, 189, 191, 194
Wutaishan, 229

Y.M.C.A., 69, 74, 224 f.
Y.W.C.A., 502
Yang Chang-chen, 419 f.
Yang Chien, 111; characterized, 113–14; murder of, 113, 120
Yang Hu-chen, 136, 141, 144 ff.
Yang Kwei-fei, 134 f.
Yang, Miss, 266

Yang, Mr., 112
Yang Yu-ting, 44
Yangtze, 167, 205 f., 226, 234, 237, 498; battlefields near, 237, 242; war zones of, 251, 260, 277, 298; guerrilla region near, 247–313; guerrilla expedition north of, 298–313
Yangtze gunboat patrol, American, 210
Yangtze gunboat patrol, British, 210, 233
Yangtzepoo factory district, Shanghai, 70
Yarnell, Harry, 209
Yeh Chien-ying, 147
Yeh Tao-kang, 137
Yeh Ting, 167, 250, 254 ff., 259, 299, 319, 357, 365 f., 368
Yellow Mountain, 249
Yellow River, 53, 183, 367; floods, famine, 53; dikes blasted by Chinese, 221
Yen Hsi-shan, 185, 189
Yenan, 138, 155, 158, 161, 164 ff., 167 ff., 179 ff., 182, 191, 259
"Young Marshal," *see* Chang Hsueh-liang
Youth Marching Song, 248
Youth Monthly, 352
Youth movement, 355
Yu Chou Fang, 85
Yung River, 435
Yunnan Province, 123, 166, 238

Zeitschrift für Geopolitik, 19
Zinsser, Hans, 171

TYPE NOTE

This book is set in Linotype ELECTRA. This face cannot be classified as either "modern" or "old-style." It is not based on any historical model, nor does it echo any particular period or style. It avoids the extreme contrast between "thick" and "thin" elements that marks most "modern" faces, and attempts to give a feeling of fluidity, power, and speed.

The book was composed, printed, and bound by The Plimpton Press, Norwood, Massachusetts. The typography and the binding design are by W. A. Dwiggins.

Soc
DS
777.47
S5

3 1254 00078 8410

DATE DUE	
JUN 13 1977	NOV 3 0 1985
AUG 1 ~~1977~~	DEC 0 8 2007
AUG 2 3 1977	
AUG 0 6 1990	SEP ~~~~
FEB ~~79~~	
JAN ~~1991~~ Ill grant	MAR 2 8 1995
ILL GRANT OCT 3 1 1986	
SEP 05 1989 ILL GRANT	MAR ~~1995~~
JUL 1 6 1990	
FEB ~~95~~	